Network Security

T0138099

Scott C.-H. Huang • David MacCallum
Ding-Zhu Du
Editors

Network Security

 Springer

Editors
Scott C.-H. Huang
Department of Computer Science
City University of Hong Kong
Tat Chee Avenue 83
Hong Kong
Hong Kong SAR
shuang@cityu.edu.hk

David MacCallum
Department of Computer Science
& Engineering
University of Minnesota
Union Street SE., 200
55455-0000 Minneapolis
Minnesota
4-192 EE/CS Bldg.
USA

Ding-Zhu Du
Department of Computer Science
University of Texas, Dallas
Erik Jonsson School of Engineering
& Computer Science
W. Campbell Road 800
75080 Richardson Texas
USA
dzdu@utdallas.edu

ISBN 978-1-4899-9001-3   ISBN 978-0-387-73821-5 (eBook)
DOI 10.1007/978-0-387-73821-5
Springer New York Dordrecht Heidelberg London

Printed on acid-free paper

Springer is part of Springer Science+Business Media (www.springer.com)

Preface

Over the past two decades, network technologies have been remarkably renovated and computer networks, particularly the Internet, have permeated into every facet of our daily lives. These changes also brought about new challenges, particularly in the area of security. Network security is essential to protect data integrity, confidentiality, access control, authentication, user privacy, and so on. All of these aspects are critical to provide fundamental network functionalities.

This book covers a comprehensive array of topics in network security including secure metering, group key management, DDoS attacks, and many others. It can be used as a handy reference book for researchers, educators, graduate students, as well as professionals in the field of network security. This book contains 11 refereed chapters from prominent researchers working in this area around the globe. Although these selected topics could not cover every aspect, they do represent the most fundamental and practical techniques.

This book has been made possible by the great efforts and contributions of many people. First, we thank the authors of each chapter for contributing informative and insightful chapters. Then, we thank all reviewers for their invaluable comments and suggestions that improved the quality of this book. Finally, we thank the staff members from Springer for publishing this work. Besides, *we would like to dedicate this book to our families*.

City University of Hong Kong, Hong Kong SAR   Scott C.-H. Huang
University of Minnesota, USA   David MacCallum
University of Texas at Dallas, USA   Ding-Zhu Du

Contents

Contributors

Endre Bangerter IBM Zurich Research Laboratory, Säumerstrasse 4, 8803 Rüschlikon, Switzerland, eba@zurich.ibm.com

Carlo Blundo Dipartimento di Informatica ed Applicazioni, Università di Salerno, 84081 Baronissi (SA), Italy, carblu@dia.unisa.it

Jan Camenisch IBM Zurich Research Laboratory, Säumerstrasse 4, 8803 Rüschlikon, Switzerland, jca@zurich.ibm.com

Mihaela Cardei Department of Computer Science and Engineering, Florida Atlantic University, Boca Raton, FL 33431, USA, mihaela@cse.fau.edu

Maggie Cheng Department of Computer Science, University of Missouri Rolla, MO, USA, chengm@umr.edu

Xiaochun Cheng Department of Computer Science, The University of Reading, Whiteknights, Reading RG6 6AY, England, UK, x.cheng@reading.ac.uk

Xiuzhen Cheng Computer Science Department, George Washington University, Washington, DC 20052, USA, cheng@gwu.edu

Ramkumar Chinchani Computer Science and Engineering, State University of New York at Buffalo, Amherst, NY 14260, USA, rc27@cse.buffalo.edu

Stelvio Cimato Dipartimento di Tecnologie dell'Informazione, Università di Milano, 26013 Crema, Italy, cimato@dti.unimi.it

Yi Gao School of Information Technology and Computer Science, University of Wollongong, Australia, yg70@uow.edu.au

Duc Ha Computer Science and Engineering, State University of New York at Buffalo, Amherst, NY 14260, USA, ducha@cse.buffalo.edu

Scott C.-H. Huang Department of Computer Science, University of Minnesota, MN, USA, huang@cs.umn.edu

Anusha Iyer Computer Science and Engineering, State University of New York at Buffalo, Amherst, NY 14260, USA, aa44@cse.buffalo.edu

Sushil Jajodia Center for Secure Information Systems, George Mason University, Fairfax, VA 22030, USA, jajodia@gmu.edu

Markus Jakobsson School of Informatics and Computing, Indiana University, Bloomington, IN 47408, USA, markus@indiana.edu

Jiang Li Department of Systems and Computer Science, Howard University, Washington, DC 20059, USA, lij@scs.howard.edu

Anna Lysyanskaya Computer Science Department, Brown University, Providence, RI 02912, USA, anna@cs.brown.edu

Xiaoqi Ma Department of Computer Science, The University of Reading, Whiteknights, Reading RG6 6AY, England, UK, xiaoqi.ma@reading.ac.uk

Barbara Masucci Dipartimento di Informatica ed Applicazioni, Università di Salerno, 84081 Baronissi (SA), Italy, masucci@dia.unisa.it

Filippo Menczer School of Informatics and Computing, Indiana University, Bloomington, IN 47408, USA, fil@indiana.edu

Yi Mu School of Information Technology and Computer Science, University of Wollongong, Australia, ymu@uow.edu.au

Hung Q. Ngo Computer Science and Engineering, State University of New York at Buffalo, Amherst, NY 14260, USA, hungngo@cse.buffalo.edu

Peng Ning Computer Science Department, North Carolina State University, Raleigh, NC 27695, USA, pning@ncsu.edu

Mohammad O. Pervaiz Department of Computer Science and Engineering, Florida Atlantic University, Boca Raton, FL 33431, USA, mpervaiz@fau.edu

Vincent Rijmen Department of Electrical Engineering/ESAT, Katholieke Universiteit Leuven, Leuven, Belgium, vincent.rijmen@esat.kuleuven.be

Major Jose "Manny" Rivera Computer Science Department, George Washington University, Washington, DC 20052, USA, jose.rivera@us.army.mil

Jennifer Seberry School of Information Technology and Computer Science, University of Wollongong, Australia, jennie@uow.edu.au

Shyaam Sundhar Rajamadam Srinivasan Computer Science Department, George Washington University, Washington, DC 20052, USA, shyaam@gwu.edu

Willy Susilo School of Information Technology and Computer Science, University of Wollongong, Australia, wsusilo@uow.edu.au

Shambhu Upadhyaya Computer Science and Engineering, State University of New York at Buffalo, Amherst, NY 14260, USA, shambhu@cse.buffalo.edu

Jie Wu Department of Computer Science and Engineering, Florida Atlantic University, Boca Raton, FL 33431, USA, jie@cse.fau.edu

Kai Xing School of Computer Science and Technology, Suzhou Institute for Advanced Study, University of Science and Technology of China, Hefei, Anhui, 230027 China, kxing@ustc.edu.cn

Dingbang Xu Computer Science Department, North Carolina State University, Raleigh, NC 27695, USA, dxu@ncsu.edu

Sencun Zhu Department of Computer Science, School of Information Science and Technology, The Pennsylvania State University, University Park, PA 16802, USA, szhu@cse.psu.edu

Secure Metering Schemes

Carlo Blundo, Stelvio Cimato, and Barbara Masucci

Contents

1 Introduction

The current trend on the Internet suggests that the majority of revenues of web sites come from the advertising potential of the World Wide Web. Advertising is arguably the type of commercial information exchange of the greatest economic importance in the real world. Indeed, advertising is what funds most other forms of information

C. Blundo (✉)
Dipartimento di Informatica ed Applicazioni, Università di Salerno, 84081 Baronissi (SA), Italy
e-mail: carblu@dia.unisa.it

S.C.-H. Huang et al. (eds.), *Network Security*, DOI 10.1007/978-0-387-73821-5_1,
© Springer Science+Business Media, LLC 2010

exchange, including radio stations, television stations, cable networks, magazines, and newspapers. According to the figures provided by the Internet Advertising Bureau [24] and Price Waterhouse Coopers [43], advertising revenue results for the first 9 months of 2004 totaled slightly over 7.0 billion dollars.

Advertising on the Web can be described in a scenario involving a certain number of interacting participants: *advertisers*, *servers*, and *clients*. The goals of these participants are the following:

- The *advertisers* are interested in selling products or services to clients. In order to do this, they rent advertising space from servers and put their ads on it. The goal of advertisers is to maximize the benefit per price ratio for their ads.
- The *servers* are interested in selling advertising space to advertisers. The goal of the servers is to maximize the income they receive from selling their advertising space.
- The *clients* are the parties browsing the web and possibly buying products and services in response to ads. In general, they look for the best service at the lowest price, and their choice may be influenced by the reputation of the advertiser.

Similarly, in every other advertising channel, web advertisers must have a way to measure the exposure of their ads by obtaining the usage statistics of the web sites which contain them. Indeed, the amount of money charged to display ads depends on the number of visits received by the web sites. Consequently, advertisers should prevent the web sites from inflating the count of their visits in order to demand more money. Hence, there should be a mechanism that ensures the validity and accuracy of usage measurements against fraud attempts by servers and clients. A system for measuring the amount of services performed by servers is called a *metering scheme*.

Currently, there is no single accepted standard or terminology for web measurement. For example, a visit can be defined in different ways according to the measurement context: it might be a page hit, a session lasting more than a fixed threshold of time, or any similar definition. As pointed out by Novak and Hoffman [41], standardization is a crucial first step in the way for obtaining successful commercial use of the Internet.

Statistical sampling is one of the methods used by commercial enterprises which sell services for measuring the activity of web sites. Such a method is survey-based: it picks a representing group of users, checks their usage patterns, and derives usage statistics about all the users. In traditional types of media, such as radio or television, this method makes sense since the number of options for the users are limited. On the Web, however, where the number of pages to visit is on the order of millions, sampling results do not provide meaningful data.

Alternative techniques to statistical sampling include *log analysis* and *hardware boxes*. Many Web servers have a logging mechanism that stores and tracks client visits. The server can analyze and collect data for statistical analysis of visits and ad exposure. However, servers have a financial motivation for exaggerating their popularity and could easily alter logging data to attract more advertisers. In order to avoid server log modification, advertisers could provide servers with tamper-resistant hardware verifying the correctness of server logs. A method for the verification of server access logs and statistics was suggested in [6] and [7]. In their proposal, each client request to a server is transferred to a tamper-resistant authentication device, which responds with a Message Authentication Code[1] (MAC), which is stored on an accessible medium by the server, and a binary digit B. If $B = 0$, the request is processed normally, whereas, if $B = 1$, the server is required to issue a "redirect" response to the client, instructing it to connect to a different server, controlled by an audit agency. The agency's server logs this request and redirects it back to the original server, where it is eventually serviced. The audit agency periodically verifies each MAC and checks whether requests where $B = 1$ correspond to an associated client log entry on its server. If this does not happen in a high number of cases, certification of the log file could be denied, based on the agency's policy.

Currently, the most employed measurement method to learn about the exposure of ads on the Internet is the *pay-per-click* method, which is based on the number of *click-through* on banners and other ads. Advertisers typically install a software, called the *click-through payment program*, at web servers hosting their ads to collect access information. The security of this method has been analyzed in [1] and [2] where several protocols have been described to detect *hit inflation* attacks which artificially inflate the number of click-troughs. Such an attack can be easily performed by manipulating any unsecured metered data stored on the servers or by using a robot program, which is configured to generate visits to the web servers. Since the owner of the server can charge higher rates for advertisements by showing a higher number of visits, the owner has a strong economic incentive to inflate the number of visits. The lesson learnt from software and pay-TV piracy is that big financial interests lead to corrupt behaviors which overcome any software or hardware security mechanism.

Common alternatives to pay-per-click programs include *pay-per-lead* and *pay-per-sale* programs, where servers are paid only for visits from users who perform some substantial activity or make purchases at the web sites. It is virtually impossible for servers to mount useful hit inflation attacks on these schemes, since simple clicks are worthless to servers. However, these programs are susceptible to a different form of fraud, known as *hit shaving*, where the server fails to report that the user visit is actually associated with a lead or a sale.

The Coalition for Advertising Supported Information and Entertainment (CASIE) [17] states in its guidelines for interactive media audience measurement that third party measurement is the foundation for advertiser confidence in information. It is the measurement practice of all other advertiser supported media. There are a number of companies (a partial list of these includes companies such as I/PRO [25], Nielsen [38], NetCount [37], Media Metrix [31], and Audiweb [3]) which offer third party based audit services for the Internet. Therefore, a new party

---

[1] A message authentication code is an authentication tag attached to a message, in order to provide data integrity and authentication. Such a tag is a function of the message and of a secret key, shared between the sender and the receiver.

is introduced in the scenario described at the beginning of this section: the *audit agency*, a special party responsible for measuring the interaction between clients and servers. Clients and servers do not necessarily trust each other, but they do trust the audit agency. Clearly, clients are required to register with the audit agency in order to participate in the measurement process. Such registration may have several advantages for clients. For example, after registration, the clients may access to additional services, such as receiving news on topics of interest, getting information on upcoming promotions, downloading coupons, participating in a forum, sending free SMS (Short Message Service) through a web site, disposing of free disk space and mailbox, and many others. Moreover, registration does not require clients to disclose their real identity.

Even though metering originated in the field of web advertisements, there are several other applications of secure metering schemes.

- *Network accounting*: Network accounting is very complicated since the information transmitted through the Internet is divided into packets which travel separately and are routed through many different networks. The common method of payment to data networks consists in fixed rate payments for connections. Indeed, it is very difficult to provide efficient and undisputed measurements of the amount of traffic that originated from a source and passed through different networks. The payment for this usage might be decided according to the number of packets routed by a network through several different networks. Metering schemes could be used to enable the network owner to construct a proof for the number of packets routed by the network.
- *Target audience*: Metering schemes can be used to measure the usage of a web site by a special category of users. A metering scheme can be used, for example, by an editor of text books who pays a web site to host his or her advertisements and is interested in knowing how many professors visited the site. In return, the professors receive updates on the latest releases.
- *Toll free connection*: Many companies offer toll free numbers to their customers. Similarly, they might agree to pay for the cost required to access their web sites. Franklin and Malkhi [23] suggested to use metering schemes as a method to measure the amount of money that the companies should pay to the users' ISPs.
- *Royalties*: Servers might offer content (or links to content) which is the property of other parties. Metering schemes could be used to measure the number of requests for this content in order to decide on the sum that should be paid to the content owners.
- *Coupons*: Imagine a newspaper that distributes coupons to its clients, which give them access to an online service, which is run by a service provider. The payment for this usage might be decided according to the number of coupons which have been actually used. Metering schemes could be used to enable the service provider to construct a proof for the number of coupons that have been used.

2 State of the Art

Recently, several directions for designing efficient and secure metering schemes have been proposed. Many proposals are based on various cryptographic techniques, as secure function evaluations, threshold cryptography, and secret sharing.

2.1 Client Authentication

Employing standard cryptographic methods to keep self-authenticating records of interactions between clients and servers is one of the proposals to design metering schemes. A naive implementation of an *authentication*-based metering scheme could be implemented by using digital signature schemes. Each client is required to generate a digital signature for each visit to a server. A server can present the list of the digital signatures to an audit agency as a proof for its operations.

This system is very accurate, but it does not preserve privacy since the audit agency obtains lists with signed confirmations for the clients and the servers actions. Moreover, the system is not efficient: it requires clients to perform a public key signature for each visit, and the size of a server's proof, as well as the time to verify it, is of the same order as the number of visits it had (the work of the audit agency is of the same order as the total number of visits to all servers).

Naor and Pinkas [34] suggested the use of *hash trees* [33] to design authentication based metering schemes. A hash tree could be used by any server to store the confirmations sent by clients during their visits. Later, any server could send the root of the hash tree to the audit agency. During the verification stage, the audit agency could verify the values of the random leaves. The problem of this approach is that additional care should be taken to prevent the server from storing the same value at different leaves. This could be accomplished by using families of perfect hash functions or by requiring the server to sort the leaves.

2.2 Micropayments

The use of *micropayments* for financing online services was proposed by Jarecki and Odlyzko [26]. In their schemes, each customer is issued a certificate by the bank to be used when dealing with the merchants. The first transaction between a customer and a merchant is always registered with the bank, whereas, for any consecutive transaction, the merchant decides whether to report that transaction to the bank or not. This enables the bank to maintain an accurate approximation of the customer's spending. The probability of reporting each transaction is proportional to the amount involved in that transaction and the amount of overspending that the bank is willing to risk.

In the metering scenario, micropayments would require each client to send a small amount of money to a server during a visit. The server can prove many client visits by showing that it earned a large sum of money.

However, all the current suggestions for micropayment schemes require the communication from the merchant (i.e., the server) to the bank (i.e., the audit agency) to be of the same order as the number of payments that the merchant received. This means that the amount of information that the audit agency receives is of the same order as the total number of visits to all the metered servers.

2.3 *Pricing via Processing*

This approach is similar to the suggestion of Dwork and Naor [21] for combating junk email and was proposed by Franklin and Malkhi [23] in the metering scenario. They proposed metering schemes where any server is given a large computational task by the audit agency; part of this task is performed by each client visiting the server, and the results of such computations are saved by the server along with the record of the visits, as an indication of the amount of computation performed. In particular, this approach does not rely on client authentication or on a third party. These schemes have the drawback that it is not possible for the audit agency to distinguish between computation performed by clients and computation performed by servers. Moreover, in these schemes it is not possible to distinguish between the situation in which two different clients visit a server and the situation in which there is a client visiting a server twice. Finally, these schemes offer lightweight security, i.e., clients can "fool" the audit agency with an amount of computational resources proportional to the amount of the possible fraud. Therefore, these solutions cannot be applied if servers and clients have a strong commercial interest to falsify the metering results.

2.4 *Threshold Computation of a Function*

The notion of a *threshold computation of a function* was introduced by Desmedt and Frankel [20]. The approach to the metering scenario could be the following: Each client C_i receives a share f_i of a function f. Every time the client visits a server, it computes its partial function $f_i(x)$ by using its share and sends the result to the audit agency. After receiving a certain number of partial functions, the server is able to compute the total function $f(x)$, which can be shown to the audit agency as a proof for the visits received by clients.

The problem of this approach is that known implementations of threshold computations are far too inefficient in terms of computation and communication to be applicable for metering.

2.5 Secret Sharing

A *secret sharing scheme* is a technique to share a secret among a set of n participants in such a way that only qualified subsets, pooling together their information, can reconstruct the secret; but, subsets of participants that are not enabled to recover the secret have no information about it. Secret sharing schemes were introduced by Shamir [44] and Blakley [8]. The survey by Stinson [45] contains an unified description of results in the area of secret sharing schemes. The reader can also profitably see the book [46].

Naor and Pinkas [34–36] first proposed secret sharing based metering schemes, where any server provides the audit agency with a short *proof*[2], of the visits it has received. In their scheme, which are supposed to be active for a certain number of time frames, any server which has been visited by any set of h or more clients in a time frame, where h is a parameter of the scheme, is able to compute the proof, whereas, any server receiving visits from less than h clients in a time frame has no information about its proof for that time frame. These schemes are called *threshold metering schemes*.

The work of Naor and Pinkas formed the basis for a number of subsequent research efforts. The authors of [13, 19] proposed an information-theoretic approach to metering schemes and showed lower bounds on the communication complexity of such schemes. They also proposed metering schemes offering a trade-off between the security requirements and the complexity of the information distribution. Metering schemes with pricing were considered in [12, 13, 30]. Such schemes provide a flexible payment system since they enable the audit agency to count the exact number of visits that a server has received in any time frame. Dynamic multi-threshold metering schemes were proposed in [14]. In such schemes, the number of visits required to servers to compute their proofs can be different for each server and each time frame. Metering schemes realizing general access structures[3] have been introduced in [29] and further analyzed in [4, 11, 39, 40].

3 General Framework

In this section, we present the general framework which will be used to describe metering schemes in the rest of this paper. Moreover, we specify the requirements for metering schemes.

---

[2] In metering schemes, a *proof* is a value that the server can compute only if a fixed number of clients have visited it or a client has visited it a certain number of times. Such a value is sent to the audit agency at fixed time intervals.

[3] The access structure is the family of all subsets of clients, called *qualified sets*, which enable a server to compute its proof (i.e., if a server receives visits from all clients belonging to some qualified set, then it can compute the *proof*).

A *metering scheme* consists of n clients, say $C_1, \ldots, C_n$, m servers, say $S_1, \ldots, S_m$, and an audit agency $\mathcal{A}$ whose task is to measure the interaction between the clients and the servers. The life cycle of a metering scheme is divided into a number τ of *time frames*. Any client visit to a server within a time frame is called a *regular operation*. At the end of each time frame, each server which has received visits from certain subsets of clients within that time frame can prove this fact to the audit agency and receive the payment corresponding to its services in that time frame. The *access structure* Γ of the metering scheme is the collection of subsets of clients, called *qualified sets*, whose visits to any server within each time frame will enable the server to be paid by the audit agency. In particular, any server which has been visited by at least a qualified subset of clients within a time frame will be able to provide the audit agency with a proof for the visits it has received. Moreover, if two different qualified sets of clients visit the same server within a certain time frame, the proofs computed by the server at the end of the time frame are the same, that is, the server will be paid only once.

The general structure of a metering scheme is the following:

- *Initialization.* This step is performed once by the audit agency $\mathcal{A}$. The audit agency $\mathcal{A}$ chooses a random secret key and generates an initialization message for any client, which is a function of this key and of the identity of the client. This message is sent to any client through a private channel and should be kept secret by the client.
- *Regular Operation in a Time Frame.* Every time a client C_i visits a server S_j in a time frame t, it uses its private information to compute a message which is sent to the visited server.
- *Proof Computation for a Time Frame.* At the end of a time frame any server uses the information provided by a qualified subset of clients within the time frame and the information provided by the audit agency at the beginning of the time frame to compute a proof. Such a proof is sent to the audit agency.
- *Proof Verification for a Time Frame.* During this stage, the audit agency verifies if the proofs received by the servers are consistent with its private information. In this case, the audit agency pays the server for its services, otherwise, it does not provide any money.

This is the most general form of a metering scheme. There are metering schemes which also require other kinds of information exchanges among the parties, for example, some schemes require the audit agency to send some initialization information to servers at the beginning of each time frame. There are also schemes requiring the audit agency to "help" servers in the proof computation, by sending them some information at the end of each time frame.

3.1 Assumptions and Requirements

In the following section, we consider the assumptions regarding the parties involved in a metering scheme.

- AUDIT AGENCY. We assume that the audit agency is a trusted third party and that the information sent by the audit agency to each client, by means of private channels, is correct. Clearly, clients are required to register with the audit agency in order to participate to the metering process.
- CLIENTS. The metering scenario contemplates the existence of a certain number of *corrupt clients*. While honest clients are expected to keep their private information secret and to send correct information to servers during their visits, corrupt clients could cooperate with corrupt servers in order to help them inflate the count of their visits within a certain time frame. A corrupt client can donate to a corrupt server the whole private information received by the audit agency during the initialization phase. Moreover, in several schemes corrupt clients can also attempt to defraud a honest server by sending incorrect information during a regular operation. In this case, servers also need a method to verify the correctness of the information sent by corrupt clients.
- SERVERS. The scenario also contemplates the existence of a certain number of *corrupt servers*. While honest servers are expected to keep secret the proofs computed by using the information received by clients, corrupt servers could cooperate with other corrupt servers to inflate the count of their visits within a certain time frame. In particular, within a time frame t, a corrupt server can donate to another corrupt server the information that it has received during time frames $1, \ldots, t$. Such information includes the sets of client visits received by the server within time frames $1, \ldots, t$.

A metering scheme should meet the following requirements:

- SECURITY. The system should protect the audit agency from servers that claim they received more visits than they did. Moreover, servers should be protected from corrupt clients which will not help them compute their proof. The security of a metering scheme can rely either on the computational infeasibility of breaking it (*computational security*), or on the theoretical impossibility of breaking it, even using infinite computing power (*information-theoretic or unconditional security*).
- NONREPUDIATION. The audit agency should not doubt the proofs computed by the servers. In case of a dispute, the servers should be able to show evidence of the received visits.
- ACCURACY. The results of the metering process should reflect the real interaction between clients and servers as closely as possible.
- EFFICIENCY. The computation and storage requirements for the parties should be minimal, especially for the clients, which do not have a direct gain from the metering system.
- PRIVACY. The system should preserve clients, privacy by preventing tracking and retrieving unnecessary details of client behaviors.
- ANONYMITY. The system should enable client anonymity, that is, each server should not be able to tell whether several visits were performed by the same client.

It is important to notice that none of the existing metering scheme satisfies all requirements listed above.

3.2 Complexity Measures

The main resources one has to consider when analyzing a metering scheme are the following:

- *Communication Complexity.* Metering schemes involve distributing information to clients and servers. The clients receive some information from the audit agency and such information is used to compute the information sent to the servers when visiting them. Since such information distribution affects the overall communication complexity, a major goal is to construct metering schemes whose overhead to the overall communication is as small as possible.
- *Space Complexity.* The problem of establishing bounds on the size of the private information distributed to clients has received considerable attention by several researchers. The practical relevance of this issue is based on the following observations: First, the security of any system tends to degrade as the amount of information that must be kept secret, that is, the private information held by clients, increases. Second, if the private information given to clients is too long, the memory requirements for the clients will be too severe, and, at the same time, the initialization phase will become inefficient. Therefore, it is important to derive significant upper and lower bounds on the size of information distributed to clients.
- *Randomness Complexity.* During the initialization phase of any metering scheme, the audit agency has to choose a *random* secret key in order to generate the private information to be distributed to each client. Since truly random bits are hard to obtain (they require the use of a natural source of randomness, such as an unbiased coin, a radioactive source, or a noise diode), the problem of estimating the amount of random bits needed by the audit agency to set up a metering scheme has also received considerably attention.

4 Unconditionally Secure Metering Schemes

In this section we describe metering schemes which are *unconditionally secure* against servers trying to inflate the number of clients they served: this means that any server which has not been visited by a qualified set of clients in a time frame has *no information* at all about its proof for that time frame. In this setting, the amount of resources that corrupt servers and clients can afford in order to forge a server's proof is unbounded, that is, they can use as much time and space they need. Although the servers are so powerful, the only thing they can do in order to compute a proof is to guess the proof itself.

4.1 Threshold Metering Schemes

Naor and Pinkas [34] first proposed metering schemes based on threshold secret sharing schemes. In a threshold secret sharing scheme, a secret is shared among n participants in such a way that any set of participants having cardinality greater than or equal to a fixed threshold h can recover it, whereas, sets of cardinality less than h have no information about the secret. Particular threshold secret sharing schemes proposed by Shamir [44] are based on polynomial interpolation in a finite field Z_q, where $q > n$ is a prime number. The construction is the following: let $S \in Z_q$ be the secret to be shared. To set up the scheme, the dealer, who is the party performing the secret sharing, randomly chooses $h - 1$ coefficients $a_1, \ldots, a_{h-1}$ in Z_q and constructs the polynomial $Q(x) = S + \sum_{j=1}^{h-1} a_j x^j \bmod q$. The share distributed to the i-th participant is equal to $y_i = Q(i)$. Any h participants, pooling together their shares, can reconstruct the polynomial $Q(x)$ (and hence recover the secret $s = Q(0)$) by solving a system of h linear equations in h unknowns. An alternative method for the reconstruction of the polynomial $Q(x)$, given the shares $y_{i_1}, \ldots, y_{i_h}$ and the identities $i_1, \ldots, i_h$ of any h participants, is based on the Lagrange interpolation formula

$$Q(x) = \sum_{j=1}^{h} y_{i_j} \prod_{1 \le k \le h, k \ne j} \frac{x - i_k}{i_j - i_k}$$

and requires $O(h^2)$ steps. In particular, since the h participants are only interested in recovering the secret, they do not need to recover the whole polynomial, but just its constant term. Therefore, they can use the following formula

$$S = Q(0) = \sum_{j=1}^{h} y_{i_j} \prod_{1 \le k \le h, k \ne j} \frac{i_k}{i_k - i_j}.$$

On the other hand, any $h - 1$ participants have no information about the secret. Indeed, by pooling together their shares, they will obtain a system of $h - 1$ linear equations in h unknowns. Since, for any hypothesized value S' of the secret, there will be a unique polynomial $Q'(x)$, which is consistent with the $h - 1$ shares and such that $Q'(0) = S'$, no value of the secret can be ruled out. Hence, the participants have no information about the secret.

As shown by Naor and Pinkas, threshold secret sharing schemes can be used in the metering scenario in the following way: the audit agency splits a secret into n shares (where n is the number of clients) and gives a share to each client. When a client visits a server, it gives its share to the server. If the server receives h different shares from h different clients, then it is able to reconstruct the secret. This secret is shown to the audit agency as a *proof* for h client visits. This straightforward implementation of a metering scheme works if the measurement is performed in a single time frame and if there are no corrupt clients or servers. Indeed, the proof (i.e., the secret) is the same for all servers. Therefore, the above construction cannot be used if there are corrupt servers or clients or several time frames. What is needed in this case is a method enabling different servers to reconstruct different proofs in different time frames.

To accommodate many servers and many time frames, Naor and Pinkas proposed a metering scheme based on a modified version of the polynomial secret sharing scheme of Shamir [44]. Their scheme uses a bivariate polynomial rather than a univariate one to share many secrets, which serve as proofs for different servers in different time frames. In their scheme, the qualified subsets of clients are those of cardinality larger than or equal to h, where h is a parameter of the scheme. Their scenario contemplates the presence of a certain number $c \leq h - 1$ of corrupt clients and a certain number $s \leq m$ of corrupt servers which could cooperate in order to inflate the count of visits received by servers. Let $q > n$ be a prime number. In the following, we use the term *regular visit* to indicate visits performed by non-corrupt clients. Moreover, we denote by "∘" an operator mapping each pair (j, t), with $j = 1, \ldots, m$ and $t = 1, \ldots, \tau$, to an element of Z_q, having the property that no distinct two pairs (j, t) and (j', t') are mapped to the same element. The scheme is described in Fig. 1.

In the following section we analyze the randomness, space, and communication complexities of the above scheme. In order to set up the scheme, the audit agency has to choose a random bivariate polynomial over Z_q, having degree $h - 1$ in x and $s\tau - 1$ in y. Therefore, it has to choose $hs\tau$ random coefficients in Z_q, requiring a total amount of $hs\tau \log q$ random bits. Concerning to clients, they are required to store a polynomial of degree $s\tau - 1$ over Z_q. Hence, the size of the information kept secret by clients is equal to $s\tau \log q$ bits. During a regular operation in time frame t, each server S_j receives the pair $(i, Q(i, j \circ t))$ from a client C_i. However, in order to evaluate the communication complexity, the space needed to store the identity i

---

Initialization:

- The audit agency $\mathcal{A}$ chooses a random bivariate polynomial $Q(x, y)$ over Z_q of degree $h - 1$ in x and degree $s\tau - 1$ in y.
- The audit agency $\mathcal{A}$ sends the polynomial $Q(i, y)$, whose degree is $s\tau - 1$, to each client C_i.

Regular Operation for Time Frame t:
When the client C_i visits the server S_j in time frame t, it sends the pair $(i, Q(i, j \circ t))$ to S_j.

Proof Generation for Time Frame t:

- Assume that the server S_j has been visited by at least h different clients in time frame t.
- The server S_j can perform a Lagrange interpolation on the polynomial $Q(x, j \circ t)$ and compute the proof as $Q(0, j \circ t)$.
- The server S_j sends the value $Q(0, j \circ t)$ to the audit agency.

Proof Verification for Time Frame t:
The audit agency $\mathcal{A}$ verifies the proof received by S_j by evaluating the polynomial $Q(x, y)$ at the point $(0, j \circ t)$.

Fig. 1 Naor–Pinkas threshold metering scheme (NP-U)

of the client will not be considered. Indeed, such an identity could be substituted by the IP address of the client since the IP address will be revealed to the server during the communication with the client. Clearly, each client must have a static IP address and not a dynamic one. It follows that the size of the information sent from clients to servers is equal to $\log q$ bits. The IP address of the client will be mapped by the server to a value in Z_q. Finally, the proof computed by each server S_j at the end of the time frame t is an element in Z_q, having size $\log q$ bits. Moreover, in the above scheme, clients do relatively little additional work (they evaluate a polynomial over a small field and send its result to the audit agency) and are not required to change their communication pattern. The amount of work performed by servers is similar to prove that a certain number of clients visited it, any server sends to the audit agency the result of an interpolation of a polynomial over a small field (and the audit agency can efficiently verify it by evaluating the polynomial $Q(x, y)$ at the point $(0, j \circ t)$).

An Example We want to set up a metering scheme to check if any server received at least $h = 1.000$ visits in a certain number $\tau = 100$ of time frames. The scheme should be secure against a coalition of up to $s = 10$ corrupt server. Let $q = 2^{31} - 1$ and let $Q(x, y)$ be a polynomial over Z_q of degree $h - 1 = 999$ in x and $s \cdot \tau - 1 = 999$ in y. As the finite field Z_q is small, the basic arithmetic operations on its elements, which are 32-bit words, are very efficient.

In order to set up the scheme, the audit agency has to choose $hs\tau \log q = 32.000$ random bits, hence the randomness complexity of the scheme is 4 Mbytes. The share held by each client consists of a polynomial of degree 999, whose storage requires 4 Kbytes. In order to perform a regular operation, each client has to perform a polynomial evaluation. The result of such evaluation, which is a 32-bit word, is sent to the visited server. After receiving 1.000 client visits within a time frame, a server can compute its proof by interpolating a polynomial of degree 999. The proof generated by each server, which is a 32-bit word, can be verified by the audit agency by evaluating a polynomial of degree 1.000.

4.1.1 An Entropy Based Model

In this section, we describe Naor–Pinkas threshold metering schemes by using an information-theoretic approach. Such an approach, proposed in [19], can be used to describe any unconditionally secure metering scheme.

With a boldface capital letter, say $\mathbf{X}$, we denote a random variable taking value on a set, denoted with the corresponding capital letter X, according to some probability distribution $\{Pr_{\mathbf{X}}(x)\}_{x \in X}$. The values such a random variable can take are denoted with the corresponding lower case letter. Given a random variable $\mathbf{X}$, we denote with $H(\mathbf{X})$ the Shannon entropy of $\{Pr_{\mathbf{X}}(x)\}_{x \in X}$ (for some basic properties of entropy, consult the Appendix).

During the initialization phase, the audit agency provides each client with some information about the server's proofs. For any $i = 1, \ldots, n$, we denote by c_i the information that the audit agency $\mathcal{A}$ gives to the client $\mathcal{C}_i$ during the initialization phase. Moreover, we denote by C_i the set of all possible values that c_i can assume. Given a set of client indices $X = \{i_1, \ldots, i_\ell\} \subseteq \{1, \ldots, n\}$, where $i_1 < i_2 < \ldots < i_\ell$, we denote by C_X the Cartesian product $C_{i_1} \times \cdots \times C_{i_\ell}$.

During a regular operation, a client uses the information received in the initialization phase to compute the information passed to servers when visiting them. For any $i = 1, \ldots, n$, $j = 1, \ldots, m$, and $t = 1, \ldots, \tau$, we denote by $c_{i,j}^t$ the information that the client C_i sends to the server S_j when visiting it in time frame t. Moreover, we denote by $C_{i,j}^t$ the set of all possible values that $c_{i,j}^t$ can assume. Given a set of client indices $X = \{i_1, \ldots, i_\ell\} \subseteq \{1, \ldots, n\}$, where $i_1 < i_2 < \ldots < i_\ell$, we denote by $C_{X,j}^t$ the Cartesian product $C_{i_1,j}^t \times \cdots \times C_{i_\ell,j}^t$.

During the proof computation phase, servers compute the proofs to be sent to the audit agency. For any $j = 1, \ldots, m$ and $t = 1, \ldots, \tau$, we denote by p_j^t the proof computed by the server S_j when it has been visited by a subset of clients having cardinality larger than or equal to h in time frame t. Moreover, we denote by P_j^t the set of all values that p_j^t can assume. Given a set of server indices $B = \{j_1, \ldots, j_\beta\} \subseteq \{1, \ldots, m\}$, where $j_1 < j_2 < \ldots < j_\beta$, we denote by P_B^t the cartesian product $P_{j_1}^t \times \cdots \times P_{j_\beta}^t$.

A *corrupt* server can be assisted by corrupt clients and other corrupt servers in order to inflate the count of its visits. A corrupt client C_i can donate to a corrupt server the whole private information received by the audit agency during the initialization phase. In time frame t, where $t = 1, \ldots, \tau$, a corrupt server can donate to another corrupt server the information that it has received during time frames $1, \ldots, t$. For any $i = 1, \ldots, n$ and $t = 1, \ldots, \tau$, we denote by $V_j^{[t]}$ the *view* of the server S_j at time frame t. Such information includes the sets of client visits received by server S_j in time frames $1, \ldots, t$. We also define $V_j^{[0]} = \emptyset$, for any corrupt server S_j. Given a set of server indices $B = \{j_1, \ldots, j_\beta\} \subseteq \{1, \ldots, m\}$, where $j_1 < j_2 < \ldots < j_\beta$, we denote by $V_B^{[t]}$ the cartesian product $V_{j_1}^{[t]} \times \cdots \times V_{j_\beta}^{[t]}$.

An (n, m, τ, c, s, h) *threshold metering scheme* is a protocol to measure the interaction between n clients and m servers during τ time frames in such a way that the following properties are satisfied:

- **Visit Computation.** For any time frame $t = 1, \ldots, \tau$, any client is able to compute the information needed to visit any server in time frame t:
  Formally, for $i = 1, \ldots, n$, $j = 1, \ldots, m$, and $t = 1, \ldots, \tau$, it holds that

$$H(\mathbf{C}_{i,j}^t | \mathbf{C}_i) = 0.$$

- **Proof Computation.** For any time frame $t = 1, \ldots, \tau$, any server which has been visited by h different clients in time frame t can compute its proof for t:
  Formally, for $j = 1, \ldots, m$, $t = 1, \ldots, \tau$, and any $X \subseteq \{1, \ldots, n\}$ such that $|X| \geq h$, it holds that

$$H(\mathbf{P}_j^t | \mathbf{C}_{X,j}^t) = 0.$$

- **Security.** Consider a coalition of at most s corrupt servers and at most c corrupt clients. Assume that in some time frame t each corrupt server in the coalition has been visited by less than h honest clients. Then, the corrupt servers have no information about their proofs for time frame t, even if they are helped by the corrupt clients.

  Formally, for any $B = \{j_1, \ldots, j_\beta\} \subseteq \{1, \ldots, m\}$, $X_1, \ldots, X_\beta, Y \subseteq \{1, \ldots, n\}$, such that $|B| = \beta \leq s$, $|Y| \leq c$, $|X_j| \leq h - 1$ and $|X_j \cup Y| \leq h - 1$, for any $j = 1, \ldots, \beta$, and any $t = 1, \ldots, \tau$, it holds that

$$H(\mathbf{P}_B^t | \mathbf{C}_Y \, \mathbf{C}_{X_1, j_1}^t \cdots \mathbf{C}_{X_\beta, j_\beta}^t \, \mathbf{V}_B^{[t-1]}) = H(\mathbf{P}_B^t).$$

The problem of establishing bounds on the communication and randomness complexities of metering schemes has been addressed in several papers (see [12, 14, 19, 29, 30]). In particular, in [19], it was shown that if the proofs for the servers are uniformly chosen in a finite field F, then the size of the information that any client passes to any server during a visit is lower bounded by $\log |F|$, that is,

$$\log |C_{i,j}^t| \geq \log |F| \text{ for any } i = 1, \ldots, n, \ j = 1, \ldots, m, \text{ and } t = 1, \ldots, \tau. \quad (1)$$

Moreover, if also the proofs for the servers are statistically independent, then the size of the information distributed to any client during the initialization phase is lower bounded by $s\tau \log |F|$, that is

$$\log |C_i| \geq s\tau \log |F| \text{ for any } i = 1, \ldots, n. \quad (2)$$

Finally, in [30], it was shown that in the same hypothesis as the above result, the number of random bits needed by the dealer to set up an (h, n)-threshold metering scheme is lower bounded by $hs\tau \log |F|$, that is

$$\log |C_1 \times \cdots \times C_n| \geq hs\tau \log |F|. \quad (3)$$

It is easy to see that the scheme of Fig. 1 meets the above bounds.

4.2 Metering Schemes with Pricing

Threshold metering schemes can be used to check if a server received at least h visits, where h is a predefined parameter of the schemes. Indeed, in such schemes, a server that has received a number of visits less than h is in the same situation as a server which has received no visit, that is, it has absolutely no information about its proof. Consequently, the audit agency will pay nothing to a server that has been visited by less than h clients.

Metering schemes with pricing were introduced in [12, 13] and further analyzed in [30]. Compared to threshold metering schemes, these schemes enable a more flexible payment system since they allow to count the exact number of visits received by each server, which is paid accordingly. In these schemes, there are two thresholds ℓ and h, where $\ell < h \leq n$, and any server can be in three different situations: (1) the server is visited by a number of clients greater than or equal to h; (2) the server is visited by a number of clients smaller than or equal to ℓ; (3) the server is visited by a number r of clients between $\ell + 1$ and h. The audit agency would pay all the negotiated amount for the exposure of the ads in case 1; it would pay nothing in case 2; and it would pay a smaller sum, which depends on the number of visits r, in case 3.

A Non-Interactive Scheme In the metering scheme proposed in [12, 13], there is a proof associated to any number of client visits between $\ell + 1$ and h, for any server and for any time frame. Moreover, each server can compute its proof as a function of the information provided by the clients visiting it and does not need any interaction with the audit agency. The scheme uses $h - \ell$ independent Naor and Pinkas metering schemes, with thresholds $\ell + 1, \ldots, h$. The scheme is described in Fig. 2.

In the following, we analyze the randomness, space, and communication complexities of the scheme. In order to set up the scheme, the audit agency has to choose $h - \ell$ random bivariate polynomials $Q_{\ell+1}(x, y), \ldots, Q_h(x, y)$ over Z_q, where, for $z = \ell + 1, \ldots, h$, the polynomial $Q_z(x, y)$ has degree $z - 1$ in x and $s\tau - 1$ in y. Therefore, it has to choose $s\tau \sum_{z=\ell+1}^{h} z$ random coefficients in Z_q, requiring a total amount of $s\tau \sum_{z=\ell+1}^{h} z \log q$ random bits. Concerning to clients, they are required to store $h - \ell$ polynomials of degree $s\tau - 1$ over Z_q. Hence, the size of the information kept secret by clients is equal to $(h - \ell)s\tau \log q$ bits. During a regular

---

Initialization:

- The audit agency $\mathcal{A}$ chooses $h - \ell$ random bivariate polynomials $Q_{\ell+1}(x, y), \ldots, Q_h(x, y)$ over Z_q, where, for $z = \ell + 1, \ldots, h$, the polynomial $Q_z(x, y)$ is of degree $z - 1$ in x and degree $s\tau - 1$ in y.
- The audit agency $\mathcal{A}$ sends to each client C_i the $h - \ell$ polynomials $Q_{\ell+1}(i, y), \ldots, Q_h(i, y)$, which are of degree $s\tau - 1$.

Regular Operation for Time Frame t:

When the client C_i visits the server S_j in time frame t, it sends the $h - \ell$ values $Q_{\ell+1}(i, j \circ t)$, $\ldots, Q_h(i, j \circ t)$ to S_j.

Proof Generation and Verification for Time Frame t:

- Assume that the server S_j has been visited by a number r of clients, $\ell < r \leq h$, in time frame t.
- The server S_j can perform a Lagrange interpolation on the polynomial $Q_r(x, j \circ t)$ and compute the r-proof $Q_r(0, j \circ t)$.
- The server S_j sends the pair $(Q_r(0, j \circ t), r)$ to the audit agency.
- The audit agency $\mathcal{A}$ verifies the proof by evaluating the polynomial $Q_r(x, y)$ at the point $(0, j \circ t)$.

Fig. 2 A non-interactive metering scheme with pricing (NI)

operation in time frame t, each server S_j receives from a client an $(h - \ell)$-tuple of elements of Z_q. Hence, the size of the information sent from clients to servers is equal to $(h - \ell) \log q$ bits. Finally, the r-proof computed by each server S_j which has received r client visits in time frame t is an element in Z_q, having size $\log q$ bits.

An Interactive Scheme A different kind of metering scheme with pricing was presented in [30]. In such a scheme, for any server S_j and any time frame t, there is a unique proof p_j^t associated to the server in that time frame. If the server is visited by a number of clients between ℓ and $h - 1$ in time frame t, it gains *some information* about its proof for t. The uncertainty of a server with respect to its proof for t decreases linearly as the number of client visits in time frame t increases between ℓ and $h - 1$. Consequently, any server receiving a number of visits less than h in a time frame is not able to compute its proof, but needs to interact with the audit agency at the end of the time frame. Only after receiving some information from the audit agency the server will be able to compute its proof. The pricing payment system depends on the amount of information that the audit agency sends to the server before the computation of the proof. The scheme is described in Fig. 3.

In the following section, we analyze the randomness, space, and communication complexities of the above scheme. In order to set up the scheme, the audit agency

---

Initialization:

- Let $f_1, \ldots, f_{h-\ell}$ be preselected elements of Z_q distinct from $1, \ldots, n$, which are known to any client and any server.
- The audit agency $\mathcal{A}$ chooses a random bivariate polynomial $Q(x, y)$ over Z_q, of degree $h - 1$ in x and degree $s\tau - 1$ in y.
- The audit agency $\mathcal{A}$ sends the polynomial $Q(i, y)$ to each client C_i.

Regular Operation for Time Frame t:
When the client C_i visits the server S_j in time frame t, it sends the value $Q(i, j \circ t)$ to S_j.

End of Time Frame t:

- Let r be the number of visits received by S_j in time frame t. Then, S_j sends the message "I received r visits in time frame t" to $\mathcal{A}$.
- If $r \leq \ell$ or $r \geq h$, then $\mathcal{A}$ does not send any message to S_j; whereas, if $\ell < r < h$, then $\mathcal{A}$ evaluates the polynomial $Q(x, j \circ t)$ in $h - r$ points other than $1, \ldots, n, f_1, \ldots, f_{h-\ell}$ and sends the results to S_j.

Proof Generation for Time Frame t:

- Assume that the server S_j has been visited by $r > \ell$ different clients in time frame t.
- Then, knowing the $h - r$ points of $Q(x, j \circ t)$ received by $\mathcal{A}$, S_j can perform a Lagrange interpolation on the polynomial $Q(x, j \circ t)$ and compute the proof as the $(h - \ell)$-tuple $(Q(f_1, j \circ t), \ldots, Q(f_{h-\ell}, j \circ t))$.

Proof Verification and Pricing Evaluation for Time Frame t:

- The audit agency verifies the proof received by S_j by computing $Q(f_v, j \circ t)$, for $v = 1, \ldots, h - \ell$. If the proof is correct, then $\mathcal{A}$ decides on the amount of money to be paid to S_j based on the number of values sent to S_j at the end of the time frame.

Fig. 3 An interactive metering scheme with pricing (I)

has to choose a random bivariate polynomial over Z_q, of degree $h - 1$ in x and $s\tau - 1$ in y. Therefore, it has to choose $hs\tau$ random coefficients in Z_q, requiring a total amount of $hs\tau \log q$ random bits. Concerning to clients, they are required to store a polynomial of degree $s\tau - 1$ over Z_q. Hence, the size of the information kept secret by clients is equal to $s\tau \log q$ bits. During a regular operation in time frame t, each server S_j receives from a client C_i the value $Q(i, j \circ t)$, which is an element of Z_q. Hence, the size of the information sent from clients to servers is equal to $\log q$ bits. At the end of a time frame, a server which has received r visits from client, where $\ell < r < h$, receives from the audit agency other $h - r$ points of the polynomial $Q(x, j \circ t)$. Hence, the size of the information sent from the audit agency to servers is equal to $(h-r) \log q$ bits. Finally, the proof computed by each server S_j in time frame t is an $(h - \ell)$-tuple of elements in Z_q, having size $(h - \ell) \log q$ bits. Compared to the scheme presented in [12], this scheme distributes less information to clients and servers. The drawback of the scheme is that it requires servers to interact with the audit agency in order to compute their proofs.

4.3 Metering Schemes for General Access Structures

The measures considered in previous metering schemes are simple thresholds. In other words, these measures can distinguish between two cases: either the server has received at least a required number of visits or it has not. The authors of [29] considered a more general situation. They showed how to construct a metering scheme realizing any access structure, where the access structure is the family of all subsets of clients, called *qualified sets*, which enable a server to compute its proof. The construction uses as building blocks threshold metering schemes proposed by Naor and Pinkas. The proofs are points of a finite field Z_q where q is a sufficiently large prime number. Let $\Gamma = \{A_1, \ldots, A_\ell\}$ be a monotone access structure on the set of clients $\{C_1, \ldots, C_n\}$, and let $h_r = |A_r|$, for any $r = 1, \ldots, \ell$. The scheme is described in Fig. 4.

The authors of [29] also proved several lower bounds on the communication complexity of metering schemes realizing monotone access structures. In particular, they proved that if the proofs for the servers are uniformly chosen in a finite field F, then the size of the information that any client passes to any server during a visit is lower bounded by $\log |F|$, that is,

$$\log |C_{i,j}^t| \geq \log |F| \quad \text{for any } i = 1, \ldots, n, \ j = 1, \ldots, m, \text{ and } t = 1, \ldots, \tau. \quad (4)$$

Moreover, if also the proofs for the servers are statistically independent, then the size of the information distributed to any client during the initialization phase is lower bounded by $s\tau \log |F|$, that is

$$\log |C_i| \geq s\tau \log |F| \quad \text{for any } i = 1, \ldots, n. \quad (5)$$

Initialization:

- The audit agency A chooses a polynomial $P_1(x, y)$ over $GF(q)$, which is of degree $h_1 - 1$ in x and $s\tau - 1$ in y.
- For $r = 2, \ldots, \ell$, A chooses a polynomial $P_r(x, y)$ over $GF(q)$, which is of degree $h_r - 1$ in x and $s\tau - 1$ in y and such that $P_r(0, y) = P_1(0, y)$.
- Afterwards, for any $r = 1, \ldots, \ell$, A gives the polynomial $P_r(i, y)$ to each client $C_i \in \mathcal{A}_r$.

Regular Operation for Time Frame t:

When a client C_i visits a server S_j during a time frame t it gives the values $P_r(i, j \circ t)$, for any $r \in \{1, \ldots, \ell\}$ such that $C_i \in \mathcal{A}_r$, to S_j.

Proof Generation and Verification:

- If during a time frame t a server S_j has received visits from a qualified set $\mathcal{A}_r$, for some $r \in \{1, \ldots, \ell\}$, then it can interpolate the polynomial $P_r(x, j \circ t)$ and compute the proof $P_r(0, j \circ t)$.
- When the audit agency receives the value $P_r(0, j \circ t)$, it can easily verify if this is the correct proof for server S_j.

Fig. 4 A metering scheme for any access structure (GA)

A metering scheme realizing an access structure Γ is said to be *optimal* if both the bounds (4) and (5) are met with equality. If there is any access structure Γ for which there exists an optimal metering scheme realizing, it is called an *optimal access structure*.

The construction of Fig. 4 in general gives schemes which are not optimal with respect to the communication complexity. Indeed, the amount of information received by a client during the initialization phase and that of the information distributed by the client during a visit to a server depend on the number of qualified subsets that the client belongs to. For any client C_i, let d_i be the number of sets $X \in \Gamma$ such that $C_i \in X$. In the construction of Fig. 4, the proofs are points of a finite field Z_q where q is a sufficiently large prime number. In order to set up the scheme, the audit agency has to choose $s\tau \sum_{r=+1}^{\ell}(h_r - 1)$ random coefficients in Z_q, requiring a total amount of $s\tau \sum_{r=1}^{\ell}(h_r - 1) \log q$ random bits. Moreover, the information distributed to client C_i by the audit agency consists of $d_i s\tau$ points of Z_q, that is, its size is equal to $d_i s\tau \log q$ bits. Finally, the information given from client C_i to a server S_j during a visit in a time frame consists of d_i points of Z_q. that is, its size is equal to $d_i \log q$ bits. If we construct a metering scheme realizing a threshold access structure Γ with threshold h by using the construction of Fig. 4, then the information distributed to each client by the audit agency consists in $\binom{n-1}{h-1}s\tau$ points of Z_q, that is, its size is equal to $\binom{n-1}{h-1}s\tau \log q$ bits. Moreover, the information distributed by any client to any server during a visit consists in $\binom{n-1}{h-1}$ points of Z_q, that is, its size is equal to $\binom{n-1}{h-1} \log q$ bits. This construction is very inefficient compared to the construction proposed by Naor and Pinkas [34].

The authors of [11] showed a general construction for optimal metering schemes realizing general access structures. Their construction is based on the Brickell vector space construction for secret sharing schemes [16] and can be applied if there exists a linear function ϕ describing the access structure realized by the metering scheme. In the following, given a set G of vectors, we denote by $\langle G \rangle$ the linear space spanned by the vectors in G. Let $d \geq 2$, let $e_1 = (1, 0, \ldots, 0)$ be a d-dimensional vector, and let $(Z_q)^d$ be the vector space of all d-tuples over Z_q, where q is a prime number. Let Γ be an access structure such that there exists a function $\phi : C \rightarrow (Z_q)^d$ which satisfies the property

$$e_1 \in < \phi(C_i) : C_i \in X > \; \Leftrightarrow \; X \in \Gamma. \tag{6}$$

In other words, the vector e_1 can be expressed as a linear combination of the vectors in the set $\{\phi(C_i) : C_i \in X\}$ if and only if X is a qualified subset. Notice that a general upper bound on the parameter d is not known, and in some cases, d can be quite large. However, in our scheme, the information that each client has to keep secret does not depend on d, but only on s and τ. In Fig. 5, we show how to construct an optimal metering scheme realizing the access structure Γ.

The scheme meets the bounds (4) and (5). Indeed, the information distributed to any client by the audit agency consists of $s\tau$ points of Z_q, whereas, the information given from any client to any server during a visit consists of a single point of Z_q.

Initialization:

- For any client C_i the audit agency $\mathcal{A}$ constructs the d-dimensional vector $v_i = \phi(C_i)$. This vector is sent to client C_i over a public channel.
- For any server S_j the audit agency $\mathcal{A}$ constructs the matrix B_j with $s\tau$ rows and τ columns, whose t-th column is the $s\tau$-dimensional vector $b_j^t = (1, j \circ t, (j \circ t)^2, \ldots, (j \circ t)^{s\tau-1})$, for $t = 1, \ldots, \tau$. For the sake of simplicity, we assume that the matrix B_j is made public by the audit agency, but it could be computed by the server S_j itself (and also by the other servers and clients), since its structure is known.
- Afterwards, $\mathcal{A}$ constructs a random matrix M with d rows and $s\tau$ columns. This matrix is kept secret by $\mathcal{A}$.
- For any client C_i, $\mathcal{A}$ computes the $s\tau$-dimensional vector $c_i = v_i \cdot M$. This vector is sent to client C_i over a private channel.

Regular Operation for Time Frame t:

- Let b_j^t be the t-th column of the matrix B_j and let $g_j^t = M \cdot b_j^t$ be a d-dimensional vector.
- When a client C_i visits a server S_j during a time frame t it computes the value $c_{i,j}^t = c_i \cdot b_j^t = (v_i \cdot M) \cdot b_j^t = v_i \cdot (M \cdot b_j^t) = v_i \cdot g_j^t$. This value is sent to S_j.

Proof Generation for Time Frame t:

- Let $X \in \Gamma$ be a qualified set of clients visiting a server S_j in time frame t.
- Then, the server S_j can compute its proof for time frame t as $p_j^t = \sum_{i:C_i \in X} a_i c_{i,j}^t$, where each $a_i \in Z_q$ and is such that the d-dimensional vector e_1 can be expressed as $e_1 = \sum_{i:C_i \in X} a_i v_i$.

Fig. 5 An optimal metering scheme (OPT)

The vector space construction for optimal metering schemes realizing an access structure Γ can be applied if there exists a function ϕ such that property (6) is satisfied. The problem of the existence of such a function ϕ has been extensively studied by several researchers in the area of secret sharing schemes (see [16] and [45]). Karchmer and Wigderson [27] generalized Brickell's construction, showing how to construct a linear secret sharing scheme realizing any general access structure. Their scheme is at least as efficient as any other linear secret sharing scheme (see Chap. 4 of [5]). Therefore, in order to construct a not necessarily optimal metering scheme realizing any general access structure, we could use Karchmer and Wigderson construction instead than Brickell's one. Indeed, the authors of [15] proposed a linear algebraic approach to design metering schemes realizing any access structure. Namely, given any access structure, they presented a method to construct a metering scheme realizing it from any linear secret sharing scheme with the same access structure. Besides, they proved some properties about the relationship between metering schemes and secret sharing schemes. These properties provide some new bounds on the communication complexity of metering schemes. According to these bounds, the optimality of the metering schemes obtained by their method relies upon the optimality of the linear secret sharing schemes for the given access structure.

In the following, we show how to construct the function ϕ for some access structures. Consequently, the vector space construction can be applied to obtain optimal metering schemes realizing these access structures.

Threshold Structures Naor and Pinkas [34] showed how to construct optimal metering scheme realizing a *threshold access structure*, that is, such that the qualified subsets of clients are those having cardinality greater than or equal to a certain threshold h. It is interesting to observe that their scheme is a special case of the vector space construction. To see this, let $d = h$ and let $\phi(C_i) = (1, x_i, x_i^2, \ldots, x_i^{h-1})$ for any client C_i. It is easy to see that the function ϕ satisfies (6), that is, the h-dimensional vector e_1 belongs to the subspace $\langle \phi(C_i) : C_i \in X \rangle$ if and only if X is a set containing h clients.

In the following, we show that the resulting scheme is equivalent to the Naor and Pinkas scheme [34]. The coefficients of the random bivariate polynomial $Q(x, y)$ can be seen as the coefficients of the random matrix M in the vector space construction, while, for any client C_i, the coefficients of the univariate polynomial $Q(x_i, y)$ can be seen as the coefficients of the vector c_i. Similarly, for any server S_j and any time frame t, the coefficients of the polynomial $Q(x, j \circ t)$ correspond to the coefficients of the vector g_j^t and the proof $Q(0, j \circ t)$ corresponds to the value p_j^t.

Multilevel Structures In a *multilevel access structure*, there are u disjoint classes of clients (also called *levels*), $L_1, \ldots, L_u$, where each class $L_r \subseteq \{C_1, \ldots, C_n\}$ is associated to a positive integer $h_r \leq n_r = |L_r|$, for $r = 1, \ldots, u$, and such that $h_1 < h_2 < \cdots < h_u$. A multilevel access structure consists of those subsets which contain at least h_r clients all of level *at most* L_r for some $r \in \{1, \ldots, u\}$. Therefore, in any metering scheme realizing a multilevel access structure, any server is able to compute its proof for a given time frame if and only if it has received at least h_r visits from clients of level *at most* L_r for some $r \in \{1, \ldots, u\}$ during that time frame.

The authors of [29] showed how to construct an optimal metering scheme realizing any multilevel access structure. Their scheme can be obtained by the vector space construction letting $d = h_u$ and $\phi(C_i) = (1, x_i, x_i^2, \ldots, x_i^{h_r-1},$ $0, \ldots, 0)$, where $x_i \in Z_q$ is chosen by $\mathcal{A}$, for any client $C_i \in L_r$ and any $r = 1, \ldots, u$. Following the line of Theorem 1 in [16], it can be proved that if

$$q > (h_u - 1)\binom{n}{h_u - 1},$$ then it is possible to choose the value $x_i \in Z_q$ associated

to any client C_i in such a way that (6) is satisfied (i.e., the h_u-dimensional vector e_1 belongs to the subspace $< \phi(C_i) : C_i \in X >$ if and only if X is a set of h_r clients of level *at most* L_r, where $r \in \{1, \ldots, u\}$).

Compartmented Structures In a *compartmented access structure*, there are u disjoint classes of clients (also called *compartments*), $G_1, \ldots, G_u$, where each class $G_r \subseteq \{C_1, \ldots, C_n\}$ is associated to a positive integer $h_r \leq n_r = |G_r|$, for $r = 1, \ldots, u$. The compartmented access structure consists of those subsets which contain at least h_r clients from compartment G_r, *for any* $1 \leq r \leq u$. Therefore, in any metering scheme realizing a compartmented access structure, any server S_j is able to compute its proof for a given time frame if and only if it has received at least h_r visits from clients in compartment G_r, for any $1 \leq r \leq u$, during that time frame.

The authors of [29] showed how to construct an optimal metering schemes realizing any compartmented access structure. Their construction is based on polynomial interpolation on a finite field. In the following, we propose a construction for optimal metering schemes realizing compartmented access structures which is based on the general vector space construction. In our construction, any server receiving at least h_r visits from clients in compartment G_r, for any $1 \leq r \leq u$, is also required to receive a total of at least h client visits in a time frame, where h is a positive integer, in order to compute its proof. It is easy to see that if $h = \sum_{r=1}^{u} h_r$, we obtain the construction proposed in [29].

Our construction is obtained by the vector space construction, letting $d = h$. Without loss of generality, assume that $t = h - \sum_{r=1}^{u} h_r \geq 0$. Let $t_0 = t$, and let $t_r = t + \sum_{j=1}^{r} h_j$ for $1 \leq r \leq u$. For any index $r = 1, \ldots, u$, denote by $C_{r,i}$ the clients in compartment G_r. For each client $C_{r,i}$, the audit agency chooses a value $x_{r,i} \in Z_q$ and constructs the h-dimensional vector $\phi(C_{r,i}) = (1, x_{r,i}, x_{r,i}^2, \ldots, x_{r,i}^{t-1}, 1, \ldots, 1, x_{r,i}^t, \ldots, x_{r,i}^{t+h_i-1}, 1, \ldots, 1)$ where the values $x_{r,i}^t, \ldots, x_{r,i}^{t+h_i-1}$ correspond to the coordinates of indices $t_{i-1} + 1, \ldots, t_i$.

Following the line of Theorem 3 in [16], it can be proved that if $q > \binom{n}{h}$, then

it is possible to choose the value $x_i \in Z_q$ associated to any client C_i in such a way that (6) is satisfied (i.e., the h-dimensional vector e_1 belongs to the subspace $< \phi(C_i) : C_i \in X >$ if and only if X is a set containing h_r clients of compartment G_r, for any $1 \leq r \leq u$, and h clients in total).

5 Computationally Secure Metering Schemes

In this section, we describe metering schemes whose security is based on un-proven specific computational assumptions. In this setting, the amount of resources that corrupt servers and clients can afford in order to forge a server's proof is bounded. In particular, a corrupt party can perform only feasible computations, that is, procedures which require time and space upper bounded by a polynomial $p(n)$, where $n = |x|$ is the size of the instance x of the problem which is solved by the procedure.

5.1 Naor and Pinkas Scheme

Naor and Pinkas [34] proposed a computationally secure variant of their metering scheme, allowing the audit agency to reuse the same polynomial for an unlimited number of time frames. The security of their scheme relies on the difficulty of solv-ing the computational Diffie–Hellman problem, which is a well-known assumption used in cryptography. Let q and p be two prime numbers and let g be a generator of a subgroup of Z_q^* of order p, such that extracting discrete logarithms to the base g in this subgroup is hard. The computational Diffie–Hellman assumption states that given g, g^a, and g^b, it is difficult to compute g^{ab}, where a and b are random integers.

The key idea on which the scheme depicted in Fig. 6 is based is to do interpolation in the exponents. Since, as we have seen before, Lagrange's interpolation formula

---

Initialization:

- The audit agency $\mathcal{A}$ chooses a random polynomial $Q(x)$ over Z_q of degree $h - 1$ in x.
- The audit agency $\mathcal{A}$ sends the value $Q(i)$ to each client C_i.

Beginning of a Time Frame t:
The audit agency $\mathcal{A}$ randomly chooses a value r_j and sends the challenge g^{r_j} to each server S_j.

Regular Operation for Time Frame t:
When the client C_i visits the server S_j, it receives the value g^{r_j} and computes the value $g^{r_j \cdot Q(i)}$, to be sent to S_j.

Proof Generation for Time Frame t:

- Assume that the server S_j has been visited by at least h different clients in time frame t.
- The server S_j performs a Lagrange interpolation on the polynomial $g^{r_j \cdot Q(x)}$ and computes the proof as $g^{r_j \cdot Q(0)}$.
- The server S_j sends the value $g^{r_j \cdot Q(0)}$ to the audit agency.

Proof Verification for Time Frame t:
The audit agency $\mathcal{A}$ verifies the proof received by S_j by evaluating the polynomial $g^{r_j \cdot Q(x)}$ at the point $x = 0$.

Fig. 6 Naor–Pinkas computational metering scheme (NP-C)

for a polynomial $Q(x)$ of degree $h - 1$ says that from any h points $y_{i_1}, \ldots, y_{i_h}$ of $Q(x)$ we can compute the point

$$Q(0) = \sum_{j=1}^{h} y_{i_j} \lambda_j,$$

where, for $j = 1, \ldots, h$, the value λ_j can be expressed as $\lambda_j = \prod_{1 \leq k \leq h, k \neq j} \frac{i_k}{i_k - i_j}$, then we can also compute the point

$$g^{Q(0)} = g^{\sum_{j=1}^{h} y_{i_j} \lambda_j} = \prod_{j=1}^{h} g^{y_{i_j} \lambda_j}.$$

Interpolation in the exponents was first used by Feldman in [22] in order to enable each participant in a secret sharing scheme to verify its own share, received from a possibly dishonest dealer, with no loss in security. Such a property was guaranteed by the difficulty of computing the discrete logarithm in certain finite multiplicative groups. Since then, interpolation in the exponents has been used in several papers. In the metering scheme proposed by Naor and Pinkas, it allows the audit agency to use the same polynomial in just one variable for several time frames. Indeed, instead of changing the polynomial each time a new time frame starts, the audit agency sends at the beginning of a time frame a challenge g^{r_j} to each server S_j, where r_j is a random integer. Each client C_i visiting the server S_j during the time frame receives the challenge g^{r_j} from the server and computes $g^{r_j \cdot Q(i)}$ by using the value $Q(i)$ received by the audit agency in the initialization phase. At the end of the time frame, any server S_j which has been visited by at least h different clients in that time frame is able to compute the proof $g^{r_j \cdot Q(0)}$ by using the values provided by the clients during their visits.

It is possible to show that it is computationally infeasible that a server S_j, knowing a polynomial number of challenges and their answers and knowing a challenge g^{r_j} and less than h answers of the form $g^{r_j \cdot Q(i)}$, can compute the proof $g^{r_j \cdot Q(0)}$ (unless he is also able to break the computational DH assumption). We refer to [34] for the details.

In the previous scheme, each client C_i is required to perform little additional work during the interaction with a server S_j since it has to compute $g^{r_j \cdot Q(i)}$ from the challenge g^{r_j} and his private value $Q(i)$. Similarly, the amount of work done by servers is comparable to the work done for the unconditional setting. The interpolation of the polynomial over a small field is performed replacing the additions and multiplications operations on elements of the field with multiplications and exponentiations, respectively. Finally, the audit agency can verify the value received from the server by performing a polynomial evaluation and an exponentiation.

Let us now analyze the randomness, space, and communication complexities of the above scheme. During the initialization phase, the audit agency has to choose a random polynomial over Z_q of degree $h - 1$. Moreover, for each time frame t and for each server S_j, it has to choose a random value r_j to be used for the computation of the challenge g^{r_j}. Therefore, it has to choose $h + m\tau$ coefficients in Z_q. Clients are required to store a single value, hence the size of the information kept secret by each client amounts to $\log q$ bits. Each time a client interacts with the server during a regular operation, it has to send a value in Z_q. Then, the size of the information sent from clients to servers is equal to $\log q$ bits. Finally, the size of the proof is also equal to $\log q$ bits.

5.2 Ogata–Kurosawa Scheme

Ogata and Kurosawa [42] proposed a *robust* computational metering scheme with the aim to prevent malicious behaviors of the clients. Indeed, clients could cheat the servers by providing fake values and prevent them to compute the proof. Robust schemes were first introduced by Naor and Pinkas as a variant to their basic scheme [34]. Their idea was to let servers have a way to authenticate the values sent by clients during the interaction. To allow a client to communicate a value $u \in Z_q$ to a server in an authenticated way, the audit agency chooses two random values $a, b \in Z_q$ and computes $v = au + b \bmod q$. The pair (a, b) is sent to the server, whereas, the pair (u, v) is sent to the client. Later on, the client sends the pair (u, v) to the server, which can check whether $v = au + b \bmod q$. However, in [42], an attack to such scheme is shown allowing two malicious clients to prevent a server from correctly computing a proof.

The robust scheme proposed by Ogata and Kurosawa is computationally secure under the computational Diffie–Hellman assumption and is described in Fig. 7. In such scheme, the audit agency chooses a random polynomial $Q(x, y, z)$, having degree 1 in x, degree $s\tau - 1$ in y, and $h - 1$ in z. Each client is then provided with the bivariate polynomial $Q(x, y, i)$, while each server is provided with the polynomial $Q(r_j, j, z)$, where r_j is a random integer chosen in $Z_q \setminus \{0\}$. At the beginning of a time frame, $\mathcal{A}$ publishes a challenge g^{u_j} for any server $\mathcal{S}_j$, where u_j is a random integer, so that if $\mathcal{C}_i$ wants to access $\mathcal{S}_j$'s site, it has to evaluate the given polynomial at the point j (i.e., it has to compute the polynomial $Q(x, j, i)$), obtaining two coefficients $a_{i,j}$ and $b_{i,j}$, and provide $\mathcal{S}_j$ with the values $g^{u_j a_{i,j}}$ and $g^{u_j b_{i,j}}$. The server $\mathcal{S}_j$ is able to verify the validity of the values sent by $\mathcal{C}_i$ since $g^{u_j a_{i,j}} \cdot (g^{u_j b_{i,j}})^{r_j} = g^{u_j(a_{i,j} + b_{i,j} r_j)} = g^{u_j Q(r_j, j, i)}$. At the end of a time frame, if $\mathcal{S}_j$ has been visited by h or more clients, then can collect a number of values of the form $g^{u_j a_{i,j}} = g^{u_j Q(0, j, i)}$ and can compute the proof $g^{u_j Q(0, j, 0)}$ by using polynomial interpolation. The audit agency $\mathcal{A}$ verifies the value sent by $\mathcal{S}_j$ simply comparing it with the evaluation of $g^{u_j Q(x, y, i)}$ at the point $(0, j, 0)$.

It is possible to show that server $\mathcal{S}_j$, after receiving h visits during time frame t, can compute its proof for that time frame, even if the adversary corrupts all the clients and all the servers other than $\mathcal{S}_j$. At the same time, it is possible to show that a corrupt server receiving less than h visits during a time frame t cannot compute a proof, even if $h - 1$ clients and s servers are corrupt. We refer the reader to [42] for the details.

Initialization:

- The audit agency $\mathcal{A}$ chooses a random polynomial $Q(x, y, z)$ over Z_q of degree 1 in $x, s\tau - 1$ in y and $h - 1$ in z.
- The audit agency $\mathcal{A}$ sends the bivariate polynomial $Q(x, y, i)$ to each client C_i.
- The audit agency $\mathcal{A}$ chooses a random value $r_j \in Z_q \backslash \{0\}$ and sends the polynomial $Q(r_j, j, z)$ and the value r_j to each server S_j.

Beginning of a Time Frame t:
The audit agency chooses a random number u_j for each server S_j an publishes the challenge g^{u_j}.

Regular Operation for Time Frame t:

- When the client C_i visits the server S_j, it computes $Q(x, j, i) = a_{i,j} + b_{i,j} \cdot x$ and sends the values $d_{i,j} = g^{u_j a_{i,j}}$ and $e_{i,j} = g^{u_j b_{i,j}}$ to S_j.
- The server S_j checks whether $(d_{i,j})(e_{i,j})^{r_j} = g^{u_j \cdot Q(r_j, j, i)}$.

Proof Generation for Time Frame t:

- Assume that the server S_j has been visited by at least h different clients in time frame t.
- The server S_j performs a Lagrange interpolation on $g^{u_j Q(0, j, i)}$ and computes the proof as $g^{u_j Q(0, j, 0)}$.
- The server S_j sends the value $g^{u_j Q(0, j, i)}$ to the audit agency.

Proof Verification for Time Frame t:
The audit agency $\mathcal{A}$ verifies the proof received by S_j by evaluating the polynomial $g^{u_j Q(x, y, z)}$ at the point $(0, j, 0)$.

Fig. 7 Ogata–Kurosawa computational metering scheme (OK)

Let us now analyze the randomness, space, and communication complexities of the scheme in Fig. 7. During the initialization phase, the audit agency has to choose a random polynomial over Z_q, of degree 1 in x, $s\tau - 1$ in y, and $h - 1$ in z and a random value r_j for each server S_j, for a total of $2s\tau h + m$ elements in Z_q. Moreover, it has to choose a random value u_j for each time frame and for each server S_j. Therefore, the total number of random bits chosen by the audit agency is equal to $(2hs + m)\tau + m$. Clients are required to store a bivariate polynomial of degree 1 in x and $s\tau - 1$ in y, for a total of $2s\tau \log q$ bits. Each time a client interacts with the server during a regular operation, it has to send two values in Z_q. Then, the size of the information sent from clients to servers is equal to $2 \log q$ bits. Finally, since the proof for a server S_j is $g^{u_j Q(0, j, 0)}$, it is $\log q$ bits long.

In [42], a similar approach has also been shown for the unconditionally secure setting. Indeed, Ogata and Kurosawa proposed a robust unconditionally secure metering scheme which is a variant of the robust scheme in [34].

5.3 Hash-Based Scheme

Computationally secure metering scheme based on the well known idea of *hash chains* [28] were proposed in [9, 10]. Hash chains are collections of values where each value (except for the initial one) is computed after the application of a one-way hash function to the previous value. In this case, it is easy to follow the chain in one direction, knowing the initial seed of the chain, but it is computationally infeasible to compute the previous value in the chain, knowing just the next value.

To setup such schemes, the parties agree on a one-way hash function $\mathcal{H}$ with the following additional properties [32]:

- *Pre-image resistance*: for every output $y = \mathcal{H}(x)$, it is computationally infeasible to find any pre-image x' such that $\mathcal{H}(x') = y$;
- *2nd-pre-image resistance*: for every input x, it is computationally infeasible to find another in put $x' \neq x$ such that $\mathcal{H}(x') = \mathcal{H}(x)$;
- *Collision resistance*: it is computationally infeasible to find any two distinct inputs x, x' such that $\mathcal{H}(x) = \mathcal{H}(x')$.

During the initialization phase, the audit agency sets, for each client C_i willing to visit server S_j, a new hash chain having length $k_{i,j}$, where $k_{i,j}$ is the number of granted accesses for C_i to S_j. For the sake of simplicity, in the following, we assume that the number of granted accesses is the same, that is, $k_{i,j} = k$, for any client C_i and any server S_j. Then, A sends to C_i the initial point $w_{i,j}$ of the hash chain, and to S_j the final point $w_{i,j}^k = \mathcal{H}^k(w_{i,j})$, where $\mathcal{H}^k(x)$ denotes the application of k cascade hashing operations starting from x. During a visit to server S_j, the client C_i computes and sends the value of the hash chain requested for the r-th visit. The server can verify the correctness of the received value by comparing it with the value resulting from the application of the hash function to the last value stored and associated with the client C_i. The proof for the audit agency consists of the last value which a server stored during the interaction with the client. The scheme is described in Fig. 8.

Initialization:

- For each client C_i and any server S_j, the audit agency A chooses a random seed $w_{i,j}$ and computes $w_{i,j}^k = \mathcal{H}^k(w_{i,j})$, where $\mathcal{H}^k(x)$ denotes the application of k cascade hashing operations starting from x.
- For each server S_j, the audit agency A sends the tuple $[k, j, w_{i,j}]$ to client C_i.
- For each client C_i, the audit agency A sends the tuple $[k, i, w_{i,j}^k]$ to server S_j.

Regular Operation for Time Frame t:

- When the client C_i visits the server S_j, for the r-th time, it computes and sends $w_{i,j}^{k-r}$ to S_j.
- The server S_j verifies that $w_{i,j}^{k-r} = \mathcal{H}(w_{i,j}^{k-r+1})$ and stores $w_{i,j}^{k-r}$.

Proof Generation for Time Frame t:

- Assume that the server S_j has been visited r times by the client C_i.
- The server S_j sends the value $[i, j, r, w_{i,j}^{k-r}]$ to the audit agency.

Proof Verification for Time Frame t:
The audit agency A verifies the proof received by S_j by evaluating $\mathcal{H}^{k-r}(w_{i,j})$.

Fig. 8 Hash based metering scheme (H)

Hash chains are very powerful cryptographic tools, since the operations of generation of the values and verification can be very efficiently performed. Indeed, little additional work is done by clients during the regular operation, that is, the repeated application of the hash function (unless the client decides to pre-compute and store the values composing the hash chain). To verify the validity of the value sent by the client, the server has to evaluate the hash function. The operations involved are very simple, and the time spent and the size of the additional message do not alter the original communication pattern. Despite of other proposed metering systems, the number of proofs that each server sends to the audit agency is of the order of the number of registered clients (not of the number of the visits).

The number of visits presented by S_j is the real number of times that each client visited it since no cheating is possible from any of the players acting in the framework. Indeed, the server cannot change the number of received visits because of the properties of the function $\mathcal{H}$. Furthermore, only authorized clients can access the server, since they are able to provide a valid token. Notice that the proof sent by servers to the audit agency cannot be repudiated, since each server is able to show that the proof belongs to the hash chain whose final value has been provided by $\mathcal{A}$ itself. Furthermore, each server should not be able to reconstruct the hash chain, as far as it does not know the starting random seed for a given client C_i. Only $\mathcal{A}$ and C_i know the seed, but both of them are willing to protect and maintain this secret for obvious reasons.

In the following, we analyze the randomness, space, and communication complexities of the hash based scheme. Denote by d the bit-length of the output of the hash function $\mathcal{H}$ (standard hash functions outputs are 128, 160, 256, or 512 bits long). The audit agency, for each client and each server, has to choose a random seed for the hash chain, requiring then mnd random bits. The values computed and exchanged during the different operations of the scheme are rings of the chain. Then, the size of the information kept secret by each client is md, whereas the size of the information exchanged among clients, servers, and the audit agency is of d bits.

6 Conclusions

Secure metering schemes face the problem of measuring the interaction between servers and clients on the Web. Practical applications are measuring the exposure of Web sites as well as the impact of online advertising campaigns. In this work, we considered practical and theoretical aspects of metering schemes, addressing issues of *security*, *efficiency*, and *complexity*. In Fig. 9, the main features of the metering schemes presented in this paper are listed. The values denote the amount of random bits needed by the audit agency to setup the scheme, the amount of space needed by clients to store their private information, the communication complexity, and the size of the proof that each server should send at the end of each time frame. However, since the schemes presented in this paper have been designed for different scenarios, the complexity measures of such schemes are not directly comparable.

Scheme	Randomness	Space	Comm. C.	Proof Size
NP-U	$hs\tau \log q$	$s\tau \log q$	$\log q$	$\log q$
NI	$s\tau \sum_{z=\ell+1}^{h} z \log q$	$(h-\ell)s\tau \log q$	$(h-\ell)\log q$	$\log q$
I	$hs\tau \log q$	$s\tau \log q$	$\log q$	$(h-\ell)\log q$
GA	$s\tau \sum_{r=1}^{\ell}(h_r - 1)\log q$	$d_i s\tau \log q$	$d_i \log q$	$\log q$
NP-C	$(h+m\tau)\log q$	$\log q$	$\log q$	$\log q$
OK	$((2hs+m)\tau + m)\log q$	$2s\tau \log q$	$2\log q$	$\log q$
H	nmd	md	d	d

Fig. 9 Main features of the metering schemes presented in this paper

In the unconditional and computational metering schemes presented by Naor and Pinkas and Ogata and Kurosawa (NP-U and NP-C, and OK, respectively) a server receiving a number of visits less the fixed threshold h is in the same situation as a server which has received no visit. Consequently, the audit agency will pay nothing to a server that has been visited by less than h clients. A more flexible situation is considered for metering schemes with pricing, for which both non interactive (NI) and interactive (I) versions have been presented. These schemes enable a more flexible payment system, since they allow to count the exact number of visits received by each server, which is paid accordingly. A more general situation is considered for metering schemes realizing an access structure on the set of clients (GA). In such schemes, the audit agency is able to verify if a server has received visits by at least a qualified set of clients. Finally in hash-based metering schemes (H), servers are able to request payments corresponding to the exact number of visits received during the considered time frame.

Appendix

Information Theory Background

In this Appendix, we review the basic concepts of Information Theory used in our definitions and proofs. For a complete treatment of the subject, the reader is advised to consult [18].

Information Theory is a mathematical theory based on probability theory. In almost all applications of probability theory, one considers a *discrete random experiment* which is defined by a finite or countably infinite set called the *sample space*, consisting of all elementary events, and a *probability measure* assigning a non-negative real number to every elementary event, such that the sum of all these probabilities is equal to 1.

A *discrete random variable* $\mathbf{X}$ is a mapping from the sample space to a certain range X and is characterized by its *probability distribution* $\{Pr_{\mathbf{X}}(x)\}_{x \in X}$ that assigns to every $x \in X$ the probability $Pr_{\mathbf{X}}(x)$ of the event that $\mathbf{X}$ takes on the value

x. In this paper with a boldface capital letter, say $\mathbf{X}$, we denote a random variable taking value on a set denoted with the corresponding capital letter X according to some probability distribution $\{Pr_{\mathbf{X}}(x)\}_{x \in X}$. The values such a random variable can take are denoted with the corresponding lower letter x.

Given a probability distribution $\{Pr_{\mathbf{X}}(x)\}_{x \in X}$ on a set X, the Shannon *entropy* of $\mathbf{X}$, denoted by $H(\mathbf{X})$, is defined asv

$$H(\mathbf{X}) = - \sum_{x \in X} Pr_{\mathbf{X}}(x) \log Pr_{\mathbf{X}}(x)$$

(all logarithms in this paper are to the base 2). The entropy $H(\mathbf{X})$ is a measure of the average uncertainty one has about which element of the set X has been chosen when the choices of the elements from X are made according to the probability distribution $\{Pr_{\mathbf{X}}(x)\}_{x \in X}$. It is well known that $H(\mathbf{X})$ is a good approximation to the average number of bits needed to faithfully represent the elements of X.

The entropy satisfies the following property:

$$0 \le H(\mathbf{X}) \le \log|X|, \tag{7}$$

where $H(\mathbf{X}) = 0$ if and only if there exists $x_0 \in X$ such that $Pr_{\mathbf{X}}(x_0) = 1$; whereas, $H(\mathbf{X}) = \log|X|$ if and only if $Pr_{\mathbf{X}}(x) = 1/|X|$, for all $x \in X$.

Given two sets X and Y and a joint probability distribution on their cartesian product, the *conditional entropy* $H(\mathbf{X}|\mathbf{Y})$, is defined as

$$H(\mathbf{X}|\mathbf{Y}) = - \sum_{y \in Y} \sum_{x \in X} Pr_{\mathbf{Y}}(y) Pr(x|y) \log Pr(x|y).$$

From the definition of conditional entropy, it is easy to see that

$$H(\mathbf{X}|\mathbf{Y}) \ge 0. \tag{8}$$

We have $H(\mathbf{X}|\mathbf{Y}) = 0$ when the value chosen from Y completely determines the value chosen from X; whereas, $H(\mathbf{X}|\mathbf{Y}) = H(\mathbf{X})$ means that choices from X and Y are independent, that is, the probability that the value x has been chosen from X, given that from Y we have chosen y, is the same as the a priori probability of choosing x from X. Therefore, knowing the values chosen from Y does not enable a Bayesian opponent to modify an a priori guess regarding which element has been chosen from X.

The *mutual information* between $\mathbf{X}$ and $\mathbf{Y}$ is given by

$$I(\mathbf{X}; \mathbf{Y}) = H(\mathbf{X}) - H(\mathbf{X}|\mathbf{Y}).$$

Since $I(\mathbf{X}; \mathbf{Y}) = I(\mathbf{Y}; \mathbf{X})$ and $I(\mathbf{X}; \mathbf{Y}) \ge 0$, it is easy to see that

$$H(\mathbf{X}) \ge H(\mathbf{X}|\mathbf{Y}). \tag{9}$$

References

1. V. Anupam, A. Mayer, K. Nissim, B. Pinkas, and M. K. Reiter, On the Security of Pay-Per-Click and Other Web Advertising Schemes, in Proceedings of *The 8th International World Wide Web Conference – WWW8*, Toronto, Canada, (Elsevier 1999), pp. 1091–1100.
2. V. Anupam, A. Mayer, and M. K. Reiter, Detecting Hit Shaving in Click-through Payment Schemes, in Proceedings of *The 3rd USENIX Workshop on Electronic Commerce*, Boston, Massachusetts, USA, (Usenix Assoc. 1998), pp. 155–166.
3. Audiweb, `http://www.audiweb.it`.
4. S. G. Barwick, W. Jackson, and K. Martin, A General Approach to Robust Web Metering, *Designs, Codes, and Cryptography*, Vol. 36, No. 1, (2005), pp. 5–27.
5. A. Beimel, *Secure Schemes for Secret Sharing Schemes and Key Distribution*, PhD Thesis, Dept. of Computer Science, Technion, 1996. Available at `http://www.cs.bgu.ac.il/~beimel/pub.html`.
6. F. Bergadano and P. De Mauro, Third-party Certification of HTTP Service Access Statistics, in Proceedings of *Security Protocols Workshop*, Lecture Notes in Computer Science, Vol. 1550, (Springer, Berlin 1998), pp. 94–99.
7. F. Bergadano and P. De Mauro, Method and Apparatus for the Verification of Server Access Logs and Statistics, US Patent 6.574.627, June 2003.
8. G. R. Blakley, Safeguarding Cryptographic Keys, in Proceedings of *AFIPS 1979 National Computer Conference*, 1979, pp. 313–317.
9. C. Blundo and S. Cimato, SAWM: A Tool for Secure and Authenticated Web Metering, in Proceedings of *The 14th International Conference on Software Engineering and Knowledge Engineering – SEKE 2002*, Ischia, Italy, (ACM 2002), pp. 641–648.
10. C. Blundo and S. Cimato, A Software Infrastructure for Authenticated Web Metering, *IEEE Computer*, Vol. 37, No. 664, (IEEE 2004), pp. 28–33.
11. C. Blundo, S. Cimato, and B. Masucci, A Note on Optimal Metering Schemes, *Information Processing Letters*, Vol. 84, No. 6, 2002, pp. 319–326.
12. C. Blundo, A. De Bonis, and B. Masucci, Metering Schemes with Pricing, in Proceedings of *The 14th International Conference on Distributed Computing – DISC 2000*, Toledo, Spain, M. Herlihy (Ed.), Lecture Notes in Computer Science, Vol. 1914, (Springer, Berlin 2000), pp. 194–208.
13. C. Blundo, A. De Bonis, and B. Masucci, Bounds and Constructions for Metering Schemes, *Communications in Information and Systems*, Vol. 2, No. 1, (2002), pp. 1–28.
14. C. Blundo, A. De Bonis, B. Masucci, and D. R. Stinson, Dynamic Multi–Threshold Metering Schemes, in Proceedings of *The 7th Annual Workshop on Selected Areas in Cryptography – SAC 2000*, Waterloo, Canada, D. R. Stinson, S. Tavares (Eds.), Lecture Notes in Computer Science, Vol. 2012, (Springer, Berlin 2001), pp. 130–144.
15. C. Blundo, S. Martin, B. Masucci, and C. Padró, A Linear Algebraic Approach to Metering Schemes, *Designs, Codes, and Cryptography*, Vol. 33, (2004), pp. 241–260.
16. E. F. Brickell, Some Ideal Secret Sharing Schemes, *The Journal of Combinatorial Mathematics and Combinatorial Computing*, Vol. 6, (1989), pp. 105–113.
17. Coalition for Advertising Supported Information and Entertainment, CASIE Guiding Principles of Interactive Media Audience Measurement. Available at `http://www.commercepark.com/AAAA/casie/gp/guiding_principles.html`
18. T. M. Cover and J. A. Thomas, *Elements of Information Theory*, (Wiley, New York, 1991).
19. A. De Bonis and B. Masucci, An Information Theoretical Approach to Metering Schemes, in Proceedings of *The 2000 IEEE International Symposium on Information Theory – ISIT 2000*, Sorrento, Italy, (2000).
20. Y. Desmedt and Y. Frankel, Threshold Cryptosystems, in Proceedings of *Advances in Cryptology – CRYPTO '89*, G. Brassard (Ed.), Lecture Notes in Computer Science, Vol. 435, (Springer, Berlin 1990), pp. 307–315.
21. C. Dwork and M. Naor, Pricing via Processing or Combatting Junk Mail, in Proceedings of *Advances in Cryptology – CRYPTO '95*, E. F. Brickell (Ed.), Lecture Notes in Computer Science, Vol. 740, (Springer, Berlin 1993), pp. 139–147.

22. P. Feldman, A Practical Scheme for Non-Interactive Secret Sharing, in Proceedings of the *28-th IEEE Symposium on Foundations of Computer Science*, pp. 427–437, 1987.
23. M. Franklin and D. Malkhi, Auditable Metering with Lightweight Security, *Journal of Computer Security*, Vol. 6, No. 4, (1998), pp. 237–225.
24. Internet Advertising Bureau, `http://www.iab.net`
25. I/PRO, `http://www.ipro.com`
26. S. Jarecki and A. Odlyzko, An Efficient Micropayment System Based on Probabilistic Polling, in Proceedings of *Financial Cryptography '97*, R. Hirschfeld (Ed.), Lecture Notes in Computer Science, Vol. 1318, (Springer, Berlin 1997), pp. 173–191.
27. M. Karchmer, A. Wigderson, On Span Programs, in Proceedings of the *8th Annual IEEE Symposium on Structure in Complexity*, pp. 102–111, 1993.
28. L. Lamport, Password Authentication with Insecure Communication, In *Communications of the ACM*, Vol. 24, pp. 770–771, 1981.
29. B. Masucci and D. R. Stinson, Metering Schemes for General Access Structures, in Proceedings of *The 6th European Symposium on Research in Computer Security – ESORICS 2000*, Toulouse, France, F. Cuppens, Y. Deswarte, D. Gollmann, M. Waidner (Eds.), Lecture Notes in Computer Science, Vol. 1895, (Springer, Berlin 2000), pp. 72–87.
30. B. Masucci and D. R. Stinson, Efficient Metering Schemes with Pricing, *IEEE Transactions on Information Theory*, Vol. 47, No. 7, (IEEE 2001), pp. 2835–2844.
31. MediaMetrix, `http://www.mediametrix.com`
32. A. Menezes, P. van Oorschot, and S. Vanstone, *Handbook of Applied Cryptography*, CRC, Boca Raton, 1996.
33. R. Merkle, A Certified Digital Signature, in Proceedings of *Advances in Cryptology – CRYPTO '89*, G. Brassard (Ed.), Lecture Notes in Computer Science, Vol. 435, (Springer, Berlin 1990), pp. 218–238.
34. M. Naor and B. Pinkas, Secure and Efficient Metering, in Proceedings of *Advances in Cryptology – EUROCRYPT '98*, K. Nyberg (Ed.), Lecture Notes in Computer Science, Vol. 1403, (Springer, Berlin 1998), pp. 576–590.
35. M. Naor and B. Pinkas, Secure Accounting and Auditing on the Web, *Computer Networks and ISDN Systems*, Vol. 40, Issues 1–7, (1998), pp. 541–550.
36. M. Naor and B. Pinkas, Method for Secure Accounting and Auditing on a Communications Network, US Patent 6.055.508, June 1998.
37. NetCount, `http://ww.netcount.com`
38. Nielsen Media Research, `http://www.nielsenmedia.com`
39. V. Nikov, S. Nikova, B. Preenel, and J. Vandewalle, Applying General Access Structure to Metering Scheme, Cryptology eprint Archive 2002/12.
40. V. Nikov, S. Nikova, and B. Preenel, Robust Metering Schemes for General Access Structures, in Proceedings of *The 2004 International Conference on Information and Communications Security – ICICS 2004*, Lecture Notes in Computer Science, Vol. 3269, (Springer, Berlin 2004), pp. 53–66.
41. T. Novak and D. Hoffman, New Metrics for New Media: Towards the Development of Web Measurement Standards, September 1996. Available at `http://www2000.ogsm.vanderbilt.edu/novak/web.standards/webstands.html`
42. W. Ogata and K. Kurosawa, Provably Secure Metering Scheme, in Proceedings of *ASIACRYPT 2000*, T. Okamoto (Ed.), Lecture Notes in Computer Science, Vol. 1976, (Springer, Berlin 2000), pp. 388–398.
43. PriceWaterhouseCoopers, `http://www.pwcglobal.com`
44. A. Shamir, How to Share a Secret, *Communications of the ACM*, Vol. 22, (1979), pp. 612–613.
45. D. R. Stinson, An Explication of Secret Sharing Schemes, *Design, Codes, and Cryptography*, Vol. 2, (1992), pp. 357–390.
46. D. R. Stinson, *Cryptography Theory and Practice*, (CRC, Boca Raton 1995).

A Cryptographic Framework for the Controlled Release Of Certified Data

Endre Bangerter, Jan Camenisch, and Anna Lysyanskaya

Contents

1   Introduction

The problem of privacy protection is to control the dissemination of personal data. There exist various privacy principles that describe at a conceptual level what measures have to be taken to protect privacy. Examples of these principles are an individual's right to access and to request correction of data about oneself and the requirement for an individual to consent to the disclosure of her personal data. Another principle is that of data minimization: It states that an individual should only

E. Bangerter (✉)
IBM Zurich Research Laboratory, Säumerstrasse 4, 8803 Rüschlikon, Switzerland
e-mail: eba@zurich.ibm.com

S.C.-H. Huang et al. (eds.), *Network Security*, DOI 10.1007/978-0-387-73821-5_2,
© Springer Science+Business Media, LLC 2010

disclose the minimal necessary data for a given purpose. Determining these data is often a difficult task, and one usually needs to balance an individual's privacy interests and the legitimate interest of other parties in the individual's data. An example of this trade-off is an individual's wish to be anonymous conflicting with her requirements imposed by law enforcement to be able to identify and get hold of criminals. Such trade-offs impose limits on privacy that cannot be overcome by any technology.

When data are stored in digital form, the privacy problem is more severe than with paper based processes. Once data are disclosed in digital form, they can be easily stored, distributed, and linked with various other data. While the use of digital media aggravates the privacy problem, it also offers new opportunities and technologies to implement principles of privacy protection. Today's electronic transaction systems essentially reproduce the non-privacy protecting paper-based business processes and thereby most often fail to take advantage of the digital media as a privacy enabler.

Incorporating privacy principles in digital media calls for a *privacy architecture*. While certain aspects of privacy protection are well understood and corresponding technologies are known, no comprehensive and stable privacy architecture exists yet. Various efforts to enhance privacy in digital media are underway. Examples are the NSF-funded PORTIA project [1] or the European project PRIME [2]. The latter aims, among other things, to develop a comprehensive framework and architecture to enable privacy in digital media. One can expect that a standard privacy architecture will materialize in the near future. Such a privacy architecture will consist of a combination of various technologies ranging from software technologies such as access control, auditing, and policy management to more theoretical cryptographic techniques.

In this paper, we take a step towards enabling privacy in digital media and present a cryptographic framework that enables data minimization. In this framework, for each transaction, there is a precise specification of what data get revealed to each participant. This is called "controlled release of data". In our framework, the key feature is that the data in question is certified. That is to say, its validity can be verified by the recipient.

Besides the framework, we also describe cryptographic building blocks that allow one to efficiently implement electronic transactions with our framework. That is, we describe particular encryption schemes [22, 31], commitment schemes [33, 46], and signature schemes [18, 19]. These schemes are all discrete logarithm which allows for their combination with various efficient zero-knowledge proof techniques. For an overview of such techniques, we refer to [24].

The framework turns out to be usable for the realization of a large number of privacy enabling applications. For instance, it can be used to construct anonymous credential systems [16,27,44,49], group signature schemes [4,23,30], and electronic cash [9, 29].

2 A Cryptographic Framework for the Controlled Release of Certified Data

A (digital) certificate consists of *data items*, provided by a *user*, and a digital signature by a *(certificate) issuer* on the *data items*. By signing the user's data items, the issuer certifies, for instance, the user's authorization to perform some given task and that it has verified the validity of (some of) the user's data items. To demonstrate its authorization and the validity of the data items, the user can, for instance, show the certificate to a *verifier* who checks the certificate's validity by verifying the correctness of its signature. The verifier will accept the claims associated to a certificate as far as he trusts the issuer w.r.t. these claims.

In the following, we describe desirable properties of (non-traditional) certificates allowing the user to control what data items are disclosed to the issuer and verifier of certificates.

Required Properties when Showing a Certificate By showing a certificate, we mean the process whereby a user using a certificate she possesses to convince a verifier of the contents of the certificate. We stress that during this process the user does not necessarily send the actual certificate to the verifier.

We require a process that allows the user to show certificate such that the following properties are met.

Multi-show unlinkability: Conventional (public-key) certificates are represented (encoded) by unique strings. Thus, when the user would just send the certificate obtained from the issuer to the verifier, the issuer and the verifier can link the transactions. Furthermore, multiple showings of the same certificate to the same or different verifiers are linkable. We would like to emphasize that linkability is an inherent property of traditional certificates, which is independent of the data items contained in a certificate. In particular, even so-called pseudonymous certificates, i.e., certificates that do not contain personally identifying data items, are linkable. Linkability is known to be a serious threat to the privacy of individuals. We require that the showing of a certificate cannot be linked to the issuing of the certificate as well as to other showings of the same certificate, unless of course the data items being disclosed allow for such linking.

Selective show of data items: Given a certificate, we require that the user in each showing of the certificate can select which data items she wants to disclose (and which data items she does not want to disclose) to the verifier. For numerical data items, we require that it be possible to show that a data item lies in some interval without revealing the exact value of the data item. As an example, consider a driver's license certificate consisting of the user's name, address, and date of birth. When stopped on the road at a police checkpoint, the user shows that the certificate is valid, i.e., that she is authorized to drive, without disclosing her name, address, and date of birth. Using the same certificate, in a supermarket when purchasing alcohol, the user shows the certificate such that she only discloses that she is not underage.

Conditional showing of data items: We require that the user be able to conditionally disclose certified data, when showing a certificate. More precisely, let us assume that there is a third party, and that prior to certificate showing, the user picks the data items she wishes to show conditionally to the issuer; also the user and the verifier agree on the conditions under which the verifier may learn the selected data items. In a conditional showing, the user discloses to the verifier information (on the conditionally shown data elements) such that the verifier cannot recover the conditionally shown data items from the information. Yet, the verifier can be assured that, when asked to do so, the third party is able to recover the data items.

Hence, if the third party recovers the data items only if the mentioned condition is fulfilled (where we assume that it knows the condition), then the above mechanism implements showing of (certified) data under the agreed condition.

As an example, consider a user accessing a university library's reading room with valuable books and the third party being the university administration. The user's identity, e.g., contained in her student identity certificate, will be disclosed to the librarian only under the condition that books are stolen from the reading room. To find out the user's identity, the librarian will need to involve the university administration.

Proving relations between data items: When showing multiple certificates by different issuers, the user should be able to demonstrate that data items in the certificates are related without disclosing the data items. For instance, when showing her drivers certificate and her credit card certificate to a car rental company, the user should not need to disclose her name contained in the certificates, but only to demonstrate that both certificates are issued to the same name.

Desirable Properties of Certificate Issuing. We now describe the properties we require of the process where the user gets issued a certificate by an issuer. Let $\{m_1, \ldots, m_l\}$ denote a set of data items and H a subset of these data items. It should be possible for the user to obtain certificate on $\{m_1, \ldots, m_l\}$ such that the issuer does not learn any information on the data items H, while it learns the other data items, i.e., $\{m_1, \ldots, m_l\} \setminus H$. We refer to such an issuing as *blind certification*.

Obviously, the data items in H are chosen by the user; however, the other data items could be chosen by the issuer or by the user. For the data items that remain hidden from the issuers, we require that the user is able to assert that some of them were previously certified by another issuer. An example where this property is useful is e-cash with online double spending tests. Here, the user chooses a random and unique number that is certified by the bank (issuer) such that the bank does not learn the number (c.f. Sect. 3.2).

2.1 A Framework of Cryptographic Primitives

In this section, we illustrate how a framework of encryptions, commitments, signatures, and zero-knowledge proofs can be used to implement certificates having properties as described above. The presentation is (quite) informal and intended to be accessible for non-specialists in cryptography. We first recall the abstract properties of encryptions, commitments, signatures, and zero-knowledge proofs of knowledge.

By $\omega = A(\alpha)$, we denote that ω is output by the (probabilistic polynomial-time) algorithm A on input α.

An *(asymmetric) encryption scheme* consists of the algorithms SetupEnc, Enc, and Dec with properties as follows. The *key-generation algorithm* SetupEnc outputs an encryption and decryption key pair (EK, DK). The *encryption algorithm Enc* takes as input a message m, a label L, and the encryption key EK and outputs a encryption E of m, i.e., $E = \text{Enc}(m, L; EK)$. The *decryption algorithm Dec* takes as input an encryption E, a label L and the decryption key DK and outputs the message m, i.e., $m = \text{Dec}(E; DK)$. An encryption scheme is secure, if an encryption $E = \text{Enc}(mEK)$ does not contain any computational information about m to an adversary who is given E and EK, even if the adversary is allowed to interact with the decryptor. (For more on definitions of security for cryptosystems, see, for example, Goldreich [39].) The notion of encryptions with labels was introduced in [31]. Labels allow to bind some public data to the ciphertext at both encryption and decryption time. In our applications, user would attach a label to an encryption E that indicates the conditions under which should be decrypted.

A *commitment scheme* consists of the algorithms Commit and VerifyCommit with properties as follows. The *commitment algorithm Commit* takes as input a message m, a random string r, and outputs a commitment C, i.e., $C = \text{Commit}(m, r)$. The *(commitment) verification algorithm VerifyCommit* takes as input a C, m and r and outputs 1 (accept) if C is equal to $commit(m, r)$ and 0 (reject) otherwise. The security properties of a commitment scheme are as follows. The *hiding property* is that a commitment $C = \text{Commit}(m, r)$ contains no (computational) information on m. The *binding property* is that given C, m, and r, where $1 = \text{VerifyCommit}(C, m, r)$, it is (computationally) impossible to find a message m' and a string r' such that $1 = \text{VerifyCommit}(C, m', r')$.

A *signature scheme* consists of algorithms: SetupSign, Sign, VerifySign as follows. The *key-generation algorithm* SetupSign outputs a verification and signing and pair (VK, SK). The *signing algorithm Sign* takes as input a message m and a signing key SK and outputs an signature S on m, i.e., $S = \text{Sign}(m; SK)$. The *(signature) verification algorithm VerifySign* takes as input an alleged signature S, the message m, and the verification key VK; it decides whether to accept or reject the signature. A signature scheme is secure [41] if, on input VK, no adversary can produce a valid signature on *any* message m even after a series of adaptive queries to the signing algorithm (provided that the adversary did not explicitly ask for a signature on m). In a variant we use, Sign takes as input a *list* of messages $m_1, \ldots, m_l$ and a signing key SK and outputs an signature S on $m_1, \ldots, m_l$, i.e., $S = \text{Sign}(m_1, \ldots, m_l; SK)$. The verification algorithm also looks at a list of messages and a purported signature. For our purposes, we also require an extended signature scheme which additionally features a two party protocol HiddenSign between a signer and a (signature) requestor. Let be given messages

$m_1, \ldots, m_l$ and commitments $C_1 = \text{Commit}(m_1), \ldots, C_l = \text{Commit}(m_{l'})$ with $l' \leq l$. The common input to the protocol are $C_1, \ldots, C_{l'}$ and $m_{l'+1}, \ldots, m_l$ and the signer's input is a signing key SK. At the end of the protocol, the requestor's output is a signature S on $m_1, \ldots, m_l$. We denote such a protocol execution by $S = \text{HiddenSign}(C_1, \ldots, C_{l'}, m_{l'+1}, \ldots, m_l; SK)$. We see that by the hiding property of commitments the signer does not learn any information on the messages $m_1, \ldots, m_{l'}$ in the protocol HiddenSign.

Finally, we consider *zero-knowledge proofs of knowledge*. Let W denote an arbitrary boolean predicate, i.e., a function that on input some string α either outputs 1 (true) or 0 (false). A proof of knowledge is a two party protocol between a prover and a verifier, where the common input is a predicate W, and the prover's input is a string w for which W is true, i.e., $1 = W(w)$. At the end of the protocol, the verifier either outputs 1 (accept) or 0 (reject). The protocol has the property that if the verifier accepts, then it can be assured that the prover knows a string w' such that $W(w') = 1$. The protocol is zero-knowledge if the verifier does not learn any (computational) information about the provers input w. We denote such a zero-knowledge proof of knowledge by $\text{PK}\{(w) : W(w) = 1\}$. Often we use proofs of knowledge where W is a composite predicate in multiple variables. Our notational convention is that the elements listed in the round brackets denote quantities the knowledge of which is being proved. These are (in general) not known to the verifier, and the protocol is zero-knowledge with respect to these parameters. Other parameters mentioned in a proof of knowledge expression are known to the verifier. (In particular, the description of the predicate W is known to the verifier.) For instance, $\text{PK}\{(x, y) : W_1(x, y) = 1 \land W_2(x, z) = 1\}$ denotes a protocol where the parameters mentioned are (x, y, z); the value z is known to both parties (since it is not listed in the round brackets); the protocol is zero-knowledge with respect to (x, y). Upon completion of this protocol, the verifier will be convinced that the prover knows some x' and y' such that $W_1(x', y')$ and $W_2(x', z)$ are satisfied.

2.2 Cryptography for the Controlled Release of Certified Data

In this section, we discuss how the cryptographic building blocks discussed in the previous paragraph can be used to implement the controlled release of certified data.

By I_1 and I_2, we denote certificate issuers with verification and signing key pairs (VK_1, SK_1) and (VK_2, SK_2), respectively. The verification keys VK_1 and VK_2 shall be publicly known and authenticated. Also, we assume that the user holds a certificate $Cert_1 = \text{Sign}(m_1, \ldots, m_{l_1}; SK_1)$ from I_1 and a certificate $Cert_2 = \text{Sign}(\tilde{m}_1, \ldots, \tilde{m}_{l_2}; SK_2) = 1$ from I_2.

Multi-Show Unlinkability and Selective Show of Data Items The key idea that underlies the controlled release of certified data is to prove knowledge (in zero-knowledge) of a certificate instead of disclosing a certificate to the verifier. To show the certificate $Cert_1$ to the verifier without disclosing, e.g., the data items

$m_1, \ldots, m_{l'_1}$ (where $l'_1 \leq l_1$), the user (as the prover) and the (certificate) verifier (as the verifier in the proof of knowledge) compute a protocol such a way as follows

$$PK\{(Cert_1, m_1, \ldots, m_{l'_1}) :$$

$$VerifySign(Cert_1, m_1, \ldots, m_{l'_1}, m_{l'_1+1}, \ldots, m_{l_1}; VK_1) = 1\}. \quad (1)$$

Protocol (1) proves that the user has (knows) a valid certificate with respect to the verification key VK_1. By the zero-knowledge property of the protocol, the verifier does not learn any information on $Cert_1$ and the data items $m_1, \ldots, m_{l'_1}$. ¿From this observation, it follows that multiple showings of the certificate $Cert_1$ using Protocol (1) are unlinkable, unless the data items $m_{l'_1+1}, \ldots, m_{l_1}$ disclosed to the verifier are linkable. The ability to selectively show data items follows trivially, as the user can choose, in each execution of Protocol (1), which data items to disclose to the verifier and of which data items to proof knowledge.

Proving Relations Between Data Items This property is straightforward to achieve by using protocols such as the following one

$$PK\{(Cert_1, m_1, \ldots, m_{l'_1}, Cert_2, \tilde{m}_2, \ldots, \tilde{m}_{l_2}) :$$

$$VerifySign(Cert_1, m_1, \ldots, m_{l'_1}, m_{l'_1+1}, \ldots, m_{l_1}; VK_1) = 1$$

$$\wedge VerifySign(Cert_2, m_1, \tilde{m}_2, \ldots, \tilde{m}_{l'_2}, m_{l'_2+1}, \ldots, \tilde{m}_{l_2}; VK_2) = 1\}. \quad (2)$$

Using protocol (2), the user can prove that she possesses a certificate $Cert_1$ from I_1 and a certificate $Cert_2$ from I_2. Additionally, she proves that the first data items m_1 and $\tilde{m}_1$ of the certificates are equal. Yet, by the zero-knowledge property, the verifier does not learn the respective data items. Thus we see that demonstrating relations between certified attributes is achieved using techniques to prove knowledge of relations, such as equality.

Conditional Showing of Data Items Let us assume that there is a third party which, using the algorithm SetupEnc, has created the encryption and decryption key pair (EK, DK). The encryption key EK shall be publicly known and authenticated. To show, e.g., the data item m_1 contained in $Cert_1$ conditionally, the user encrypts m_1 under the encryption key EK of the third party, i.e., $E = Enc(m_1, Cond; EK)$. Here, $Cond$ denotes a label that describes the condition under which the user agrees m_1 to be released to the verifier. Then, the user and the verifier execute the following protocol

$$PK\{(Cert_1, m_1, \ldots, m_{l'_1}) :$$

$$VerifySign(Cert_1, m_1, \ldots, m_{l'_1}, m_{l'_1+1}, \ldots, m_{l_1}; VK_1) = 1$$

$$\wedge E = Enc(m_1, Cond; EK)\}. \quad (3)$$

Besides of showing the certificate $Cert_1$, the user demonstrates in the protocol (3) that E is an encryption of the first data item contained in the certificate under the encryption key EK (such proofs are referred to as verifiable encryption). ¿From the zero-knowledge property of the protocol and security property of the encryption scheme, it follows that the verifier does not get any (computational) information on the value encrypted in E.

To obtain the data item m_1, the verifier sends E and $Cond$ to the third party. The third party verifies if the condition $Cond$ is fulfilled, and if so, he returns the decryption $m_1 = \mathrm{Dec}(E; DK)$ of E. We note that by the security property of the encryption scheme, the third party can not be fooled to decrypt under a condition other than the one described by $Cond$.

Blind Certification Let us see how the user can get a certificate $Cert_3$ on data items m_1 and m' from issuer I_2 without disclosing m_1 to I_2, whereas the issuer I_2 can be asserted that m_1 is a data item certified by I_1; the data item m' is disclosed to the issuer. We recall that $Cert_1 = \mathrm{Sign}(m_1, \dots, m_{l_1}; SK_1)$. To this end, the user commits to m_1, i.e., $C = \mathrm{Commit}(m_1, r)$. Then, the user (as prover) and issuer (as verifier) execute the following protocol

$$PK\{(Cert_1, r, m_1, \dots, m_{l_1'}) : \quad C = \mathrm{Commit}(m_1, r) \;\wedge$$

$$\mathrm{VerifySign}(Cert_1, m_1, \dots, m_{l_1'}, m_{l_1'+1}, \dots, m_{l_1}; VK_1) = 1\}. \quad (4)$$

With this protocol, the user demonstrates the issuer that C is a commitment to the first data item contained in the certificate $Cert_1$ issued by I_1. From the zero-knowledge property of the protocol and the hiding property of the commitment scheme, it follows that the issuer does not get any information on the data item m_1. If protocol (4) is accepted by the issuer, then he issues the certificate $Cert_3$ on m' and hidden m_1 using the protocol

$$Cert_3 = \mathrm{HiddenSign}(C, m'; SK_2), \quad (5)$$

where it is important to note that C is the same commitment as used in (4). ¿From the properties of HiddenSign, it follows that in protocol (5) the issuer learns m' but does not learn any information on m_1.

Finally, the user checks the correctness of $Cert_3$ by evaluation if

$$\mathrm{VerifySign}(m_1, m'; SK_2) = 1.$$

3 Example Applications of the Framework

The controlled disclosure techniques described above have a large number of applications to privacy protection, such as anonymous credential systems [16,27,44,49], group signature schemes [4,23,30], and electronic cash [9,29].

In this section, we sketch how one can use these techniques to implement an anonymous credential system with identity revocation and e-cash with offline double-spending tests.

3.1 An Anonymous Credential System with Anonymity Revocation

The key idea underlying the implementation of anonymous credentials is that every user is represented by a unique identifier *ID*, which remains the user's secret throughout the lifetime of a credential system.

Now, a credential from an organization simply is a certificate on the identifier *ID* (issued by the organization). Credentials are shown by using protocols of the form (1), such that the user's identifier *ID* is not disclosed to the verifier. Then, the *unlinkability* of credentials follows from the (multi-show) unlinkability property of certificates discussed above. Credentials are issued using blind certification such that the user's *ID* is not disclosed to the issuing organization. The *unforgeability* of credentials trivially follows from the unforgeability property of the signature scheme being used for blind certification.

A credential system is called *consistent*, if it is impossible for different users to team up and to show some of their credentials to an organization and obtain a credential for one of them that a user alone would not have gotten [17, 43, 44]. We achieve consistency as follows. When the user shows multiple credentials from different organizations, she proves that the same identifer *ID* underlies all credentials being shown, i.e., that the credentials belong to the same user. To this end, we use combined showing techniques as in protocol (2). When issuing credentials, the issuer asserts that the identifier *ID* that is blindly signing is the same as in existing credentials of the user. This can be achieved using the blind certification protocols described in (4) and (5).

Optionally, credentials can have attributes. Examples of credential attributes are an expiration date, the users age, a credential subtype. When showing a credential, the user can choose which attribute(s) to prove something about, and what to prove about them. For example, when showing a credential that has attributes (*expdate* = 2002/05/19, *age* = 55), the user can decide to prove only that *age* > 18. Credential attributes are implemented by adding data items (additional to the user's identifier *ID*) to certificates. When showing credentials, the user can decide what information on attributes she discloses using the selective showing techniques described above.

Finally, in many applications of credentials, it is desirable that under certain conditions the user's anonymity is revoked. Anonymity revocation can be implemented using our conditional showing techniques by conditionally disclosing the user's identity.

3.2 Anonymous e-cash

Let us sketch an implementation of an anonymous e-cash system with offline double-spending tests. Such a system consists of banks issuing e-coins, users spending e-coins at shops, which in turn deposit spent coins at the bank.

An e-coin is a certificate issued by the bank. To retrieve an e-coin, the user identifies herself at the bank. The bank assigns a unique number ID to the user. The user secretly chooses a random serial number s and a random blinding number b. The bank issues a certificate $Cert_{ecoin}$ on the data items ID, s, and b using blind certification such that it does not learn s and b.

At a shop, the user spends the e-coin $Cert_{ecoin}$ as follows. The shop chooses a random integer challenge c. The user computes $u = ID \cdot c + b$ and uses the following variant of a selective showing protocol

$$PK\{(Cert_{ecoin}, ID, b, ID', b') :$$

$$VerifySign(Cert_{ecoin}, ID, s, b; VK) = 1$$

$$\wedge u = (ID' \cdot c + b') \wedge ID = ID' \wedge b = b'\}, \qquad (6)$$

where VK is the bank's signature verification key. We note that the shop learns the value of s in the proof (6). Here, we additionally assume that the proof (6) can be carried out non-interactively, i.e., it can be represented in terms of string Π which is sent from the user to the shop. Such a non-interactive proof can be validated by the shop by applying an appropriate verification algorithm on Π. Also, in analogy to the zero-knowledge property of interactive proofs, a non-interactive proof shall not reveal any (computational) information on $Cert_{ecoin}$, ID, and b.

To deposit the e-coin, the shop sends the tuple (c, s, u, Π) to the bank. The bank first verifies the non-interactive proof Π to see if the tuple (c, s, u, Π) corresponds to a valid spending of an e-coin. In case of double spending, the bank can recover the cheating user's ID as follows. The bank verifies if there already exists an e-coin with serial number s in its database of deposited e-coins. If so, it retrieves the corresponding tuple (c', s, u', Π'). We may safely assume that $c \neq c'$, and also we recall that by (6) the validity of Π asserts that $u = ID \cdot c + b$ and $u' = ID \cdot c' + b$. Therefore, from u, u', c, and c', the bank can compute the user's identity $ID = (u - u')/(c - c')$. Thus, we see why non-interactive proofs are needed: it is because the bank itself needs to be able to verify the correctness of the proof (6) to ensure it correctly reveals a cheating user's identity ID.

Other desirable properties of e-cash, such as unforgeability and anonymity immediately follow from the properties of our certificates and the associated controlled disclosure techniques discussed above.

4 Concrete Framework

In theory, one could use any secure signature and encryption scheme for our framework, their combination by zero-knowledge proofs as described in the previous sections would in general not be efficient at all. Therefore, we describe in this section concrete implementations of these schemes can be efficiently combined. That is, they are all amendable to efficient proofs of knowledge of discrete logarithms.

4.1 Preliminaries

4.1.1 Notation

In the sequel, we will sometimes use the notation introduced by Camenisch and Stadler [23] for various proofs of knowledge of discrete logarithms and proofs of the validity of statements about discrete logarithms. For instance,

$$PK\{(\alpha, \beta, \gamma) : y = g^\alpha h^\beta \ \wedge \ \tilde{y} = \tilde{g}^\alpha \tilde{h}^\gamma \ \wedge \ (u < \alpha < v)\}$$

denotes a "*zero-knowledge Proof of Knowledge of integers α, β, and γ such that $y = g^\alpha h^\beta$ and $\tilde{y} = \tilde{g}^\alpha \tilde{h}^\gamma$ holds, where $u < \alpha < v$,*" where $y, g, h, \tilde{y}, \tilde{g}$, and $\tilde{h}$ are elements of some groups $G = \langle g \rangle = \langle h \rangle$ and $\tilde{G} = \langle \tilde{g} \rangle = \langle \tilde{h} \rangle$. The convention is that Greek letters denote quantities of the knowledge of which is being proved, while all other parameters are known to the verifier. Using this notation, a proof-protocol can be described by just pointing out its aim while hiding all details. ¿From this protocol notation, it is easy to derive the actual protocol as the reader can see from the example we give below.

In the random oracle model, such protocols can be turned into signature schemes using the Fiat–Shamir heuristic [36, 47]. We use the notation $SPK\{(\alpha) : y = g^\alpha\}(m)$ to denote a signature obtained in this way and call it proof signature.

Throughout, we use ℓ_s as a parameter controlling the statistical indistinguishability between distributions, ℓ_n as the length for RSA moduli that are hard to factor, and ℓ_q as a parameter such that discrete logarithms in a subgroup of order $q > 2^{\ell_q - 1}$ are hard to compute. Finally, we use ℓ_c as a parameter to denote the length of the challenges in the PK protocols.

Let a be a real number. We denote by $\lfloor a \rfloor$ the largest integer $b \leq a$, by $\lceil a \rceil$ the smallest integer $b \geq a$, and by $\lfloor a \rceil$ the largest integer $b \leq a + 1/2$. For positive real numbers a and b, let $[a]$ denote the set $\{0, \ldots, \lfloor a \rfloor - 1\}$ and $[a, b]$ denote the set $\{\lfloor a \rfloor, \ldots, \lfloor b \rfloor\}$ and $[-a, b]$ denote the set $\{-\lfloor a \rfloor, \ldots, \lfloor b \rfloor\}$.

4.1.2 Bi-Linear Maps

Suppose that we have a setup algorithm BiLinMapSetup that, on input the security parameter ℓ_q, outputs the setup for $G = \langle g \rangle$ and $\mathsf{G} = \langle \mathsf{g} \rangle$, two groups of prime order $q = \Theta(2^{\ell_q})$ that have a non-degenerate efficiently computable bilinear map e. More precisely: We assume that associated with each group element, there is a unique binary string that represents it. (For example, if $G = \mathbb{Z}_p^*$, then an element of G can be represented as an integer between 1 and $p - 1$.) Following prior work (for example, Boneh and Franklin [7]), e is a function, $e : G \times G \to \mathsf{G}$, such that

- (Bilinear) For all $P, Q \in G$, for all $a, b \in \mathbb{Z}$, $e(P^a, Q^b) = e(P, Q)^{ab}$.
- (Non-degenerate) There exists some $P, Q \in G$ such that $e(P, Q) \neq 1$, where 1 is the identity of G.
- (Efficient) There exists an efficient algorithm for computing e.

We write: $(q, G, \mathsf{G}, g, \mathsf{g}, e) \in_R \text{BiLinMapSetup}(\ell_q)$. It is easy to see, from the first two properties and from the fact that G and G are both of the same prime order q, that whenever g is a generator of G, $\mathsf{g} = e(g, g)$ is a generator of G.

Such groups, based on the Weil and Tate pairings over elliptic curves (see Silverman [48]), have been extensively relied upon in cryptographic literature over the past few years (cf. [7, 8, 38, 42] to name a few results).

4.2 Commitment Scheme

4.2.1 Pedersen's Commitment Scheme

There are several commitment schemes that are suitable for our purposes. The first one is due to Pedersen [46]. It uses elements g and h of prime order q such that $g \in \langle h \rangle$, where q is an ℓ_q-bit number.

To commit to a message $m \in_R \mathbb{Z}_q$, one chooses a random $r \in_R \mathbb{Z}_q$ and computes the commitment $C := g^m h^r$. The commitment can be opened by revealing m and r. To prove knowledge of the value contained in a commitment C, one can use the protocol denoted $PK\{(\mu, \rho) : C = g^\mu h^\rho\}$.

The Pedersen commitment scheme is information theoretically hiding and computationally binding. That is, a commitment does not leak *any* information about the committed message but someone who is able to compute the discrete logarithm $\log_h g$ can open the commitment to different messages. However, the commitment scheme can be turned into one that is computationally hiding and unconditionally binding: Let $C = (C_1, C_2) = (g^m h^r, g^r)$. Such a commitment can be opened by revealing m and r, and $PK\{(\mu, \rho) : C_1 = g^\mu h^\rho \wedge C_2 = g^\rho\}$ can be used to prove knowledge of the message committed by it.

4.2.2 An Integer Commitment Scheme

The Pedersen commitment scheme can be used only to commit to elements of $\mathbb{Z}_q$. However, we sometimes need to commit to elements from $\mathbb{Z}$. Therefore, we describe the integer commitment scheme due Damgård and Fujisaki [33].

Let $\mathfrak{n}$ be the product of two safe $(\ell_n/2)$-bit primes $\mathfrak{p} = 2\mathfrak{p}' + 1$ and $\mathfrak{q} = 2\mathfrak{q}' + 1$, and $\mathfrak{g}$ and $\mathfrak{h}$ be two generators of $\mathfrak{G}_{\mathfrak{n}'} \subset \mathbb{Z}_\mathfrak{n}^*$, where $\mathfrak{n}' = \mathfrak{p}'\mathfrak{q}'$. Note that $\mathfrak{G}_{\mathfrak{n}'}$ is the subgroup of $\mathbb{Z}_\mathfrak{n}^*$ of order $\mathfrak{n}'$.

Assume that one is given $\mathfrak{n}$, $\mathfrak{g}$, and $\mathfrak{h}$ such that the factorization of $\mathfrak{n}$ as well as the value $\log_\mathfrak{h} \mathfrak{g}$ are unknown to at least the party computing the commitment. The parameters $\mathfrak{n}$, $\mathfrak{g}$, and $\mathfrak{h}$ could be for instance provided by a trusted third party. Then, one can commit to an integer $m \in \{0, 1\}^{\ell_m}$, where ℓ_m is some public parameter, as follows: Choose a random $r \in_R [\mathfrak{n}/4]$ and compute the commitment $\mathfrak{C} := \mathfrak{g}^m \mathfrak{h}^r$. The commitment can be opened by revealing m and r. To prove knowledge of the value contained in a commitment C, one can use the protocol $PK\{(\mu, \rho) : \mathfrak{C} \equiv \mathfrak{g}^\mu \mathfrak{h}^\rho \pmod{\mathfrak{n}}\}$.

4.2.3 Proving the Length of a Discrete Logarithm

Assume the availability of n, g, $\mathfrak{h}$ as above. Let $G = \langle g \rangle$ be a group of prime order q and let $y = g^m$ such that $-2^{\ell_m} < m < 2^{\ell_m}$, where $2^{\ell_m} < q2^{-\ell_s-\ell_c-1}$. To convince a verifier that $-2^{\ell_s+\ell_c+\ell_m} < m < 2^{\ell_s+\ell_c+\ell_m}$, the prover commits to x using the above integer commitment scheme, i.e., chooses a random $r \in_R [n/4]$,d computes $\mathfrak{C} := g^m \mathfrak{h}^r$, and then runs the protocol

$$PK\{(\mu, \rho) : y = g^\mu \wedge \mathfrak{C} \equiv g^\mu \mathfrak{h}^\rho \pmod{n} \wedge -2^{\ell_m+\ell_s+\ell_c} < \mu < 2^{\ell_m+\ell_s+\ell_c}\}$$

with the verifier. As an example of how such a protocol can be derived from its notations, we spell this one out below.

The input to both the parities is g, y, n g, $\mathfrak{h}$, $\mathfrak{C}$, ℓ_m, ℓ_s, and ℓ_c, where ℓ_s and ℓ_c are two security parameters. The prover, in addition get m and r in its input.

1. The prover chooses a random $r_\mu \in \{0, 1\}^{\ell_s+\ell_c+\ell_m}$ and $r_\rho \in \{0, 1\}^{\ell_s+\ell_c+\ell_n}$, where ℓ_n is the length of $n/4$, and computes $\tilde{y} := g^{r_\mu}$ and $\tilde{\mathfrak{C}} := g^{r_\mu} \mathfrak{h}^{r_\rho} \bmod n$ and sends $\tilde{y}$ and $\tilde{\mathfrak{C}}$ to the verifier.
2. The verifier replies with a randomly chosen $c \in \{0, 1\}^{\ell_c}$.
3. The prover computes $s_\mu := r_\mu + cm$ and $s_\rho := r_\rho + cr$ and sends these values to the verifier.
4. The verifier accepts if the equations

$$\tilde{y} = y^{-c} g^{s_\mu}, \quad \tilde{\mathfrak{C}} \equiv \mathfrak{C}^{-c} g^{s_\mu} \mathfrak{h}^{s_\rho} \pmod{n}, \quad \text{and} \quad s_\mu \in \{0, 1\}^{\ell_s+\ell_c+\ell_m}$$

hold. Otherwise, the verifier rejects.

For the analysis of why the protocol indeed proves that $-2^{\ell_m+\ell_s+\ell_c} < \log_g y < 2^{\ell_m+\ell_s+\ell_c}$, we refer the reader to [22].

The above protocol can be extended to one that proves equality of discrete logarithms in two groups $\langle g_1 \rangle$ and $\langle g_2 \rangle$ of different order, say q_1 and q_2. That is, for $y_1 = g_1^m$ and $y_2 = g_2^m$ with $m0 \in \{0, 1\}^{\ell_m}$ and ℓ_m such that $2^{\ell_m+\ell_s+\ell_c+1} < \min\{q_1, q_2\}$, it is not hard to see that the protocol

$$PK\{(\mu, \rho) : y_1 = g_1^\mu \wedge y_2 = g_2^\mu \wedge$$
$$\mathfrak{C} \equiv g^\mu \mathfrak{h}^\rho \pmod{n} \wedge -2^{\ell_m+\ell_s+\ell_c} < \mu < 2^{\ell_m+\ell_s+\ell_c}\}$$

achieves this goal, where $\mathfrak{C}$ is a commitment to m as above.

4.3 The SRSA-CL Signature Scheme and Its Protocols

We now present the first signature scheme that is suited for our framework. The signature scheme has been proposed by Camenisch and Lysyanskaya and proven secure under the strong RSA assumption [18]. The strong RSA assumption was put forth by Baric and Pfitzmann [5] as well as by Fujisaki and Okamoto [37] and has been proven to be hard in the generic algorithms model [34]. Together with the signature scheme, Camenisch and Lysyanskaya have also put forth protocols to obtain a signature on committed messages and to prove knowledge of a signature on committed messages. In the following, however, we present more efficient protocols that use some research results that have appeared since.

4.3.1 The SRSA-CL Signature Scheme

Let ℓ_n, ℓ_m, and $\ell_e = \ell_m + 3$ be parameters. The message space of the signature scheme is the set $\{(m_1, \ldots, m_L) : m_i \in \pm\{0, 1\}^{\ell_m}\}$.

Key generation. On input 1^{ℓ_n}, choose a ℓ_n-bit RSA modulus $n = pq$, where $p = 2p' + 1, q = 2q' + 1, q'$, and p' are primes of similar size. Choose, uniformly at random $S \in_R QR_n$ and $R_1, \ldots, R_L, Z \in_R \langle S \rangle$. Provide non-interactive proofs that $R_1, \ldots, R_L, Z \in_R \langle S \rangle$, e.g., run

$$\text{SPK}\{(\rho_1, \ldots, \rho_L, \zeta) : \ R_1 \equiv S^{\rho_1} \pmod{n} \ \wedge \ \ldots$$
$$\ldots \wedge \ R_L \equiv S^{\rho_L} \pmod{n} \ \wedge \ Z \equiv S^{\zeta} \pmod{n}\}$$

using $\ell_c = 1$. Output the public key $(n, R_1, \ldots, R_L, S, Z, \ell_m)$ and the secret key p.

Signing algorithm. On input $m_1, \ldots, m_L$, choose a random prime number e of length $\ell_e + \ell_s + \ell_c + 1 > \ell_m + \ell_s + \ell_c + 3$, and a random number v of length $\ell_v = \ell_n + \ell_m + \ell_r$, where ℓ_r is a security parameter [18]. Compute the value A such that $Z \equiv R_1^{m_1} \ldots R_L^{m_L} S^v A^e \pmod{n}$. The signature on the message $(m_1, \ldots, m_L)$ consists of (e, A, v).

Verification algorithm. To verify that the tuple (e, A, v) is a signature on messages $(m_1, \ldots, m_L)$, check that $Z \equiv A^e R_1^{m_1} \ldots R_L^{m_L} S^v \pmod{n}$, and check that $2^{\ell_e + \ell_s + \ell_c + 2} > e > 2^{\ell_e + \ell_s + \ell_c + 1}$.

Theorem 4.1 ([18]). *The signature scheme is secure against adaptive chosen message attacks [41] under the strong RSA assumption.*

The original scheme considered messages in the interval $[0, 2^{\ell_m} - 1]$. Here, however, we allow messages from $[-2^{\ell_m} + 1, 2^{\ell_m} - 1]$. The only consequence of this is that we need to require that $\ell_e > \ell_m + 2$ holds instead of $\ell_e > \ell_m + 1$. Also, in the above scheme, we require that $e > 2^{\ell_e + \ell_s + \ell_c + 1}$, whereas in the original scheme $e > 2^{\ell_e - 1}$ was sufficient.

Furthermore, an analysis of the security proofs shows that it is in fact sufficient if to chose the parameter v from $\mathbb{Z}_e$ [14]. However, if one uses this scheme to sign committed messages, then v should be chosen from a larger interval such that these messages are statistically hidden (cf. next paragraph).

Finally, to allow for a protocol to prove knowledge of a signature that is zero-knowledge, Camenisch and Lysyanskaya [18] required the signer to prove that n is the product of two safe primes, whereas due to the improved protocols presented below we require the signer only to prove that $R_i, Z \in \langle S \rangle$, which is considerably more efficient.

4.3.2 Obtaining of a Signature on Committed Messages

Let $c_1 = g^{m_1} h^{r_1}, \ldots, c_{L'} = g^{m_{L'}} h^{r_{L'}}$ be commitments to messages and let $m_{L'+1}, \ldots, m_L$ be messages known to (and possibly chosen by) the signer. To get a signature on these messages, the signer and the recipient of the signature can execute the following protocol (cf. [18]):

The parties' common inputs are $c_1, \ldots, c_{L'}, m_{L'+1}, \ldots, m_L, (n, R_1, \ldots, R_L, S, Z, \ell_m)$. The signer's secret input is p and q, and the recipient secret input is $m_1, \ldots, m_{L'}, r_1, \ldots, r_{L'}$. The parties execute the following steps.

1. The recipient chooses a random integer $v' \in_R \{0,1\}^{\ell_n + \ell_s}$, computes $C := R_1^{m_1} \ldots R_{L'}^{m_{L'}} S^{v'} \mod n$, and sends C to the signer.
2. The recipient runs the following proof protocol with the signer:

$$PK\{(\varepsilon, \mu_1, \ldots, \mu_{L'}, \rho_1, \ldots, \rho_{L'}, v) : c_1 = g^{\mu_1} h^{\rho_1} \wedge \ldots \wedge$$

$$c_{L'} = g^{\mu_{L'}} h^{\rho_{L'}}, \wedge C \equiv R_1^{\mu_1} \ldots R_{L'}^{\mu_{L'}} S^v \pmod{n} \wedge$$

$$\mu_1, \ldots, \mu_{L'} \in \{0,1\}^{\ell_m + \ell_c + \ell_s}\}$$

3. The signer chooses a random ℓ_e-bit integer e' such that $e := 2^{\ell_e + \ell_c + \ell_s + 1} + e'$ is a prime. The signer also chooses a random $v'' \in \mathbb{Z}_e$, computes

$$A := \left(\frac{Z}{C R_{L'+1}^{m_{L'+1}} \ldots R_L^{m_L} S^{v''}} \right)^{1/e} \mod n$$

and sends (A, e, v') to the recipient.
4. To convince the signer that $A \in \langle S \rangle$, she runs following proof protocol with the recipient.

$$PK\left\{(\delta) : A \equiv \pm \left(\frac{Z}{C R_{L'+1}^{m_{L'+1}} \ldots R_L^{m_L} S^{v''}} \right)^{\delta} \pmod{n}\right\}$$

5. The recipient verifies that $e > 2^{\ell_e + \ell_c + \ell_s + 1}$ is prime and stores $(A, e, v := v' + v'')$ as signature on the message tuple $(m_1, \ldots, m_L)$.

Compared to the protocol presented in [18], the signer proves to the recipient that $A \in \langle S \rangle$. This is necessary to assure that the recipient can prove knowledge of a signature on committed messages such that the proof does not reveal any information about the signature or messages. The method we apply to prove $A \in \langle S \rangle$ was put forth in [12] to which we refer for details on why this proof actually works.

4.3.3 Prove Knowledge of a Signature on Committed Messages

Let $c_1 = g^{m_1} h^{r_1}, \ldots c_{L'} = g^{m_{L'}} h^{r_{L'}}$, be commitments to the messages $m_1, \ldots, m_{L'}$ that are not revealed to the verifier; and let $m_{L'+1}, \ldots, m_L$ be the messages that are revealed to the verifier. Let (e, A, v) is a signature on the messages $(m_1, \ldots, m_L)$, $L \geq L'$. To prove knowledge of this signature, keeping the messages $m_1, \ldots, m_{L'}$ secret, the prover and the verifier can use the protocol below which uses ideas put forth in [14].

The parties' common inputs are $c_1, \ldots, c_{L'}, m_{L'+1}, \ldots, m_L, (n, R_1, \ldots, R_L, S, Z, \ell_m)$. The prover's secret input is $m_1, \ldots, m_{L'}, r_1, \ldots, r_{L'}$, and (e, A, v). The parties execute the following steps.

1. The prover chooses a random $r_A \in_R \{0, 1\}^{\ell_n + \ell_s}$, computes $\tilde{A} := A S^{r_A}$, and sends $\tilde{A}$ to the verifier.
2. The prover executes the proof protocol

$$\mathrm{PK}\{(\varepsilon, \mu_1, \ldots, \mu_{L'}, \rho_1, \ldots, \rho_{L'}, \nu) : c_1 = g^{\mu_1} h^{\rho_1} \wedge \ldots \wedge c_{L'} = g^{\mu_{L'}} h^{\rho_{L'}} \wedge$$

$$\frac{Z}{\tilde{A}^{2^{\ell_e + \ell_c + \ell_s + 1}} R_{L'+1}^{m_{L'+1}} \ldots R_L^{m_L}} \equiv \tilde{A}^{\varepsilon} R_1^{\mu_1} \ldots R_{L'}^{\mu_{L'}} S^{\nu} \pmod{n} \wedge$$

$$\varepsilon \in \{0, 1\}^{\ell_e + \ell_c + \ell_s} \wedge \mu_1, \ldots, \mu_{L'} \in \{0, 1\}^{\ell_m + \ell_c + \ell_s}\}$$

with the verifier.

4.4 The BM-CL Signature Schemes and Its Protocols

We now describe the second signature scheme that is suited for our purpose. The scheme was put forth by Camenisch and Lysyanskaya [19] and is based on the LSRW assumption introduced by Lysyanskaya et al. [44]: Let $G = \langle g \rangle$ be a group of prime order q, and let $X, Y \in G$, $X = g^x$, and $Y = g^y$. Now, the assumption states that given triples $(a_i, a_i^y, a_i^{x+m_i xy})$ with randomly chosen a_i, but for adaptively chosen messages $m_i \in \mathbb{Z}_q$, it is hard to computes a (a, a^y, a^{x+mxy}) with $m \neq m_i$ for all i. The assumption was proved to hold in the generic algorithms model [44]. The BM-CL signature scheme uses this assumption in the setting of bi-linear maps.

4.4.1 The Signature Scheme

The message space of the signature scheme is the set $\{(m_1, \ldots, m_L) : m_i \in \mathbb{Z}_q\}$. Its algorithms are as follows.

Key generation. Run the BiLinMapSetup algorithm to generate $(q, G, \mathsf{G}, g, \mathsf{g}, e)$. Choose $x \in_R \mathbb{Z}_q$, $y \in_R \mathbb{Z}_q$, and for $1 \le i \le L$, $z_i \in_R \mathbb{Z}_q$. Let $X = g^x$, $Y = g^y$ and, for $1 \le i \le L$, $Z_i = g^{z_i}$ and $W_i = Y^{z_i}$. Set $SK = (x, y, z_1, \ldots, z_L)$, $VK = (q, G, \mathsf{G}, g, \mathsf{g}, e, X, Y, \{Z_i\}, \{W_i\})$.

Signature. On input $(m_1, \ldots, m_L) \in \mathbb{Z}_q^L$, secret key $SK = (x, y, z_1, \ldots, z_L)$, and public key $VK = (q, G, \mathsf{G}, g, \mathsf{g}, e, X, Y, \{Z_i\}, \{W_i\})$ do:

1. Choose a random $v \in_R \mathbb{Z}_q$.
2. Choose a random $a \in_R G$.
3. Let $A_i = a^{z_i}$ for $1 \le i \le L$.
4. Let $b = a^y$, $B_i = (A_i)^y$.
5. Let $c = a^{x+xyv} \prod_{i=1}^{L} A_i^{xym_i}$.

   Output $\sigma = (a, \{A_i\}, b, \{B_i\}, c, v)$.

Verification. On input $VK = (q, G, \mathsf{G}, g, \mathsf{g}, e, X, Y, \{Z_i\}, \{W_i\})$, a message tuple $(m_1, \ldots, m_L) \in \mathbb{Z}_q^L$, and purported signature $\sigma = (a, \{A_i\}, b, \{B_i\}, c, v)$, check the following:

1. $\{A_i\}$ were formed correctly: $e(a, Z_i) = e(g, A_i)$.
2. b and $\{B_i\}$ were formed correctly: $e(a, Y) = e(g, b)$ and $e(A_i, Y) = e(g, B_i)$.
3. c was formed correctly: $e(X, a) \cdot e(X, b)^v \cdot \prod_{i=1}^{L} e(X, B_i)^{m_i} = e(g, c)$.

Theorem 4.2 ([19]). *The above signature scheme is correct and secure under the LRSW assumption.*

4.4.2 Obtaining of a Signature on Committed Messages

Let $c_1 = g^{m_1} h^{r_1}, \ldots, c_{L'} = g^{m_{L'}} h^{r_{L'}}$ be commitments to messages $m_1, \ldots, m_{L'}$ that are chosen by the recipient and are not known the signer; and let $m_{L'+1}, \ldots, m_L$ be messages known to (or chosen by) the signer. To get a signature on these messages, the signer and the recipient of the signature can execute the following protocol (cf. [18]):

The parties' common inputs are $c_1, \ldots, c_{L'}, m_{L'+1}, \ldots, m_L, \ell_m$ and $(q, G, \mathsf{G}, g, \mathsf{g}, e, X, Y, \{Z_i\}, \{W_i\})$. The signer's secret input is $(x, y, z_1, \ldots, z_L)$, and the recipient secret input is $m_1, \ldots, m_{L'}, r_1, \ldots, r_{L'}$. The parties execute the following steps.

1. The recipient chooses a random $v \in_R \mathbb{Z}_q$ and computes $M := g^v \prod_{i=1}^{L} Z_i^{m_i}$. Next, the user gives a zero-knowledge proof of knowledge that M contains the same messages as the commitments $c_1, \ldots, c_{L'}$:

$$PK\{(v, \rho_1, \ldots, \rho_{L'} \mu_1, \ldots, \mu_{L'}) : c_1 = g^{\mu_1} h^{\rho_1} \wedge \ldots \wedge$$

$$c_{L'} = g^{\mu_{L'}} h^{\rho_{L'}} \wedge M = g^v \prod_{i=1}^{L'} Z_i^{\mu_i}\}.$$

2. The signer

    a. Chooses $\alpha \in_R \mathbb{Z}_q, a = g^{\alpha}$.

    b. For $1 \leq i \leq L$, lets $A_i = a^{z_i}$, sets $b = a^y$, and for $1 \leq i \leq L$, lets $B_i = A_i^y$.

    c. Sets $c = a^x M^{\alpha xy}$.

    d. Sends the recipient the values $(a, \{A_i\}, b, \{B_i\}, c)$.

3. The recipient stores the signature $\sigma = (a, \{A_i\}, b, \{B_i\}, c, v)$.

4.4.3 Prove Knowledge of a Signature on Committed Messages

Let $c_1 = g^{m_1} h^{r_1}, \ldots c_{L'} = g^{m_{L'}} h^{r_{L'}}$, be commitments to the messages $m_1, \ldots, m_{L'}$ that are not revealed to the verifier; and let $m_{L'+1}, \ldots, m_L$ be the messages that are revealed to the verifier. Let $(a, \{A_i\}, b, \{B_i\}, c, v)$ be a signature on messages $(m_1, \ldots, m_L), L \geq L'$. To prove knowledge of this signature, keeping the messages $m_1, \ldots, m_{L'}$ secret, the prover and the verifier can use the protocol below.

The parties' common inputs are $c_1, \ldots, c_{L'}, m_{L'+1}, \ldots, m_L, (q, G, \mathsf{G}, g, \mathsf{g}, e, X, Y, \{Z_i\}, \{W_i\})$. The prover's secret input is $m_1, \ldots, m_{L'}, r_1, \ldots, r_{L'}$, and $(a, \{A_i\}, b, \{B_i\}, c, v)$. The parties execute the following steps.

1. The prover computes a blinded version of her signature σ: She chooses random $r, r' \in_R \mathbb{Z}_q$ and forms $\tilde{\sigma} = (\tilde{a}, \{\tilde{A}_i\}, \tilde{b}, \{\tilde{B}_i\}, \tilde{c})$ as follows:

$$\tilde{a} = a^r, \quad \tilde{b} = b^r \text{ and } \tilde{c} = c^r$$

$$\tilde{A}_i = A_i^r \text{ and } \tilde{B}_i = B_i^r \text{ for } 1 \leq i \leq L$$

    Further, she blinds $\tilde{c}$ to obtain a value $\hat{c}$ that is distributed independently of everything else: $\hat{c} = \tilde{c}^{r'}$.
    She then sends $(\tilde{a}, \{\tilde{A}_i\}, \tilde{b}, \{\tilde{B}_i\}, \hat{c})$ to the verifier.

2. Let $\mathsf{v}_x, \mathsf{v}_{xy}, \mathsf{V}_{(xy,i)}, i = 1, \ldots, L$, and v_s be as follows:

$$\mathsf{v}_x = e(X, \tilde{a}), \quad \mathsf{v}_{xy} = e(X, \tilde{b}), \quad \mathsf{V}_{(xy,i)} = e(X, \tilde{B}_i), \quad \mathsf{v}_s = e(g, \hat{c}).$$

The prover and verifier compute these values (locally) and then carry out the following zero-knowledge proof protocol:

$$PK\{(\varepsilon, \mu_1, \ldots, \mu_{L'}, \rho_1, \ldots, \rho_{L'}, \nu, \rho) :$$

$$c_1 = g^{\mu_1} h^{\rho_1} \wedge \ldots \wedge c_{L'} = g^{\mu_{L'}} h^{\rho_{L'}} \wedge$$

$$\mathsf{v}_x^{-1} \prod_{i=L'+1}^{L} (\mathsf{V}_{(xy,i)})^{-m_i} = (\mathsf{v}_s)^{-\rho} (\mathsf{v}_{xy})^{\nu} \prod_{i=1}^{L'} (\mathsf{V}_{(xy,i)})^{\mu_i}\}.$$

The Verifier accepts if it accepts the proof above and (a) $\{\tilde{A}_i\}$ were formed correctly: $e(\tilde{a}, Z_i) = e(g, \tilde{A}_i)$; and (b) $\tilde{b}$ and $\{\tilde{B}_i\}$ were formed correctly: $e(\tilde{a}, Y) = e(g, \tilde{b})$ and $e(\tilde{A}_i, Y) = e(g, \tilde{B}_i)$.

4.5 The CS Encryption and Verifiable Encryption

We finally describe an encryption scheme that fits our framework. The scheme was proposed by Camenisch and Shoup [22], who also provided a protocol that allows an encrypter to efficiently prove that a ciphertext contains a discrete logarithm (or an element of a representation). Camenisch and Shoup further provided the analogue, i.e., a protocol that allows a decryptor to prove that the decryption of a given ciphertext revealed a discrete logarithm. Such a protocol could for instance be used to ensure that a trusted third party behaves correctly. However, we do not present the latter protocol here.

The Camenisch–Shoup encryption scheme is based on Paillier's Decision Composite Residuosity (DCR) assumption [45] is that given only n, it is hard to distinguish random elements of $\mathbb{Z}^*_{n^2}$ from random elements of the subgroup consisting of all n-th powers of elements in $\mathbb{Z}^*_{n^2}$.

4.5.1 The Encryption Scheme

Let ℓ be a further security parameter. The scheme makes use a hash function $\mathcal{H}(\cdot)$ that maps a triple $(u, \{e_i\}, L)$ to a number in the set $[2^\ell]$. It is assumed that $\mathcal{H}$ is collision resistant, i.e., that it is computationally infeasible to find two triples $(u, \{e_i\}, L) \neq (u', \{e'_i\}, L')$ such that $\mathcal{H}(u, \{e_i\}, L) = \mathcal{H}(u', \{e'_i\}, L')$. Let abs : $\mathbb{Z}^*_{n^2} \to \mathbb{Z}^*_{n^2}$ map $(a \bmod n^2)$, where $0 < a < n^2$, to $(n^2 - a \bmod n^2)$ if $a > n^2/2$, and to $(a \bmod n^2)$, otherwise. Note that $v^2 = (\mathrm{abs}(v))^2$ holds for all $v \in \mathbb{Z}^*_{n^2}$.

We now describe the key generation, encryption, and decryption algorithms of the encryption scheme, as they behave for a given value of the security parameter ℓ.

Key Generation. Select two random ℓ-bit Sophie Germain primes p' and q', with $p' \neq q'$, and compute $p := (2p' + 1)$, $q := (2q' + 1)$, $n := pq$, and $n' := p'q'$. Choose random $x_{(1,1)}, \ldots, x_{(1,L')}$, x_2, $x_3 \in_R [n^2/4]$, choose a random $g' \in_R \mathbb{Z}^*_{n^2}$, and compute $g := (g')^{2n}$, $y_{(1,i)} := g^{x_{(1,i)}}$ for $i = 1, \ldots, L'$, $y_2 := g^{x_2}$, and $y_3 := g^{x_3}$. The public key is $(n, g, \{y_{(1,i)}\}, y_2, y_3)$. The secret key is $(n, \{x_{(1,i)}\}, x_2, x_3)$.
Below, let $h = (1 + n \bmod n^2) \in \mathbb{Z}^*_{n^2}$ which is an element of order n.

Encryption. To encrypt a message tuple $(m_1, \ldots, m_{L'})$, $m_i \in [n]$, with label $L \in \{0, 1\}^*$ under a public key as above, choose a random $r \in_R [n/4]$ and compute

$$u := g^r, \quad e_i := y^r_{(1,i)}h^{m_i} \quad (i = 1, \ldots, L'), \quad \text{and} \quad v := \mathrm{abs}((y_2 y_3^{\mathcal{H}(u, \{e_i\}, L)})^r).$$

The ciphertext is $(u, \{e_i\}, v)$.

Decryption. To decrypt a ciphertext $(u, \{e_i\}, v) \in \mathbb{Z}_{n^2}^* \times (\mathbb{Z}_{n^2}^*)^{L'} \times \mathbb{Z}_{n^2}^*$ with label L under a secret key as above, first check that $\mathrm{abs}(v) = v$ and $u^{2(x_2 + \mathcal{H}(u, \{e_i\}, L) x_3)} = v^2$. If this does not hold, then output reject and halt. Next, let $t = 2^{-1} \bmod n$, and compute $\hat{m}_i := (e_i / u^{x(1,i)})^{2t}$. If all the $\hat{m}_i$ are of the form h^{m_i} for some $m_i \in [n]$, then output $m_1, \ldots, m_{L'}$; otherwise, output reject.

Theorem 4.3 ([22]). *The above scheme is secure against adaptive chosen ciphertext attack provided the DCR assumption holds, and provided $\mathcal{H}$ is collision resistant.*

4.5.2 Verifiable Encryption of Discrete Logarithms

Let $c_1 = g^{m_1} h^{r_1}, \ldots c_{L'} = g^{m_{L'}} h^{r_{L'}}$, be commitments to the messages $m_1, \ldots, m_{L'} \in \mathbb{Z}_q$. We now present a protocol that allows a prover to encrypt $m_1, \ldots, m_{L'} \in \mathbb{Z}_q$ and then to convince a verifier that the resulting ciphertext indeed encrypts the values contained in these commitment.

The protocol requires an integer commitment scheme, i.e., the auxiliary parameters $\mathfrak{n}$, and $\mathfrak{g}$ and $\mathfrak{h}$ such that the prover is not privy to the factorization of $\mathfrak{n}$.

Recall that ℓ_c is a security parameter controlling the size of the challenge space in the PK protocols. Finally, we require that $q < n2^{-\ell_s - \ell_c - 3}$ holds, i.e., that $m_i \in \mathbb{Z}_q$ "fits into an encryption". (If this condition is not meet, the m_is could be split into smaller pieces, each of which would then be verifiable encrypted. However, we do not address this here.)

The common input of the prover and verifier is the public key $(n, g, \{y_{(1,i)}\}, y_2, y_3)$ of the encryption scheme, the additional parameters $(\mathfrak{n}, \mathfrak{g}, \mathfrak{h})$, a group element (δ), a ciphertext $(u, \{e_i\}, v) \in \mathbb{Z}_{n^2}^* \times (\mathbb{Z}_{n^2}^*)^{L'} \times \mathbb{Z}_{n^2}^*$, and label L. The prover has additional inputs $m_1, \ldots, m_{L'} \in \mathbb{Z}_q$ and $r \in_R [n/4]$ such that

$$u = g^r, \qquad e = y_{(1,i)}^r h^{m_i}, \quad \text{and} \qquad v = \mathrm{abs}((y_2 y_3^{\mathcal{H}(u,e,L)})^r).$$

The protocol consists of the following steps.

1. The prover chooses a random $s \in_R [\mathfrak{n}/4]$ and computes $\mathfrak{k} := \mathfrak{g}^m \mathfrak{h}^s$. The prover sends $\mathfrak{k}$ to the verifier.
2. Then, the prover and verifier engage in the following protocol.

$$PK\{(r, m, s) : (v, \rho_1, \ldots, \rho_{L'} \mu_1, \ldots, \mu_{L'}) :$$

$$c_1 = g^{\mu_1} h^{\rho_1} \wedge \ldots \wedge c_{L'} = g^{\mu_{L'}} h^{\rho_{L'}} \wedge$$

$$u^2 = g^{2r} \wedge v^2 = (y_2 y_3^{\mathcal{H}(u,e,L)})^{2r} \wedge$$

$$e^2 = y_{(1,1)}^{2r} h^{2\mu_1} \wedge \ldots \wedge e^2 = y_{(1,L')}^{2r} h^{2\mu_{L'}} \wedge$$

$$\mathfrak{k}_1 = \mathfrak{g}^{\mu_1} \mathfrak{h}^s \wedge \ldots \wedge \mathfrak{k}_{L'} = \mathfrak{g}^{\mu_{L'}} \mathfrak{h}^s \wedge -\mathfrak{n}/2 < \mu_i < \mathfrak{n}/2\}.$$

5 Bibliographic Notes

Chaum pioneered privacy-preserving protocols that minimize the amount of personal data disclosed. His work put forth the principles of anonymous credentials [25, 27, 28], group signatures [30], and electronic cash [26]. The inventions of zero-knowledge proofs [11, 40] and zero-knowledge proofs of knowledge [6] have made a tremendous impact in this area. In particular, Damgård gave the first proof of concept [35] of an anonymous credential where a credential was represented by a signature on an individual's name, obtained in a way that kept the name hidden from the issuer; while showing a credential was carried out via a zero-knowledge proof of knowledge. These first developments were of great theoretical interest, but did not suggest solutions that were usable in practice.

Brands [10] invented efficient techniques for proving relations among committed values. The applications of these include electronic cash and a system where individuals do not have to disclose all attributes of their public keys in all contexts, but can choose which subset of attributes to disclose, or can choose to prove more complex relations among attributes. His techniques fell short of a full-fledged privacy framework as we described above because they did not have multi-show unlinkability. That is, if a user used his public key in several transactions, even though in each transaction he had a choice of which attributes to disclose, still in every transaction he had to disclose some information uniquely linkable to his public key.

Research on group signatures further contributed to the development of the key techniques for our privacy framework. In a group signature scheme, each member of the group can sign on behalf of the entire group such that one cannot determine which signer produced a given signature, or even whether two given signatures were produced by the same signer. What makes it non-trivial is that, in case of an emergency, a group signature can be traced to its signer with the help of a trusted third party. Camenisch and Stadler [23] came up with the first group signature scheme where the size of the public key was independent of the size of the group. Subsequent work in this area [21, 24] put forth a more general framework for group signatures. Finally, Ateniese et al. [4] invented the first provably secure group signature scheme (see also Camenisch and Michels [20] and Cramer and Shoup [32] that paved the way for the Ateniese et al. scheme).

Anonymous credential systems as described above were introduced by Lysyanskaya et al. [44]. The first efficient and provably secure scheme was put forth by Camenisch and Lysyanskaya [17], whose construction was largely inspired by the Ateniese et al. group signature scheme construction.

The foundation of our framework and the first key building block – a signature scheme with efficient protocols – was identified as such in a further study on anonymous credentials. Generalizing prior work [17], Lysyanskaya [43] showed how to obtain an anonymous credential system using this building block. The SRSA-CL signature scheme [18, 43] described in this paper emerged as a generalization of the techniques needed for anonymous credentials. Camenisch and Groth [14] made further improvements to the parameters of this signature and to the associated protocols; the parameters and protocols described in the present paper reflect these improvements. This signature scheme and associated protocols have since been implemented as part of the Idemix project at IBM [15] and incorporated into the TCG standard as part of the direct anonymous attestation protocol [12]. The BM-CL signature scheme described above was invented very recently [19]. It has not been implemented yet, but it is also quite practical.

The other key building block – verifiable encryption – was introduced by Camenisch and Damgård [13] and independently by Asokan et al. [3], as part of efforts in group signature scheme design and fair exchange of digital signatures, respectively. The verifiable encryption scheme described here is due to Camenisch and Shoup [22] and is the state-of-the-art.

Acknowledgement The information in this document is provided as is, and no guarantee or warranty is given that the information is fit for any particular purpose. The user thereof uses the information at its sole risk and liability. Part of the work reported in this paper is supported by the IST PRIME project; however, it represents the view of the authors only. The PRIME project receives research funding from the Community's Sixth Framework Programme and the Swiss Federal Office for Education and Science. Anna Lysyanskaya is supported by NSF Career grant CNS-0347661.

References

1. Portia project, website. crypto.stanford.edu/portia.
2. PRIME project, website. www.prime-project.eu.org.
3. N. Asokan, V. Shoup, and M. Waidner. Optimistic fair exchange of digital signatures. *IEEE Journal on Selected Areas in Communications*, 18(4):591–610, Apr. 2000.
4. G. Ateniese, J. Camenisch, M. Joye, and G. Tsudik. A practical and provably secure coalition-resistant group signature scheme. In M. Bellare, editor, *Advances in Cryptology – CRYPTO 2000*, volume 1880 of *Lecture Notes in Computer Science*, pages 255–270. Springer, Berlin 2000.
5. N. Barić and B. Pfitzmann. Collision-free accumulators and fail-stop signature schemes without trees. In W. Fumy, editor, *Advances in Cryptology – EUROCRYPT '97*, volume 1233 of *Lecture Notes in Computer Science*, pages 480–494. Springer, Berlin 1997.
6. M. Bellare and O. Goldreich. On defining proofs of knowledge. In E. F. Brickell, editor, *Advances in Cryptology – CRYPTO '92*, volume 740 of *Lecture Notes in Computer Science*, pages 390–420. Springer, Berlin 1992.
7. D. Boneh and M. Franklin. Identity-based encryption from the Weil pairing. In J. Kilian, editor, *Advances in Cryptology – CRYPTO 2001*, volume 2139 of *Lecture Notes in Computer Science*, pages 213–229. Springer, Berlin 2001.
8. D. Boneh and A. Silverberg. Applications of multilinear forms to cryptography. In *Topics in Algebraic and Noncommutative Geometry, Contemporary Mathematics*, volume 324, pages 71–90. American Mathematical Society, Providence, RI 2003.
9. S. Brands. Untraceable off-line cash in wallets with observers. In D. R. Stinson, editor, *Advances in Cryptology – CRYPTO '93*, volume 773 of *Lecture Notes in Computer Science*, pages 302–318, Springer, Berlin 1993.
10. S. Brands. *Rethinking Public Key Infrastructure and Digital Certificates– Building in Privacy*. PhD thesis, Eindhoven Institute of Technology, Eindhoven, The Netherlands, 1999.
11. G. Brassard, D. Chaum, and C. Crépeau. Minimum disclosure proofs of knowledge. *Journal of Computer and System Sciences*, 37(2):156–189, Oct. 1988.
12. E. Brickell, J. Camenisch, and L. Chen. Direct anonymous attestation. Technical Report Research Report RZ 3450, IBM Research Division, Mar. 2004.

13. J. Camenisch and I. Damgård. Verifiable encryption, group encryption, and their applications to group signatures and signature sharing schemes. In T. Okamoto, editor, *Advances in Cryptology – ASIACRYPT 2000*, volume 1976 of *Lecture Notes in Computer Science*, pages 331–345. Springer, Berlin 2000.

14. J. Camenisch and J. Groth. Group signatures: Better efficiency and new theoretical aspects. In *Proceedings of SCN '04*, volume 3352 of LNCS, pages 120–133, Springer, Berlin 2004.

15. J. Camenisch and E. V. Herreweghen. Design and implementation of the *idemix* anonymous credential system. Technical Report Research Report RZ 3419, IBM Research Division, May 2002.

16. J. Camenisch and A. Lysyanskaya. Efficient non-transferable anonymous multi-show credential system with optional anonymity revocation. Technical Report Research Report RZ 3295, IBM Research Division, Nov. 2000.

17. J. Camenisch and A. Lysyanskaya. Efficient non-transferable anonymous multi-show credential system with optional anonymity revocation. In B. Pfitzmann, editor, *Advances in Cryptology – EUROCRYPT 2001*, volume 2045 of *Lecture Notes in Computer Science*, pages 93–118. Springer, Berlin 2001.

18. J. Camenisch and A. Lysyanskaya. A signature scheme with efficient protocols. In S. Cimato, C. Galdi, and G. Persiano, editors, *Security in Communication Networks, Third International Conference, SCN 2002*, volume 2576 of *Lecture Notes in Computer Science*, pages 268–289. Springer, Berlin 2003.

19. J. Camenisch and A. Lysyanskaya. Signature schemes and anonymous credentials from bilinear maps. In M. K. Franklin, editor, *Advances in Cryptology – CRYPTO 2004*, volume 3152 of *Lecture Notes in Computer Science*, pages 56–72. Springer, Berlin 2004.

20. J. Camenisch and M. Michels. A group signature scheme with improved efficiency. In K. Ohta and D. Pei, editors, *Advances in Cryptology – ASIACRYPT '98*, volume 1514 of *Lecture Notes in Computer Science*, pages 160–174. Springer, Berlin 1998.

21. J. Camenisch and M. Michels. Separability and efficiency for generic group signature schemes. In M. Wiener, editor, *Advances in Cryptology – CRYPTO '99*, volume 1666 of *Lecture Notes in Computer Science*, pages 413–430. Springer, Berlin 1999.

22. J. Camenisch and V. Shoup. Practical verifiable encryption and decryption of discrete logarithms. In D. Boneh, editor, *Advances in Cryptology – CRYPTO 2003*, volume 2729 of *Lecture Notes in Computer Science*, pages 126–144, Springer, Berlin 2003.

23. J. Camenisch and M. Stadler. Efficient group signature schemes for large groups. In B. Kaliski, editor, *Advances in Cryptology – CRYPTO '97*, volume 1296 of *Lecture Notes in Computer Science*, pages 410–424. Springer, Berlin 1997.

24. J. L. Camenisch. *Group Signature Schemes and Payment Systems Based on the Discrete Logarithm Problem*. PhD thesis, ETH Zürich, 1998. Diss. ETH No. 12520, Hartung Gorre Verlag, Konstanz.

25. D. Chaum. Untraceable electronic mail, return addresses, and digital pseudonyms. *Communications of the ACM*, 24(2):84–88, Feb. 1981.

26. D. Chaum. Blind signatures for untraceable payments. In D. Chaum, R. L. Rivest, and A. T. Sherman, editors, *Advances in Cryptology – Proceedings of CRYPTO '82*, pages 199–203. Plenum, New York, 1983.

27. D. Chaum. Security without identification: Transaction systems to make big brother obsolete. *Communications of the ACM*, 28(10):1030–1044, Oct. 1985.

28. D. Chaum and J.-H. Evertse. A secure and privacy-protecting protocol for transmitting personal information between organizations. In M. Odlyzko, editor, *Advances in Cryptology – CRYPTO '86*, volume 263 of *Lecture Notes in Computer Science*, pages 118–167. Springer, Berlin 1987.

29. D. Chaum, A. Fiat, and M. Naor. Untraceable electronic cash. In S. Goldwasser, editor, *Advances in Cryptology – CRYPTO '88*, volume 403 of *Lecture Notes in Computer Science*, pages 319–327. Springer, Berlin 1990.

30. D. Chaum and E. van Heyst. Group signatures. In D. W. Davies, editor, *Advances in Cryptology – EUROCRYPT '91*, volume 547 of *Lecture Notes in Computer Science*, pages 257–265. Springer, Berlin 1991.

31. R. Cramer and V. Shoup. A practical public key cryptosystem provably secure against adaptive chosen ciphertext attack. In H. Krawczyk, editor, *Advances in Cryptology – CRYPTO '98*, volume 1642 of *Lecture Notes in Computer Science*, pages 13–25, Springer, Berlin 1998.

32. R. Cramer and V. Shoup. Signature schemes based on the strong RSA assumption. In *Proceedings of the 6th ACM Conference on Computer and Communications Security*, pages 46–52. ACM, Nov. 1999.

33. I. Damgård and E. Fujisaki. An integer commitment scheme based on groups with hidden order. In *Advances in Cryptology – ASIACRYPT 2002*, volume 2501 of *Lecture Notes in Computer Science*. Springer, Berlin 2002.

34. I. Damgård and M. Koprowski. Generic lower bounds for root extraction and signature schemes in general groups. In L. Knudsen, editor, *Advances in Cryptology – EUROCRYPT 2002*, volume 2332 of *Lecture Notes in Computer Science*, pages 256–271. Springer, Berlin 2002.

35. I. B. Damgård. Payment systems and credential mechanism with provable security against abuse by individuals. In S. Goldwasser, editor, *Advances in Cryptology – CRYPTO '88*, volume 403 of *Lecture Notes in Computer Science*, pages 328–335. Springer, Berlin 1990.

36. A. Fiat and A. Shamir. How to prove yourself: Practical solutions to identification and signature problems. In A. M. Odlyzko, editor, *Advances in Cryptology – CRYPTO '86*, volume 263 of *Lecture Notes in Computer Science*, pages 186–194. Springer, Berlin 1987.

37. E. Fujisaki and T. Okamoto. Witness hiding protocols to confirm modular polynomial relations. In *The 1997 Symposium on Cryptograpy and Information Security*, Fukuoka, Japan, Jan. 1997. The Institute of Electronics, Information and Communcation Engineers. SCSI97-33D.

38. C. Gentry and A. Silverberg. Hierarchical ID-based cryptography. In Y. Zheng, editor, *Advances in Cryptology – ASIACRYPT 2002*, volume 2501 of *Lecture Notes in Computer Science*, pages 548–566. Springer, Berlin 2002.

39. O. Goldreich. *Foundations of Cryptography II: Basic Applications*. Cambridge University Press, Cambridge 2004.

40. S. Goldwasser, S. Micali, and C. Rackoff. The knowledge complexity of interactive proof systems. In *Proceedings of the 27th Annual Symposium on Foundations of Computer Science*, pages 291–304, 1985.

41. S. Goldwasser, S. Micali, and R. Rivest. A digital signature scheme secure against adaptive chosen-message attacks. *SIAM Journal on Computing*, 17(2):281–308, Apr. 1988.

42. A. Joux. A one-round protocol for tripartite Diffie-Hellman. In *Proceedings of the ANTS-IV conference*, volume 1838 of *Lecture Notes in Computer Science*, pages 385–394. Springer, Berlin 2000.

43. A. Lysyanskaya. *Signature schemes and applications to cryptographic protocol design*. PhD thesis, Massachusetts Institute of Technology, Cambridge, Massachusetts, Sept. 2002.

44. A. Lysyanskaya, R. Rivest, A. Sahai, and S. Wolf. Pseudonym systems. In H. Heys and C. Adams, editors, *Selected Areas in Cryptography*, volume 1758 of *Lecture Notes in Computer Science*. Springer, Berlin 1999.

45. P. Paillier. Public-key cryptosystems based on composite residuosity classes. In J. Stern, editor, *Advances in Cryptology – EUROCRYPT '99*, volume 1592 of *Lecture Notes in Computer Science*, pages 223–239. Springer, Berlin 1999.

46. T. P. Pedersen. Non-interactive and information-theoretic secure verifiable secret sharing. In J. Feigenbaum, editor, *Advances in Cryptology – CRYPTO '91*, volume 576 of *Lecture Notes in Computer Science*, pages 129–140. Springer, Berlin 1992.

47. D. Pointcheval and J. Stern. Security proofs for signature schemes. In U. Maurer, editor, *Advances in Cryptology – EUROCRYPT '96*, volume 1070 of *Lecture Notes in Computer Science*, pages 387–398. Springer, Berlin 1996.

48. J. Silverman. *The Arithmetic of Elliptic Curves*. Springer, Berlin 1986.

49. E. Verheul. Self-blindable credential certificates from the weil pairing. In C. Boyd, editor, *Advances in Cryptology – ASIACRYPT 2001*, volume 2248 of *Lecture Notes in Computer Science*, pages 533–551. Springer, Berlin 2001.

Scalable Group Key Management for Secure Multicast: A Taxonomy and New Directions

Sencun Zhu and Sushil Jajodia

Contents

1 Introduction

Many multicast-based applications (e.g., pay-per-view, online auction, and teleconferencing) require a secure communication model to prevent disclosure of distributed data to unauthorized users. One solution for achieving this goal is to let all members in a group share a key that is used for encrypting data. To provide backward and forward confidentiality [23] (i.e., a new member should not be allowed to decrypt the earlier communication and a revoked user should not be able to decrypt the future communication), this shared group key should be updated and redistributed to all authorized members in a secure, reliable, and timely fashion upon a membership change. This process is referred to as *group rekeying*.

A group rekeying operation usually involves two phases. The first phase deals with the key encoding problem. To prevent passive eavesdropping attacks, a new group key must be encrypted by some key encryption keys (KEKs) prior to its

S. Zhu (✉)
Department of Computer Science, School of Information Science and Technology,
The Pennsylvania State University, University Park, PA 16802, USA
e-mail: szhu@cse.psu.edu

S.C.-H. Huang et al. (eds.), *Network Security*, DOI 10.1007/978-0-387-73821-5_3,
© Springer Science+Business Media, LLC 2010

distribution. The goal of a key encoding algorithm is to minimize the number of encrypted keys that have to be distributed. The second phase deals with the key distribution problem. The encrypted keys output from a key encoding algorithm should be distributed to group members reliably in the presence of packet losses. The scalability of group rekeying is determined by the efficiency of both key encoding and key distribution mechanisms.

A simple approach for group rekeying is one based on unicast. The key server sends the group key to each member individually and securely. Despite its simplicity, this approach is not scalable because its communication cost increases linearly with the group size. Specifically, for a group of size N, the key server needs to encrypt and send N keys when not considering packet losses. For large groups with very frequent membership changes, scalable group rekeying becomes an especially challenging issue.

In recent years, many approaches for scalable group rekeying have been proposed. Among them, Logical Key Hierarchy (LKH) [22, 23], One-way Function Trees (OFT) [2, 4], and Subset-Difference [10, 16] work on the key encoding phase; Proactive-FEC [25] and Weighted Key Assignment and Batched Key Retransmission (WKA–BKR) [21]) work on the key distribution phase. Due to different research focuses and diversity of performance metrics such as bandwidth overhead (the bandwidth used for sending or receiving new keys), rekeying latency (the time a user waits for receiving its keys after the key server distributes new keys), and storage requirement (the memory used by the key server or a user to store relevant keys), each approach has its own merits, and some of them are complementary to each other. Therefore, rather than comparing one scheme to another in detail, we are more interested in showing the previous research trends and envisioning some future research directions. We studied the existing approaches chronologically and made the following observations:

- The research interests have been moving from stateful protocols to stateless protocols. In a stateful protocol, a user normally has to receive all keys of interest in all previous rekeying operations to be able to extract the current group key, whereas in a stateless protocol, a legitimate user can readily extract the new group key from the received keying materials despite the number of previous group rekeying operations it has missed. Stateless protocols such as Subset Difference [10, 16] are hence more attractive than stateful protocols such as logical key hierarchy (LKH) [22, 23] when no feedback channel exists (e.g., unidirectional communication) or when users go off-line frequently or they experience bursty packet losses.
- Reliable key distribution has also become a research hot spot. Recently, researchers have proposed customized reliable multicast protocols for group key distribution (e.g., Proactive-FEC [25] and WKA–BKR [21]). Other schemes (e.g., ELK [17]) integrate the key encoding phase with the key distribution phase.
- Self-healing key distribution, which can also be thought of as belonging to the key distribution phase, has drawn much attention recently. A self-healing key distribution scheme [12, 19, 27] provides the property that a user is able to recover

the lost previous group keys on its own without asking the key server for retransmission, thus preventing the key server from being overwhelmed by feedback implosion.

- Several optimization schemes [1, 20, 26] have been proposed to further reduce the rekeying communication overhead by exploiting the characteristics of group members such as topology, membership durations, and loss rates.
- The study of group key management is no longer limited in the context of IP multicast. Recently, several group key management schemes have been proposed for wireless networks such as mobile ad hoc networks [13, 29] and sensor networks [28].

The remainder of this paper is organized as follows. We first introduce several existing work in more detail in Sect. 2, then discuss new research directions in Sect. 3.

2 A Taxonomy of Group Rekeying Protocols

This section describes several group rekeying schemes following our earlier observations. The schemes we discuss do not cover the literature entirely. We focus on *scalable* and *centralized* group rekeying, which has become the mainstream of research on secure multicast recently. Given the large amount of work in this direction, we believe that scalable group rekeying deserves an independent study. We do not discuss contributory group rekeying, in which every member is required to contribute a piece of information to collaboratively generate a new group key, and other tightly related issues such as multicast source authentication.

2.1 Stateful Protocols

A stateful protocol is one in which normally a member has to receive all keys of interest in all of the previous rekeying operations to be able to decrypt the new group key; otherwise, it will need to ask the key server for key retransmission. Most of the logical-key-tree-based group rekeying protocols in the literature (e.g., LKH [22,23], OFT [2], and ELK [17]) are stateful protocols. We illustrate below the LKH and OFT schemes and show why they are stateful.

Logical Key Hierarchy (LKH) The basis for the LKH approach for scalable group rekeying is a key tree data structure maintained by the key server. The root of the key tree is the group key used for encrypting data in group communications, and it is shared by all users. Every leaf node of the key tree is a secret key shared only between an individual user and the key server, and the middle level keys are key encryption keys (KEKs) used to facilitate the distribution of the root key. Of all these keys, each user owns only those keys that lie on the path from its individual leaf node to the root of the key tree. As a result, when a user joins or leaves the

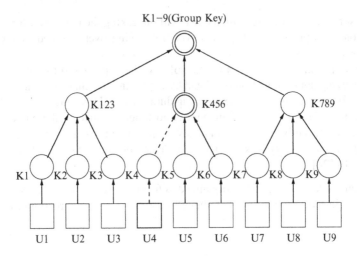

K1−9(Group Key)

Fig. 1 An example of a logical key tree. The root key is the group key, and a leaf key K_i is an individual key shared between the key server and a user U_i. Every user knows only the keys on the path from its leaf node to the root

group, all of the keys on its path have to be changed and redistributed to maintain backward and forward data confidentiality. Note that all the keys in the key tree are randomly generated, and there are no functional relationships among them.

Figure 1 shows an example key tree. Here, K_{1-9} is the group key shared by all users, $K_1, K_2, \ldots, K_9$ are individual keys, and $K_{123}, K_{456}, K_{789}$ are KEKs known only by users who are in the sub-trees rooted at these keys. We next illustrate the member join and leave procedures that are called by the key server separately when receiving a member join or leave request.

- **Join Procedure** Suppose in Fig. 1 the root key was K_{1-8} and K_{789} was K_{78} before user U_9 joined the group, and they are replaced with keys K_{1-9} and K_{789}, respectively, when U_9 joins. All the users need K_{1-9}, but only U_7, U_8 and U_9 need K_{789}. To securely distribute these new keys to the members of interest, the key server encrypts K_{1-9} with K_{1-8}, K_{789} with K_{78}, and K_{1-9} and K_{789} with K_9. Let $Enc(m, k)$ denote encrypting message m with key k, and $x|y$ denote the concatenation of messages x and y. The message multicast by the key server is:

$$Enc\{K_{1\text{-}9}, K_{1\text{-}8}\}, Enc\{K_{789}, K_{78}\}, Enc\{K_{1\text{-}9}|K_{789}, K_9\}. \qquad (1)$$

Each user can extract the keys it needs independently. For example, user U_1 decrypts the first item in the message to obtain the new group key K_{1-9}; besides K_{1-9}, user U_7 also decrypts the second item to obtain key K_{789}. Here, we can see that some users are only interested on a fraction of the rekeying payload. This is referred to as *sparseness property*.

- **Leave Procedure** When user U_4 departs from the group, the keys K_{456} and K_{1-9} need to be changed. Assume that these keys are replaced with keys K'_{456}

and K'_{1-9}, respectively. In the join procedure, an updated key can be encrypted by its old key for distribution. In the departure procedure, however, an updated key should not be encrypted by its old key for distribution because the users being revoked also know the old key. Instead, an updated key is encrypted by its child keys that are unknown to the revoked users. In this example, the key server encrypts K'_{1-9} with K_{123}, K'_{456}, and K_{789} separately, encrypts K'_{456} with K_5 and K_6 separately, and then multicasts these five encrypted keys to the group.

$$Enc\{K'_{1-9}, K_{123}\}, Enc\{K'_{1-9}, K'_{456}\}, Enc\{K'_{1-9}, K_{789}\},$$
$$Enc\{K'_{456}, K_5\}, Enc\{K'_{456}, K_6\}.$$

Also due to the sparseness property, after it receives the broadcast message, a member extracts the encryptions that are of interest to it to obtain the relevant updated keys.

Consider user U_7 in Fig. 1. During the group rekeying for adding U_9 into the group, U_7 must receive K_{789}; otherwise, it will not be able to decrypt the new group key K'_{1-9} (encrypted by K_{789}) during the group rekeying for revoking user U_4. As such, LKH is a stateful rekeying protocol.

LKH is very efficient and hence scalable for group rekeying when compared to a unicast-based naive approach. Let N be the group size and d be the degree of the key tree (the optimal degree d is shown to be 4 [22]). The communication cost in LKH is $O(\log_d N)$, whereas the unicast-based approach requires a communication cost of $O(N)$. In LKH+ [9], when a new user joins, every group member applies a one-way hash function to the affected keys instead of the key server redistributing them, thus the communication cost can be significantly reduced.

One-Way Function Trees (OFT) In OFT [2], the key server maintains a binary key tree. Unlike in LKH, in OFT, an interior key in the key tree is derived from its child keys. Each node v has a node secret x_v and a node key k_v. The node secrets of interior nodes and the node keys are computed as follows: $x_v = \langle f(x_L) \oplus f(x_R) \rangle$ and $k_v = g(x_v)$, where L and R are, respectively, the left and right children of v; f and g are special one-way functions; and $\oplus$ is bitwise exclusive-or. The node secret of the root is used as the group key. Often, $f(x_v)$ is called the blinded key of x_v because knowing $f(x_v)$ does not enable the recovery of x_v due to one-wayness of function f. Figure 2 shows the structure of an example OFT key tree.

In OFT, the key server and all members individually compute the group key. A member only knows its own node secret and the blinded keys of the sibling nodes of the nodes on its path to the root node; these keys allow a member to compute the group key through a bottom-up approach. For example, in Fig. 2, member U_4 only knows x_7 and $f(x_6)$, $f(x_2)$. It can first derive x_3 from x_7 and $f(x_6)$, then derive the group key x_1 from x_3 and $f(x_2)$.

When there is a member join or leave, the node secrets of the nodes on the path from the member to the root node must be updated. Consequently, the blinded keys of these node secrets also need to be updated. To securely distribute the updated blinded key $f(x'_v)$ of x'_v to and only to the members who need it (i.e., the members

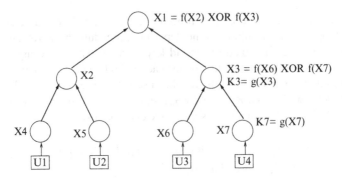

Fig. 2 An OFT key tree and the functional relationships among its node secrets and node keys

who are in the subtree rooted at v's sibling node s), the key server encrypts $f(x_v')$ with k_s, the node key of s. Note that the key server does not need to distribute x_v' to the members that are in the subtree rooted at v because these members can derive x_v' from the blinded keys of v's child nodes. As a result, the bandwidth overhead of OFT in a member join/leave is about $\log_2 N$ keys, which is half of that for revoking a member in LKH because in LKH an updated key is separately encrypted by each of its child keys.

Batched Rekeying For a large group with very dynamic membership, LKH or OFT may not scale well [18] because it performs a group rekeying for every membership change. To reduce the frequency of group rekeying operations, researchers have proposed to use batched rekeying [18, 25] instead of individual rekeying. Batched rekeying can be done in a periodic fashion so that the rekeying frequency is decoupled from the membership dynamics of a group, and hence the processing overhead at the key server can be reduced. In addition, using batched rekeying can reduce the overall bandwidth consumption significantly. This is because every compromised key in the key tree, due to member joins or leaves, only needs to be updated once despite the number of joins and leaves. For example, in Fig. 1 when users U_4 and U_6 both depart from the group during the same rekeying period, $K_{1\text{-}9}$ and K_{456} only need to be changed once.

2.2 Stateless Protocols

A stateless rekeying protocol is one that allows a legitimate group member to obtain the group key from the received rekeying material, despite the number of previous rekeying operations it has missed. The statelessness property is very desirable when no feedback channel exists (e.g., encrypted DVD distribution or stealthy radio receivers) or when group members go off-line frequently or experience high packet losses. A simplest stateless protocol, which we refer to as *flat-tree rekeying*, is one in which the key server encrypts the group key with the individual key of every member and then multicasts all the encrypted keys. Every member uses its individual key to decrypt one of the encryptions to obtain the group key. However, this scheme does not scale well with the group size. More scalable stateless protocols include subset-difference rekeying (SDR) [16] and MARKS [3], which are introduced in the following sections in more detail.

Subset-Difference Rekeying (SDR) In SDR, the key server maintains a logical binary key tree and maps every member to a leaf node of the key tree. Let V_i and V_j be two vertices in the key tree and V_i an ancestor of V_j. Let S_{ij} be a subset, which can be thought of as the set of users in the sub-tree rooted at node V_i minus the set of users in the sub-tree rooted at node V_j (see Fig. 3 for an example). Each subset is associated with a unique key that is only known to the members belonging to this subset. During a rekey operation, the key server partitions the current members of the group into a *minimal* number of non-overlapping subsets (see Fig. 4 for an example). It then encrypts the new group key with the unique key of each subset separately. Hence, the number of encrypted keys to be distributed to the users equals the number of subsets generated by the method. A group member only needs to receive exactly one encrypted key in every rekeying operation, which is the new group key encrypted with the key of a subset to which it belongs. The SDR scheme falls back to the flat-tree rekeying scheme when every subset contains one member.

In SDR, the average number of subsets is $1.25\,r$ when there are totally r revoked users in the system. The communication complexity (i.e., the number of subsets) is independent of the group size N, which makes this scheme very scalable with the

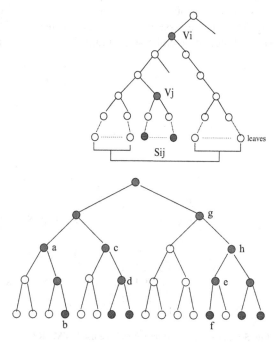

Fig. 3 The solid leaf nodes denote the revoked users. Subset S_{ij} contains the current members

Fig. 4 An example of SDR. A solid leaf node denotes a revoked user, and all the solid nodes form a minimum spanning tree that connects all the revoked users. The subsets $\{S_{ab}, S_{cd}, S_{ef}, S_{gh}\}$ cover all the remaining users

group size. However, because r always grows, the performance of SDR degrades with time. Note that in LKH the rekeying cost is determined by the group size N and the number of users being revoked since the *previous* rekeying operation; thus, LKH does not incur this performance degradation. This comparison suggests that SDR is suitable for applications in which the number of revoked users r is relatively small, particularly when $r \ll N$, whereas LKH seems to be preferable for applications that have a large number of revoked users. On the other hand, in SDR, each user stores $0.5 \log^2 N$ keys, whereas in LKH each user stores $\log N$ keys. Halevy and Shamir [10] presents a variant of SDR, which allows a tradeoff between user storage and communication cost.

MARKS MARKS is mainly designed for receiver-initiated Internet multicast applications where the membership duration of a member is known to the key server when the member joins the group (e.g., a user may subscribe to a multimedia distribution program for a certain time period). In MARKS, the key server maintains a binary hash tree that is constructed through a top-down approach using a random key as the root key. Except the root key, every other keys in the key server is derived from its parent key based on a one-way hash function. Figure 5 shows an example. $S(0,0)$ is a random key. From $S(0,0)$, the key server derives $S(1,0)$ and $S(1,1)$ as follows:

$$S(1,0) = f(S(0,0)), S(1,1) = g(S(0,0)).$$

Here, f and g are different one-way functions. Recursively, the key server derives all the other keys.

MARKS divides a multicast application into multiple sessions, and each session uses a unique group key that is a leaf key in the binary hash tree. For example, in Fig. 5, $K0$ is the session key for the time interval $[T0, T1]$, $K1$ is for $[T1, T2]$, and so on. Since the membership duration of a member is assumed to be known to the

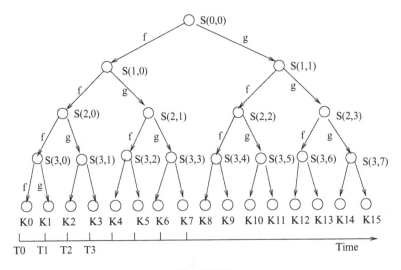

Fig. 5 An example of binary hash tree used in MARKS

key server when the member joins, the key server sends to the member the subset of leaf keys that are used for the duration. Indeed, the key server can minimize the size of the keying message by sending some interior keys instead of the leaf keys if the leaf keys can be derived from them. For example, in Fig. 5, if a member has membership duration from $T0$ to $T3$, it only needs to receive $S(2, 0)$. From $S(2, 0)$, it can derive $K0$, $K1$, $K2$, and $K3$ using the public algorithms f and g.

MARKS does not incur rekeying overhead for member leaves because it completely de-couples senders from the joining and leaving activities of all receivers. Therefore, it scales well with the group size. However, the requirement that membership durations be known in advance limits MARKS to some specific multicast applications.

2.3 Reliable Key Distribution

During a group rekeying operation based on a rekeying algorithm such as LKH, the key server first updates the compromised keys, including the group key and a fraction of KEKs; it then encrypts the updated keys with appropriate noncompromised KEKs; and finally it multicasts all of the encrypted keys to the group. A reliable key distribution protocol is designed to ensure that most (if not all) of the group members receive the keys of interest to them reliably in the presence of packet losses in a network.

Although reliable multicast transport protocols such as SRM [8] and RMTP [14] can be used for reliable delivery of keys, these protocols are complex and (in some cases) require additional support from the network infrastructure. Moreover, the reliable key delivery problem has some characteristics that can be exploited to design custom protocols that are more light-weight in nature.

Recently, several schemes have been proposed for providing reliability for key delivery. The simplest solution is to send every key multiple times (referred to as a *multi-send* scheme) to increase the probability that every user receives the keys of interest to it. The proactive FEC approach [25] and the WKA–BKR approach [21] have been shown to incur a much smaller bandwidth overhead than the multi-send approach. A key server can employ the proactive FEC, WKA–BKR, or their hybrid WFEC–BKR [27] for reliable distribution of the encrypted keys output from a key encoding algorithm such as LKH, OFT, or SDR. Below, we introduce in more detail the proactive FEC, WKA–BKR and another reliable key distribution protocol called ELK [17].

Proactive FEC-Based Key Delivery In the proactive FEC-based approach, the key server packs the encrypted keys into multiple packets. These packets are divided into FEC blocks of k packets each; the last block is padded with default packets if not full. The key server then generates $\lceil (\rho-1)k \rceil$ parity packets for each block based on Reed Solomon codes [15], where $\rho \geq 1$ is the proactivity factor determined by the loss rates of the group members. Finally, the key server broadcasts both the original packets and the parity packets.

A user interested in the packets from a certain block can recover all of the original packets in the block as long as it receives any k out of $\lceil k\rho \rceil$ packets from the block. If a user does not receive the exact packet that contains the encrypted keys of interest to it and meanwhile it only receives $t (t < k)$ other packets from the block that contains this packet, it will need to ask the key server for retransmission of $k - t$ new parity packets.

The key server collects all of the retransmission requests, and then for each block, it generates and transmits the *maximum* number of new parity packets required by users. The retransmission phase continues until all of the users have successfully received their keys.

WKA–BKR The WKA–BKR scheme uses the simple packet replication technique which sends every packet multiple times, but it exploits two properties of logical key trees. First, the encrypted keys may have different replication weights, depending on the number of users interested in them and the loss rates of these users. For example, in LKH, the keys closer to the root of the key tree are needed by more members than the keys less closer to the root, and in SDR, some subsets cover a larger number of users than other subsets do. If a key is needed by more users and these users have higher loss rates, it should be given a higher degree of replication so that most of these users will receive the key reliably and timely. Hence, in WKA–BKR, the key server first determines the weight w_i for each encrypted key K_i based on the number of users interested in that key and the loss characteristics of these users. It then packs the keys that have the same weight $\lfloor w_i \rfloor$ into a set s_i of packets. When broadcasting the packets, the key server sends $\lfloor w_i \rfloor$ times the packets in s_i. This process is called weighted key assignment (WKA).

The second exploited property is the sparseness of rekeying payload, i.e., a user typically only needs to receive a small fraction of keying messages to decode the group key. The sparseness property suggests that when a user requests for the retransmission of its lost keys, there is no need for the key server to retransmit the entire packet that contains the requested keys sent in the previous round. Instead, the key server repackages the requested keys into new packets before retransmitting them. This process is called batched key retransmission (BKR). The WKA–BKR scheme has been shown to have a lower bandwidth overhead than the multi-send and the proactive-FEC schemes in many network settings.

ELK Unlike LKH, OFT, WKA–BKR, or proactive FEC, which provides either key encoding or key distribution, ELK [17] integrates the key encoding phase and the key distribution phase. In ELK, the key server maintains a binary key tree that is similar to the one in OFT [2]. To update a key in the key tree, the key server derives the new key from the old key and contributions from both its child keys, based on pseudo-random functions. The child keys are updated, if necessary, in the same way recursively. A member can update the key in the same way if it knows the old key and the child keys.

During a group rekeying, the key server not only generates new keys but also derives some "hint" information from these new keys based on pseudo-random functions. The new keys are distributed alone without replication, whereas the hints are usually replicated and distributed together with data packets.

When a member receives both the child keys of a new key and knows the old key, it can compute the new key based on pseudo-random functions. However, if it only receives one child key but also the hint of the new key, it can recover the new key by brute-forcing a small key space (e.g., 16 bits). On the other hand, a revoked user must brute-force at least a larger key space (e.g., 44 bits) to be able to recover the same key.

ELK achieves reliability and moderate security through a tradeoff of communication overhead with member computation. Note that ELK is also a stateful rekeying protocol because a user must receive or recover the current group key to be able to decrypt the next group key.

2.4 Self-Healing Key Distribution

The reliable key delivery protocols discussed in Sect. 2.3 work well for scenarios where a user experiences random packet losses. However, a user might have to request packet retransmissions multiple times until it finally receives the encrypted keys of interest to it. In other words, there is no guarantee that it will receive the group key before the next group rekeying event occurs. This is especially true for receivers that are experiencing intermittent burst packet losses. Another similar scenario arises when a user is off-line (while still a member of the group) at the time of a group rekeying. If the user receives data that were encrypted using a group key that it has not received, it will need to obtain that group key.

A self-healing key delivery protocol allows a user to obtain missing group keys on its own without requesting a retransmission from the key server. This is accomplished by combining information from the current key update broadcast with information received in previous key update broadcasts. In this section, we discuss two such schemes. We say a scheme has *m-recoverability* if the maximum number of previous group keys a legitimate user can recover is m.

2.4.1 Polynomial-Based Self-Healing

Staddon et al. [19] proposes the first self-healing key distribution protocol that uses secret sharing techniques. In this protocol, the key server divides the lifetime of a multicast program into m sessions, each of which uses a unique session(group) key for encrypting the data distributed in the session period. A group key is divided into two shares. When rekeying the group, the key server broadcasts the current group key and shares of all the past and future group keys. To recover a missing key, a member only needs to receive two shares of the key at different rekeying operations. Figure 6 demonstrates this idea.

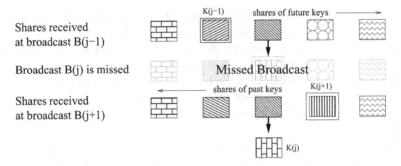

Fig. 6 The self-healing scheme. A member can recover the missing group key $K(j)$ broadcast at $B(j)$ by combining the two shares of $K(j)$ it receives from $B(j-1)$ and $B(j+1)$

Staddon et al. [19] presents a construction of this protocol with polynomial-based secret sharing techniques. Let F_q be a finite field where q is a prime number that is large enough to accommodate a cryptographic key. All the operations of this construction take place in F_q. The protocol involves three phases, as demonstrate below.

Setup   The key server randomly generates $2m$ polynomials of degree-t in $F_q[x]$, $h_1, h_2, ..., h_m, p_1, p_2, ..., p_m$, and m session keys, $K(1), K(2), ..., K(m) \in F_q$. For each $j \in \{1, m\}$, it defines a polynomial in $F_q[x]$, $q_j(x) = K(j) - p_j(x)$. The key server finally delivers $S_i = \{i, h_1(i), h_2(i), ..., h_m(i)\}$ to member i through a secure and reliable channel.

Broadcast   In session $j \in \{1, 2, ..., m\}$, the key server broadcasts $B(j)$

$$B(j): \{h_1(x) + p_1(x)\}, ..., \{h_{j-1}(x) + p_{j-1}(x)\},$$
$$\{h_j(x) + K(j)\},$$
$$\{h_{j+1}(x) + q_{j+1}(x)\}, ..., \{h_m(x) + q_m(x)\}.$$

Session Key and Shares Recovery for Session j   A member i receiving $B(j)$ can recover $K(j)$ by evaluating $h_j(x) + K(j)$ at $x = i$ and subtracting $h_j(i)$. Similarly, it can recover session key shares $p_1(i), p_2(i), ..., p_{j-1}(i), q_{j+1}(i)$, ..., $q_m(i)$. These shares allow member i to recover $K(j)$ (if it misses $B(j)$) based on a $q_j(i)$ it received earlier and a $p_j(i)$ it will receive later.

The above scheme allows self-healing key distribution, but it does not have the revocation capability because a revoked user can continue recovering the future session keys from the future broadcast messages. Staddon et al. [19] addresses this issue by combining the above self-healing scheme with a personal key distribution scheme that has revocation capability. Note that the security of this protocol is determined by t, the degree of the polynomials, because if more than t members collude with their shares, they will be able to recover the polynomials based on Lagrange interpolation, thus breaking the system. Therefore, the key server has to set t be larger than the maximal number of revoked nodes in the m sessions.

The protocol is also stateless in addition to self-healing because a member can always derive the current group key from the currently received broadcast message. The broadcast overhead of this protocol is $O(t^2m)$ key sizes. Liu et al. [12] reduces the bandwidth overhead of this protocol to $O(tm)$ by introducing a more efficient personal key distribution protocol that has revocation capability.

2.4.2 Self-Healing SDR

Zhu et al.[27] proposes a self-healing key distribution scheme for SDR. The key idea is to bind the ability of a user to recover a previous group key to its membership duration. Below, we illustrate the basic scheme through an example where $m = 5$.

Consider Fig. 7. Let $T(10)$ be the current rekeying time. The key server first generates a random key $K^5(10)$, based on which it derives a hash key chain including $K^5(10), K^4(10), ..., K^1(10), K^0(10)$, where $K^0(10) = H(K^1(10)) = H^2(K^2(10)) = ... = H^5(K^5(10))$ and H is a one-way hash function. Due to the one-wayness of a hash function, a user knowing $K^j(10)$ $(0 < j < 5)$ can compute independently all the keys between $K^{j-1}(10)$ and $K^0(10)$, but not any of the keys between $K^{j+1}(10)$ and $K^5(10)$. $K^0(10)$ is the group key that all the users should use for data encryption between $T(10)$ and $T(11)$.

The key server then divides the current members of the group into six subgroups according to their membership durations. Applying the SDR algorithm to each subgroup in the key tree, it generates and sends $K^0(10)$ to the newly joined members, $K^1(10)$ to those joining at $T(9)$, $K^2(10)$ to those joining at $T(8)$, $K^3(10)$ to those joining at $T(7)$, $K^4(10)$ to those joining at $T(6)$, and $K^5(10)$ to all those joining at or before $T(5)$. Finally, it broadcasts a message $B(10)$

$$B(10): \{K^0(5)\}_{K^0(4)\oplus K^5(10)}, \{K^0(6)\}_{K^0(5)\oplus K^4(10)}, ...,$$
$$\{K^0(8)\}_{K^0(7)\oplus K^2(10)}, \{K^0(9)\}_{K^0(8)\oplus K^1(10)}.$$

Consider a current member that joined before $T(5)$. Suppose it has received $K^0(4)$ (or any other keys in the key chain for $T(4)$) and $K^5(10)$ from the key server but missed all the intermediate keys. From $K^5(10)$, it first derives all the other keys in the key chain, i.e., $K^4(10), ..., K^1(10), K^0(10)$. It then decrypts the first item in $B(10)$ to recover $K^0(5)$, using which and $K^4(10)$ to recover $K^0(6)$, and so on to recover all other keys. If the member joined at time $T(7)$, it can only recover $K^0(8)$

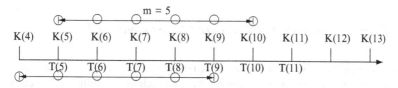

Fig. 7 An example illustrating self-healing SDR where $T(i)$ is a group rekeying time point. $T(10)$ is the current rekey time

and $K^0(9)$. This shows that the self-healing capability of a member is determined by its membership duration and is bounded by the design parameter m. Experimental results show that, in general, this protocol incurs bandwidth overhead of at most 3 m keys.

2.5 Rekeying Optimization

The logical key tree in LKH is usually required to keep balanced, so that the rekeying cost is fixed to be $log(N)$ for a group of size N. However, Selcuk et al. [20] shows that it is beneficial to use an unbalanced key tree in scenarios where group members have different membership durations. The idea is to organize the key tree with respect to the compromise probabilities of members, in a spirit similar to data compression algorithms such as Huffman and Shannon–Fano coding. Namely, the key server places a member that is more likely to be revoked closer to the root of the key tree. If the key server knows in advance or can make a good guess of the leaving probability of each member, this probabilistic organization of the LKH tree could lead to a smaller communication overhead than that in a balanced-key-tree case. Banerjee and Bhattacharjee [1] shows that organizing members in a key tree according to their topological locations could also be beneficial if the multicast topology is known to the key server.

Zhu et al. [26] shows two performance optimizations that are applicable to group key management schemes based on the use of logical key trees. These optimizations involve simple modifications to the algorithms and data structures used by the key server to maintain the logical key tree for a group. The first optimization exploits the temporal patterns of group member joins and leaves. The main idea is to split the logical key tree into two partitions–a short-term partition and a long-term partition. When a member joins the group, the key server initially places it in the short-term partition. If the member is still in the group after a certain time threshold, the key server then moves it from the short-term partition to the long-term partition. The second scheme exploits the loss probabilities of group members. The key server maintains multiple key trees and places members with similar loss rates into the same key tree. Thus, the key server separates keys needed by high loss members from those needed by low loss members when it packs keys into packets. These two optimizations are shown to reduce communication overhead over the one-key-tree scheme for applications with certain member characteristics.

2.6 Group Rekeying in Ad-hoc and Sensor Networks

Most of the previous group rekeying schemes were designed for secure multicast communications in the context of wired networks such as IP Multicast. Recently, as wireless networks such as ad hoc and sensor networks become the research hot spot, researchers have proposed several customized group rekeying schemes for wireless networks.

2.6.1 Group Rekeying for Ad-hoc Networks

An ad hoc network is a collection of wireless mobile nodes, and it can support communications in environments where no wired infrastructure exists. To communicate with parties beyond direct wireless transmission range, nodes in such a network need to cooperate to forward packets for each other; as a result, they act as both hosts and routers. In situations where no infrastructure (e.g., a wired and fixed base station) is available, such a network can be quickly and inexpensively formed to route traffic. For example, applications of ad hoc networking include voice and video communications in a battlefield, disaster relief, and ubiquitous computing. Some of these applications involve collaborative computing among a large number of nodes and are thus group-oriented in nature. For deploying such applications in an adversarial environment such as a battlefield or even in many civilian applications, it is necessary to provide support for secure group communication. As a result, we will all need to address the group key management issue.

Group key management for ad-hoc networks poses several new challenges compared to wired networks. First, group key management schemes for ad-hoc networks must be more resource-efficient, because the resources of a node such as power, computation and communication capacity, and storage are relatively constrained. Second, packet loss probability in ad-hoc networks is much higher than in wired networks. This is mainly due to the unreliable transmission links and temporary network partitions caused by node mobility. Thus, group key management schemes for ad-hoc networks must work efficiently under high packet loss rates.

These new challenges seem to rule out the stateful group rekeying protocols such as LKH and OFT that were proposed for wired networks with low packet loss rates, although no formal study on this has been conducted yet. Note that combining reliable key distribution protocols with stateful protocols does not solve the problem in the case of network partitions. Therefore, stateless protocols are preferred. However, stateless protocols such as SDR do not scale with the number of revoked nodes in the system.

Below we briefly introduce two symmetric-key-based group rekeying schemes for ad-hoc networks. The first one [13] is an energy-aware group rekeying scheme for ad hoc networks. This scheme exploits the physical locations of the member nodes when organizing the logical key tree (LKH [22]). This exploitation could save $15\% \sim 37\%$ energy in some scenarios, compared to a random LKH that does not use the physical location information. Two assumptions are made in order to use the location information. First, the network topology is assumed to be static. Second, the key server knows the exact location of every node.

The second scheme, called GKMPAN [29], exploits the property of an ad-hoc network that member nodes are both hosts and routers. In IP Multicast, all group members are end hosts, and they have no responsibility for forwarding keying material to other group members. In contrast, for group communication in an ad hoc network, the members of the group also act as routers. As such, in GKMPAN, the key server only has to deliver the new group key securely to the group members that are its immediate neighbors, and these neighbors then forward the new group key securely to their own neighboring members. In this way, a group key is propagated to all the members in a hop-by-hop fashion.

For the above scheme to work, a fundamental requirement is the existence of a secure channel between every pair of neighboring nodes. GKMPAN provides secure channels through probabilistic key pre-deployment [7, 30]. The main idea is to randomly load every node with a subset of keys from a large key pool before the node joins a network. Two nodes can establish a secure channel directly if they share a common key in their key subsets; otherwise, they can request a third node that shares a common key with each of them to establish a secure channel for them. To prevent compromised nodes from colluding to jeopardize the secure channels between other nodes, GKMPAN also includes a distributed key updating scheme for updating any compromised channels. The transmission cost per node in this scheme is close to one key and is independent of group size. Moreover, GKMPAN also provides the stateless property. Therefore, GKMPAN is much more efficient than LKH-like schemes that are used in ad-hoc networks.

2.6.2   Group Rekeying for Sensor Networks

Sensor networks can also be considered as ad-hoc networks, except that they are formed by sensor nodes that are more limited in power, computational and communication capacities, and memory. The current generation of sensor nodes such as Berkeley Mica Motes [24] have only 4 MHZ Processors, 19.2 bps bandwidth, and 4 KB RAM. In a sensor network, the network controller may broadcast missions, commands, or queries to all the nodes; therefore, a secure group communication model is also needed for sensor networks deployed in security critical environments. When compromised sensor nodes are detected, the network controller needs to update the group key and revoke the compromised nodes.

The group rekeying schemes [13, 29] for ad-hoc networks may be applied in sensor networks as well. Zhu et al. [28] introduces a more efficient group rekeying scheme. The scheme also uses hop-by-hop propagation of group keys as in GKM-PAN [29], but a secure channel between two neighboring sensor nodes is established upon other KEKs that are already in place. The transmission cost per node is shown to be one key, which is the optimal performance for node revocation.

Summary Generally speaking, stateful protocols are more bandwidth efficient than stateless protocols, whereas stateless protocols are more preferable in the presence of high packet loss or when members go off-line frequently. Both stateful and stateless protocols need a key distribution mechanism to distribute a new group key to all members reliably and in a timely fashion, and a self-healing key distribution mechanism to enable a member to recover a certain number of previous group keys on its own. The performance of group rekeying schemes could be further improved by exploiting the characteristics of group members such as their topological distribution, temporal patterns, and packet loss rates.

Compared to wired networks, ad-hoc and sensor networks are more constrained in the resources of member nodes and have higher packet loss rates. Group rekeying schemes exploiting the property that member nodes are both hosts and routers in these networks could provide significantly better performance than those adopted directly from the schemes proposed for wired networks.

3 New Research Directions

The group key management problem has been studied for about ten years in the context of IP Mutlicast, and many scalable schemes [2, 16, 22, 23] have been proposed. Each of these schemes has its own merits, subject to network size, membership dynamics, and loss characteristics. In the future, we can try to design a "perfect" group rekeying scheme. Ideally, a scalable group rekeying scheme should not only have the communication overhead close to that of a stateful protocol such as LKH or OFT but also have embedded reliability and self-healing mechanisms. If we cannot design such a perfect scheme, the alternative is to augment a stateful protocol with some lightweight plugins. For example, we have seen that a customized reliable multicast scheme such as Proactive FEC or WKA–BKR can be used to increase the reliability of key delivery for LKH, but we do not know if there is a scheme that can add self-healing to LKH, just as the scheme in [27] adding self-healing to the stateless protocol SDR.

Although IP multicast was proposed more than 10 years ago, its deployment has been very slow due to both technical and operational concerns. Recently, researchers have proposed the concept of overlay multicast (also called EndSystem multicast) [5, 6], which shifts multicast support from routers to end systems. Overlay multicast is a promising technique because it is independent of the underlying physical topology and therefore bypasses the limitations of IP multicast. We may directly deploy the existing group key management schemes proposed for IP multicast in overlay multicast, but these schemes might not provide the optimal performance. Therefore, further research study in this direction is needed.

For ad-hoc and sensor networks, if secure channels between neighboring nodes cannot be established efficiently (e.g., through key pre-deployment [29]), it is unclear, with respect to energy consumption, if a group rekeying scheme exploiting the same property as in GKMAPN [29] will outperform those designed for wired networks. For example, in [11], the secure channels are established upon public-key cryptography, which is very expensive in terms of computational and communication cost. Therefore, research that investigates issues such as which scheme is the best in what networks with what kind of loss probability and mobility models would be very helpful.

A related open issue is to distribute key serving responsibility over several key servers to improve reliability and survivability. This is especially important in the context of mobile ad-hoc networks where a key server may not be accessible due to node mobility. Having multiple replica key servers could address this issue, but it introduces the security weakness of compromising one key server breaking the system. An alternative solution is to use threshold cryptography, in which multiple key servers have to collaborate to perform group key management tasks. So far no efficient schemes have been proposed for this purpose.

Another related open issue is node compromise detection in ad-hoc and sensor networks. The key server initiates a group rekeying operation when it knows some node has been compromised. However, node compromise detection is a very challenging issue, especially for sensor networks that are often deployed in unattended environments.

References

1. S. Banerjee, and B. Bhattacharjee. Scalable Secure Group Communication over IP Multicast. In Proceedings of International Conference on Network Protocols (ICNP) 2001, Riverside, California, November 2001.
2. D. Balenson, D. McGrew, and A. Sherman. Key Management for Large Dynamic Groups: One-Way Function Trees and Amortized Initialization. IETF Internet draft (work in progress), August 2000.
3. B. Briscoe. MARKS: Zero Side Effect Multicast Key Management Using Arbitrarily Revealed Key Sequences. In Proceedings of First International Workshop on Networked Group Communication, NGC 1999.
4. R. Canetti, J. Garay, G. Itkis, D. Micciancio, M. Naor, and B. Pinkas. Multicast Security: A Taxonomy and Some Efficient Constructions. In Proceedings of IEEE INFOCOM'99, March 1999.
5. Y. Chu, S. Rao, S. Seshan, and H. Zhang. Enabling Conferencing Applications on the Internet Using an Overlay Multicast Architecture. In Proceedings of ACM SIGCOMM 2001, August 2001.
6. Y. Chu, S. Rao, and H. Zhang. A Case for EndSystem Multicast. In Proceedings of ACM Sigmetrics, June 2000.
7. L. Eschenauer, and V. Gligor. A Key-Management Scheme for Distributed Sensor Networks. In Proceedings of ACM CCS 2002.
8. S. Floyd, V. Jacobson, C. Liu, S. McCanne, and L. Zhang. A Reliable Multicast Framework for Lightweight Session and Application Layer Framing. IEEE/ACM Transactions on Networking, December 1997.
9. H. Harney, and E. Harder. Logical Key Hierarchy Protocol Internet Draft, draft-harney-sparta-lkhp-sec-00.txt, March 1999.
10. D. Halevy, and A. Shamir. The LSD Broadcast Encryption Scheme. In Proceedings of Advances in Cryptology - CRYPTO 2002.
11. T. Kaya, G. Lin, G. Noubir, and A. Yilmaz. Secure Multicast Groups on Ad Hoc Networks. In Proceedings of ACM Workshop on Security of Ad Hoc and Sensor Networks (SASN'03), 2003.
12. D. Liu, P. Ning, and K. Sun. Efficient Self-Healing Group Key Distribution with Revocation Capability. In Proceedings of the 10th ACM Conference on Computer and Communications Security (CCS'03), pp. 231–240, Washington, DC, October 2003.
13. L. Lazos, and R. Poovendran. Energy-Aware Secure Multicast Communication in Ad-hoc Networks Using Geographic Location Information. In Proceedings of IEEE ICASSP'03, Hong Kong, China, April 2003.
14. J. Lin, and S. Paul. RMTP: A Reliable Multicast Transport Protocol, In Proceedings of IEEE INFOCOM'96, March 1996.

15. A. Mcauley. Reliable Broadband Communications Using a Burst Erasure Correcting Code. In Proceedings of ACM SIGCOMM'90, Philadelphia, PA, September 1990.

16. D. Naor, M. Naor, and J. Lotspiech. Revocation and Tracing Schemes for Stateless Receivers. In Advances in Cryptology - CRYPTO 2001, LNCS 2139, pp. 41–62, Springer, 2001.

17. A. Perrig, D. Song, and D. Tygar. ELK, a new protocol for efficient large-group key distribution. In Proceedings of the IEEE Symposium on Security and Privacy 2001, Oakland, CA, May 2001.

18. S. Setia, S. Koussih, S. Jajodia, and E. Harder. Kronos: A Scalable Group Re-Keying Approach for Secure Multicast. In Proceedings of the IEEE Symposium on Security and Privacy, Oakland, CA, May 2000.

19. J. Staddon, S. Miner, M. Franklin, D. Balfanz, M. Malkin, and D. Dean. Self-Healing Key Distribution with Revocation. In Proceedings of the IEEE Symposium on Security and Privacy, Oakland, CA, May 2002.

20. A. Selcuk, C. McCubbin, and D. Sidhu. Probabilistic Optimization of LKH-based Multicast Key Distribution Schemes. Draft-selcuk-probabilistic-lkh-01.txt, Internet Draft, January 2000.

21. S. Setia, S. Zhu, and S. Jajodia. A Comparative Performance Analysis of Reliable Group Rekey Transport Protocols for Secure Multicast. In Performance Evaluation, 49(1/4):21–41, 2002. Special issue Proceedings of Performance 2002, Rome, Italy, September 2002.

22. C. Wong, M. Gouda, and S. Lam. Secure Group Communication Using Key Graphs. In Proceedings of SIGCOMM 1998, pp. 68–79, Vancouver, British Columbia.

23. D. Wallner, E. Harder, and R. Agee. Key Management for Multicast: Issues and Architecture. Internet Draft, draft-wallner-key-arch-01.txt, September 1998.

24. The Xbow Company. URL: Http://www.xbow.com.

25. Y. Yang, X. Li, X. Zhang, and S. Lam. Reliable group rekeying: Design and Performance Analysis. In Proceedings of ACM SIGCOMM 2001, pp. 27–38, San Diego, CA, USA, August 2001.

26. S. Zhu, S. Setia, and S. Jajodia. Performance Optimizations for Group Key Management Schemes. In Proceedings of the 23rd IEEE ICDCS 2003, Providence, RI, May 2003.

27. S. Zhu, S. Setia, and S. Jajodia. Adding Reliable and Self-Healing Key Distribution to the Subset Difference Group Rekeying Method for Secure Multicast. In Proceedings of 5th International Workshop on Networked Group Communications (NGC 2003), Germany, September 2003.

28. S. Zhu, S. Setia, and S. Jajodia. LEAP: Efficient Security Mechanisms for Large-Scale Distributed Sensor Networks. In Proceedings of the 10th ACM Conference on Computer and Communications Security (CCS'03), Washington, DC, October 2003.

29. S. Zhu, S. Setia, S. Xu, and S. Jajodia. GKMPAN: An Efficient Group Key Management Scheme for Secure Multicast in Ad-hoc Networks. In Proceedings of the 1st International Conference on Mobile and Ubiquitous Systems (Mobiquitous'04), Boston, Massachusetts, August 22–25, 2004.

30. S. Zhu, S. Xu, S. Setia, and S. Jajodia. Establishing Pair-wise Keys For Secure Communication in Ad Hoc Networks: A Probabilistic Approach. In Proceedings of the 11th IEEE International Conference on Network Protocols (ICNP'03), Atlanta, Georgia, November 4–7, 2003.

Web Forms and Untraceable DDoS Attacks

Markus Jakobsson and Filippo Menczer

Contents

1 Introduction

The competitive advantage of most industrialized nations depends on a well-oiled and reliable infrastructure, much of which depends on the Internet to some extent. We show how one very simple tool can be abused to bring down selected sites, and argue how this in turn – if cunningly performed – can do temporary but serious damage to a given target. Here, the target may be a person, business, or institution

---

M. Jakobsson (✉)
School of Informatics and Computing, Indiana University, Bloomington, IN 47408, USA
e-mail: markus@indiana.edu

S.C.-H. Huang et al. (eds.), *Network Security*, DOI 10.1007/978-0-387-73821-5_4,
© Springer Science+Business Media, LLC 2010

relying on the Internet or the telephone network for its daily activities, but may also be more indirectly dependent on the attacked infrastructure. In the latter situation, the target may not be the least prepared for an attack of the type it would suffer. For example, if voters are allowed to cast votes using home computers or phones (as in recent trials in Britain [10]), then an attack on *some* voters or servers may invalidate the *entire* election, requiring all voters to cast their votes again – for fairness, this would include even those who used traditional means in the first place. Other potential examples of secondary damage include the general mobile phone system, the infrastructure for delivery of electricity from power plants to consumers, and the traffic-balancing of the interstate highway system, given that these allow for load balancing via the Internet in many places.

When assessing the damage a potential attack can inflict, it is important to recognize that attacks may carry a substantial cost to society even if they do not obliterate their targets – in particular if repeatedly perpetrated, which becomes easier if the attacks are difficult to trace back to their perpetrators. Furthermore, one should not only take the direct costs into account but also the indirect costs associated with not being able to rely on the infrastructure.

Approach The attack described here is illustrated in Fig. 1. It involves Web crawling agents that, posing as the victim, fill forms on a large set of third party Web sites (the "launch pads") causing them to send emails or SMSs to the victim or have phone calls placed. The launch pads do not intend to do damage; they are mere tools in the hands of the attacker. This idea is not new – it is similar to sending pizzas to someone else's address. However, we demonstrate how easily one can exploit Web forms to do real damage and quantify such damage.

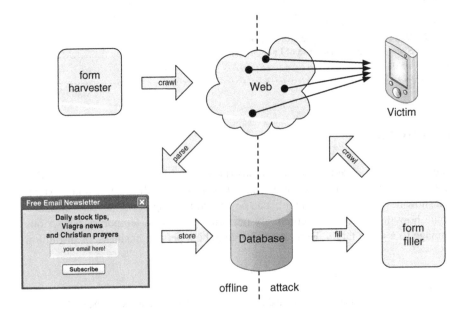

Fig. 1 Illustration of the attack

Our attack takes advantage of the absence in the current Web infrastructure of a (non-interactive) technique for verifying that the submitted email address or phone number corresponds to the user who fills in the form. This allows an automated attacker to enter a victim's email or number in a tremendous number of forms, causing a *huge* volume of messages to be directed to the victim's mailbox. Depending on the quantity of generated messages, this may cost the victim anything from lost time (sorting out what messages to delete); to lost messages (if the mailbox fills up, causing the Internet Service Provider (ISP) to bounce legitimate emails); to a crash or other unavailability of some of the victim's or ISP's machines.

Potential victims An attacker could target any user with a known or guessable email address. The list of targets that are vulnerable to the attack because of public email addresses is large. It includes banks, journalists, law enforcement officers, customer service and technical support centers, email-based chatrooms, and politicians. An attacker could target people with certain opinions or inclinations by harvesting email addresses from selected bulletin boards or by performing a focused crawl for given keywords on personal Web pages. Given that many companies use predictable formatting for email addresses, it may be possible to mount an attack on people believed to work for a company, or on people with common names, which in the end may amount to an attack of the company itself. The attack can also be used to affect the outcome of online auctions: some eBay users appear to use their email addresses as identifiers, making it trivial to block these from any competition during an auction. A large portion of the remaining set of eBay users can be conned into giving out their email address: simply ask them an innocuous question relating to a previous transaction of theirs (using the supplied Web interface) and the reply will contain their email address.

Our attack is also applicable to mobile devices, such as cell phones and PDAs, by targeting addresses that result in text messages being sent to those devices. Not only does this generate network congestion and unwanted costs but it also causes the text messaging feature of a mobile phone to be disabled once memory is filled up. According to a quick test of ours, the memory of a common cell phone model fills up after around 80 messages – an attack we performed in a few seconds. We note that an attacker would not have to know what cell phone numbers are in use in order to mount a general attack on the *service provider* – he or she can simply attack large quantities of numbers at random, many of which will be actual numbers given the high density of used numbers. Beyond inconveniencing everyday users of SMS, an attacker could stop medical doctors from being paged. If a large number of random mobile devices are attacked during an electronic election, it is highly probable that some voters will be unable to cast their vote. This may cause the fairness of the results to be questioned. This may especially be so if the targeted phone numbers correspond to particularly rich or poor voting districts, or to districts with higher proportions of certain minorities. Moreover, an attacker can target all email accounts with names likely to correspond to a given corporate leader and thereby render his or her mobile device unable to receive meaningful messages.

The common telephony infrastructure (both mobile and wired) can be attacked in an analogous manner: by agents entering a victim's *phone number* in numerous forms. If the remaining entered information is not consistent or accurate, this may result in a representative of the corresponding company placing a phone call to straighten things out, possibly after trying to send one or more messages to the email address entered in the form. Given the higher cost of placing a phone call – compared to sending an email – many companies prefer responding by email, which is likely to require a larger number of forms to be filled in by an attacker, in order to cause a comparable call frequency. On the other hand, phone calls being more disruptive than email messages, the impact of the attack types may be comparable for a given attack size.

Defenses What complicates the design of countermeasures is the fact that there is nothing *per se* that distinguishes a malicious request for information from a desired request in the eyes of the launch pad site, making the latter oblivious to the fact that it is being used in an attack. This also makes legislation against unwanted emails, SMSs, and phone calls [9] a meaningless deterrent: without the appropriate technical mechanisms to distinguish valid requests from malicious ones, how could a site be held liable when used as a launch pad? To further aggravate the issues, and given that our attack is a type of DDoS attack, it will not be possible for the victim (or nodes acting on its behalf) to filter out high-volume traffic emanating from a suspect IP address, even if we ignore the practical problems associated with spoofing of such addresses.

The "double opt-in" defense routinely employed by mailing list managers against impersonation of users is not useful to avoid the generation of network traffic. Some sites attempt to establish that a request emanated with a given user by sending the user an email to which he or she is to respond in order to complete the registration or request. However, as far as our attack is concerned, it makes little difference whether the emails sent to a victim are responses to requests, or simply emails demanding an acknowledgment.

While it may appear that the simplicity and generality of the attack would make it difficult to defend against, this is fortunately not the case. We propose (1) simple extensions of known techniques whereby well-intentioned Web sites can protect themselves from being exploited as launch pads for our attack, and (2) a set of heuristic techniques whereby users can protect themselves against becoming victims. Our countermeasures are light-weight and simple, require no modifications of the communication infrastructure, and can be deployed gradually.

2 Related Work

The automatic recognition and extraction of forms from Web pages using simple heuristics is not a new concept. For example, it has been applied to the design of comparison shopping agents aimed at searching for products from multiple vendor sites [4]. The problem is only a bit harder if an account must be set up before a a form can be submitted. For instance, many sites allow only registered users to send SMSs to any number. However, setting up an account is free and can easily be automated – this is why, for example, Hotmail and Yahoo use CAPTCHAs to prevent spammers from setting up fake accounts automatically.

During a denial of service attack, a large number of connections are set up with a victim, thereby exhausting the resources of the latter. A distributed denial of service attack is mounted from multiple directions, thereby making it more difficult to defend against. There exist many automated tools to mount DDoS attacks [2, 3, 5]. These require that the attacker takes control of a set of computers from which he or she will launch the attack. This, in turn, makes DDoS attacks more difficult to perform for a large portion of potential offenders. It also offers a certain degree of traceability since the take-over of launch pad computers may set off an alarm. The poor man's DDoS attack illustrated here can be mounted without the need to take over any launch pad computer, and offers the offender an almost certain guarantee of untraceability – due both to its swiftness and to the fact that it utilizes only steps that are also performed by benevolent users.

The attack we describe herein [6] is an extension and variant of the recent work by Byers et al. [1], in which an attack was described where victims are inundated by *physical* mail. While the underlying principles are the same – to request something for somebody else – the ways the attacks are performed, and what they achieve, are different. By generalizing to mostly all types of communication, our attack becomes a weapon in the hands of an attacker wishing to attack secondary targets as well as primary ones. This, along with the "real-time" aspect of our attack, makes it a potential threat to national security as well as to our communication infrastructure, and companies relying on the latter.

The defenses proposed in [1] and [6] vary considerably, given both the difference in threat situations and the difference in terms of the systems to be secured. The work of [1] discusses how to secure sites against being exploited as launch pads, but for the physical attack, they describe only mitigating measures seem possible. On the other hand, for the email based attacks described here, we show that the vulnerability of current Web forms can easily and completely be eliminated. Furthermore, we also consider how to secure entities against becoming victims. This strengthens our defenses in the face of poorly behaved Web sites, and non-compliant sites. Given that most sites are likely to belong to this category, the defense mechanisms described in [1] do not offer a good degree of protection against our variant of the attack.

Yet another difference between the two studies lies in the analysis; while no analysis is performed in [1], we describe experimental results illustrating the strength of our attack. These results show how long it takes for a typical adversary (a person with access to a standard computer and Internet connection) to disable a typical account. From this, it can be extrapolated how long it takes for a more powerful adversary to mount larger attacks. This highlights the danger of malware mounting a synchronized large-scale attack from multiple infected machines.

3 The Attack

3.1 Description of Vulnerability

Many sites allow a visitor to request information or subscribe to a newsletter. A user initiates a request by entering his or her contact information in a form, possibly along with additional information. Figure 2 shows the HTML code for a typical form.

Our attack takes advantage of the fact that, in the current Web infrastructure (e.g., HTTP protocol), there is no way to verify that the information a user enters corresponds to the true identity or address of the user. Thus, it is possible to request information on behalf of another party. Agents – or automated scripts acting as users – allow this to be performed on a large scale, thereby transforming the illegitimate requests from a poor practical joke to an attack able to bring down the victim's site.

3.2 Finding the Victim

In many instances, the attacker may know the email address or phone number of the victim, or may be able to extract it from postings to newsgroups, replies in an auction setting, etc. In other cases, the address may be unknown. If the attacker wishes to target the corporate leaders of a given company, he or she has to determine what their likely addresses are, which typically are limited to a few combinations of first and last names. In order to target mobile devices, such as Blackberries, the attacker would also target the appropriate wireless service providers, again targeting all names that match the victim(s). In order to target a service provider, a massive attack of this type is also possible. To wreak havoc in an electronic election in which users are allowed to use their own computers and wireless devices, it suffices to target a few voters who will later complain that they were locked out. It is even possible for an attacker to block his or her own device (stopping *himself* from voting) in order to later be able to lodge a complaint and have the election results questioned.

Fig. 2 HTML code of a typical Web form that can be exploited by our attack; this can be used to detect, parse, and submit the form

```
<form action="newsletter.php"
    method="POST">
<input type="text"
    name="Email"
    value="your email here!">
<input type="submit"
    name="submit"
    value="Subscribe">
</form>
```

3.3 Phase I: Harvesting Suitable Forms

Many Web sites use forms to execute scripts that will collect one or more email addresses and add them to one or more lists. There are many legitimate ways in which the collected emails can be used: mailing lists for newsletters, alert services, postcards, sending articles or pages to friends, etc. There are less legitimate uses as well, for example, many sites collect emails by advertising freebies of various sorts, and then sell the email lists to spammers as "opt-in" requests.

One way for an attacker to automatically locate and collect forms to be used as launch pads is by employing a topic-driven crawler [7, 8]. Such a software searches the Web in a focused way trying to find pages similar to a given description. The description could be a query that yields many pages with email-collecting forms.

An even more straightforward approach is for an agent to harvest forms from the Web by posting appropriate queries directly to some search engine. The agent can then fetch the hit pages to extract forms. For example, search engines return millions of hits for queries such as ``free newsletter'' or ``send this'' and hundreds of thousands of hits for ``send SMS''. However, search engines often do not return more than a maximum number of hits (say, 1,000). One way for the attacker's software to get around this obstacle is to create many query combinations by including positive and/or negative term requests. These combinations can be designed to yield large sets of hits with little overlap. Figure 3 illustrates how to create such queries automatically.

Once a potential page is identified, it must be parsed by the agent to extract form information. The page may actually not contain a form, or contain a form that cannot be used as a launch pad. A heuristic approach can be used to identify suitable forms. For example, there must be at least one text input field and either its name or its default value must match a string like "email." Such a heuristic identifies potential launch pad forms with high probability. In our experiments, using a search engine with queries as shown in Fig. 3 leads to a form harvest rate of about 40%. In other words, the heuristic yields about 4 potential launch pad forms from each ten search engine hits.

Once suitable Web form URLs are collected, they could be shared among attackers much like email address lists are exchanged among spammers. The harvest rate

```
base = (free email newsletter);
list = (alert subscribe opt-in list spam porn contest
    prize stuff travel ezine market stock joke sign
    verify money erotic sex god christ penis viagra
    age notify news recipe gratis libre livre);
foreach set = subset(list) {
    query(base plus(set) minus(list - set));
}
```

Fig. 3 Pseudocode illustrating how queries can be designed to harvest Web forms from a search engine

would then be 100%. It is easy to write software that parses the HTML code of a Web page and extracts form information. This consists of a URL for the form action, the method (GET/POST), and a set of input fields, each with a name, a type/domain, and possibly a default value. The form information can be stored in a database. This first phase of the attack can be carried out off-line, before the victim is even identified (cf. left-hand side of Fig. 1).

3.4 Phase II: Automatically Filling Forms

A form can be filled and submitted automatically, either immediately upon discovery, or at a later time based on the stored form's information. Heuristics can be used to assign values to the various input fields. These include the victim's email address and, optionally, other information such as name, phone, etc. Other text fields can be left blank or filled with junk. Fields that require a single value from a set (radio buttons, drop-down menus) can be filled with a random option. Fields that allow multiple values (checkboxes, lists) can be filled in with all options.

Once all input names have an associated value, an HTTP request can be assembled based on the form's method. Finally, sending the request for the action URL corresponds to submitting the filled form. For efficiency, forms can be filled and submitted in parallel by concurrent processes or threads.

This second phase of the attack (cf. right-hand side of Fig. 1) requires a form database, which could be a simple text file, and a small program that fills forms acting like a Web user agent (browser). The program could be executed from a public computer, for example, in a library or a coffee shop. All that is required is an Internet connection. The program could be installed from a floppy disk, downloaded from a Web or FTP server, or even invoked via an applet or a virus.

3.5 Poorly Behaved Sites

There are many poorly behaved sites that may not care whether the entered contact information corresponds to the Web page visitor or a potential victim. The reason is simple: these sites derive benefit from the collection of valid email addresses, whatever their origin may be. The benefit may be the actual use of these addresses, or the sale of the same. For example, it is believed that the age verification scripts of many porn sites are simply disguised collectors of email addresses. We note that posting an email address to such a site may result in what we refer to as a *snowball effect*, that is, a situation in which a submitted email address results in several emails, as the email address is bought, sold, and used.

The snow-ball effect can be exploited to maximize damage by generating a large-volume, persistent stream of email toward the victim. An efficient approach to maximize the number of spammers who obtain the victim's email is to post it on newsgroups and chatrooms, which are regularly and automatically scanned by spammers to harvest fresh email addresses. This approach does not even require one to collect and fill Web forms; but it has a more delayed, long-term effect.

3.6 Well Behaved Sites

While it is evident that the vulnerability we describe is made worse if the launch pads of the attack are poorly behaved sites, we argue that an attacker also can take advantage of well behaved sites. These are sites that may not sell the email address entered in the form, and who may wish to verify that it corresponds to a legitimate request for information. However, as previously mentioned, the double opt-in procedure typically involves sending an email to the address entered in the form, requesting an acknowledgment before more information is sent. This email, while perhaps not as large as the actual requested information, also becomes part of the attack as confirmation messages flood the victim's mailbox.

Moreover, if the intention of the form is to allow a user to send information to a friend, the above measures of caution are not taken. Examples of sites allowing such requests are electronic postcard services, many online newspapers, and more.

An attacker may also pose as a buyer to an e-commerce site, entering the victim's email address along with other information, such as an address and potentially incorrect credit card information. This would cause one or more emails to be sent to the victim. Given that the victim would not likely respond to any of these, the company may attempt to call the phone number entered in the form, which would constitute a potential attack in itself.

3.7 On the Difficulty of Tracing an Attacker

As described, the attack consists of two phases: one in which suitable forms are harvested, and a second in which the forms are filled and submitted. While it is possible for a site to determine the IP address of a user filling a form, not all sites may have the apparatus in place to do so. Moreover, given the very short duration of the second phase (see Sect. 4), it is easy for an attacker to perform this part of the attack using a public machine as shown above.

While the first phase of the attack typically takes more time, this can be performed once for a large number of consecutive attacks. Even if the first phase of the attack takes place from an identifiable computer and using a search engine, it is difficult for the search engine to recognize the intent of an attacker from the queries, especially considering the large numbers of queries handled. And it is impossible for a launch pad site to determine how its form was found by the attacker, whether a search engine was used, which one, and in response to what query. In other words, the second phase of the attack cannot be traced to the first (possibly traceable) phase.

Finally, the possibility of an attack – or parts thereof – being mounted by a virus (and therefore, from the machine of an innocent person) further frustrates any remaining hopes of meaningful traces.

4 Experimental Data

4.1 Experimental Setup

Here, we report on a number of contained experiments carried out to demonstrate the ease of mounting the attack and its potential damage. We focus on email (as opposed to SMS) attacks in these experiments. We are interested in how many email messages, and how much data, can be targeted to a victim's mailbox as a function of time since the start of an attack. We also want to measure how long it would take to disable a typical email account.

Clearly these measurements, and the time taken to mount an attack, depend on the number of forms used. It would not be too difficult to mount an attack with, say, 10^5 or 10^6 forms. However, much smaller attacks suffice to disable a typical email account by filling its inbox. Furthermore, experimenting with truly large-scale attacks would present ethical and legal issues that we do not want to raise. Therefore, we limit our experiments to very contained attacks, aiming to observe how the potency of an attack scales with its computational and storage resource requirements. We created a number of temporary email accounts and used them as targets of attacks of different sizes. Each attack used a different number of Web forms, sampled randomly from a collection of about 4,000 launch pads, previously collected.

In the collection phase of the attack, we used a "form-sniffing" agent to search the Web for appropriate forms based on hits from a search engine, using the technique described in Sect. 3. The MSN search engine was used because it did not disallow crawling agents via the robot exclusion standard.[1] This was done only once.

The collection agent was implemented as a Perl script using no particular optimizations (e.g., no timeouts) and employing off-the-shelf modules for Berkeley database storage, HTML parsing, and the LWP library for HTTP. The agent crawled approximately 110 hit pages per minute, running on a 466 MHz PowerMac G4 with a shared 10 Mbps Internet connection. This configuration is not unlike what would be available at a copy store. From our sample we measured a harvest rate of 40% (i.e., 40 launch pad forms per 100 search engine hits) with a standard error of 3.5%. At this harvest rate, the agent collected almost 50 launch pad forms per minute, and almost 4,000 forms in less than 1.5 h. If run in the background (e.g., in the form of a virus), this would produce as many as 72,000 forms in one day, or a million forms in two weeks – probably in significantly less time with some simple optimizations.

---

[1] We wanted to preserve the ethical behavior of the agent used in our experiments; an actual attacker could use any search engine since the robot exclusion standard is not enforceable.

The second phase, repeated for attacks of different size, was carried out using the same machinery and similarly implemented code. A "form-filling" agent took a victim's information (email and name) as input, sampled forms from the database, and submitted the filled forms. The agent filled approximately 116 forms per minute. We call *attack time* the time required to mount an attack with a given number of forms. All the attack simulation experiments took place in April 2003.

4.2 Results

Figure 4 illustrates how the number of messages in the victim's inbox and the inbox grow over time after the attack is mounted. The plots highlight two distinct dynamic phases. While the attack is taking place, some fraction of the launch pad forms generate immediate messages toward the target. These responses correspond to an initial high growth rate. Shortly after the attack is over, the initial responses cease and a second phase begins in which messages continue to arrive at a lower, constant rate. These are messages that are sent by launch pads at regular intervals (e.g., daily newsletters), repeat acknowledgment requests, and spam. In the plots, we fit this dynamic behavior to the piecewise linear model:

$$M_F(t) = \begin{cases} a_F t & 0 < t < t^* \\ b_F t + (a_F - b_F)t^* & t \geq t^* \end{cases} \qquad (1)$$

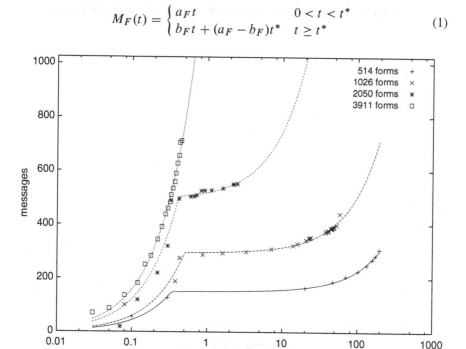

Fig. 4 Messages received by victim versus time for attacks of different size

where $M_F(t)$ is the inbox size or number of messages at time t ($t = 0$ is the start of the attack), for an attack with F forms. The short-term and long-term growth rates, a_F and b_F ($a_F > b_F$), and the transition time between the two phases, t^*, are determined by a nonlinear least-squares fit of the model to the data. In the initial phase, messages arrive at a high rate a_F. Some time after the end of the attack (determined by t^*), once the immediate responses have subsided, the arrival rate goes down to the long-term growth rate b_F.

The email traffic generated by our attacks was monitored until the size of the inbox passed a threshold of 2 MB. This is a typical quota on free email accounts such as Hotmail and Yahoo. No other mail was sent to the victim accounts, and no mail was deleted during the experiments. When an inbox is full, further email is bounced back to senders and, for all practical purposes, the email account is rendered useless unless the victim makes a significant effort to delete messages. We call *kill time* the time between the start of an attack and the point when the inbox size reaches 2 MB.

In Fig. 5, we can observe that for the three smaller attacks ($F = 514, 1026, 2050$) kill time occurs well after the attack has terminated. For the largest attack ($F = 3911$), kill time occurs while the attack is still being mounted. This is mirrored by the fact that this attack is still in the initial phase of high response rate when the inbox fills up.

One can use the data in Fig. 5 and the model of (1) to analyze how large an attack would be necessary to kill an account in a given amount of time, as a function of the account quota. Figure 6 shows the number of forms that in our experiments

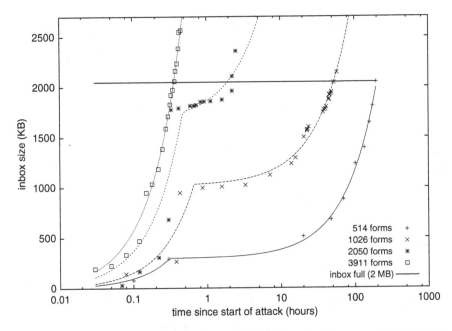

Fig. 5 Victim's inbox storage versus time for attacks of different size. The account is killed when the inbox reaches 2 MB

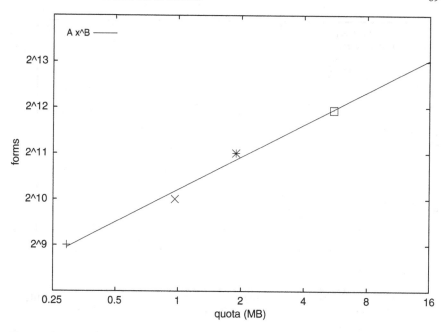

Fig. 6 Attack size necessary to kill an account in an hour versus victim's quota. The power law fit yields $R^2 = 0.9889$

would kill an account in one hour, corresponding to a *lunch hour attack*, in which the victim's machine is disabled while he or she is temporarily away. The number of forms scales sub-linearly, as a power law $F \sim q^{0.7}$ where q is the account quota. We can think of this as a manifestation of the snow-ball effect – periodic alerts and spam compound immediate responses making the attack more efficient.

Figure 7 shows how the arrival rate of email in the victim's mailbox scales with the size of the attack, for both the short and long term. The short-term arrival rate for an attack of size F is given by the growth parameter a_F, obtained by fitting the model in (1) to the data in Fig. 5. As illustrated by the regression in Fig. 7, the short-term arrival rate grows linearly with F as one would expect ($a_F \approx 1.5F$). The long-term arrival rate b_F, obtained analogously, shows a remarkable exponential growth with F ($b_F \approx 2.7e^{0.002F}$). Note that this fit is significantly stronger statistically than a linear or power law fit. Such a non-linear scaling behavior is another manifestation of the snow-ball effect. Even if the arrival rate subsides after the end of the attack, it can be made very large with small increases in attack size.

Finally, Fig. 8 shows how attack time and kill time scale with the size of the attack. As expected, attack time is proportional to F. Kill time (cf. Fig. 5) scales as a power law: $t \sim F^{-3.2}$. Again, this nonlinear scaling behavior is a consequence of the snow-ball effect, which amplifies the destructive effect of the attack and makes it possible to kill an email account efficiently. In fact the intersection between attack and kill time in Fig. 8 indicates that there is no need to mount attacks with more than $F \approx 2^{12}$ forms if the goal is to disable an account with a 2 MB quota.

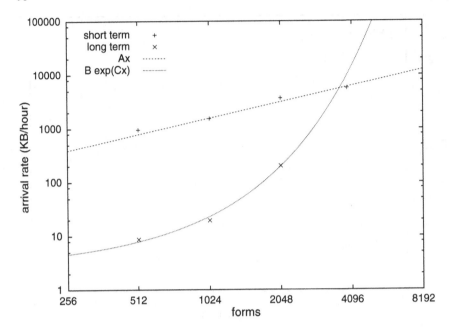

Fig. 7 Short- and long-term growth rate of victim's inbox versus attack size. The linear regression for short-term growth rate yields $R^2 = 0.9694$. The exponential fit for long-term growth rate yields $R^2 = 0.9931$

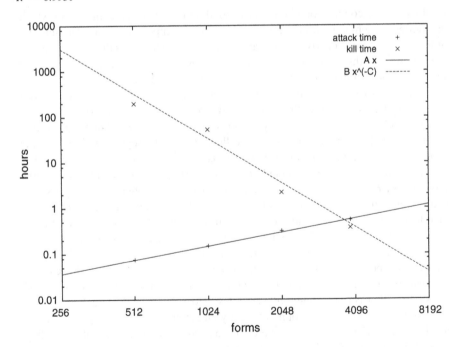

Fig. 8 Attack time and time to fill a 2 MB inbox, as a function of attack size. The linear regression for attack time and power law fit for kill time yield $R^2 = 0.9952$ and 0.977, respectively

5 Defense Mechanisms

We now describe a set of related defense techniques for our DDoS attack. A first line of defense consists of a simple *preventive* step by which Web sites can avoid being exploited as launch pads in our attack. For Web sites that have not yet complied with this preventive step, as well as unscrupulous spammer sites that have no intention to verify the legitimacy of requests, we describe a second line of defense for the *detection* and *management* of such attacks by potential victims. The second line of defense consists of a heuristic approach, whose use can be adapted to different situations of interest.

5.1 Prevention of Attacks

Many sites that allow users to subscribe to email services such as newsletters and alerts employ `mailto` links (either to a person or to a listserv manager, e.g., Majordomo). These sites cannot be exploited as launch pads, because the attacker would need a mail transport agent, for example, a machine running a SMTP server or an external mail relay. Such an attack is possible, but more difficult to carry out from a public computer and also more easily detectable and traceable. Open relays are rare and often blocked by ISPs anyway (because they are used by spammers), and a "legitimate" SMTP server requires some level of authentication that would allow to identify or trace the attacker. The obvious preventive solution to the proposed attack is thus to disable Web forms and enforce the use of email-based listserv tools such as Majordomo. However, this would disallow useful Web forms in which users can enter additional information – this cannot be done conveniently with a simple `mailto` link to a listserv.

To allow for the use of forms as appropriate while still verifying the legitimacy of email service requests, well behaved sites currently send a message to the submitted email address requesting confirmation that the address corresponds to a legitimate user request. As we observed earlier, this double opt-in procedure is exploited in our attack because confirmation requests, even if not repeated (as they often are), contribute to flooding the victim's mailbox just as any other message.

It is possible to both enable Web form requests and verify the legitimacy of requests without becoming vulnerable to our attack. Web sites would use the following simple strategy. After the form has been filled out, the Web site creates dynamically a page containing a `mailto` link with itself as an addressee. Legitimate users would send the message to validate their request. The email to the Web site would then be used by the site's mailing list manager to verify that the sender matches the email address submitted via the Web form. Although the address of the sender is not reliable because it can be spoofed in the SMTP protocol, the sender cannot spoof the IP address of its legitimate ISP's SMTP server. The site can thus verify that the email address in the form request matches the originating SMTP server in the validation message.

There are three caveats to this strategy. First, messages via open relays must be discarded by the site. Second, if an attacker could guess that a user in a given domain requests information from some site, he or she could request information from the same site for other users in the same domain, potentially spoofing the validation created by the addressee. To prevent such an attack, the validation message created by the site should contain a number with sufficient entropy that it is hard to guess. Third, one could still attack victims who share their ISP's mail server, which would not affect the attacker himself in a notable way if there are quotas. In this case, however, the attack could be traced. Furthermore, our heuristic defense mechanisms – presented next – will address such an attack. With these caveats, our preventive strategy would afford the same security as double opt-in, but without sending any email to victims.

The above technique works for forms where a party requests information to be sent to herself, but it does not cover common services such as sending newspaper articles or postcards to others. Sites wishing to allow this can use alternative defenses. Namely, well behaved sites may make the harvesting of forms more difficult by not labeling forms using HTML, but rather, using small images. This would increase the effort of finding and filling the forms. Given the relative abundance of available forms, potential attackers are then likely to turn to other sites where no image analysis has to be performed to find and fill the form. Doing this has no impact on human users, except to a very small extent on the download time of the form. A more robust version of this defense would use an inverse Turing test or CAPTCHA (Completely Automatic Public Turing test to tell Computers and Humans Apart) [11, 12], a technique already employed by many sites to prevent agents from impersonating human users.

If legislation is brought in place that makes sites liable for any attacks mounted using their facilities [9], then even poorly behaved sites may wish to employ protective measures as those described above to avoid being the defendants in lawsuits by victims of the attack we describe.

5.2 Detection and Management of Attacks

In the previous subsection, we considered how well-behaved sites can protect themselves against being used as launch pads. Since it is not likely that all sites will comply with these protective measures, we also need to consider protection against poorly behaved and otherwise noncompliant sites. This protection will reside on the machine or mail server of the potential victim and rely on three tools:

Extended Address Book. Most users maintain an address book in which they enter the email addresses of their most frequent correspondents. We consider the use of an additional *extended address book*. This contains the email addresses of all parties the user has sent email to or received email from, along with a time stamp indicating when the last email was sent or received. To reduce the required storage, we may allow users to have old entries automatically removed.

The extended address book is similar to the whitelists maintained by spam filters; the main difference is that it would only be used for filtering purposes when an attack is suspected, as described subsequently. Emails of spammers might even be included. A set of users may share one and the same extended address book.

Attack Meter. We will let the system estimate the probability that a given user is under attack at any given time. The parameters considered would be the amount of traffic to the user in relation to the normal amount of traffic to his or her, and relative to the traffic of other users; the proportion of emails arriving to the user (and his or her peers) that originate from users who are not in his their extended address books; and the number of duplicate emails received by users handled by the mail server. The calibration of the estimation may be performed with a given threat situation in mind.

Cleaner. During a clean-up, a set of suspect emails are removed from the inbox of the user. Depending on the situation, it may be that all suspect emails are removed; all suspect emails of a certain minimum size; all suspect emails from (or not from) given domains; or some other, potentially customized selection of all suspect emails.

When a user accesses his or her account, he or she would be shown the likely probability, according to the attack meter, that he or she is under attack. If the user indicates that he or she believes he is under attack, the mail server would automatically mark all emails that are from senders who are *not* in the extended address book as *suspect*, and proceed to perform a clean-up. This may also be induced by the system – without the request of the user – if the user is not available, an attack is judged to likely be under progress, and resources are scarce. If these defenses reside on the side of the service provider, as appropriate for wireless devices, the attack meter can also take the general attack situation in consideration when determining whether an individual is being attacked. We note that this solution also secures list moderators at the expense of not being able to receive messages from new posters during the time of an attack; note also that the risk of the launch pads already being in the extended address book of the moderator is slim.

For targets such as a politician, it may be typical to receive messages from users who are not in the extended address book. However, many of the constituents are likely to use accounts with one of a very small set of known ISPs. In contrast, launch pads are likely not to have the same domains. Therefore, under attack, the mail server could mark as suspect those emails that do not come from the known ISPs likely to correspond to the wanted senders. Furthermore, the mail server may mark emails as suspects if coming from other countries – when indicated by the corresponding domain – as these are also unlikely to be from constituents.

5.3 Synergy Between Defense of Launch Pads and Victims

It is important that the heuristic defense mechanisms proposed do not disrupt desired functionality, thus it must still be possible for a user to fill forms and receive information sent to him. Indeed this will still be possible – even during a detected attack – as long as the site with the form sends email from an address that is present in the extended address book of the party requesting information.

In the strategy described above to prevent Web sites from being exploited as launch pads, the user who submits a request through a form must send a validation message (dynamically created and self-addressed) to the Web site. This step causes the Web site's email address to be entered into the user's extended address book. As a result, the information sent to the user by the site is not filtered out. This creates an incentive for sites to comply with the preventive strategy, not only to avoid being exploited but also to keep their messages from being filtered out.

6 Conclusion

We investigated an automated, agent-based DDoS attack in which a victim is swamped by communication from entities believing he or she requested information. The primary tool of the attack is that of Web forms, which can be automatically harvested and filled out by an agent. We also quantified the damage such an attack could do by describing experimental results.

We described a very simple strategy by which Web sites can avoid being exploited in the poor man's DDoS attack; once a majority of Web sites comply with this strategy, such attacks will be prevented.

For the interim, we have proposed a set of heuristic techniques to inoculate users against the poor man's DDoS attack. These mechanisms only allow emails to be filtered out if they are sent from sites that are not in a user's extended address book.

We have not investigated the generation of traffic by means of posting messages, to newsgroups, chatrooms, and bulletin boards, purportedly from the victim, but believe such attacks to be similar to those we discussed, and possible to defend against in similar manners.

There are more drastic types of defense measures that can protect from the attack described in this paper. Some ISPs are considering CAPTCHA based challenge-response systems in conjunction with whitelists to combat spam.[2] While such an approach would indeed protect a potential victim from the email DDoS attack, it would also decrease the accessibility of email. For example, it would violate the Americans with Disabilities Act because CAPTCHAs discriminate against blind people. Many email-based transactions, such as e-commerce confirmations, would also be blocked. The defenses we have described are more targeted at the DDoS attack, more light-weight, and do not require modifications to the Web or email infrastructure.

At a more general level, the kind of attack described here raises new issues with social and political implications for the use of modern communication media such

---

[2] Earthlink has announced a beta version of such a system as of this writing.

as the Internet, electronic messaging, and mobile telephony. For example, if users were required to identify themselves when using the Internet in order to prevent such abuses, then one could no longer use a computer anonymously in a public place such as a library. We hope that this work will lead to solutions that can protect our inboxes as well as our privacy and freedom of speech.

References

1. S. Byers, A.D. Rubin, and D. Kormann. Defending against an Internet-based attack on the physical world. In Proceedings of ACM Workshop on Privacy in the Electronic Society, 2002.
2. S. Dietrich, N. Long, and D. Dittrich. Analyzing distributed denial of service tools: The Shaft case. In Proceedings of 14th Systems Administration Conference, 2000.
3. D. Dittrich. Distributed denial of service (DDoS) attacks/tools. http://staff.washington.edu/dittrich/misc/ddos/, 2003.
4. R.B. Doorenbos, O. Etzioni, and D.S. Weld. A scalable comparison-shopping agent for the World-Wide Web. In Proceedings of the First International Conference on Autonomous Agents, pp. 39–48, 1997.
5. K.J. Houle, G.M. Weaver, N. Long, and R. Thomas. Trends in denial of service attack technology. CERT Coordination Center White Paper, October 2001. http://www.cert.org/archive/pdf/DoS_trends.pdf.
6. M. Jakobsson, and F. Menczer. Untraceable email cluster bombs: On agent-based distributed denial of service. Technical report, http://arxiv.org/abs/cs.CY/0305042, 2003.
7. F. Menczer, G. Pant, M. Ruiz, and P. Srinivasan. Evaluating topic-driven Web crawlers. In D.H. Kraft, W.B. Croft, D.J. Harper, and J. Zobel, (Eds.), Proceedings of 24th Annual International ACM SIGIR Conference on Research and Development in Information Retrieval, pp. 241–249, New York, NY, ACM, 2001.
8. F. Menczer, G. Pant, and P. Srinivasan. Topical web crawlers: Evaluating adaptive algorithms. ACM Transactions on Internet Technology, 4(4), 2004. Forthcoming.
9. J. Silva. Spam small problem ... today. RCRNews, 2003. http://www.rcrnews.com/cgi-bin/article.pl?articleId=42294.
10. SkyNews. Elections: The final push. http://www.sky.com/skynews/article/0,,30100-12300859,00.html, 2003.
11. L. Von Ahn, M. Blum, N. Hopper, and J. Langford. CAPTCHA: Using hard AI problems for security. In Proceedings of Eurocrypt, 2003.
12. L. Von Ahn, M. Blum, and J. Langford. Telling humans and computers apart automatically. Communications of the ACM, 47(2):56–60, 2004.

Mechanical Verification of Cryptographic Protocols

Xiaochun Cheng, Xiaoqi Ma, Scott C.-H. Huang, and Maggie Cheng

Contents

1 Introduction

Information security is playing an increasingly important role in modern society, driven especially by the uptake of the Internet for information transfer. Large amount of information is transmitted everyday through the Internet, which is often the target

X. Cheng (✉)
Department of Computer Science, The University of Reading, Whiteknights,
Reading RG6 6AY, England, UK
e-mail: x.cheng@reading.ac.uk

S.C.-H. Huang et al. (eds.), *Network Security*, DOI 10.1007/978-0-387-73821-5_5,
© Springer Science+Business Media, LLC 2010

of malicious attacks. In certain areas, this issue is vital. For example, military departments of governments often transmit a great amount of top-secret data, which, if divulged, could become a huge threat to the public and to national security. Even in our daily life, it is also necessary to protect information. Consider e-commerce systems as an example. No one is willing to purchase anything over the Internet before being assured that all their personal and financial information will always be kept secure and will never be leaked to any unauthorised person or organisation.

The Internet and many other networks are vulnerable; the information going through them is subject to the threat of eavesdrop and alteration of various spies and intruders. Confidential information can be disclosed or modified without consciousness. To achieve secrecy of sensitive information, cryptography is extensively used. Before an important message is sent out, it usually needs to be encrypted, so that spies cannot read the contents of it without the corresponding key even if they intercept the encrypted information from the network.

However, cryptography can only offer protection if it is used in an appropriate way. Guidelines about how to use cryptographic technology are incorporated in the large number of security protocols that have been developed. These protocols in general contribute greatly to information security.

Unfortunately, many such protocols are inherently incorrect, or at least cannot achieve completely all that is intended of them. Indeed, some protocols considered perfect at first were found to have flaws in them many years later [5]. To evaluate and verify security protocols in a systematic way, some verification methods come to be necessary.

2 Security Protocols

Since information flowing over network is vulnerable and insecure, cryptography is introduced. It can transform human-readable *cleartext* (using some encryption key) to unreadable *ciphertext*, which seems to be "meaningless" code for people who do not know the corresponding decryption key. By this means, the important information is kept confidential from all unauthorised parties. Normally, cryptographic systems can be divided into the *public key* cryptosystem and the *private key* cryptosystem.

However, only using cryptography cannot guarantee that the encrypted data are secure. Therefore, researchers invented security protocols as guides to how to use cryptography to achieve information security.

The term *security protocol* is usually a synonym of *cryptographic protocol*, which means a protocol that uses cryptography to achieve the goals of information security, such as confidentiality, integrity, authentication and so on. We will use these two terms interchangeably. Security protocol technology is widely used in network communications.

Security protocols can be broadly divided into three categories:

- *Key establishment protocol*, which is used to establish a shared secret between different communicating parties.

- *Authentication protocol*, which is used to provide assurance of the identity of another party to one involved in the communication.
- *Authenticated key establishment protocol*, which is used to establish a shared secret with a party whose identity has been (or can be) trusted.

3 Flaws in Security Protocols

The security of protocols obviously depends on the strength of the cryptographic algorithms. However, using a strong cryptographic algorithm does not guarantee communication security. Actually, we usually assume all cryptographic algorithms are strong enough and intruders cannot break them by brute force. That is, intruders cannot exhaustively search the key space and find the correct key; the only way to read an encrypted message is to decrypt it with the corresponding decryption key.

The mostly studied protocol is probably the Needham–Schroeder public key protocol, which was proposed more than a quarter of century ago and was found a subtle flaw in it by Lowe 17 years later. Now, this protocol has become an ideal choice for demonstrating various kinds of formal verification methods, and many researchers have investigated it. This section gives the example to show how an intruder can break the Needham–Schroeder public key protocol without breaking the cryptographic algorithm, and even without knowing the secret keys of other principals.

In a vulnerable network with malicious spies and intruders, principals engaged in network communication sometimes even cannot be sure the one who is talk to is exactly the person he want to communicate with. *Authentication* is therefore used to help a principal verify the identity of the other one. In 1978, Needham and Schroeder proposed a protocol intending to provide mutual authentication [9]. The protocol was considered correct for nearly two decades and was later broken by Lowe using CSP with FDR as the model checker [5, 6].

3.1 The Needham–Schroeder Public Key Protocol

Originally, the Needham–Schroeder public key protocol involves seven steps and can be described as follows:

$$
\begin{aligned}
&1. \quad A \rightarrow S \quad : \quad A, B \\
&2. \quad S \rightarrow A \quad : \quad \{K_b, B\}_{K_s^{-1}} \\
&3. \quad A \rightarrow B \quad : \quad \{N_a, A\}_{K_b} \\
&4. \quad B \rightarrow S \quad : \quad B, A \\
&5. \quad S \rightarrow B \quad : \quad \{K_a, A\}_{K_s^{-1}} \\
&6. \quad B \rightarrow A \quad : \quad \{N_a, N_b\}_{K_a} \\
&7. \quad A \rightarrow B \quad : \quad \{N_b\}_{K_b}
\end{aligned}
$$

The aim of this protocol is to establish mutual authentication between an *initiator* A and a *responder* B, with the help of a trusted *key server* S, whose public key is known to all principals. As its name indicates, the protocol uses public key cryptography.

At the beginning, principal A sends a message to the key server S to request B's public key. This message consists of the names of two parties of the communication he or she wants to establish, namely A and B. S then responds A's request by returning B's public key K_b, together with B's name, signed with S's private key K_s^{-1} to assure A that he is the originator of this message. After A has received B's public key, he or she then composes a fresh nonce N_a and sends it to B with his or her own name, encrypted with B's public key that he or she just got from S. After B receives this message, he decrypts it and then reads the nonce N_a and knows who is seeking to communicate with him or her. B then gets A's public key K_a from the key server S in a similar way to A's. After that, B sends back a message consisting of his or her own fresh nonce N_b as well as A's nonce N_a, encrypted with A's public key K_a to A. To respond B's message, A then returns B's nonce N_b to B.

This protocol looks like "the interleaving of two logically disjoint protocols" [5]. The steps 1, 2, 4 and 5 are used to obtain public keys of each other principal, while steps 3, 6 and 7 can be considered as a "pure" authentication protocol.

Ideally, after steps 2 and 5, A and B can, respectively, assure that they have successfully got each other's public key from the key server S, since in these two steps messages are signed with S's private key, and they believe that nobody can fake S's signature. After step 6, A believes that B is responding to his or her because he or she sent N_a encrypted with B's public key to B and only B can decrypt it and read the content. Similarly, B is assured A's identity after step 7.

To make the problem simpler, some researchers assume that the public keys of all principles are known to the whole world [5, 6, 12, 14], while others stick to the original protocol [3, 8].

The simplified version of the protocol omits the steps concerning public key distribution and consists only three steps [5, 6, 12, 14]:

$$
\begin{aligned}
&1. \quad A \to B \quad : \quad \{N_a, A\}_{K_b} \\
&2. \quad B \to A \quad : \quad \{N_a, N_b\}_{K_a} \\
&3. \quad A \to B \quad : \quad \{N_b\}_{K_b}
\end{aligned}
$$

3.2 Lowe's Attack

Seventeen years after the original Needham–Schroeder public key protocol was published, Lowe found a subtle flaw in it [5].

Lowe supposes there is an intruder I in the network communication system. I pretends himself or herself as an "honest" user of the network and can receive messages from other principals and originate standard sessions with others. It is also assumed that I is so powerful and intelligent that he or she can intercept any messages in the system and introduce new messages. Lowe supposes the cryptographic system is strong enough so that I can neither decrypt a message encrypted with someone else's public key nor fake other's signature without the corresponding private key. Thus, I can only produce new messages using nonces of his own or that he or she knew previously (usually by decrypt, other principals' communication using private keys revealed to him or her).

Lowe's attack interleaves two simultaneous sessions of the protocol and allows the intruder I to impersonate another principal A to set up a false session with B. The following is how I achieves that. Note Lowe uses notation $I(A)$ to represent the intruder I impersonating A.

$$
\begin{aligned}
&1.3. \quad A \rightarrow I && : \quad \{N_a, A\}_{K_i} \\
&2.3. \quad I(A) \rightarrow B && : \quad \{N_a, A\}_{K_b} \\
&2.6. \quad B \rightarrow I(A) && : \quad \{N_a, N_b\}_{K_a} \\
&1.6. \quad I \rightarrow A && : \quad \{N_a, N_b\}_{K_a} \\
&1.7. \quad A \rightarrow I && : \quad \{N_b\}_{K_i} \\
&2.7. \quad I(A) \rightarrow B && : \quad \{N_b\}_{K_b}
\end{aligned}
$$

At first, A starts up a standard session with I by sending him or her a nonce N_a. However, A has not realised that I is an intruder. Instead of following the second step of the protocol, I uses the nonce N_a received from A to initiate a new session with another principal B, and claims to B that he or she is A. B then creates a new nonce N_b and sends it back to A together with A's nonce N_a, according to the step 2 of the simplified protocol. Unfortunately, this message is intercepted by I. I cannot decrypt it and simply forwards it to A. A decrypts the message, verifies his or her nonce N_a, reads B's nonce N_b and sends it back to I using I's public key K_i. I now can decrypt it and read the nonce N_b, and then returns it to B. B now believes that A is communicating with him, although it is actually the intruder I.

4 Existing Protocol Verification Methods

Since Burrows et al. proposed their famous BAN logic [3], designing formal methods for verifying security protocols has been a research highlight in recent years. Much research work has been conducted in this area and many good models and methods have been proposed.

Generally speaking, all these methods can be broadly divided into two categories, namely state based methods and rule based methods. Here, we give a brief description to these two kinds of methods.

4.1 State Based Methods

State based methods model security protocols as finite state machines. They will search the state space exhaustively to see whether all the reachable states are safe [11]. If some reachable state in a security protocol is proved to be unsafe, a flaw may be reported; otherwise, the protocol will be said to be correct and safe.

State based methods are efficient and usually can find attacks quickly. Many attacks have been found by this kind of methods. However, it is difficult to effectively control the size of the state space; when the protocol is large, the state space will become surprisingly huge, and it will be extremely time consuming, or even practically impossible, to search the whole space.

Two typical formal methods of this kind are described as follows.

CSP Method with FDR as the Model Checker

The Failure Divergences Refinement (FDR) Checker is a model checker for CSP, which is used to describe concurrent systems whose component processes interact with each other by communication [6]. Lowe first employed it to verify the Needham–Schroeder public key protocol and found the subtle flaw described in the previous section.

In Lowe's method, FDR takes two CSP processes, namely a specification and an implementation, as input, and tests whether the implementation refines the specification. It has been used to analyse many sorts of systems, including communication protocols and distributed databases [6].

The agents taking part in the protocol are modelled as CSP processes. It is also assumed that the intruder can interact with the protocol – he can read and intercept all the messages communicating over the network, and can use all information he knows to introduce fake messages into the system and then send them to any honest principals. The model checker FDR is used to test whether the protocols correctly achieve authentication, and to discover potential attacks upon the protocols, which allow the intruder to impersonate honest principal with another one in a run of the protocol [6].

NRL Protocol Analyzer

The NRL Protocol Analyzer developed by Meadows is a prototype special-purpose verification tool, written in Prolog. It has been developed for the analysis of cryptographic protocols that are used to authenticate principals and services and distribute keys in a network [7, 8].

As most other authentication protocol verification methods, the NRL Protocol Analyzer makes the assumption that principals communicate over a network controlled by a hostile intruder who can read, modify and destroy traffic, and also perform some operations, such as encryption, that are available to legitimate participants in the protocols such as the Needham–Schroeder public key protocol [7, 8].

In the NRL Protocol Analyzer, actions of legitimate principals are specified by the user as state transitions. Inputs to the transitions are values of local state variables and messages received by the principal, the latter assumed to have been generated or passed on by the intruder, and outputs are the new values of local state variables, and messages sent by the principal, which are subject to interception and modification by the intruder. The means by which the intruder can modify messages are specified by having the specification writer indicate which operations are performable by the intruder, and what words the intruder may be assumed to know initially [7, 8].

Instead of working forward from an initial state, it works backward from a final state. The user of the NRL Protocol Analyzer uses it to prove a security property by specifying an insecure state in terms of words known by the intruder, values of local state variables, and sequences of events that have or have not occurred. The Analyzer gives a complete description of all states that can immediately precede that state, followed by a complete description of all states that can immediately precede those, and so forth [7, 8].

4.2 Rule Based Methods

Rule based methods, also called belief logic methods in some literatures, formally express what principal can infer from messages received [11]. With this approach, the protocols, the necessary assumptions and the goals of the protocols are formulated in formal logic. Then, the security properties of the protocols can be proved by using the axioms and rules of the logic [4].

Rule based methods are generally much more efficient than state exploration methods, and they do have found many subtle flaws. However, some of them only consider single runs of the protocols and usually ignore the interleaving of two or more sessions. So there are a lot of flaws which cannot be found with these logics.

In the recent years, a number of rule based methods and belief logics have been developed. Among them, the BAN logic introduced by Burrows et al. and Bolignano's model are good representatives.

Besides that, a special kind of rule based model is also interesting. This model constructs proofs using specific rules. Paulson's inductive inference method serves as a good example.

BAN Logic

The BAN logic was proposed in 1989 [3] and named after its three creators: Michael Burrows, Martín Abadi and Roger Needham. Their aim to create this logic was to provide a theoretical tool for formally analysing protocols for the authentication of principals in distributed computing systems. It is actually the first and probably the most well-known rule based method for verifying security protocols, which began the research of protocol formal verification.

The basic idea of the BAN logic is formalising the beliefs of principals taking part in the protocols as logical statements [1]. The logic provides a number of postulates to represent inference rules. Each protocol step is transformed to an idealised form, in which a message is presented as a formula.

To analyse and verify a protocol, the protocol steps should first be changed to idealised form. And assumptions about the initial state should be written. After that, the protocol should be annotated in the way that logical formulae are attached to statements of the protocol, as assertions about the state of the system after each statement. Then, the logical postulates are applied to the assumptions and the assertions to derive the beliefs held by the participants of the protocols. This procedure may be repeated as new assumptions are found to be necessary and as the idealised protocol is refined [3].

The BAN logic provides a very elegant and concise way of proving properties of authentication protocols [2] and has many successful cases [3]. However, it also has many limitations, which have been the subject of many research activities, shown as follows:

- There is no complete semantics for the logics. This may lead to problems in modeling as some facts may have an unclear meaning [2]. It is not entirely clear what is proved, secrecy lies outside the logic's scope, and yet the proofs contain (incorrect!) assertions that the two nonces remain secret [12].
- The modelling of freshness is also particularly problematic. As in most modal logics, it is in particular not possible to distinguish between freshness of creation and freshness of receipt [16].
- The very abstract level of the BAN logic imposes, in many cases, the use of hypotheses or protocol descriptions whose relevance is hard to access [2].
- There is no systematic way for translating a protocol description into a BAN description [4].

Bolignano's Method

In 1996, Bolignano presented an approach to the verification of authentication protocols [2]. The approach is based on the use of general purpose formal methods. It is complementary with belief logic methods as it allows for a description of protocol, hypotheses and authentication properties at a finer level of precision and with more freedom [2].

In this method, different principals involved in the protocol can be classified into two categories: some principals are considered as *trustable* (or *reliable*) while others are not. Communication media can be considered as principals that receive message on one end and emit other messages at another end. They are usually taken to be non-trustable as messages can usually be spied upon, replayed, removed or created by intruders. Bolignano models the media as a single principal and call it "the external world" or more concisely the *intruder* [2].

Data communicated between principals are modelled as sets. A number of deduction rules and properties are also given to describe what kind of information can be deduced from the known information. Bolignano then uses a "chemical abstract machine paradigm" to formalise the protocols as sets of "atomic actions which may be applied repeatedly and in any order and whenever pre-condition holds". Then, several authentication properties are proved to show whether the protocol is secure [2].

Although Bolignano claimed that he has considered cases of parallel multi-sessions [2], his model cannot find some protocol flaws involving two or more sessions, for example the flaw corresponding to Lowe's attack on Needham–Schroeder public key protocol.

Paulson's Inductive Method

The motivation for Paulson to develop the inductive method is that it "can be applied to many nondeterministic processes" [11].

Paulson introduced several message analysis and synthesis operators, namely parts, analz and synth, which can be inductively defined. These operators can be used to described what information a principal can get and produce from his knowledge. Paulson assumes that the intruder observes all traffic in the network and sends fraudulent messages he can synthesise [11].

Protocols can be modelled as traces in which each step has the form Says A B X, meaning A says message X to B. Each agent's state is represented by its initial knowledge and what it can read from the traffic. Honest principals can only read messages sent to themselves, while the intruder can read all messages over the network [11].

Before the security properties of protocols can be proved, some lemmas and theorems should be proved at first. The first group of lemmas are regularity properties. They concern occurrences of a particular item as a possible message component. Unicity lemmas are special regularity lemmas that specified items can occur only once in a trace. For example, a nonce cannot be used twice unless it has been known to the intruder [10, 11].

After that, secrecy theorems need to be proved. They state that certain information (such as a principal's private key or a nonce) is always kept secret, that is, prevented from being known by the intruder. These theorems are more difficult to prove than the regularity properties [10, 11].

With all the lemmas and theorems, the final security guarantees can then be proved. If something wrong happens in the proof of security guarantees, it may imply flaws in the protocol. According to on which theorem we fail to prove, we may identify the flaw [12].

Paulson's inductive approach has proved to be an outstanding formal method. It found many flaws in existing protocols [11–15]. However, as stated before, it is not easy to master this method, and verifying protocols with this method is time-consuming.

5 A Knowledge Based Verification Framework

We propose a new knowledge based framework to prove secure properties of crypto-graphic protocols and to verify them or find flaws in them. This framework focuses on the knowledge of all participants in the protocol. We describe their initial knowl-edge and infer what they can know and can never know with the progress of the protocol, processing this knowledge in formal logic. In other words, it concerns the knowledge analysis of all participants. This framework is implemented in Isabelle to enable mechanical verification.

The framework is composed of a number of basic notations, predicates, action functions, assumptions and rules, which are described as follows.

5.1 Basic Notations and Data Structures

We call all participants taking part in network communications *principals*. They can be divided into three categories: the *server*, the *friends*, which stand for all "honest" principals, and the *spy*, which is also called the *adversary* or *intruder* in some literatures. In Isabelle notation, they can be described as follows:

datatype `principal = Server | Friend nat | Spy`

In the above definition, different friends are represented as different natural numbers.

Random numbers chosen by principals serve as *nonces* to identify protocol runs uniquely and avoid replay attack [14]. Nonces are normally denoted as N_a, N_b, etc., where the subscripts imply the producers of the nonces.

Every principal has some keys. In public key cryptosystem, the principal A basi-cally has a *public key* and a corresponding *private key*, which are denoted as K_a and K_a^{-1}, respectively. On the other hand, in symmetric key cryptosystem, two commu-nicating principals A and B normally share a sessions key, denoted as K_{ab}.

In Isabelle notation, all the nonces and keys are simply represented as natural numbers.

One of the most important concepts is the *message*. A message is a piece of information sent from one principal to another. A message can consist of names of principals, nonces, keys, encrypted messages, signed messages, hashed messages or a combination of these. It is recursively defined in Isabelle as follows:

datatype `message = Principal principal`
`                     | Nonce nonce | Key key`
`                     | MPair message message`
`                     | Encrypt message key | Sign`
`                        message key`
`                     | Hash message`

Paired messages can be abbreviated using curly braces. For example, `MPair M1 M2` can be written as {`M1`, `M2`}. A compound message consisting of more than two components can be understood as a nested compound message. For example, {`M1`, `M2`, `M3`} is the abbreviation of {`M1`, {`M2`, `M3`}}.

5.2 Action Functions and Predicates

We define a number of useful *functions* and *predicates*. Among them are *key functions*. Function `Kpb` has the type `principal ⇒ key`, mapping a principal to its public encryption key. Functions `Kpv`, `Spb` and `Spv` similarly map a principal to its private encryption key, public signature key and private signature key, respectively. Both `Kpb` and `Spb` are injective functions.

Function `Nonce_of` maps a principal to its nonce. It is also an injective function.

To determine whether a message is a part of another one, we introduce a function `msg_part`. For a non-compound message, only itself is a part of it. For a compound message, this function can be recursively defined:

```
''msg_part M1 {M2, M3} = (M1 = {M2, M3}
                   ∨ msg_part M1 M2
                   ∨ msg_part M2 M1''
```

The predicate `Know` has the type `principal ⇒ message ⇒ bool`, describing a principal's knowledge state about a certain message. Similarly, the predicate `Auth` with the type `principal ⇒ principal ⇒ message ⇒ bool` describes the first principal's authentication state about the second one on a certain message, that is, whether the message is sent by the second principal to the first one and is unmodified.

To describe cryptographic protocols, two *action functions* need to be introduced. One is `Send` with the type `principal ⇒ principal ⇒ message ⇒ bool`, representing that one principal sends a message to another principal. Correspondingly, the other function is `Rcv` with the type `principal ⇒ message ⇒ bool`, meaning that a principal receives a certain message from others.

5.3 Assumptions

Our method is based on a number of assumptions, which are widely accepted by most researchers in this field.

The most important assumptions are *key assumptions*. In public cryptosystems, the public key of any principal is known to all other principals:

axioms `KeyAssump1`: ''∀ X Y. Know X (Key (Kpb Y))''

On the contrary, any principal's private key is initially secret from others except itself:

KeyAssump2: `'∀ X. Know X (Key (Kpv X))''`
KeyAssump3: `'∀ X Y. ((X ≠ Y) → ¬ (Know X (Key`
`(Kpv X))))''`

We also assume that any principal's name is open to the world:

axioms *KnowName:* `'∀ X Y. Know X (Principal Y)''`

Besides that, any principal knows its own nonce:

axioms *KnowNonce:* `'∀ X. Know X (Nonce (Nonce_of X))''`

According to the definition of spy, it is not honest principal, so we have:

axioms *Honest_not_Spy:* `'∀ n. Spy ≠ Friend n''`

In addition, we also have some other assumptions, which are described as follows:

- The spy always observes all messages sent through the network. It tries to use all the keys it knows to decrypt the message on the network and to send forged messages to others. It can also intercept messages sent from one principal to another. That is, the spy has the "full" control over the network.
- There is only one spy in the network.
- The spy cannot read an encrypted message without the corresponding decryption key; that is, secret keys are not guessable.
- A honest principal only reads information addressed to it.
- A principal never sends messages to itself.
- Nonces are always different from each other.

5.4 Rules

We introduce a group of inference rules into the method to infer new knowledge from the old. All these rules can be divided into four categories.

The first is the *encryption/decryption rule*, which includes two rules.

When a principal knows a message and a key, it can use this key to encrypt the message and get the encrypted message:

Rule1_1 : `'Know X M ∧ Know X (Key K)`
`⇒ Know X (Encrypt M K)''`

When a principal knows a message encrypted with a key and the reverse of the key, it can use the reverse of the key to get the original message:

Rule1_2 : `'Know X (Encrypt M K) ∧ Know X (Key (invKey K))`
`⇒ Know X M''`

The second category is the *message combination/separation rule*, which also includes two rules.

When a principal knows two messages, it can know the combination of them:

$$Rule2\_1 \; : \; ''Know \; X \; M1 \; \wedge \; Know \; X \; M2 \; \Rightarrow \; Know \; X \; \{M1, \; M2\}''$$

When a principal knows the combination of two messages, it can know them separately:

$$Rule2\_2 \; : \; ''Know \; X \; \{M1, \; M2\} \; \Rightarrow \; Know \; X \; M1 \; \wedge \; Know \; X \; M2''$$

These two rules can be used inductively to deal with compound messages consisting of more than two components.

The third category is the *message sending/receiving rule*, which includes four rules.

If a principal sends a message to another one, the object principal will eventually receive it:

$$Rule3\_1 \; : \; ''Send \; X \; Y \; M \; \Rightarrow \; Rcv \; Y \; M''$$

As one of our assumptions describes, the spy can observe all information flowing over the network:

$$Rule3\_2 \; : \; ''Send \; X \; Y \; M \; \Rightarrow \; Rcv \; Spy \; M''$$

After a principal receives a message, it will know it:

$$Rule3\_3 \; : \; ''Rcv \; X \; M \; \Rightarrow \; Know \; X \; M''$$

If a principal sends a message to another one, it must know it first:

$$Rule3\_4 \; : \; ''Send \; X \; Y \; M \; \Rightarrow \; Know \; X \; M''$$

The fourth category is the *authentication rule*, which still includes two rules.

If principal Y knows a message encrypted with principal X's public key, X receives this encrypted message, and all other principals (including the spy) do not know it, then X can authenticate that the message was sent by Y and is unmodified:

$$Rule4\_1 \; : \; ''Know \; Y \; (Encrypt \; M \; (Kpb \; X))$$
$$\wedge \; Rcv \; X \; (Encrypt \; M \; (Kpb \; X))$$
$$\wedge \; (\forall \; Z. \; ((Z \neq X \; \wedge \; Z \neq Y) \; \rightarrow \; \neg (Know \; Z \; M)))$$
$$\Rightarrow \; Auth \; X \; Y \; M''$$

If another principal knows the message, then X will unauthenticate it:

$$Rule4\_2 \; : \; ''\forall \; X \; Y. \; (\exists \; Z. \; (Z \neq X \; \wedge \; Z \neq Y \; \wedge \; Know \; Z \; M))$$
$$\Rightarrow \; \neg \; (Auth \; X \; Y \; M)''$$

The above notations, data structures, functions, predicates, assumptions and rules form the basic framework of the knowledge-based security protocol verification method.

6 Verifying Needham–Schroeder–Lowe Protocol Mechanically

To verify the Needham–Schroeder public key authentication protocol with Lowe's fix (we call it Needham–Schroeder–Lowe protocol), we first need to model it in our framework, then prove a number of important lemmas and properties, and ultimately prove the final guarantees.

6.1 Modelling the Protocol

Normally, the protocol can be formalised as three steps for all honest principals:

1. First, principal A sends a compound message consisting of its nonce and name to principal B:

   ```
   NS1 : ''Send A B (Encrypt {Nonce (Nonce_of A),
             Principal A} (Kpb B))''
   ```

2. Second, if the first step has been successfully carried out, principal B will correspondingly send a compound message consisting of A's nonce, its own nonce and name to principal A:

   ```
   NS2 : ''Send A B (Encrypt {Nonce (Nonce_of A),
             Principal A} (Kpb B))''
         ⇒ Send B A (Encrypt {Nonce (Nonce_of A),
           Nonce (Nonce_of B), Principal B} (Kpb A)
   ```

3. Lastly, if the second step has been successfully carried out, principal A will correspondingly send B's nonce back to principal B:

   ```
   NS3 : ''Send B A (Encrypt {Nonce (Nonce_of A),
             Nonce (Nonce_of B), Principal B} (Kpb A)
         ⇒ Send A B (Encrypt {Nonce (Nonce_of B)) (Kpb B)''
   ```

These three steps are enough for honest principals. However, the spy does not necessarily obey these rules. As we stated in the assumptions previously, it may send out forged messages to other honest principals, that is, it may send any messages it knows to any other principals as if they are according to the protocol:

axioms *Fake :* ''Know Spy X ⇒ Send Spy X''

Since the spy can send out forged messages which seem to be valid protocol messages and fool honest principals, these honest principals may respond to the forged messages innocently. If such responses are made, we can infer that the spy must have sent forged messages to corresponding principals. So we have two extra rules:

axioms
```
NS2_response_to_Spy : ''Send B Spy (Encrypt {Nonce
           (Nonce_of D), Nonce (Nonce_of B), Principal B}
           (Kpb Spy))
```

```
⇒ Send Spy B (Encrypt {Nonce (Nonce_of D),
   Principal F} (Kpb B))''
```

axioms
```
NS3_response_to_Spy : ''Send A Spy (Encrypt (Nonce
   (Nonce_of E)) (Kpb Spy))
⇒ Send Spy A (Encrypt {Nonce (Nonce_of D),
Nonce (Nonce_of E), Principal F} (Kpb A))''
```

In the original Needham–Schroeder public key protocol, the spy can break it by interleaving two sessions. Lowe fixed the flaw by adding the principal's name B to the second protocol step [5], therefore A can decide whether this message is forged by the spy. If the name in the message is not the name of the sender, A should decline the message and terminate the protocol session:

axioms `NS2_decline : ''Send B A (Encrypt {Nonce`
```
   (Nonce_of D), Nonce (Nonce_of E), Principal C}
   (Kpb A))
⇒ B = C''
```

Additionally, since it is a two-part authentication protocol, only two honest principals are involved. If a principal does not equate to either of them, it must be the spy.

axioms `other_principal :`
```
''[| X ≠ Friend 1; X ≠ Friend 2 |] ⇒ X = Spy''
```

6.2 Some Important Lemmas

To prove the final guarantees for the two participating principals, we need to first prove some lemmas. Most of them are straightforward and can be proved automatically in Isabelle. For example, if principal A sends to B a message encrypted by B's public encryption key, B will be able to read the content of this message.

Besides these straightforward properties, there are a number of important ones which need to be explained.

One of these lemmas is that if a principal knows a message M, and M_1 is a part of M, then it should know the message M_1 as well:

lemma `know_part_imply [simp] :`
```
''Know A M ∧ msg_part M1 M → Know A M1''
```

Due to the inductive definition of the data type `message`, we need to prove this lemma by induction. Seven subgoals have been produced after we apply the induction command. The subgoals concerning principal, nonce, key and encrypted,

signed and hashed massages can be simply proved by using the implication introduction, conjunction elimination and conjunction introduction rules of higher order
logic provided by Isabelle. However, the subgoal concerning compound messages
is a little more complex. In this case, after decomposing all compound parts into
pieces, we use the *blast* method to prove the subgoals.

With the lemma *know_part_imply*, it is easy to prove the lemma
know_encrypted_part which is a simplification rule:

> **lemma** *know_encrypted_part [simp]* :
> ``[| Know B (Encrypt M (Kpb B)); msg_part M1 M |]*
> ⇒ Know B M1''

Another important lemma states that if a principal sends to another principal a
compound message encrypted with the second principal's public encryption key, the
latter will eventually know the parts of it:

> **lemma** *know_send_encrypted_part [simp]* :
> ``[| Send A B (Encrypt M (Kpb B)); msg_part M1 M |]*
> ⇒ Know B M1''

This lemma can be easily proved using the lemma *know_encrypted_part*
together with rules 3_3 and 3_1 of our framework. In doing so, it simplifies the final
proof greatly.

6.3 Secrecy of Nonces

The correctness of the Needham–Schroeder–Lowe protocol relies greatly on the
secrecy of the nonces used by A and B [12]. So the key point for proving
the Needham–Schroeder–Lowe protocol is to prove the secrecy of nonces of A
and B.

Our proofs base these nonce secrecy lemmas on such an assumption: if nobody
sends out a nonce encrypted by the spy's public key, the spy will never get a chance
to read the contents of the nonce, assuming that nonces will never be sent out in
plain text:

> **axioms** *spy_know_encrypted_nonce* :
> ``Know Spy (Encrypt (Nonce (Nonce_of
> (Friend n))) (Kpb (Friend n)))*
> ⇒ Send C Spy (Encrypt (Nonce
> (Nonce_of (Friend n))) (Kpb Spy))''

The first lemma *spy_not_know_nonce_2* is that the spy will never see *B*'s nonce:

lemma *spy_not_know_nonce_2* :
            ``¬ Know Spy (Nonce (Nonce_of (Friend 2)))``

We prove this lemma by the "negative approach", that is, if the spy knows *B*'s nonce, it may send to *B* this nonce encrypted by *B*'s public key, which will never happen. This impossibility is guaranteed by *B*'s name in the second protocol introduced by Lowe and the above axiom *NS2_decline*.

The other lemma *spy_not_know_N1N2* states that the spy will never see the contents of a compound message consisting of *A* and *B*'s nonces and *B*'s name which is the second protocol message:

lemma *spy_not_know_N1N2* :
      ``¬ Know Spy {Nonce (Nonce_of (Friend 1)),
        Nonce (Nonce_of (Friend 2)), Principal
        (Friend 2)}``

This lemma is supported by the first one, since if the spy knows such a compound message, it must know *B*'s nonce.

We have to point out that the spy may intercept and know *A*'s nonce. But it does not decrease the secrecy of the second protocol message sent from *B* to *A*.

6.4 Proving Guarantee for B

The guarantee for *B* after step 3 is that *B* authenticates that *A* really has sent *B*'s nonce (encrypted by *B*'s public encryption key) to *B* and this message has not been modified by the spy:

theorem *B_trust_NS3* : ``'Auth (Friend 2)
        (Friend 1) (Nonce (Nonce_of (Friend 2)))``

With all above lemmas and properties, the proof is not difficult. Rule 4_1 is applied first. It produces three subgoals:

- *A* knows *B*'s nonce encrypted by *B*'s public key;
- *B* has received such a message;
- No other principal knows *B*'s nonce.

For the first subgoal, since principal *B* has sent its nonce to *A* (together with *B*'s own name and *A*'s nonce, and encrypted by *A*'s public encryption key), *A* must have got and read the content of it. *A* can encrypt it using *B*'s public encryption key. Step 3 of the protocol guarantees the second subgoal. The third subgoal is shown by the lemma *spy_not_know_nonce_2*. With all the subgoals resolved, the guarantee for *B* is proved.

6.5 Proving Guarantee for A

Correspondingly, the guarantee for A after step 2 is that A authenticates that B really has sent A's nonce, B's nonce and B's name (encrypted by A's public encryption key) to A, and this message has not been modified by the spy:

theorem A_trust_NS2 :
```
''Auth (Friend 1) (Friend 2) {Nonce (Nonce_of
(Friend 1))), (Nonce (Nonce_of (Friend 2))),
(Principal (Friend 2))}''
```

Again, rule 4_1 is applied. Another three subgoals are produced:

- B knows the compound message consisting of A's nonce, B's nonce and B's name encrypted by A's public encryption key;
- A has received such a compound message;
- No other principal knows such a compound message.

When step 1 finishes, B has received A's nonce. B also knows B's nonce and name. B can then encrypt it using A's public encryption key. Step 2 of the protocol guarantees that A receives the message. The third subgoal has been shown by the lemma spy_not_know_N1N2.

6.6 Summary

Using our knowledge-based framework, we model the Needham–Schroeder–Lowe protocol into logic formulae and infer it by analysing principals knowledge – what they can know and what they can never know. To improve the efficiency of the verification, we implement it using Isabelle. We have implemented all the data structures, functions, predicates, assumptions and inference rules in Isabelle. With this implementation, we are able to prove the correctness of the Needham–Schroeder–Lowe protocol and other protocols – modelling the protocols, proving necessary lemmas and properties and proving the final guarantees. All the proving details are generated by Isabelle, thereby saving users a significant amount of time. In addition, our framework also takes the cases concerning multiple interleaving sessions into consideration, making the method more powerful.

References

1. G. Bella. Inductive Verification of Cryptographic Protocols, PhD Thesis, University of Cambridge, Cambridge, UK, 2000.
2. D. Bolignano. An Approach to the Formal Verification of Cryptographic Protocols, In Proceedings of the 3rd ACM Conference on Computer and Communications Security, pp. 106–118, New Delhi, India, March 1996.

3. M. Burrows, M. Abadi, and R. Needham. A Logic of Authentication, in ACM Transactions on Computer Systems, 8(1):18–36, February 1990.
4. A. Liebl. Authentication in Distributed Systems: A Bibliography, in ACM SIGOPS Operating Systems Review, 27(4):122–136, October 1993.
5. G. Lowe. An Attack on the Needham-Schroeder Public-Key Authentication Protocol, in Information Processing Letters, 56(3):131–133, November 1995.
6. G. Lowe. Breaking and Fixing the Needham-Schroeder Public-Key Protocol using FDR, in Margaria and Steffen (Eds.) Tools and Algorithms for the Construction and Analysis of System, Vol. 1055 of Lecture Notes in Computer Science, pp. 147–166. Springer, 1996.
7. C.A. Meadows. Analyzing the Needham-Schroeder Public-Key Protocol: A Comparison of Two Approaches, in E. Bertino, H. Kurth, G. Martella and E. Montolivo (Eds.) Computer Security ESORICS 96, Vol. 1146 of Lecture Notes in Computer Science, pp. 351–346. Springer, 1996.
8. C.A. Meadows. The NRL Protocol Analyzer: An Overview, in Journal of Logic Programming, 26(2):113–131, February 1996.
9. R. Needham, and M. Schroeder. Using Encryption for Authentication in Large Networks of Computers, in Communications of the ACM, 21(12):993–999, 1978.
10. T. Nipkow, L.C. Paulson, and M. Wenzel. Isabelle/HOL: A Proof Assistant for Higher-Order Logic, Springer, 2003.
11. L.C. Paulson. Proving Properties of Security Protocols by Induction, in Proceedings of the 10th Computer Security Foundations Workshop, pp. 70–83, Rockport, Massachusetts, June 1997.
12. L.C. Paulson. Mechanized Proofs of Security Protocols: Needham-Schroeder with Public Keys, Technical Report 413, Computer Laboratory, University of Cambridge.
13. L.C. Paulson. Mechanized Proofs for a Recursive Authentication Protocol, in Proceedings of the 10th Computer Security Foundations Workshop, pp. 84–95, Rockport, Massachusetts, June 1997.
14. L.C. Paulson. The Inductive Approach to Verifying Cryptographic Protocols, in Journal of Computer Security, 6(1–2):85–128, 1998.
15. L.C. Paulson. Proving Security Protocols Correct, in Proceedings of the 14th Annual IEEE Symposium on Logic in Computer Science, pp. 370–383, Trento, Italy, July 1999.
16. E. Snekkenes. Roles in Cryptographic Protocols, in Proceedings of the 1992 IEEE Computer Society Symposium on Research in Security and Privacy, pp. 105–119, Oakland, California, USA, May 1992.

Routing Security in Ad Hoc Wireless Networks

Mohammad O. Pervaiz, Mihaela Cardei, and Jie Wu

Contents

M.O. Pervaiz (✉)

Department of Computer Science and Engineering, Florida Atlantic University,
Boca Raton, FL 33431, USA
e-mail: mpervaiz@fau.edu

S.C.-H. Huang et al. (eds.), *Network Security*, DOI 10.1007/978-0-387-73821-5_6,
© Springer Science+Business Media, LLC 2010

1 Introduction to Ad Hoc Wireless Networks

Wireless networks provide rapid, untethered access to information and computing, eliminating the barriers of distance, time, and location for many applications ranging from collaborative, distributed mobile computing to disaster recovery (such as fire, flood, earthquake), law enforcement (crowd control, search, and rescue), and military communications (command, control, surveillance, and reconnaissance). An ad hoc network is a collection of wireless mobile hosts forming a temporary network without the aid of any established infrastructure or centralized administration [11].

In ad hoc wireless networks, every device has the role of router and actively participates in data forwarding. Communication between two nodes can be performed directly if the destination is within the sender's transmission range or through intermediate nodes acting as routers (multi-hop transmission) if the destination is outside sender's transmission range.

Some of the characteristics which differentiate ad hoc wireless networks from other networks are:

1. **Dynamic Network Topology.** This is triggered by node mobility, nodes leaving or joining the network, node inoperability due to the lack of power resources, etc. Nonetheless, the network connectivity should be maintained in order to allow applications and services to operate undisrupted.
2. **Fluctuating Link Capacity.** The effects of high bit error rate are more profound in wireless communication. More than one end-to-end path can use a given link in ad hoc wireless networks, and if the link were to break, it could disrupt several sessions during the period of high bit transmission rate.
3. **Distributed Operations.** The protocols and algorithms designed for an ad hoc wireless network should be distributed in order to accommodate a dynamic topology and an infrastructureless architecture.
4. **Limited Energy Resources.** Wireless devices are battery powered; therefore, there is a limited time they can operate without changing or replenishing their energy resources. Designing energy efficient mechanisms is thus an important feature in designing algorithms and protocols. Mechanisms used to reduce energy consumption include (a) having nodes enter sleep state when they cannot send or receive data, (b) choose routing paths that minimize energy consumption, (c) selective use of nodes based on their energy status, (d) construct communication and data delivery structures that minimize energy consumption, and (e) reduce networking overhead.

Designing communication protocols in the ad hoc wireless networks is challenging because of the limited wireless transmission range, broadcast nature of the wireless medium (hidden terminal and exposed terminal problems [14]), node mobility, limited power resources, and limited physical security. Advantages of using an ad hoc wireless networks include easy and speedy deployment, robustness (no infrastructure required), and adaptive and self-organizing network.

In this chapter, we are concerned with the security of routing protocols in ad hoc wireless networks. Routing is an important operation, providing the communication protocol for data delivery between wireless devices. Assuring a secure routing protocol (SRP) is a challenging task since ad hoc wireless networks are highly vulnerable to security attacks due to their unique characteristics. Traditional routing protocol designs do not address security, and are based on a mutual trust relationship between nodes.

The rest of this chapter is organized as follows. We continue with an overview of the routing protocols in ad hoc wireless networks in Sect. 2. Security services and challenges in an ad hoc network environment are presented in Sect. 3. We continue with a classification and description of the main attacks on routing in Sect. refattacks, followed by a description of the state-of-the-art security mechanisms for routing protocols in Sect. 5. Our article ends in Sect. 6 with conclusions.

2 Overview of Routing Protocols in Ad Hoc Wireless Networks

Routing is an important operation, being the foundation of data exchanging between wireless devices. Each wireless node acts as a router and participate in the routing protocol. Routing relies therefore on an implicit trust relationship among participating devices. Main routing responsibilities are exchanging the routing information, finding a feasible path between source and destination based on various metrics, and path maintenance.

The major requirements [14] of a routing protocol are (1) minimum route acquisition delay, (2) quick route reconfiguration in the case of path breaks, (3) loop-free routing, (3) distributed routing protocol, (4) low control overhead, (5) scalability with network size, (6) QoS support as demanded by the application, (7) support of time-sensitive traffic, and (8) security and privacy.

There are a number of challenges [14] triggered by the unique characteristics of ad hoc wireless networks. Node mobility affects network topology and may incur packet lose, path disconnection, network partition, and difficulty in resource allocation. Wireless nodes are in general resource constrained, in terms of battery power, memory and computing power. Wireless channel has a high bit error rate (10^{-5}–10^{-3}) compared with wired counterparts (10^{-12}–10^{-9}). Wireless channel is shared by the nodes in the same broadcast area, thus the link bandwidth available per node is limited, and varies with the number of nodes present in that area. The design of routing protocols should take these factors into consideration.

Based on the routing information update mechanism, routing protocols in ad hoc wireless networks can be classified as proactive (or table-driven) protocols, reactive (or on-demand) protocols, and hybrid routing protocols. In the next three subsections, we present important features of each category and short descriptions of several representative routing protocols.

2.1 Proactive Routing Protocols

In proactive routing protocols, nodes exchange routing information periodically in order to maintain consistent and accurate routing information. When a node has to transmit data to a destination, the path can be computed rapidly based on the updated information available in the routing table. The disadvantage of using a proactive protocol is high overhead needed to maintain an up to date routing information. In ad hoc wireless networks, node mobility triggers a dynamic topology that might require a large number of routing updates. This has a negative impact on resource constrained wireless devices, bandwidth utilization, and throughput.

The protocols in this category are typical extensions of the wired network routing protocols. Examples include Destination Sequence Distance Vector (DSDV) [18], Wireless Routing Protocol (WRP) [13], Optimized Links State Routing (OLSR) [3], etc.

Next, we present the main features of DSDV [18]. A security enhancement mechanism Secure Efficient Ad hoc Distance Vector (SEAD [6]) for DSDV will be detailed later in Sect. 5.1. Similar with other distance vector protocols, DSDV finds the shortest paths between nodes using a distributed version of the Bellman–Ford algorithm. Each node maintains a routing table, with an entry for each possible destination in the network. For each entry, the following fields are maintained: the destination address, next hop on the shortest path to that destination, shortest known distance to this destination, and a destination sequence number that is created by the destination itself. To maintain an updated view of the network topology, each node sends periodically to each of its neighbors its routing table information. Based on the routing information received from its neighbors, each node updates its routing table to reflect current status of the network.

Sequence numbers play an important role in DSDV and are used for preventing loop formation. Each entry in the routing table has a sequence number. This is the most recent sequence number known for that destination and is included in the periodic routing updates. If a node receives an update with a smaller sequence number, then that update is ignored. A newly advertised path is adopted if it has a greater sequence number, or if it has the same sequence number but a lower metric.

Besides the periodic updates, there are triggered updates, issued when important routing updates should be transmitted. When a broken link is detected, the node creates a routing update with next odd sequence number and metric value of infinity. Routing update messages can be full dump, when information for all destination is sent, or incremental when only information changed from the last full dump is sent.

Main advantage of using DSDV is that routes to all destinations are always available, without requiring a route discovery process. Main disadvantage of DSDV is high overhead due to the periodic routing updates.

2.2 Reactive Routing Protocols

In the reactive routing protocols, a route discovery mechanism is initiated only when a node does not know a path to a destination it wants to communicate with. In the case of mobile ad hoc network, reactive routing protocols have been demonstrated to perform better with significantly lower overheads than proactive routing protocols since they are able to react quickly to the many changes that may occur in node connectivity, and yet are able to reduce (or eliminate) routing overhead in periods or areas of the network in which changes are less frequent.

A reactive routing protocol has two main operations, route discovery (usually broadcasting using a form of controlled flooding) and route maintenance. Various reactive protocols have been proposed in the literature such as Ad Hoc On-demand Distance Vector (AODV) [19], Dynamic Source Routing (DSR) [11], Temporally Ordered Routing Algorithm (TORA) [17], etc. We present next the main features of DSR and AODV. Security supporting mechanisms for these protocols are presented later in Sect. 5.

DSR [11] is a source routing protocol and thus has the property that each data packet carries the source-destination path in its header. Using this information, intermediate nodes can determine who is the next hop this packet should be forwarded to. Each node maintains a routing cache that contains routing information that the node learned from routing information forwarded or overheard. Every entry has an expiration time after which the entry is deleted in order to avoid stale information.

DSR performs route discovery by having the sender broadcasts by flooding a *RouteRequest* packet. Each *RouteRequest* contains a sequence number generated by the source node in order to prevent loop formation and to avoid multiple retransmissions by a node of the same *RouteRequest* packet. An intermediate node checks the sequence number and appends its own identifier and forwards the *RouteRequest* only if this message is not a duplicate. The receiver, upon receiving the *RouteRequest*, sends back a *RouteReply* packet along the reverse route recorded in *RouteRequest*. Upon receiving the *RouteReply*, the sender starts sending data to the receiver.

As part of the route maintenance, if a node detects a failure (e.g., broken link), it sends a *RouteError* message to the source. All intermediate nodes hearing the *RouteError* update their routing cache and all routes that contain this hop are truncated. If the source does not have an alternative path to the destination, it has to re-initiate the path discovery mechanism.

DSR has several optimization techniques. First, it allows intermediate nodes that know a path to the destination to reply to the *RouteRequest* message instead of forwarding the request. This speeds up the route discovery. Second, path discovery can use an expanding ring search mechanism when sending the *RouteRequest* messages. This is especially useful for close destinations, thus avoiding broadcasting in the whole network.

Advantages of DSR include (1) route maintenance apply only to active routes, (2) route caching can speed up and reduce overhead of route discovery, and (3) a single route discovery might yield more routes to the destination when intermediate nodes reply from local caches. Disadvantages of DSR are (1) adding the source-destination path in each packet incurs overhead, especially for long paths and small data (2) the flooding used in route discovery is unreliable, redundant, may introduce collisions, contentions; and (3) intermediate nodes might send *RouteReply* from stale routing caches, thus polluting other caches as well.

AODV [19] implements the same main operations as DSR. It discovers a path to a destination using a *RouteRequest* and *RouteReply* sequence, and performs route maintenance for link failures by propagating a *RouteError* message to the source. AODV tries to improve on DSR by maintaining routing tables at the nodes, such that data packets do not contain the source-destination path. Each node maintains a routing table for each destination of interest, including the following fields: destination, next hop, number of hops, destination sequence number, and expiration time.

When a source node broadcasts a *RouteRequest* to discover a path to a destination, intermediate nodes that forward the message set up a reverse path, pointing toward the node from which the request was received. In this way, *RouteReply* travels along the reverse paths set-up when *RouteRequest* was forwarded, without carrying the full path in the header. When *RouteReply* travels along the reverse path, each node sets up forward links that will be used later to forward data packets between the source and destination. When a source node sends a *RouteRequest*, it assigns a higher sequence number for that destination. Intermediate nodes are allowed to reply with *RouteReply* only if they know a recent path to the destination (with the same or higher sequence number). The reverse and forward paths are purged from the routing tables if they are not used within a specific time interval.

The advantages of AODV can be summarized as follows: (1) paths are not included and carried in the packet headers, (2) nodes maintain routing tables with entries only for the active routes (if not used for specific time interval they are purged), and (3) AODV uses a destination sequence number mechanism to limit the chances of an intermediate node replying with stale information to a *RouteRequest* packet.

2.3 Hybrid Routing Protocols

Some ad hoc network routing protocols are hybrid of proactive and reactive mechanisms. Examples of hybrid routing protocols are Zone Routing Protocol (ZRP) [5], Core Extraction Distributed Ad Hoc Routing Protocol (CEDAR) [22], etc.

ZRP [5] is a hybrid of proactive and reactive routing protocols. The network is divided in zones, where every zone is a r-hop neighborhood of a node. The intrazone routing protocol is a proactive routing protocol, while the inter-zone routing protocol is a reactive routing protocol. By varying r, we can control the routing update control traffic. When a node wants to transmit data to a destination within the same zone, then this is done directly using the proactive routing protocol and the information already available in routing tables.

If the destination is in another zone, then the source node bordercasts the *RouteRequest* (e.g., this message is forwarded by the border routers) until it reaches the destination zone. Then, the border node of the destination zone sends back a *RouteReply* message. Any node forwarding the *RouteRequest* appends its address to it. This information is used when sending *RouteReply* back to the source.

If a broken link is detected, the path reconstruction can be done locally, and then a path update is sent to the source, or can be done globally by having the source re-initiate the path discovery.

ZRP efficiently explores the features of proactive and reactive protocols. It reduces the control overhead by maintaining the proactive protocols within zones and reduces the flooding drawbacks by deploying the reactive protocol and border-cast mechanism only between the zones. Particular attention should be considered when selecting the zone radius r, since this can significantly impact the routing performance.

2.4 Broadcasting in Ad Hoc Wireless Networks

Broadcasting refers to the operation of sending a message to all other hosts in the network. Broadcasting is used for the route discovery in reactive routing protocols. In a mobile environment, broadcasting is expected to be used more frequently since nodes mobility might trigger path disconnecting and thus route discovery is invoked as part of the path maintenance procedure.

Broadcasting operation has the following characteristics [25]: (1) the broadcast is spontaneous, that means that each node can start broadcasting at any time, and (2) broadcasting is unreliable. No acknowledgment packet is sent for example in IEEE 802.11 by a node upon receiving a broadcast message.

One straightforward method used to implement broadcasting is through a form of controlled flooding. In this method, each node retransmits a broadcast message when it receives it first time. Transmitting a broadcast through flooding in a *CSMA/CA* network triggers a numbers of issues, commonly referred to as the *broadcast storm problem* [25]:

1. **Redundant rebroadcast.** A node resends a broadcast message even if all its neighbors have already received the message from some other neighbors.
2. **Contention.** The neighbors of a transmitting node receive the message at approximately the same time, and when resending the message, they contend for the wireless communication medium.
3. **Collision.** Collisions are more likely to occur because of the lack of back-off mechanism and the lack of RTS/CTS dialogue. Such an example is when more neighbors retransmit at the same time a message recently received.

The work of [25] proposes several schemes to alleviate the *broadcast storm problem* by limiting the cases when a node rebroadcasts a message: (1) probabilistic scheme, when each node rebroadcasts a message with a specific probability; (2) counter-based scheme, when a node retransmits a message if it was received less than a threshold number of times over a fixed interval; (3) distance-based scheme, when a message is resent only if it is received from neighbors farther away than a specific threshold distance; and (4) location-based scheme, when a node retransmits a message only if the additional area covered is larger than a specific threshold area.

The work of [26] proposes several local and deterministic schemes where a subset of nodes, called forward nodes, is selected locally while ensuring broadcast coverage. In one scheme, each node decides its own forwarding status, whereas in another scheme, the status of each node is determined by neighbors jointly.

In Sect. 5.11, we discuss few mechanisms proposed recently in literature to secure the broadcast operation.

3 Security Services and Challenges in Ad Hoc Wireless Networks

In order to assure a reliable data transfer over the communication networks and to protect the system resources, a number of security services are required. Based on their objectives, the security services are classified into five categories [23]: availability, confidentiality, authentication, integrity, and nonrepudiation.

- **Availability:** Availability implies that the requested services (e.g., bandwidth and connectivity) are available in a timely manner even though there is a potential problem in the system. Availability of a network can be tampered, for example, by dropping off packets and by resource depletion attacks.
- **Confidentiality:** Confidentiality ensures that classified information in the network is never disclosed to unauthorized entities. Confidentiality can be achieved by using different encryption techniques so that only the legitimate communicating nodes can analyze and understand the transmission. The content disclosure attack and location disclosure attack reveal the contents of the message being transmitted and physical information about a particular node respectively.
- **Authenticity:** Authenticity is a network service to determine a user's identity. Without authentication, an attacker can impersonate any node, and in this way, one by one node, it can gain control over the entire network.
- **Integrity:** Integrity guarantees that information passed on between nodes has not been tampered in the transmission. Data can be altered both intentionally and accidentally (e.g., through hardware glitches or in case of ad hoc wireless connections through interference).
- **Non-repudiation:** Non-repudiation ensures that the information originator cannot deny having sent the information. This service is useful for detection and isolation of compromised nodes in the network. Many authentication and secure routing algorithms implemented in ad hoc networks rely on trust-based concepts. The fact that a message can be attributed to a specific node helps making these algorithms more secure.

Designing a secure ad hoc wireless networks communication is a challenging task due to (1) insecure wireless communication links, (2) absence of a fixed infrastructure, (3) resource constraints (e.g., battery power, bandwidth, memory, and CPU processing capacity), and (4) node mobility that triggers a dynamic network topology.

The majority of traditional routing protocol designs fail to provide security. The main requirements [14] of a SRP are (1) detection of malicious nodes, such nodes should be avoided in the routing process; (2) guarantee of correct route discovery; (3) confidentiality of network topology, if an attacker learns the network topology, he can attack the bottleneck nodes, detected by studying the traffic patters. This will result in disturbing the routing process and denial of service (DoS); and (4) stability against attacks, the routing protocol must be able to resume the normal operation within a finite amount of time after an attack.

4 Security Attacks on Routing Protocols in Ad Hoc Wireless Networks

Providing a secure system can be achieved by preventing attacks or by detecting them and providing a mechanism to recover for those attacks. Attacks on ad hoc wireless networks can be classified as active and passive attacks, depending on whether the normal operation of the network is disrupted or not.

1. **Passive Attack:** In passive attacks, an intruder snoops the data exchanged without altering it. The attacker does not actively initiate malicious actions to cheat other hosts. The goal of the attacker is to obtain information that is being transmitted, thus violating the message confidentiality. Since the activity of the network is not disrupted, these attackers are difficult to detect. Powerful encryption mechanism can alleviate these attackers by making difficult to read overheard packets.

2. **Active Attack:** In active attacks, an attacker actively participates in disrupting the normal operation of the network services. A malicious host can create an active attack by modifying packets or by introducing false information in the ad hoc network. It confuses routing procedures and degrades network performance. Active attacks can be divided into internal and external attacks:

   External Attacks are carried by nodes that are not legitimate part of the network. Such attacks can be defended by using encryption, firewalls, and source authentication. In external attacks, it is possible to disrupt the communication of an organization from the parking lot in front of the company office.

   Internal Attacks are from compromised nodes that were once legitimate part of the network. Since the adversaries are already part of the ad hoc wireless network as authorized nodes, they are much more severe and difficult to detect when compared to external attacks.

A large number of attacks have been identified in the literature that affect the routing in ad hoc wireless networks. Solutions and mechanism that defense against various attacks are presented later in Sect. 5. Next, we classify routing attacks into five categories: attacks using impersonation, modification, fabrication, replay, and DoS.

4.1 Attacks Using Impersonation

In impersonation attacks, an intruder assumes the identity and privileges of another node in order to consume its resources or to disturb normal network operation. An attacker node achieves impersonation by misrepresenting its identity. This can be done by changing its own IP or Message Authentication Code (MAC) address to that of some other legitimate node. Some strong authentication procedures can be used to stop attacks by impersonation.

Man-in-the-Middle Attack
In this attack, a malicious node reads and possibly modifies the messages between two parties. The attacker can impersonate the receiver with respect to the sender, and the sender with respect to the receiver, without having either of them realize that they have been attacked.

Sybil Attack
In the Sybil attack [15], an attacker pretends to have multiple identities. A malicious node can behave as if it were a larger number of nodes either by impersonating other nodes or simply by claiming false identities. Sybil attacks are classified into three categories: direct/indirect communication, fabricated/stolen identity, and simultaneity. In the direct communication, Sybil nodes communicate directly with legitimate nodes, whereas in the indirect communication, messages sent to Sybil nodes are routed through malicious nodes. An attacker can fabricate a new identity or it can simply steal it after destroying or temporarily disabling the impersonated node. All Sybil identities can participate simultaneously in the network or they may be cycled through.

4.2 Attacks Using Modification

This attack disrupts the routing function by having the attacker illegally modifying the content of the messages. Examples of such attacks include redirection by changing the route sequence number and redirection with modified hop count that can trigger the black hole attack. Some other modification based attacks are presented next.

Misrouting Attack
In the misrouting attack, a non-legitimate node sends data packet to the wrong destination. This type of attack is carried out by modifying the final destination address of the data packet or by forwarding a data packet to the wrong next hop in the route to the destination.

Detour Attack

In this type of attack, the attacker adds a number of virtual nodes in to a route during the route discovery phase. As a consequence, the traffic is diverted to other routes that appear to be shorter and might contain malicious nodes which could create other attacks. The attacking node can save energy in a detour attack because it does not have to forward packets to that destination itself. This attack is specific to source routing protocols.

Blackmail Attack

Blackmail attack causes false identification of a good node as malicious node. In ad hoc wireless networks, nodes usually keep information of perceived malicious nodes in a *blacklist*. An attacker may blackmail a good node and tell other nodes in the network to add that node to their blacklists as well, thus avoiding the victim node in future routes.

4.3 Attacks Using Fabrication

In fabrication attacks, an intruder generates false routing messages, such as routing updates and route error messages, in order to disturb network operation or to consume other node resources. A number of fabrication messages are presented next.

Resource Consumption Attack

In this attack, a malicious node deliberately tries to consume the resources (e.g., battery power, bandwidth, etc.) of other nodes in the network. The attack can be in the form of unnecessary route requests, route discovery, control messages, or by sending stale information. For example, in *routing table overflow* attack, a malicious node advertises routes to nonexistent nodes, thus causing routing table overflow. By using *packet replication* attack, an adversary consumes bandwidth and battery power of other nodes.

Routing Table Poisoning

In this attack, a malicious node sends false routing updates, resulting in suboptimal routing, network congestion, or network partition.

Rushing Attack

A malicious node in rushing attack attempts to tamper *RouteRequest* packets, modifying the node list, and hurrying its packet to the next node. Since in on demand routing protocol, only one *RouteRequest* packet is forwarded, if the route requests forwarded by the attacker are first to reach target (destination), then any route found by the route discovery mechanism will include a path through the attacker.

Black Hole

In this type of attack, a malicious node advertise itself as having the shortest path to all nodes in the network (e.g., the attacker claims that it is a level-one node).

The attacker can cause DoS by dropping all the received packets. Alternately, the attacker can monitor and analyze the traffic to find activity patterns of each node. Sometimes, the black hole becomes the first step of a man-in-the-middle attack.

Gray Hole
Under this attack, an attacker drops all data packets but it lets control messages to route through it. This selective dropping makes gray hole attacks much more difficult to detect than blackhole attack.

4.4 Replay Attacks

In the replay attack, an attacker retransmits data to produce an unauthorized effect. Examples of replay attacks are wormhole attack and tunneling attack.

Wormhole Attack
In the wormhole attack [10], two compromised nodes can communicate with each other by a private network connection. The attacker can create a vertex cut of nodes in the network by recording a packet at one location in network, tunneling the packet to another location, and replaying it there. The attacker does not require key material as it only needs two transceivers and one high quality out-of-band channel. The wormhole can drop packets, or it can selectively forward packets to avoid detection. It is particularly dangerous against different network routing protocols in which the nodes consider themselves neighbor after hearing a packet transmission directly from some node.

Tunneling Attack
In a tunneling attack [21], two or more nodes collaborate and exchange encapsulated messages along existing data routes. For example, if a *RouteRequest* packet is encapsulated and sent between two attackers, the packet will not contain the path traveled between the two attackers. This would falsely make the receiver conclude that the path containing the attackers is the shortest path available.

4.5 Denial of Service

In the DoS attack [14], an attacker explicitly attempts to prevent legitimate users from using system services. This type of attack impacts the availability of the system. An ad hoc wireless network is vulnerable to DoS attacks because of its dynamic changing topology and distributed protocols. Examples of DoS attacks include:

Consumption of Scarce Resources
Attacker can consume valuable network resources (e.g., bandwidth, memory and access points) so that the entire network becomes unavailable to users.

Destruction or Alteration of Configuration Information

In this DoS attack, an attacker attempts to alter or destroy configuration information, thus preventing legitimate users from using the network. An improperly configured network may not perform well or may not operate at all.

5 Security Mechanisms and Solutions for Routing Protocols in Ad Hoc Wireless Networks

Message encryption and digital signatures are two important mechanisms for data integrity and user authentication.

There are two types of data encryption mechanisms, symmetric and asymmetric (or public key) mechanisms. Symmetric cryptosystems use the same key (the secret key) for encryption and decryption of a message, and asymmetric cryptosystems use one key (the public key) to encrypt a message and another key (the private key) to decrypt it. Public and private keys are related in such a way that only the public key can be used to encrypt messages and only the corresponding private key can be used for decryption purpose. Even if attacker comprises a public key, it is virtually impossible to deduce the private key.

Any code attached to an electronically transmitted message that uniquely identifies the sender is known as digital code. Digital signatures are key component of most authentication schemes. To be effective, digital signatures must be non-forgeable. Hash functions are used in the creation and verification of a digital signature. It is an algorithm which creates a digital representation or *fingerprint* in the form of a *hash value* (or *hash result*) of a standard length which is usually much smaller than the message and unique to it. Any change to the message will produce a different hash result even when the same hash function is used. In the case of a secure hash function, also known as a *one-way hash function*, it is computationally infeasible to derive the original message from knowledge of its hash value.

In ad hoc wireless networks, the secrecy of the key does not ensure the integrity of the message. For this purpose, MAC [1] is used. It is a hashed representation of a message and even if MAC is known, it is impractical to compute the message that generated it. A MAC, which is a cryptographic checksum, is computed by the message initiator as a function of the secret key, and the message being transmitted, and it is appended to the message. The recipient re-computes the MAC in the similar fashion upon receiving the message. If the MAC computed by the receiver matches the MAC received with the message, then the recipient is assured that the message was not modified.

Next, we present security mechanisms specifically tailored for specific routing mechanisms.

5.1 Secure Efficient Ad hoc Distance Vector

SEAD [6] is a proactive routing protocol, based on the design of DSDV [18]. Besides the fields common with DSDV, such as destination, metric, next hop, and sequence number, SEAD routing tables maintain a hash value for each entry, as described below. This paper is concerned with protecting routing updates, both periodic and triggered, by preventing an attacker to forge better metrics or sequence numbers in such update packets.

The key feature of the proposed security protocol is the use of one-way hash chains, using a one way hash function H. Each node computes a list of hash values $h_0, h_1, \cdots, h_n$, where $h_i = H(h_{i-1})$ and $0 < i \leq n$, based on an initial random value h_0. The paper assumes the existence of a mechanism for distributing h_n to all intended receivers. If a node knows H and a trusted value h_n, then it can authenticate any other value $h_i, 0 < i \leq n$ by successively applying the hash function H and then comparing the result with h_n.

To authenticate a route update, a node adds a hash value to each routing table entry. For a metric j and a sequence number i, the hash value h_{n-mi+j} is used to authenticate the routing update entry for that sequence number, where $m - 1$ is the maximum network diameter. Since an attacker cannot compute a hash value with a smaller index than the advertised value, he or she is not able to advertise a route to the same destination with a greater sequence number, or with a better metric.

SEAD provides a robust protocol against attackers trying to create incorrect routing state in other node by modifying the sequence number or the routing metric. SEAD does not provide a way to prevent an attacker from tampering next hop or destination field in a routing update. Also, it cannot prevent an attacker to use the same metric and sequence number learned from some recent update message, for sending a new routing update to a different destination.

5.2 ARIADNE

ARIADNE [7], an efficient on-demand SRP, provides security against arbitrary active attackers and relies only on efficient symmetric cryptography. It prevents attackers from tampering uncompromised routes consisting of uncompromised nodes.

ARIADNE ensures point-to-point authentication of a routing message by combining a shared key between the two parties and MAC. However, for secure authentication of a routing message, it relies on the TESLA [20] (see Sect. 5.11) broadcast authentication protocol.

Design of ARIADNE is based on DSR (see Sect. 2.1). Similar with DSR, it consists of two basic operations, route discovery and route maintenance. ARIADNE makes use of efficient combination of one way hash function and shared keys. It assumes that sender and receiver share secret (non-TESLA) keys for message authentication. The initiator (or sender) includes a MAC computed with an end-to-end key and the target (or destination) verifies the authenticity and freshness of the request using the shared key. Pre-hop hashing mechanism, a one-way hash function that verifies that no hop is omitted, is also used in Ariadne. In the case of any dead link, a *RouteError* message is sent back to the initiator. Errors are generated just as regular data packets, and intermediate nodes remove routes that use dead links in the selected path.

ARIADNE provides a strong defense against attacks that modify and fabricate routing information. When it is used with an advanced version of TESLA called TIK (see Sect. 5.9), it is immune to wormhole attacks. However, it is still vulnerable to selfish node attack. General security mechanisms are very reliable, but key exchanges are complicated, making ARIADNE infeasible in the current ad hoc environments.

5.3 Security Aware Routing

Security Aware Routing (SAR) [12] is an on demand routing protocol based on AODV (see Sect. 2.2). It integrates the trust level of a node and the security attributes of a route to provide an *integrated security metric* for the requested route. By incorporating a Quality of Protection (*QoP*) as a routing metric, the route discovery can return quantifiable secure routes. The *QoP* vector used is a combination of security level and available cryptographic techniques.

SAR introduces the notion of a *trust hierarchy*, where nodes of the ad hoc wireless network are divided into different trust levels such that an initiator can impose a minimum trust level for all the nodes participating in the source-destination communication. Note that a path with the required trust level might not exist even if the network is connected. Even if SAR discovers fewer routes than AODV, they are always secured.

The initiator of the route in SAR includes a security metric in the route request. This security metric is the minimum trust level of the nodes that can participate in the route discovery. Consequently, only those nodes that have this minimum security level can participate in the route discovery. All other nodes that are below that trust level will drop the request packets. If an end-to-end path with the required security is found, the intermediate node or destination sends a suitably modified *RouteReply*. In the case of multiple paths satisfying the required security attributes, SAR selects the shortest of such routes. If route discovery fails, then a message can be sent to the initiator so that it can lower the trust level.

In the case of a successful path search, SAR always finds a route with quantifiable guarantee of security. This can be done by having nodes of a trust level share a key. Thus, a node that does not have a particular trust level will not possess the key for that level, and as a result it will not be able to decrypt the packets using the key of that level. Therefore, it will not have any other option but to drop the packet.

SAR uses sequence numbers and timestamps to stop replay attacks. Threats such as interception and subversion can be prevented by trust level key authentication. Modification and fabrication attacks can be stopped by verifying the digital signatures of the transmitted packets.

One of the main drawbacks of using SAR is the excessive encrypting and decrypting required at each hop during the path discovery. In a mobile environment, the extra processing leads to an increased power consumption.

A route discovered by SAR may not be the shortest route in terms of hop-count, but it is secure. Such a path ensures that only the nodes having the required trust level will read and re-route the packets, but at the same time, malicious node can steal the required key, a case in which the protocol is still open for all kinds of attacks.

5.4 Secure Routing Protocol

SRP [16] is another protocol extension that can be applied to many of the on demand routing protocols used today. SRP defends against attacks that disrupt the route discovery process and guarantees to identify the correct topological information.

The basic idea of SRP is to set up a security association (SA) between a source and a destination node without the need of cryptographic validation of the communication data by the intermediate nodes. SRP assumes that this SA can be achieved through a shared key K_{ST} between the source S and target T. Such a security association should exist prior to the route initiation phase.

The source S initiates the route discovery by sending a route request packet to the destination T. The SRP uses an additional header called SRP header to the underlying routing protocol (e.g., AODV) packet. SRP header contains the following fields: the query sequence number Q_{SEC}, query identifier number Q_{ID}, and a 96 bit MAC field.

Intermediate nodes discard a route request message if SRP header is missing. Otherwise, they forward the request toward destination after extracting Q_{ID}, source, and destination address. Highest priority is given to nodes that generate requests at the lowest rates and vice versa.

When the target T receives this request packet, it verifies if the packet has originated from the node with which it has SA. If Q_{SEC} is greater or equal to Q_{MAX}, the request is dropped as it is considered to be replayed. Otherwise, it calculates the keyed hash of the request fields, and if the output matches SRP MAC, then authenticity of the sender and integrity of the request are verified.

On the reception of a route reply, S checks the source address, destination addresses, Q_{ID}, and Q_{SEC}. It discards the route reply if it does not match the currently pending query. In case of a match, it compares reply IP source-route with the exact reverse of the route carried in reply packet. If the two routes match, then S calculates the MAC by using the replied route, the SRP header fields, and the secure key between source and destination. If the two MAC match, then the validation is successful, and it confirms that the reply did came from the destination T.

SRP suffers from the lack of validation mechanism for route maintenance messages as it does not stop a malicious node from harming routes to which that node already belongs to. SRP is immune to IP spoofing because it secures the binding of the MAC and IP address of the nodes, but it is prone to wormhole attacks and invisible node attacks.

5.5 Secure Routing Protocol for Ad Hoc Networks

A Secure Routing Protocol for Ad Hoc Networks (ARAN) [21] is an on-demand protocol designed to provide secure communications in managed-open environments. Nodes in a managed-open environment exchange initialization parameters before the start of communication. Session keys are exchanged or distributed through a trusted third party like a certification authority.

Each node in ARAN receives a certificate after securely authenticating its identity to a trusted certificate server T. Nodes use these certificates to authenticate themselves to other nodes during the exchange of routing messages. The certificate contains the node's IP address, its public key, as well as the time of issuing and expiration. These fields are concatenated and signed by the server T. A node A receives a certificate as: $T \rightarrow A : cert_A = [IP_A, K_{A+}, t, e] K_{T-}$.

In the authentication phase, ARAN ensures the existence of a secure path to the destination. Each intermediate node in the network stores the route pair (previous node, the destination node). All the fields are concatenated and signed with source node I's private key. A combination of the nonce number (N_I) and timestamp (t) is used to obtain data freshness and timeliness property. Each time I performs a route discovery, it monotonically increases the nonce. The signature prevents spoofing attacks that may alter the route or form loops. Source node I broadcasts a Route Discovery Packet (RDP) for a destination D as $I \rightarrow brdcst$:[RDP, IP_D, $cert_I$, N_I, t]K_{I-}.

Each node that receives the RDP for the first time removes any other intermediate node's signature, signs the RDP using its own key, and broadcasts it to all its neighboring nodes. This continues until destination node D eventually receives the packet.

After receiving the RDP, the destination node D sends a Reply (REP) packet back along the reverse path to the source node I. If J is the first node on the reverse path, REP packet is sent as $D \rightarrow J$:[REP, IP_I, $cert_D$, N_I, t] K_{D-}.

When the source node I receives the REP packet, it verifies the destination's signature K_{D-} and nonce N_I. When there is no traffic on an existing route for some specific time, then that route is deactivated in the routing table. Nodes use an ERR message to report links in active routes broken due to node movement.

Using predetermined cryptographic certificates, ARAN provides network services like authentication and non-repudiation. Simulations show that ARAN is efficient in discovering and maintaining routes, but routing packets are larger in size and overall routing load is high. Due to heavy asymmetric cryptographic computation, ARAN has higher cost for route discovery. It is not immune to wormhole attack and if nodes do not have time synchronization, then it is prone to replay attacks as well.

5.6 Security Protocols for Sensor Network

Security Protocols for Sensor Network (SPINS) [24] is a suite of two security
building blocks which are optimized for ad hoc wireless networks. It provides important network services such as data confidentiality, two party data authentication,
and data freshness through Secure Network Encryption Protocol (SNEP) and secure broadcast through Micro Timed Efficient Stream Loss-tolerant Authentication
(μTESLA).

Most of the current protocols are not practical for secure broadcast as they use
asymmetric digital signatures. These signatures have high cost of creation and verification. SPINS introduces μTESLA (see Sect. 5.11), an enhanced version of TESLA
which uses symmetric cryptographic techniques for authentications and asymmetry
cryptography only for the delayed disclosure of keys. Tight lower bound on the key
disclosure delay and robustness against DoS attacks makes μTESLA a very efficient
and secure protocol for data broadcast.

SNEP provides point to point communication in the wireless network. It relies on
a shared counter between a sender and a receiver in order to ensure semantic security. Thus, it protects message contents of encrypted messages from eavesdroppers.
Since both nodes share the counter and increment it after each block, the counter
does not need to be sent with the message. In this way, the same message is encrypted differently each time. A receiver node is assured that the message originated
from the legitimate node if the MAC verifies successfully. The counter value in the
MAC eliminates replaying of old messages in the network.

SPINS is the first secure and lightweight broadcast authentication protocol. The
computation costs of symmetric cryptography are low, and the communication overhead of 8 bytes per message is almost negligible when compared to the size of a
message. SNEP ensures semantic security, data authentication, replay protection,
and message freshness whereas μTESLA provides authentication for secure data
broadcast.

5.7 Cooperation Of Nodes Fairness In Dynamic
Ad-hoc NeTworks

Cooperation Of Nodes Fairness In Dynamic Ad-hoc NeTworks (CONFIDANT) [2]
protocol is designed as an extension to reactive source-routing protocol such as
DSR. It is a collection of components which interact with each other for monitoring,
reporting, and establishing routes by avoiding misbehaving nodes. CONFIDANT
components in each node include a network monitor, reputation system, trust manager, and a path manager.

Each node in this protocol monitors its neighbors and updates the reputation
accordingly. If nodes detect any misbehaving or malicious node, they can inform
other *friend* nodes by sending an ALARM message. When a node receives such an

ALARM either directly from another node or by listening to the ad hoc network, it calculates how trustworthy the ALARM is based on the source of the ALARM and the total number of ALARM messages about the misbehaving node.

Trust manager sends alarm messages to other nodes to warn them of malicious nodes. Incoming alarms are checked for trustworthiness. Trust manager contains an alarm table, trust level table, and a *friend* list of all trust worthy nodes to which a node will send alarms.

Local rating lists and black lists are maintained in the reputation system. These lists are exchanged with friend nodes, and timeouts are used to avoid old lists. A node gives more importance to its own experience than to those events which are observed and reported by others. Whenever the threshold for certain behavior is crossed, path manager does the re-ranking by deleting the paths containing malicious nodes and ignoring any request from misbehaving nodes. At the same time, it sends an alert to the source of the path so that it can discover some other route.

When DSR is fortified with the CONFIDANT protocol extensions, it is very scalable in terms of the total number of nodes in the network, and it performs well even if more than 60% of the nodes are misbehaving. The overhead for incorporating different security components is manageable for ad hoc environment. However, detection based reputation system has few limitations, and routes are still vulnerable to spoofing and Sybil attacks.

5.8 Defense Mechanisms Against Rushing Attacks

Rushing attacks [8] (see Sect. 4.3) are mostly directed against on demand routing protocols such as DSR. To counter such attacks, a generic secure route discovery component called Rushing Attack Prevention (RAP) is used. RAP combines the following mechanisms: *Secure Neighbor Detection*, *Secure Route Delegation*, and *Randomized Route Request Forwarding*. Any on demand routing protocol such as ARIADNE can be used as underlying protocol to RAP.

In *Secure Neighbor Detection*, a three round mutual authentication procedure is used between a sender and a receiver to check if they are within normal communication range of each other. First, a node forwards a *Neighbor Solicitation* packet to the neighboring node which replies with a *Neighbor Reply* packet and finally, the initial node sends *Neighbor Verification* packet to confirm that both nodes are neighbors.

Secure Route Delegation verifies that all the steps in *Secure Neighbor Detection* phase were carried out. Before sending a route update to its neighbor, it signs a route attestation, delegating the rights to the neighbor to further propagate the update.

In *Randomize Message Forwarding*, a node buffers k route requests, and then it randomly forwards only one of these k requests. By limiting the total number of requests sent by a node, it prevents flood attacks in the network. Each request carries the list of all the nodes traversed by that request. Furthermore, bi-directional verification is also used to authenticate the neighbors.

By using efficiently combining these three mechanisms, RAP can find usable routes when other protocols cannot. When it is enabled, it has higher overhead than other protocols, but currently, it is the only protocol that can defend against rushing attacks. However, network is still prone to rushing attacks if an attacker can compromise k nodes.

5.9 Defense Mechanisms Against Wormhole Attacks

In order to prevent the wormwhole attacks (see Sect. 4.4), the *packet leashes* mechanism [10] proposes to add additional information (referred as *leashes*) to the packets in order to restrict packet's maximum allowed transmission distance.

Geographical leash and *temporal leash* can be used to detect and stop wormhole attacks. Geographical leash insures that the recipient of the packet is within a certain distance from the sender while temporal leash is used to enforce an upper bound on the packet's life time, thus restricting packet's maximum travel distance. Temporal leash uses packet's expiration time to detect a wormhole. The expiration time is computed based on the allowed maximum transmission distance and the speed of light. A node will not accept any packet if this expiration time has passed.

TIK (TESLA with Instant Key Disclosure) protocol is an extension of TESLA (see Sect. 5.11), and it is implemented with temporal leashes to detect wormholes. It requires each communicating node to know one public key for each other node in the network. The TIK protocol uses an efficient mechanism *Merkle Hash* tree [9] for key authentication. The root value m of the resulting hash tree commits to all the keys and is used to authenticate any leaf key efficiently. Hash trees are generally large so only the upper layers are stored while lower layers can be computed on demand.

The TIK packet is transmitted by sender S as $S \rightarrow R : HMAC_{K_i}(M), M, T, K_i$, where M is the message payload, T are the tree authentication values, and K_i is the key used to generate the HMAC. After the receiver R receives the HMAC value, it uses the hash tree root m and the hash tree values T to verify that the key K_i at the end of the packet is authentic, and then uses the key K_i to verify the HMAC value in the packet. The receiver R only accepts the packet as authentic if all these verifications are successful.

A receiver can verify the TESLA security condition as it receives the packet, thereby eliminating the authentication delay of TESLA. Packet leashes are effective mechanisms, but TIK is not feasible in resource constraint networks due to the expensive cryptographic mechanisms implemented. The lack of accurate time synchronization in today's systems prevent TIK from providing a usable wormhole detection mechanism. Another potential problem with leashes using a timestamp in a packet is that the sender may not know the precise time at which it will transmit the packet and generating a digital signature in that time may not be possible.

5.10   Defense Mechanisms Against Sybil Attacks

In a Sybil attack [15] (see Sect. 4.1), a malicious node acts on behalf of a larger number of nodes either by impersonating other nodes or simply by claiming false identities. Most of the secure protocols are prone to this type of attack. However, there are various key distribution mechanisms which can be used efficiently to defend against Sybil attacks.

Sybil nodes can carry out a variety of attacks. For example, network nodes use *voting* for many purposes. With enough Sybil nodes, an attacker may be able to determine the outcome of every vote. Sybil nodes, due to their larger number, are allocated more resources, and they can create DoS for legitimate nodes. Ad hoc wireless networks can use *misbehavior detection* property to detect any malfunctioning node. An attacker with many Sybil nodes can spread the blame and pass unnoticed, having only small misbehavior actions associated with each identity.

There are a number of ways to detect Sybil attacks. In *radio resource testing*, it is assumed that nodes have only one radio and are not capable of sending or receiving on more than one channel. If a node wants to verify whether its neighbors are Sybil nodes, then it assigns to each of its neighbors a different channel to broadcast messages. Then the node listens to one of the channels. If a message is received, this is an indication of a legitimate neighbor, whereas an idle transmission is an indication of a Sybil node.

A more authentic way of defending against Sybil attacks is *random key predistribution*. A random set of keys are assigned to each node and then every node can compute the common keys it shares with its neighbors. If two nodes share q common keys, they can establish a secure link. A *one-way Pseudo Random hash Function* (PRF) is used for validation. Thus, an attacker cannot just gather a bunch of keys and claim an identity since PRF is a one way hash function.

There are two types of key distribution mechanisms [4] to counter Sybil attacks. In *single-space pairwise key distribution*, each pair of nodes is assigned a unique key. A node i stores unique public information U_i and private information V_i. The node i computes its key from $f(V_i, U_j)$ where U_j is the public key of neighboring node j. Validation is successful if a node has the pairwise key between itself and the verifier. In *multi-space pairwise key distribution*, each node is assigned, by the network, k out of m random key spaces. If two neighboring nodes have at least one key space in common, then they can compute their pairwise secret key using the corresponding single space scheme.

This is the first work that proposes various defense mechanisms against the Sybil attacks, such as *radio resource testing* and *random key predistribution. Random key predistribution* is already required in many applications to secure radio communication. The most effective against Sybil attacks is the *multi-space pairwise key distribution* mechanism.

5.11   Security Mechanisms for Broadcast Operation

Timed Efficient Stream Loss-tolerant Authentication (TESLA) [20] is an efficient broadcast authentication protocol with low communication and computation overhead. It can scale to large numbers of receivers, can tolerate packet loss, and uses loose time synchronization between sender and receivers.

TESLA mainly uses purely symmetric cryptographic functions, however, it achieves asymmetric properties from clock synchronization and delayed key disclosure. In this way, it does not require to compute expensive one-way functions. For this purpose, it needs sender and receivers to be loosely time-synchronized and for a secure authentication, either the receiver or the sender must buffer some messages.

For secure broadcasting, a sender chooses a random initial key K_N and generates a one-way key chain by repeatedly computing the one-way hash function H on the starting value $K_{N-1} = H[K_N]$, $K_{N-2} = H[K_{N-1}], \ldots, K_0 = H[K_1]$. In general, $K_i = H[K_{i+1}] = H^{N-i}[K_N]$ where $H^i[x]$ is the result of applying the function H to x, for i times.

The sender node predetermines a schedule at which it discloses each key of its one-way key chain. Keys are disclosed in the reverse order from generation, i.e., $K_0, K_1, K_2, \ldots, K_N$ then the MAC computed using the key K_i is added to the packet. When the packet reaches the receiver, it checks the security condition of the key disclosure. If the key K_i used to authenticate the packet was not disclosed, then it buffers the packet and waits for the sender to disclose K_i, while using an already disclosed key to authenticate the buffered packets. However, if the key is already disclosed, then receiver will discard the packet.

Even though TESLA is efficient, it still has few drawbacks. It authenticates the initial packet with a digital signature which is too expensive for wireless nodes and disclosing a key in each packet requires too much energy for sending and receiving. TESLA is vulnerable to DoS attacks as malicious nodes can create *buffer overflow* state in the receiver while it waits for the sender to disclose its keys.

SPINS [24] introduces Micro Timed Efficient Stream Loss-tolerant Authentication (μTESLA), a modified version of TESLA which only uses symmetric mechanisms for packet authentication, and it discloses the key once per epoch. μTESLA is different from TESLA as it allows a receiver to authenticate the packets as soon as they arrive, and it replaces receiver buffering with sender buffering. Immediate authentication as well as buffering only at the sender makes it a secure protocol against DoS. It has very low security overhead. The computation, memory, and communication costs are also small. Since the data authentication, freshness, and confidentiality properties require transmitting only 8 bytes per message, μTESLA is considered a very effective and robust protocol for secure data broadcasting.

TESLA with Instant Key Disclosure (TIK) [10] is another protocol for secure broadcasting implemented with temporal leashes in order to detect wormholes (see Sect. 5.9). TIK requires accurate time synchronization between all communicating parties. It works almost in the same manner as the base protocol TESLA, but in TIK, the receiver can verify TESLA security condition as it receives the packet.

By eliminating the authentication delay of TESLA, it allows sender to disclose the key in the same packet. TIK is therefore a more robust protocol than TESLA since it eliminates the waiting time imposed by disclosing the keys only after the packet was received.

6 Conclusions

Achieving a SRP is an important task that is being challenged by the unique characteristics of an ad hoc wireless network. Traditional routing protocols fail to provide security and rely on an implicit trust between communicating nodes.

In this chapter, we discussed security services and challenges in an ad hoc wireless network environment. We examined and classified major routing attacks and presented a comprehensive survey on the state-of-the-art mechanisms and solutions designed to defeat such attacks. A summary of the secure routing mechanisms surveyed is presented in Table 1. The current security mechanisms, each defeats one or few routing attacks. Designing routing protocols resistant to multiple attacks remains a challenging task.

Table 1 Comparison and summary of different routing security mechanisms

Protocol	Security mechanisms	Attacks prevented	Comments
SEAD [6]	– One-way hash chains	– Prevents an attacker from forging better metrics or sequence numbers in routing update packets	– Used with DSDV – Designed to protect routing update packets – Does not prevent an attacker from tampering other fields or from using the learned metric and sequence number for sending new routing updates
Ariadne [7]	– One-way hash chains	– Prevents attackers from tampering uncompromised routes consisting of uncompromised nodes – Immune to wormhole attack	– Used with DSR – Provides a strong defense against attacks that modify and fabricate routing information – Prone to selfish node attack
SAR [12]	– Quality of Protection (QoP) metric	– Uses sequence numbers and timestamps to stop replay attacks in routing update packets	– Used with AODV – Route discovered may not be the shortest route in terms of hop-count, but it is always secured – Defends gainst modification and fabrication attacks

(continued)

Table 1 (continued)

Protocol	Security mechanisms	Attacks prevented	Comments
SRP [16]	– Secure certificate server	– Defends against attacks that disrupt the route discovery process and guarantees to identify the correct topological information	– Used with DSR, ZRP – Lack of validation mechanism for route maintenance messages – Prone to wormhole attacks and invisible node attacks
ARAN [21]	– Secure certificate server	– Provides network services like authentication and non-repudiation	– Used with AODV, DSR – Heavy asymmetric cryptographic computation – Prone to wormhole attack if accurate time synchronozation is not available
CONFID-ANT [2]	– Monitor – Reputation System – Path Manager – Trust Manager	– Attacks on packet forwarding and routing are defended efficiently	– Used with DSR – Detection based reputation system has few limitations – Vulnerable to spoofing and sybil attacks
Rushing Attacks and Defenses [8]	– Secure Neighbor Detection – Secure Route Delegation – Randomized Route Request Forwarding	– By limiting the total number of requests sent by a node and random forwarding, it prevents rushing attack to a certain level	– Used with DSR, ARIADNE – Network is still prone to rushing attacks if an attacker can compromise k nodes – Higher overhead than other protocols, but currently it is the only protocol that can defend against rushing attacks
Wormhole Attacks and Defenses [10]	– Packet Leashes – Merkle Hash Tree – One-way Hash Chains	– TIK when implemeted with packet leaches, effectively stops wormhole and DoS attacks	– Not feasible in resource constraint networks due to the expensive cryptographic mechanisms implemented – Accurate time synchronization is not easy to obtain
Sybil Attacks and Defenses [15]	– Radio Resource Testing – Random Key Predistribution – one-way Pseudo Random Hash Function	– Multi-space Pairwise Key Distribution is most effective mechanism against sybil attack	– First work that proposes various defense mechanisms against the Sybil attacks
TESLA [20]	– One-way Hash Chain	– Uses loose time synchronization and delayed time synchronization to provide secure broadcast	– Vulnerable to DoS attacks as malicious nodes can create buffer overflow state – Accurate time synchronization is not easy to obtain

Acknowledgement This works was supported by the DoD Defense-wide RDTE grant on Secure Telecommunication Networks.

References

1. J. Barkley, NIST Special Publication: Symmetric Key Cryptography, http://csrc.nist.gov/publications/nistpubs/800-7/node208. html
2. S. Buchegger and J. L. Boudec, Performance Analysis of the CONFIDANT Protocol Cooperation Of Nodes Fairness In Dynamic Ad-hoc NeTworks, *In Proc. of IEEE/ACM Symposium on Mobile Ad Hoc Networking and Computing (MobiHOC)*, Jun. 2002.
3. T. H. Clausen, G. Hansen, L. Christensen, and G. Behrmann, The Optimized Link State Routing Protocol, Evaluation Through Experiments and Simulation, *Proc. of IEEE Symp. on Wireless Personal Mobile Communications 2001*, Sep. 2001.
4. W. Du, J. Deng, Y. S. Han, and P. K. Varshney, A Pairwise Key Pre-distribution Scheme for Wireless Sensor Networks, *ACM CCS 2003*, Oct. 2003, pp. 42–51.
5. Z. J. Haas, The Routing Algorithm for the Reconfigurable Wireless Networks, *Proc. of ICUPC 1997*, Vol 2, Oct. 1997, pp. 562–566.
6. Y. -C. Hu, D. B. Johnson and A. Perrig, SEAD: Secure Efficient Distance Vector Routing for Mobile Wireless Ad Hoc Networks, *Fourth IEEE Workshop on Mobile Computing Systems and Applications (WMCSA'02)*, Jun. 2002.
7. Y. -C. Hu, D. B. Johnson, and A. Perrig, Ariadne: A Secure On-Demand Routing Protocol for Ad Hoc Networks, *Mobicom'02*, 2002.
8. Y. -C. Hu, D. B. Johnson, and A. Perrig, Rushing Attacks and Defense in Wireless Ad Hoc Network Routing Protocols, *WiSe 2003*, 2003.
9. Y. -C. Hu, D. B. Johnson, and A. Perrig, Efficient Security Mechanisms for Routing Protocols, *The 10th Annual Network and Distributed System Security Symp. (NDSS)*, Feb. 2003.
10. Y. -C. Hu, A. Perrig, and D. B. Johnson, Packet Leashes: A Defense against Wormhole Attacks in Wireless Networks, *Infocom* 2003.
11. D. B. Johnson and D. A. Maltz, Dynamic Source Routing in Ad Hoc Wireless Networks, *Mobile Computing*, Kluwer, Dordrecht, Vol 353, 1996, pp. 153–181.
12. R. Kravets, S. Yi, and P. Naldurg, A Security-Aware Routing Protocol for Wireless Ad Hoc Networks, *In ACM Symp. on Mobile Ad Hoc Networking and Computing*, 2001.
13. S. Murthy and J. J. Garcia-Luna-Aceves, An Efficient Routing Protocol for Wireless Networks, *ACM Mobile Networks and Applications Journal, Special Issue on Routing in Mobile Communication Networks*, Vol 1, No 2, Oct. 1996, pp. 183–197.
14. C. S. R. Murthy and B. S. Manoj, Ad Hoc Wireless Networks: Architectures and Protocols, Prentice Hall PTR, 2004.
15. J. Newsome, E. Shi, D. Song, and A. Perrig, The Sybil Attack in Sensor Networks: Analysis & Defenses, *Proc. of the 3rd Intl. Symp. on Information Processing in Sensor Networks*, 2004.
16. P. Papadimitratos and Z. J. Haas, Secure Routing for Mobile Ad hoc Networks, *In Proc. of the SCS Communication Networks and Distributed Systems Modeling and Simulation Conference (CNDS 2002)*, Jan. 2002.
17. V. D. Park and M. S. Corson, A Highly Adaptive Distributed Routing Algorithm for Mobile Wireless Networks, *IEEE Infocom 1997*, Apr. 1997, pp. 1405–1413.
18. C. E. Perkins and P. Bhagwat, Highly Dynamic Destination-Sequenced Distance-Vector Routing (DSDV) for Mobile Computers, *SIGCOMM'94 Conf. on Communications Architectures, Protocols and Applications*, Aug. 1994, pp. 234–244.
19. C. E. Perkins and E. M. Royer, Ad Hoc On-Demand Distance Vector Routing, *IEEE Workshop on Mobile Computing Systems and Applications 1999*, Feb. 1999, pp. 90–100.
20. A. Perrig, R. Canetti, D. Tygar, and D. Song, The TESLA Broadcast Authentication Protocol, RSA Cryptobytes *(RSA Laboratories)*, Vol 5, No 2, Summer/Fall 2002, pp. 2–13.

21. K. Sanzgiri, B. Dahill, B. N. Levine, C. Shields, and E. M. Belding-Royer, A Secure Routing Protocol for Ad hoc Networks, *The 10th IEEE Intl. Conf. on Network Protocol (ICNP)*, Nov. 2002.
22. P. Sinha, R. Sivakumar, and V. Bharghavan, CEDAR: A Core Extraction Distributed Ad Hoc Routing Algorithm, *IEEE Journal On Selected Areas in Communications*, Vol 17, No 8, Aug. 1999, pp. 1454–1466.
23. W. Stallings, Cryptography and Network Security: Principles and Practices, 3rd edition, Prentice Hall, New Jersey, 2003.
24. R. Szewczyk, V. Wen, D. Culler, J. D. Tygar, and A. Perrig, SPINS: Security Protocols for Sensor Networks, *In 7th Annual ACM Intl. Conf. on Mobile Computing and Networks (Mobicom 2001)*, 2001.
25. Y. -C. Tseng, S.-Y. Ni, Y.-S. Chen, and J.-P. Sheu, The Broadcast Storm Problem in a Mobile Ad Hoc Network, *ACM Wireless Networks*, Vol 8, No 2, Mar. 2002, pp. 153–167.
26. J. Wu and F. Dai, A Generic Distributed Broadcast Scheme in Ad Hoc Wireless Networks, *IEEE Transactions on Computers*, Vol 53, No 10, Oct. 2004, pp. 1343–1354.

Insider Threat Assessment: Model, Analysis and Tool

Ramkumar Chinchani, Duc Ha, Anusha Iyer, Hung Q. Ngo, and Shambhu Upadhyaya

Contents

1 Introduction

Insider threat is typically attributed to legitimate users who maliciously leverage their system privileges, and familiarity and proximity to their computational environment to compromise valuable information or inflict damage. According to the annual CSI/FBI surveys conducted since 1996, internal attacks and insider abuse

R. Chinchani (✉)
Computer Science and Engineering, State University of New York at Buffalo, Amherst, NY 14260, USA
e-mail: rc27@cse.buffalo.edu

S.C.-H. Huang et al. (eds.), *Network Security*, DOI 10.1007/978-0-387-73821-5_7,
© Springer Science+Business Media, LLC 2010

form a significant portion of reported incidents. The strongest indication yet that insider threat is very real is given by the recent study [2] jointly conducted by CERT and the US Secret Service; the first of its kind, which provides an in-depth insight into the problem in a real-world setting. However, there is no known body of work which addresses this problem effectively. There are several challenges, beginning with understanding the threat.

- **Insider threat is a low base rate problem.** Perpetrators of insiders attacks are users with legitimate authorization, and therefore, it is difficult to predict or protect against these attacks. Consequently, security officers view these attacks as unpreventable, resulting in inaction.
- **Insider threat is misperceived.** Organizations often concentrate on external attacks, almost exclusively, mainly because security audit tools and modeling techniques are readily available which aid in finding vulnerabilities and fixing them. On the other hand, insider threat is not correctly perceived because it is difficult to *measure*, and the lack of tools and techniques does not help the situation. Therefore, any good model or assessment methodology is already a significant advance.
- **Insider threat is high impact.** Although insider attacks may not occur as frequently as external attacks, they have a higher rate of success, can go undetected, and pose a much greater risk than external attacks. This is due to the fact that insiders enjoy certain important advantages over external adversaries. They are familiar about their targets and the security countermeasures in place. Therefore, very damaging attacks can be launched with only a short or nonexistent reconnaissance phase.

In a nutshell, insider threat is a complex problem involving both computational elements and human factors. As a long-term process to mitigate this threat, steps such as pre-hire screening of employees, training, and education can be undertaken. While all these practical measures will reduce the threat, they cannot eliminate it altogether, and some incidents can still occur. A possible solution it would seem is an overall increase in monitoring, logging, and security countermeasures. However, it only leads to general inconvenience. Moreover, in an organization, it sends wrong signals of distrust between the management and the employees. We seek a methodology by which very specific and targeted countermeasures can be deployed. This approach occupies a sweet spot between complete inaction and intrusive solutions. Central to such an approach is an effective threat modeling methodology, accompanied by threat assessment and analysis, with the goal of discovering likely tactics and strategy of an adversary so that appropriate countermeasures can be taken.

Insiders can cause damage either by: (1) remaining within their default set of privileges or (2) exceeding them by seeking new information and capability through a repertoire which contains not only common attacks but also unconventional ones such as social engineering. The problem of insider threat assessment is precisely the problem of evaluating the damage which can potentially occur in these two cases.

Threat assessment methodologies are not new in general, and techniques such as attack graphs [23, 28, 31, 32] and privilege graphs [10, 26] are already known. However, these techniques have been proposed to primarily model external attacks and hence, have a limited appeal to insider threat. Moreover, there are also scalability concerns regarding both model specification as well as subsequent threat analysis. Specifying a model requires information in very exact detail, making it impractical to generate the model manually. Instead, current approaches generate models automatically [31] via information obtained from live penetration testing of an organization network. However, given the possibility of systemic failures, a large part of the network is typically excluded during testing, resulting in an abbreviated model instance. Consequently, any further inferences drawn from the model are questionable. Also, threat analysis following model specification very quickly runs into the problem of intractability. To summarize, these modeling techniques are not suitable for addressing insider threat both for technical and practical reasons. We seek to devise a more appropriate modeling and assessment methodology.

1.1   Summary of Contributions

There are two prominent contributions in this chapter[1]. As our first contribution, we propose a new threat model called *key challenge graph*. The main idea behind insider threat modeling is to focus on a legitimate user's view of an organization's network. In order to estimate the threat when insiders remain within their privilege levels, we only need to represent the basic network connectivity and access control mechanisms that are in place. Additionally, to assess the threat when insiders exceed their privilege levels, we also need to represent knowledge and location of key information and capability, not normally accessible, which may assist him in his attack. The overall goal, like attack graphs, is to understand insider threat from a global perspective rather than just single-point incidents. In terms of threat variety, our model supports not only conventional attacks, but also more complex scenarios such as social engineering. One important design consideration is the granularity of information and the nature of representation. Due to the unavailability of tools to scan for weaknesses in the context of insider threat, a significant portion of the model specification task can fall upon the security analyst. Our modeling methodology allows models to be manually specified, and the resulting model instances are only polynomially-sized with respect to the input size. To demonstrate applications of our model, we have constructed some typical scenarios motivated by the CERT/USS insider threat study which analyzed threats in the banking and financial sector.

---

[1] Parts of this chapter have appeared and will appear in our papers [7, 8].

As our next contribution, we investigate and analyze the problem of automated threat analysis. It turns out that the problem is **NP**-hard, even to approximate to within a large ratio. Nevertheless, we have designed two algorithms for this purpose - one which solves the problem to optimality but takes exponential time, and the other which is a polynomial-time heuristic. We benchmark the algorithms for scalability and quality of threat analysis. The impact of threat analysis is manyfold. Given an organization network and its people, it is possible to assess whether existing security countermeasures are adequate. If not, threat analysis allows recommendations to be made to improve security. In the face of insider threat, sometimes, the only countermeasure is installing monitoring and logging systems for non-repudiability. Finally, if several intrusion detection systems are installed, threat analysis can also assign appropriate weights to intrusion detection sensors based on the likely areas of insider activity inside the organization.

1.2 Chapter Organization

The rest of the chapter is organized as follows. We present our model in Sect. 3 and show its application on representative illustrations in Sect. 4. Next, we describe the threat analysis methodology in Sect. 5 and also present insights into the complexity of the problem. Related work is discussed in Sect. 6, and finally, closing remarks are in Sect. 7.

2 Insider Threat: A Review

Defining the term "insider" in an airtight manner is hard because the boundary between insiders and outsiders is fuzzy. In the current literature, the term "insider" has been used in a very broad sense. Neumann et al. [25] pointed out that there are various classes of insiders depending on the criteria chosen. For example, based on the nature of access, an insider can be termed as someone who is employed by an organization or an individual who breaks into an organization's network and masquerades as a legitimate user. Insider misuse could either be a deliberate attack or accidental, such as an inadvertent virus download. Nevertheless, both have significant security implications. A position paper by Brad Wood [34] is a comprehensive commentary on the various facets of insider threat. An insider is accurately described in terms of attributes such as knowledge, privileges, skills, risk, and tactics. One of the notable and relevant statements made is that an insider can no longer be assumed to be bound by physical confines. The paper rightly concludes with an observation that there is a gap between academic research and operator requirement in the field due to the lack of practical tools and techniques.

We assume that every legitimate user is an insider. Note that the term "insider" can have both physical and logical connotation. Physical outsiders can be logical insiders and vice versa. For example, an authorized user who may be physically far away from an organization but has wireless or VPN connectivity. Similarly, users may be physically inside an organization but have no authorized access to use the computation infrastructure. Insiders are in a unique position with the privileges entrusted to them and the knowledge about their computational environment, and this already translates directly to a certain amount of capability. Insider abuse can occur within this default capability, but more dangerous scenarios occur when an insider widens his or her realm of capability. Since insiders have access privileges to use the computational infrastructure, it represents resources at their disposal that can be used against the parent organization, so resources for an insider attack are freely available. Unlike external attackers who use the Internet as an umbrella of anonymity and can be sloppy, insiders have a strong incentive to avoid detection. They are a part of an organization and bound by the organization policy, and if caught, an organization has all the necessary information about the insider and the legal resources to prosecute him or her. External attackers can become insiders too by compromising an internal system and learning about the computers in the neighborhood. However, there is an inherent risk to the attacker that the compromise may be discovered and the corresponding security hole patched.

The insider threat study [2] reports that financial gain is the main motivating factor behind most insider attacks; any other motive is simply not worth the risk. The financial gain can be realized in different ways depending on the organization. In a financial institution such as a bank, likely targets are customer account records or perhaps company accounts, where there is a direct access to funds. In other cases, an insider may not obtain immediate monetary gain, such as in a software company where the real value lies in the proprietary software code. While it is possible to envision several other scenarios, it is not realistic to expect that each and every one of them can be modeled, mainly because it entails a significant effort on the part of the security officer.

3 Modeling Insider Threat

In this section, we elaborately discuss our modeling methodology. But before that we state some working assumptions based on generally accepted notions about insider threat along with results from the recent study [2].

3.1 Model Overview

In our model, we assume that an attacker is goal-oriented. Also, he or she is already aware of the location of his or her potential targets and how to reach them, obviating the need for reconnaissance. These assumptions closely model an insider, and this is one of the reasons why our model is most suitable for this class of threats. We also assume that a successful compromise of a target is not possible if there is no channel of interaction. Finally, an attacker may not be able to use an existing channel of interaction with a potential target due to a strong security mechanism in place on that channel. This may force attacker to seek alternate routes to reach the target. Each sub-target that is compromised requires extra effort but can provide the attacker with additional information/capability and another front to continue the attack. Given a model specification, the goal of vulnerability analysis is to exhaustively find the different ways in which attacker can reach the target.

Prior to the formal definition of our model, which we call a *key challenge graph*, we describe the various components.

- Any physical entity on which some information or capability can be acquired is represented as a *vertex* of a graph, which shall be called the *key challenge graph*. Let V be the set of vertices. Typically, vertices are points in the network where some information may be gained such as a database server or simply any computer system whose resources can be used or misused.

- Each piece of information or capability present at any vertex v is represented as a *key* called Key$_v$. Let $\mathcal{K}$ denote the set of keys. For example, records in a database, passwords stored on a computer, or computational resources of a computer can be represented as keys. When an attacker visits a vertex, he is empowered with this additional information or capability. Note that this key should not be confused with cryptographic keys. A key in our model is only an abstraction.

- If there is a channel of access or communication between two physical entities which facilitates interaction, then a *directed edge* is created between the two corresponding vertices, pointing to the direction of the allowed interaction. Multiple channels of communication are possible, hence there can be multiple edges between two vertices. For example, a channel of communication exist between an "ssh" server and a client computer, which induces an edge in our graph model. Let E denote the set of edges.

- The presence of a security measure or an enforced security policy protects the resources and allows only authorized interaction. This deterrence is represented as a *key challenge* on the corresponding channel of communication. An example of a key challenge is the password authentication required prior to accessing to a server. A key challenge is an abstraction to capture access control.

- If a user does not have the right key to the key challenge, then he incurs a significant *cost* in breaking or circumventing the security policy; legitimate access incurs only a smaller cost of meeting the key challenge. For example, when password authentication is used, if a user knows the password, he incurs little or no cost, while another user who does not know the password will incur a higher cost in breaking the password. The cost metric is a relative quantity signifying the amount of deterrence offered by one security measure over another. It has been abstracted as a non-negative integer for the purposes of our model. Figure 1 illustrates the building block of our model.

- The starting point of an attack could be one or more vertices in the graph, which are assumed to be initially compromised by the attacker. Let V_s denote this set.

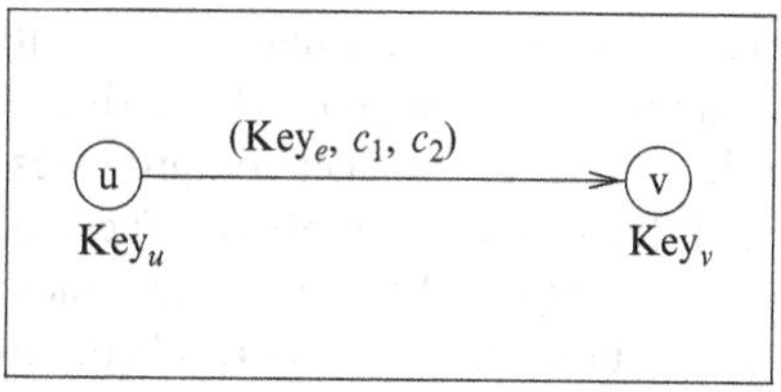

Fig. 1 Basic building block of a key challenge graph. Key_e is the key challenge of the edge $e = (u, v)$, c_1 is the cost one has to pay to traverse (u, v) without having Key_e, and $c_2 < c_1$ is the corresponding cost if the attacker has the key

Table 1 Model components and the captured abstractions

Model Component	Abstraction
Vertex	Hosts, People
Edge	Connectivity, Reachability
Key	Information, Capability
Key Challenge	Access Control
Starting Vertex	Location of insider
Target Vertex	Actual target
Cost of Attack	Threat analysis metric

- The target of an attack could also be one or more vertices in the graph. In case of multiple targets, the goal is to compromise all of them. Let the set of target vertices be denoted by V_t. An example of a target is a source code repository for a commercial product.

Table 1 provides a summary of all the abstractions captured by our model.

3.2 The Min-Hack Problem

In what follows, we formalize the aforementioned concepts.

Definition 3.1 (Key Challenge Graph). A *Key Challenge Graph G* is a tuple:

$$G = (V, E; \mathcal{K}, V_s, V_t, \kappa, \delta),$$

where V is the set of vertices, E is the set of directed edges (we allow multi-edges, i.e., G is a multi-graph), V_s is the initial set of compromised vertices, and V_t is the set of target vertices ($V_t \cap V_s = \emptyset$), $\kappa : V \to \mathcal{K}$ is a function that assigns keys to vertices, $\delta : E \to \mathcal{K} \times \mathbb{N} \times \mathbb{N}$ is a function that assigns key challenges and costs to edges.

For instance, $\kappa(v_1) = k_0$ means that the key k_0 can be obtained at vertex v_1, $\delta(e_1) = (k_1, c_1, c_2)$ implies an assignment of a key challenge to edge e_1, which requires an attacker to produce the key k_1. If he or she cannot do so, then he or she incurs a cost c_1; otherwise, he or she incurs a smaller cost c_2. An adversary begins his or her attack at some point in the set of compromised nodes in the graph and proceeds by visiting more and more vertices until the target(s) is reached. At each visited vertex, the attacker adds the corresponding key to his or her collection of keys picked up at previous vertices. Once an attacker compromises a vertex, he continues to have control over it until the attack is completed. Therefore, any vertex appears exactly once in the attack description. While a trivial attack can be performed by visiting all reachable vertices until the target is reached, cost constraints occlude such free traversals.

Definition 3.2 (Attacks and successful attacks). An *attack* is a finite and ordered sequence of a vertices $(v_1, v_2, \ldots, v_m)$ satisfying the following conditions:

1. For each $i \in \{1, \ldots, m\}$, there is some vertex $u \in V_s \cup \{v_1, \ldots, v_{i-1}\}$ such that $(u, v_i) \in E$,
2. $V_s \cap \{v_1, \ldots, v_m\} = \emptyset$,

The first condition is meant to say that the attacker must get to a new vertex v_i via a visited (or compromised) vertex u. A *successful attack* is an attack that contains all target nodes in V_t

The next important aspect of the model is the cost metric. Although an attack is defined exclusively in terms of vertices, the cost incurred by the attacker at a vertex is mainly dependent on the edge that he or she chooses to visit the vertex. We first define the cost of traversing an edge and then the cost of visiting a new vertex. The latter is the basic unit of cost metric in our model.

Definition 3.3 (Cost of Traversing an Edge). Let V^* be the set of visited vertices so far, including the initially compromised vertices, i.e., $V_0 \subseteq V^*$. For $u \in V^*$ and $v \notin V^*$, the *cost of traversing the edge* $e = (u, v) \in E$, given that $\delta(e) = (k, c_1, c_2)$, is c_1 if $k \notin \{\kappa(w) \mid w \in V^*\}$; otherwise, it is c_2. (In general, $c_1 > c_2$.)

If $e = (u, v) \notin E$, for technical convenience, we assume that $\delta(e) = (k, \infty, \infty)$, where k is some unique key no node has.

Definition 3.4 (Cost of Visiting a New Vertex). Define V^* as above. The *cost of visiting a new vertex* $v \notin V^*$ is defined to be

$$\alpha(v, V^*) = \min\{\text{cost of traversing } (u, v) \mid u \in V^*\}. \tag{1}$$

The cost of an entire attack is measured as a sum of the effort required to compromise individual vertices by attempting to counter the key challenges on the edges with or without the keys that an attacker has already picked up.

Definition 3.5 (Cost of an attack). The *cost of an attack* $(v_1, \ldots, v_m)$ is defined as:

$$\text{MINHACK}(v_1, \ldots, v_m) = \sum_{i=1}^{m} \alpha(v_i, V_i), \tag{2}$$

where $V_i = V_s \cup \{v_1, \ldots, v_{i-1}\}$.

The MIN-HACK problem is the problem of finding a minimum cost successful attack, given a key challenge graph.

4 Modeling Methodology and Applications

In this section, we describe the applications of our modeling methodology. First we dispel concerns which are normally attributed to most theoretical modeling methodologies regarding their practicality. Later, we demonstrate through illustrations the relevance of our model in capturing different types of threat scenarios.

4.1 Practical Considerations

One major benefit of using theoretical models is that they are inexpensive and do not require actual system implementation and testing. However, such benefits can be offset if the model is difficult to use or if several facets of the modeling methodology are unclear. We answer some of outstanding questions which may arise.

How is a model generated? Model specification begins by identifying the scope of the threat; it could be a very small part of the organization or the whole organization itself. The algorithm BUILD-MODEL below gives a step-by-step procedure to construct a model instance. Note that the resulting model instance has a size which is only polynomial in the input information.

BUILD-MODEL(Network Information)
1. Identify potential target nodes denoted by set T.
2. $\forall v \in T$, identify all hosts/people denoted by u having access to v.
   Add (u, v) to the set of edges E.
3. $\forall (u, v) \in E$, identify key challenges and calibrate costs.
   Add the key challenge to the set δ.
4. $\forall$ keys in δ, identify nodes containing these keys.
   Add each such node to T and goto Step 1.
5. Repeat until no new nodes are added to T.

Who constructs the model? The model is constructed by someone who is aware of the organization network and location of various resources. This is typically the system administrator and/or the security analyst. Note that for the purposes of evaluating security, we assume that whatever a security analyst can model, an insider can model as well. In terms of the time and effort required to construct the model, since our model takes a high-level view of the network, the model instance is not significantly larger than the actual network representation. Given an OPNET-like tool to assist in instantiating a model, we expect that a security analyst will not have to invest a substantial effort. We are currently implementing one such tool. Figure 2 shows snapshots of our tool in action.

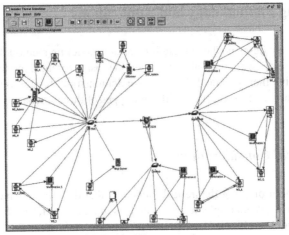

(a) Physical Representation

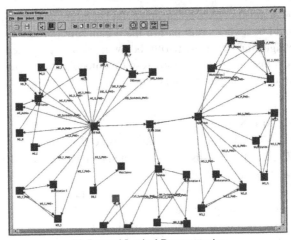

(b) Internal Logical Representation

Fig. 2 Representing an example physical network and converting it into an instance of key challenge graph

How are costs defined? Costs in our framework are a metric representative of the resistance put up by an access control mechanism. In cases such as cryptographic access control mechanisms, there are standards to go by. For example, the strength of a cryptographic algorithm is indicative of the time required for an adversary to break it. However, in other cases, the solution may be more systemic such as intrusion detection systems, where the actual costs may not be very clear. In such cases, a value relative to known standards can be used. Note that it is quite possible for two security analysts to assign different costs, and it will depend on what each perceives is the more appropriate value.

4.2 Illustrations

We now turn to the application of our model to specific examples. We have performed small scale modeling of banking environments based on [1] and [2].

A Financial Institution Example. Consider the following description. From his workstation, every teller can perform sundry personal accounting tasks. Each personal account transaction cannot exceed US$ 5,000. A manager has to endorse any larger transactions and personally handles accounts involving business organizations. The business accounts database is kept separate from the one that houses personal accounts. Any bank transaction, either by the teller or the manager, which operates on a database is encrypted. The communication between the teller's computer and the personal accounts database is frequent but not of high value, so it uses a lower strength symmetric encryption. On the other hand, the manager authenticates himself or herself to a PKI server with his or her credentials and obtains a session key to talk to the database and complete the transaction. Both the databases are protected behind a firewall to prevent any external attacks. Another key piece of information known to the teller is that the manager does not apply security patches to his or her computer frequently, and that the manager's computer could be vulnerable.

Now, consider an insider threat that manifests in the form of a rogue teller and the target being the business account database. Using the modeling methodology described earlier, we convert this description into our model (shown in Fig. 3).

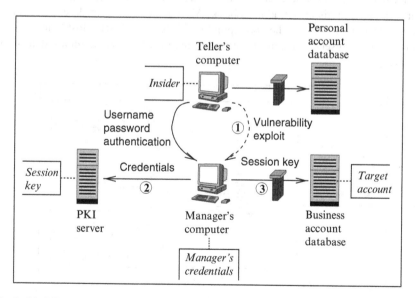

Fig. 3 Modeling an example of insider threat scenario

Using our KG model representation, the steps taken by an insider (shown numerically in Fig. 3) can be easily seen. The most likely sequence of steps is: (1) use a vulnerability exploit to compromise the manager's computer, (2) use the manager's credentials to obtain a session key from the PKI server, and (3) use the session key to attack the business account database. Simply with a key piece of information, an insider is able to launch a very damaging attack, and our KG model is able to provide a very intuitive view of the attack. The solution in this scenario is trivial, i.e., the manager's computer is to be patched.

We point out a few properties based on the example. The sequence of steps taken by the attacker is generally *not* a path. This is a striking departure from the attack graph model, where attacks appear as paths in the graph. Also, note that a very damaging insider attack is possible even with only one vulnerability in the network description.

A Resource-based Attack. We present a illustration of a denial of service (DoS) flood attack on a mail server through email worms. This attack example is based on our modeling experience in an academic environment. Transmitted via email, the most commonly used medium, these worms are one of the most effective types of social engineering attacks. They exploit a recipient's curiosity to open a virus attachment. At this point, the virus replicates and sends a copy to every entry in the recipient's address book. The flood of emails eventually overloads the mail server and results in a successful DoS attack.

Consider the following scenario (see Fig. 4). A single mail server provides email service to users User1, User2, and User3 in the organization. Each user has the other user's email id in his or her address book. All mails to and from these users must travel via the mail server. The corresponding hosts, i.e., Host1, Host2, and Host3 from which the users work, are running resource usage based anomaly detection

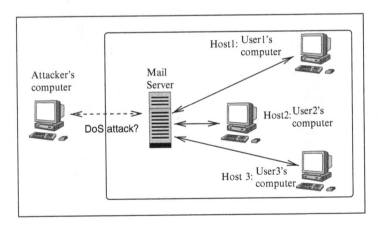

Fig. 4 A Mail server configuration

Fig. 5 Modeling the email
scenario

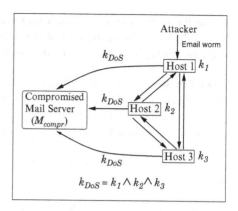

$$k_{DoS} = k_1 \wedge k_2 \wedge k_3$$

systems, and spikes in resource usage or outgoing connections are quickly flagged. Currently known email worms are stealthy, and they spread by using very little resources and limiting the number of connections made to the mail server. Due to these reasons, a mail flood on the mail server cannot be caused by infecting just one host. However, the maximum number of connections that a mail server can tolerate before being overwhelmed is less than or equal to the sum total of the maximum allowed outgoing rates of all three infected hosts. Therefore, a successful DoS attack entails the infection of all three host machines.

The KG model specification is shown in Fig. 5. Each physical entity reachable via email becomes a node. Here, the nodes are (1) the three client machines, (2) the attacker's machine, and (3) the mail server. Reaching any entity signifies that it is infected. There is an edge between two hosts (X,Y) if Y is in X's address book. Security policies enforced on individual nodes translate into the cost of traversing an edge into that node. Now, we model the threat of a DoS attack through a malicious email initiated from an attacker. There is an edge from the attacker to Host 1, signifying that the attacker will initially release the worm to Host 1. Compromising a host gives the attacker a certain capability in terms of resources, represented by the keys K_i, $i = \{1,2,3\}$. Finally, bringing down the mail server requires the compromise of all three clients. Therefore, the minimal key challenge for any edge to achieve a flooded mail server M_{compr} is $k_{DoS} = (k_1 \wedge k_2 \wedge k_3)$. We have omitted the costs because infecting a host is trivial and there is very little cost involved.

From the KG model specification, it can be seen that a distributed denial of service attack can be prevented if the mail server is instructed to randomly drop mail connections from at least one target, i.e., at least one k_i is not reached. A more permanent fix would require updating the anti-virus signatures when they are released. In our approach, since we model DoS attacks through potential targets and accrued capability, we are able to easily ask whether an attacker has gained critical mass to launch the DoS attack. Referring to attack graphs and model checking, DoS attacks violate the liveness property that a user will eventually have access to a service. Model checking [20] in its current state has certain limitations. While modeling safety properties is easily done, modeling "liveness" properties is hard.

Social Engineering Attacks. The KG model allows for a very general kind of communication channel. This means that it is possible to represent not only wired and wireless network media, but also channels such as telephone lines, and this still falls within the framework of our model. For example, when a customer calls a credit card company, a representative poses a key challenge in the form of date of birth or social security number and divulges information only when the right information is presented.

Colluding Insiders. In order to improve the chances of a successful attack, two or more attackers controlling different vertices may collude and share the keys that they possess. In this case, the set V_0 contains all these vertices and $|V_0| > 1$. This situation is no different from the one where a single attacker may initially have control over multiple vertices. This would not complicate the analysis of the model as an attack is represented not as a path but rather as a sequence of compromised vertices.

5   Threat Analysis

In this section, we address various aspects of threat analysis. Looking at this task from an algorithmic complexity viewpoint, a good attacking strategy for an insider is in some sense equivalent to a good algorithm or approximation algorithm [14] to find a minimum-cost attack on the key challenge graph. An insider is unlikely to adopt any other strategy because it will lead to an attack that is easily detected.

We are first interested in knowing the computational difficulty of analyzing a general instance of a key challenge graph. This provides very useful insight into the problem based on which automated threat analysis algorithms can be developed.

5.1   On the Complexity of Analyzing Key Challenge Graphs

We will first address the question of how hard it is to approximate MIN-HACK to within some ratio. We will show that MIN-HACK is not approximable to within $g_c(n) := 2^{(\log n)^{1-\delta}}$, where $\delta = 1 - \frac{1}{\log\log^c n}$, for any $c < 1/2$. This negative result will be shown via three independent reductions, which are of independent interests at least for pedagogical reason. The reductions are from MINIMUM LABEL COVER (MLC), from a PCP characterization of **NP** (mimicking an idea of Dinur and Safra [12]), and from the MINIMUM MONOTONE SATISFYING ASSIGNMENT (MMSA) problem. In fact, there is an hierarchy of MMSA numbered from

MMSA_i, $i = 1, 2, \ldots$ Our reduction shows that MIN-HACK is on top of this hierarchy, namely for any $i \geq 4$,

$$\text{PCP} \ll \text{MMSA}_3 \ll \text{MLC} \ll \text{MMSA}_4 \ll \cdots \ll \text{MMSA}_i \ll \text{MIN-HACK},$$

where $\ll$ denote the relation "polynomially related approximation ratio." Although quite unlikely, if MIN-HACK can be approximated to within $g_c(n)$, then the hierarchy collapses. We have not been able to reduce any problem in "class 4" to MIN-HACK. (Class 4 consists of problems with non-approximability ratio n^8 like MAX-CLIQUE and COLORING [6].)

5.1.1 Approximation Algorithms and Approximation Ratios

More detailed definitions and notations relating to optimization problems and approximation algorithms can be found in several books such as [14,27,33]. We briefly define related concepts here.

Following [9], an NP optimization problem Φ is a 4-tuple $(I, \text{sol}, \text{cost}, \text{OPT})$, where

- I is the set of polynomial-time recognizable instances of Φ.
- For each $x \in I$, $\text{sol}(x)$ is the set of feasible solutions for x. Feasible solutions are polynomially bounded in size and polynomial-time decidable.
- For each $x \in I$, $y \in \text{sol}(x)$, $\text{cost}(x, y)$ – a positive integer – is the objective value of the solution y. The objective function cost is polynomial-time computable.
- Lastly, $\text{OPT} \in \{\min, \max\}$ refers to the goal of the optimization problem: finding a feasible solution maximizing or minimizing the objective value.

The class of NP optimization problems is denoted by NPO. The class NPO PB consists of NPO problems whose objective functions are polynomially bounded.

We use $\Phi(x)$ to denote the optimal objective value of an instance x of problem Φ. Given a feasible solution y for an instance x of Φ, the approximation ratio of y is

$$R(x, y) := \max \left\{ \frac{\text{cost}(x, y)}{\Phi(x)}, \frac{\Phi(x)}{\text{cost}(x, y)} \right\}.$$

Given a function $r : \mathbb{N} \to \mathbb{R}^+$, an $r(n)$-approximation algorithm A for Φ is a polynomial-time algorithm which, on input instance $x \in I$, returns a feasible solution y for x such that $R(x, y) \leq r(|x|)$. We will use $A(x)$ to denote $\text{cost}(x, y)$, the cost of the solution returned by A on x.

5.1.2 MINIMUM LABEL COVER$_p$

Given $p \in \mathbb{N}^+$, an instance to the MLC$_p$ problem consists of:

(1) A bipartite graph $G = (U \cup V; E)$,
(2) Two sets B_1 and B_2 of labels, one for U and one for V, and

(3) For each edge $e \in E$, a relation $\Pi_e \subseteq B_1 \times B_2$ which defines admissible pairs of labels for that edge.

A *labeling* (f_1, f_2) is a pair of functions: $f_1 : U \rightarrow 2^{B_1}$ and $f_2 : V \rightarrow 2^{B_2} \setminus \{\emptyset\}$. Basically, a labeling associates a set of labels to each $u \in U$, and a non-empty set of labels to each $v \in V$. A labeling *covers* an edge $e = (u, v) \in E$ if, for every label b_2 assigned to v, there is some label b_1 assigned to u such that $(b_1, b_2) \in \Pi_e$. A labeling is a *complete cover* (or *complete label cover*) if it covers all edges. Let $U = \{u_1, \ldots, u_n\}$. The L_p-*cost* of a labeling (f_1, f_2) is the L_p-norm of the vector $(|f_1(u_1)|, \ldots, |f_1(u_n)|) \in \mathbb{Z}^n$. Specifically,

$$L_p\text{-cost}(f_1, f_2) = (|f_1(u_1)|^p + \cdots + |f_1(u_n)|^p)^{1/p} .$$

And, L_∞-cost$(f_1, f_2) = \max\{|f_1(u_i)| : 1 \le i \le n\}$. The MLC$_p$ *problem* is to find a complete cover with minimum L_p-cost.

It is not necessary to assign more than one label to any vertex $v \in V$. If a complete label cover assigns multiple labels to some vertex $v \in V$, then the labeling obtained by removing all but one label from v is also a complete covering. Consequently, henceforth, we can impose the condition that vertices in V get only one label each.

Hardness results for this problem were devised in [5, 12, 21]. The current best result is that of [12], which says that MLC$_p$ is NP-hard to approximate to within $\Theta\left(2^{(\log n)^{1-\delta}}\right)$, where $\delta = (\log \log n)^{-c}, \forall c < 1/2$.

5.1.3 Minimum Monotone Satisfying Assignment

A *monotone boolean formula* F is a boolean formula over the basis $\{\wedge, \vee\}$, i.e., F uses only binary connectives $\wedge$, and $\vee$. Equivalently, F is a rooted binary tree where each internal node is labeled with either $\wedge$ or $\vee$ and has exactly two children, and each leaf is a boolean variable.

The MINIMUM MONOTONE SATISFYING ASSIGNMENT (MMSA) was considered in [3] in relation to the problem of finding the length of a propositional proof. The MMSA problem is the problem of finding a truth assignment satisfying a monotone boolean formula which minimizes the number of TRUE variables. The problem was shown to be at least as hard as LABEL–COVER.

For each positive integer i, MMSA$_i$ is the restriction of MMSA to formulas of depth i. For instance, MMSA$_3$'s instances are monotone boolean formulas of the form AND of OR's of AND's. Following [12], let $\ll$ denote the relation "polynomially related approximation-ratio". The authors showed that, for all $i \ge 4$,

$$\text{PCP} \ll \text{MMSA}_3 \ll \text{MLC} \ll \text{MMSA}_4 \ll \cdots \ll \text{MMSA}_i \qquad (3)$$

5.1.4 Reducing MMSA to MIN-HACK

We need to quote the following result from Dinur and Safra [12].

Theorem 5.1. *It is NP-hard to approximate* $MMSA_3$ *to within a ratio of* $\Theta(g_c(n))$ *for any* $c < 1/2$, *where*

$$g_c(n) := 2^{(\log n)^{1-\delta}}, \quad \delta = 1 - \frac{1}{\log \log^c n}. \tag{4}$$

Thus, MMSA in general is not approximable to within $g_c(n)$, assuming P $\neq$ NP. We now describe a reduction from MMSA to MIN-HACK so that the approximation ratio is preserved (with a linear blow-up in input size).

Given a monotone boolean formula $\phi(x_1, \ldots, x_m)$, it is useful to think of ϕ as a full binary tree T, each of whose internal node is either an AND or an OR, and each of whose leaves is labeled with one of the variables $x_1, \ldots, x_m$. We give a name to each internal node of T (beside the label AND or OR) to distinguish all nodes of T.

The key challenge graph $G_\phi = (V, E; \mathcal{K}, V_s, V_t, \kappa, \delta)$ is constructed from ϕ as follows. (Refer to Fig. 6 for an illustration of the reduction.)

The key set $\mathcal{K}$ is the set of all labels of nodes in T, along with three dummy keys s, k, and k'. The three dummy keys are not the key challenge of any edge in G_ϕ.

The compromised node set V_s consists of just a node s. We abuse notations a little bit here by naming this node with the key it has.

The target node set V_t consists of a node t whose key is the label of the root of T. The idea is that getting to this node is the same as verifying that ϕ is satisfied by some truth assignment.

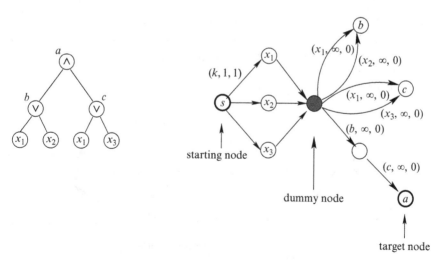

Fig. 6 Example of the reduction from MMSA to MIN-HACK

The graph G_ϕ consists of two main stages: the *truth assignment* and the *verification* stages.

The truth assignment stage consists of m edges from s to m nodes with keys $x_1, x_2, \ldots, x_m$. One always has to pay a cost of 1 to get to any of these nodes. These edges have key challenge k (a dummy key). Getting to node x_i corresponds to assigning x_i to be TRUE. Hence, the number of keys from $\{x_1, \ldots, x_k\}$ the attacker gets is the same as the number of TRUE variables in a truth assignment for ϕ. For convenience, all nodes x_1 to x_m are connected to a dummy node which has key k', another dummy key not used anywhere else. The cost to get to the dummy node is always 0. The key challenges of edges leading to the dummy node is, again, k.

The verification stage is designed to make sure that the combination of keys that the attacker gets from the first stage corresponds to a truth assignment satisfying ϕ. There are two types of components for this stage: the AND components and the OR components. For every internal node a with children b and c of T, we construct a component corresponding to a.

If a is an AND node, then connect the dummy node to a node with key a via another auxiliary node. See Fig. 7 for an illustration. The idea is that, to get the key a, one needs the keys of both of its children b and c, otherwise one pays a price of ∞. Node that, one can use a cost of $m + 1$ to represent ∞. This point will become more obvious later.

If a is an OR node, then to get the key a, we only need either key b or key c (see Fig. 8).

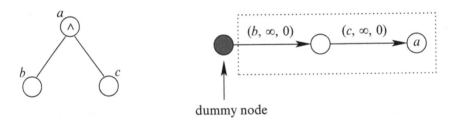

Fig. 7 AND component

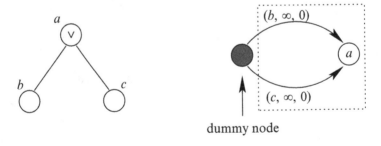

Fig. 8 OR component

Recall a note earlier saying that ∞ can be represented by $m + 1$. The proof of the following lemma asserts this point.

Lemma 5.2. *For any positive integer p. The monotone boolean formula ϕ has a truth assignment with at most p* TRUE *variables if and only if there is a successful attack on the graph G_ϕ with cost at most p.*

Proof. Note that a true assignment with all m variables assigned to TRUE would satisfy ϕ, and that a successful attack on G_ϕ of cost m can always be found (the attacker can get all keys including corresponding to a postorder traversal of T). Hence, if $p \geq m + 1$, then the theorem is trivially true. We assume $p \leq m$.

For the forward direction, assume ϕ has a truth assignment of cost p. Let X be the set of TRUE variables in this assignment. The attack in G_ϕ begins by getting all keys corresponding to variables in X with cost $p = |X|$. The internal nodes' keys can then be obtained with zero cost since ϕ is satisfied by assigning all variables in X to be TRUE. The backward direction is similar.   □

Theorem 5.3. *For every positive constant $c < 1/2$, it is NP-hard to approximate the* MIN-HACK *problem to within a ratio of $\Theta(g_c(n))$.*

Proof. This follows directly from Lemma 5.2 and Theorem 5.1.   □

We now have an "upper bound" for the hierarchy of MMSA mentioned in relation (3):

$$\text{PCP} \ll \text{MMSA}_3 \ll \text{MLC} \ll \text{MMSA}_4 \ll \cdots \ll \text{MMSA}_i \ll \text{MIN-HACK} \quad (5)$$

Consequently, if MIN-HACK is approximable to within (some constant times) $g_c(n)$, then the hierarchy collapses after MMSA_4.

5.1.5 Reducing LABEL-COVER to MIN-HACK

In this section, we present a reduction from MLC_1 to MIN-HACK which preserves the approximation ratio. Since MLC_1 was shown to be not approximable to within $g_c(n)$ for any $c < 1/2$ (unless P = NP) [12], this reduction gives another proof of the hardness result for MIN-HACK.

Consider an instance of MLC_1 consisting of a bipartite graph $G = (U \cup V, E)$, label sets B_1, B_2, and relation $\Pi_e \subseteq B_1 \times B_2$ for each edge $e \in E$. We shall construct in polynomial time an instance of MIN-HACK

$$G_{mh} = (V_{mh}, E_{mh}; \mathcal{K}, V_s, V_t, \kappa, \delta)$$

such that there is a complete covering for G_{mh} of cost at most c if and only if there is a feasible attack on G_{key} of cost at most c, for any positive integer c. Let $U = \{u_1, \ldots, u_n\}$, $V = \{v_1, \ldots, v_m\}$, $m_1 = |B_1|$, and $m_2 = |B_2|$.

Note that MLC_1 has the L_1-cost, i.e., the cost of a labeling is the total number of labels at all vertices in U, counting multiplicities. Without loss of generality, we assume that G_{mh} is feasible, namely the labeling (f_1, f_2) where $f_1(u) = B_1$, for all $u \in U$, and

$$f_2(v) \in \bigcap_{(u,v) \in E} \{b_2 \mid (b_1, b_2)\}, \quad \forall v \in V.$$

This trivial labeling has cost $m\, m_1$.

The construction of G_{mh} consists of two main components (see Fig. 9): (a) the *label acquisition* component corresponds to assigning labels to the vertices and paying the corresponding costs and (b) the *label verification* component corresponds to asserting that the labeling is valid.

The initial compromised vertex is v_s, i.e., $V_s = \{v_s\}$, and the target vertex is v_t, i.e., $V_t = \{v_t\}$. Abusing notation, we shall also use the name of a node to denote the key it possesses. (Nodes in our reduction will have different keys.)

We first define the vertices in the label acquisition component (see Fig. 10). There is a vertex (u_i, b_j^1) (whose key is (u_i, b_j^1)) for each $u_i \in U$, $b_j^1 \in B_1$, and (v_i, b_j^2)

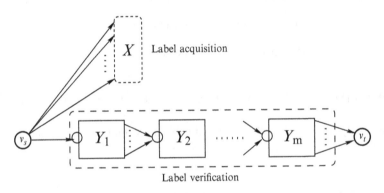

Label acquisition

Label verification

Fig. 9 Overview of the reduction from MLC_1 to MIN-HACK

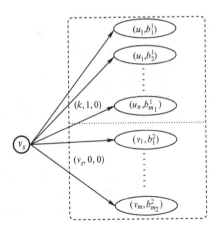

Fig. 10 The label acquisition
component

for each $v_i \in V$, and for each $b_j^2 \in B_2$. The idea is that, if vertex (w, b) is visited in an attack, then b is in the set of labels for w, where $w \in U \cup V$, and $b \in B_1 \cup B_2$. The edges in the label acquisition component are all of the form $(v_s, (w, b))$, where $w \in U \cup V$ and $b \in B_1 \cup B_2$. For each $v_i \in V$, the edges $e = (v_s, (v_i, b_j^2))$ have $\delta(e) = (v_s, 0, 0)$, namely we can assign any label b_j^2 to v_i for "free." On the other hand, for each $u_i \in U$, the edge $e = (v_s, (u_i, b_j^1))$ has $\delta(e) = (k, 1, 0)$, where k is some elusive key no vertex possesses. The idea is that adding a label b_j^1 to the set of labels of a vertex u_i imposes a cost of 1.

With the verification component, we aim to verify that, for every $v \in V$, we have picked up some label $b_2 \in B_2$ for v such that, for every edge $(u, v) \in E$, $\Pi_{(u,v)}$ contains (b_1, b_2) for some $b_1 \in B_1$ for which we do have key (u, b_1), namely b_1 was chosen to be in the label set of u. Thus, the verification component consists of a series of smaller components Y_i, each of which is meant to verify the above fact for v_i.

For any $v_j \in V$, the component Y_j consists of the following vertices (see Fig. 11):

(1) The starting vertex v_j to enter the component.
(2) A vertex (Y_j, b_l^2) for every label $b_l^2 \in B_2$.
(3) A vertex (Y_j, u_i, b_l^1) for every label $b_l^1 \in B_1$ and every $u_i \in U$ such that $(u_i, v_j) \in E$.

The edge set for component Y_j is defined as follows. There is an edge $(v_j, (Y_j, b_l^2))$ for every label $b_l^2 \in B_2$, where

$$\delta((v_j, (Y_j, b_l^2))) = ((v_j, b_l^2), m\, m_1 + 1, 0).$$

The idea is that, in order to visit (Y_j, b_l^2), we must have picked up a label b_l^2 for vertex v_j, otherwise we would be paying a very high cost. In the picture, we use ∞ to denote $mm_1 + 1$.

Let $\Gamma(v) = \{u_{i_1}, \ldots, u_{i_p}\}$ be the set of neighbors of v_j in G. There is an edge in Y_j of the form $((Y_j, b_l^2), (Y_j, u_{i_1}, b^1))$ for every label b^1 such that $(b^1, b_l^2) \in$

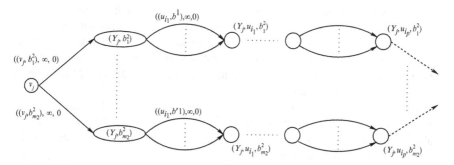

Fig. 11 The label verification component Y_j

$\Pi_{(u_{i_1}, v_j)}$. Thus, there are as many copies of this edge as there are such b^1. The copy of the edge corresponding to b^1 has key challenge (u_{i_1}, b^1); otherwise, a price of ∞ is to be paid. The idea is that, in order to walk from (Y_j, b_l^2) to (Y_j, u_{i_1}, b_l^2), we need to have one of the keys (u_{i_1}, b^1), which means the labeling has covered the edge $(u_{i_1}, v_j) \in E$. If it so happens that there is no such b^1, we put between (Y_j, b_l^2) and $(Y_j, u_{i_1}, b^1))$ an edge with the elusive key challenge k, and the "infinity" cost $mm_1 + 1$. That completes the verification that edge (u_{i_1}, v_j) is covered. We need to also check that $(u_{i_2}, v_j), \ldots, (u_{i_p}, v_j)$ are covered. This is done by serially connecting similar components, one for each $u_{i_2}, \ldots, u_{i_p}$.

This construction can clearly be done in polynomial time, and it is easy to verify that G has a complete covering of cost at most a if and only if G_{mh} has a feasible attack of cost at most a. Specifically, when $a \geq mm_1 + 1$ (the infinity cost) we use the trivial attack corresponding to the trivial cover which assigns B_1 to each vertex in U. When $a \leq mm_1$, we use the trivial correspondence between a complete labeling and a successful attack as laid out in the construction of the MIN-HACK instance.

5.1.6 Reducing PCP to MIN-HACK

In this section, we give a direct proof that MIN-HACK is not approximable to within $g_c(n)$ for any $c < 1/2$ by using a PCP characterization of NP with almost polynomially small error probability [11]. This PCP characterization can be summarized in the following theorem, which we quote from [12].

Theorem 5.4 (Dinur et al. [11]). *Let $c < 1/2$ be arbitrary and $D \leq \log\log^c n$. Let $\Psi = \{\psi_1, \ldots, \psi_n\}$ be a system of boolean constraints over variables $X = \{x_1, \ldots, x_m\}$ such that each constraint depends on D variables, and each variable takes values in a field $\mathcal{F}$ of size $O\left(2^{(\log n)^{1-1/O(D)}}\right)$. Then, it is NP-hard to decide between the following two cases:*

Yes: There is an assignment to the variables such that all $\psi_1, \ldots, \psi_n$ are satisfied.

No: No assignment can satisfy more than $O(1)/|\mathcal{F}|$ fraction of the ψ_i.

The general strategy to prove a hardness result for MIN-HACK is to show that if the MIN-HACK is approximable to within a certain ratio, then it is possible to distinguish between the YES and the NO instances of the boolean constraint satisfaction problem mentioned in Theorem 5.4. The idea is to find a "gap-preserving" reduction from Ψ to an instance of MIN-HACK. We shall follow the line of Dinur and Safra [12]. The following reduction shows that the three problems MLC_p, MMSA, and MIN-HACK are closely related.

Suppose we are given an instance $\Psi = \{\psi_1, \ldots, \psi_n\}$ as in Theorem 5.4 with m variables $X = \{x_1, \ldots, x_m\}$. For each $x \in X$, let Ψ_x denote the set of all constraints ψ which depend on x. For each constraint ψ_j, let $x_{j_1}, \ldots, x_{j_D}$ denote all the variables that ψ_j depends on.

An attack graph G_{mh} can be constructed with more or less the same format as the reduction from MLC. Figures 12 and 13 are almost self-explanatory. The graph

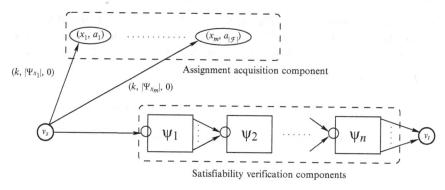

Fig. 12 Overview of the reduction from PCP to MIN-HACK

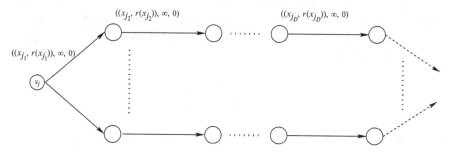

Fig. 13 The satisfiability verification component for ψ_j

G_{mh} has v_s as the initially compromised vertex, v_t the target vertex, and two types of components: the *assignment acquisition component* and a series of *satisfiability verification components*, one for each ψ_j, $1 \leq j \leq n$. (The edges or nodes with no labels are dummy edges and nodes, with dummy keys and costs zeros.)

The assignment acquisition component consists of vertices of the form (x_i, a_l), for all $x_i \in X$ and $a_l \in \mathcal{F}$. As usual, we use nodes' labels to also denote the keys the nodes have. To get the key (x_i, a_l), the attacker has to pay the price of $|\Psi_{x_i}|$.

In the satisfiability verification component for ψ_j (see Fig. 13), there are a number of parallel paths, one for each assignment $r : X \to \mathcal{F}$ which satisfies ψ_j. In order to get through this verification component for ψ_j, the attacker needs to have at least one complete set of keys $(x_{j_1}, r(x_{j_1}), \ldots, x_{j_D}, r(x_{j_D}))$ for some assignment r that satisfies ψ_j.

Lemma 5.5 (Completeness). *If Ψ is satisfiable, then there is a successful attack on G_{mh} with cost nD.*

Proof. Let r be some assignment which satisfies Ψ. A successful attack can be constructed by first grabbing all the keys $(x_i, r(x_i))$, $i = 1, \ldots, m$. The total cost of getting these keys is $\sum_{i=1}^{m} |\Psi_{x_i}| = nD$, since each constraint is dependent on D variables.

To get to v_t, the attacker can then get through the components of the ψ_j by following the path corresponding to r in each ψ_j. $\qquad\square$

Lemma 5.6 (Soundness). *Consider any $c < 1/2$, and let $g = g_c(n)$. If there is a successful attack on G_{mh} with cost at most gnD, then there is an assignment satisfying a $1/(2(2Dg)^D)$ fraction of constraints in Ψ.*

Proof. For each $x \in X$, let

$$A(x) = \{a \in \mathcal{F} \mid \text{the attacker visited node } (x, a)\}.$$

Note that visiting (x, a) incurs a cost of $|\Psi_x|$. Hence, the cost of the entire attack is

$$\sum_{x \in X} |\Psi_x||A(x)| \leq gnD. \tag{6}$$

Consider the probability distribution on X where every elements of X are chosen by first uniformly choose a constraint ψ at random, and then choose a variable x that ψ depends on at random. The probability of picking a particular x is $\frac{|\Psi_x|}{n} \frac{1}{D} = \frac{|\Psi_x|}{nD}$. Hence, relation (6) implies

$$E_x[|A(x)|] = \sum_{x \in X} \frac{|\Psi_x|}{nD} |A(x)| \leq g.$$

Call a variable x *bad* if $|A(x)| > 2Dg$. By Markov inequality,

$$\Prob_x[|A(x)| > 2Dg] \leq \Prob_x[|A(x)| > 2DE_x[|A(x)|]] < \frac{1}{2D}.$$

In other words, the probability of hitting a bad variable in this distribution is at most $1/(2D)$. We thus have

$$\frac{1}{2D} > \Prob_{\psi \in \Psi, x \in \psi}[x \text{ is bad}]$$

$$= \Prob_{\psi \in \Psi}[\psi \text{ contains a bad variable}] \cdot \Prob_{x \in \psi}[x \text{ is bad} \mid \psi \text{ contains a bad variable}]$$

$$\geq \Prob_{\psi \in \Psi}[\psi \text{ contains a bad variable}] \frac{1}{D}$$

Consequently, at least half of the ψ contains no bad variable.

To this end, define a random assignment $\bar{r} : X \to \mathcal{F}$ by assigning to x some $\bar{r}(x) \in A(x)$ uniformly. Since the attack was successful, for each ψ_j, the attacker must have gotten through one of the parallel paths in the verification component for ψ_j corresponding to some assignment r that satisfies ψ_j. The probability that $r(x) = \bar{r}(x)$ for all $x \in \psi_j$ is $\prod_{x \in \psi_j} \frac{1}{|A(x)|}$, which is at least $1/(2Dg)^D$ for the ψ_j which do not contain bad variables. Combined with the fact that at least half of the ψ_j do not contain bad variables, we conclude that there is some assignment that satisfies a $1/(2(2Dg)^D)$ fraction of Ψ as desired. $\qquad\square$

A PCP proof of Theorem 5.3. For any $c < 1/2$, we want to show that there is no $g_c(n)$ approximation for MIN-HACK, unless $P = NP$. Pick any c' such that $c < c' < 1/2$. Pick D and $\mathcal{F}$ in Theorem 5.4 such that $D = O(\log \log^{c'} n)$ and $|\mathcal{F}| = \Theta(g_{c'}(n))$. With these parameters, it is easy to see that $1/(2(2Dg)^D) > O(1)/|\mathcal{F}|$.

Consider the construction of G_{mh} described above. We will show that, if there is a g-approximation algorithm for MIN-HACK, then the algorithm can also be used to decide the YES and NO instances of the constraint satisfaction problem.

Given an instance Ψ of the constraint satisfaction problem. The strategy is to run the g-approximation algorithm on the instance G_{mh} constructed from g and report YES if the answer is at most gnD. Clearly, if Ψ is a yes-instance, then the answer is at most gnD because, by the completeness lemma the optimal solution is at most nD. On the other hand, by the soundness lemma the approximation algorithm returns an answer at most gnD only when a fraction of $> O(1)/|\mathcal{F}|$ constraints of Ψ are satisfied, implying Ψ is a yes instance. $\square$

5.2 Threat Analysis Algorithms

We have proven that solving Min-Hack to optimality is very hard. In fact, even approximating the optimal solution to a large factor is already very hard. However, it is possible to get an estimate of the optimal solution using heuristics. We present a brute force algorithm along with a heuristic algorithm for the purposes of comparison.

The brute force algorithm BRUTE-FORCE (see Table 2) generates all possible permutations of attack sequences and finds the minimum cost among them. Without loss of generality, let $V_0 = \{v_0\}$ and $V_s = \{v_s\}$. Given a set S, let PERMUTE(S) signify the set of all possible permutations of elements of S without repetitions. The running time of this algorithm is super-exponential, but it solves the Min-Hack problem to optimality.

We now describe our polynomial-time heuristic called GREEDY–HEURISTIC (see Table 3) which is based on the observation that a key sequence is structurally a path from some initial vertex to a final target vertex with zero or more branches from this backbone path, taken to collect additional keys. We use a greedy approach with the all-pairs shortest path (APSP) as the core decision-making procedure. Given

Table 2 A brute force algorithm to find cost of optimal key sequence

```
(Brute-Force)(KG)
1   min_cost ← 0
2   for each S ⊆ V − (V_0 ∪ V_s)
3   do for each s ∈ PERMUTE(S)
4       do cost ← ATTACK-COST(v_0 s v_s)
5           if cost < min_cost
6               then min_cost = cost
7   return min_cost
```

Table 3 A greedy heuristic to find cost of near-optimal key sequence

```
(Greedy-Heuristic)(KG)
 1    S ← V₀
 2    M ← UPDATED-ADJ-MATRIX(KG, π(S))
 3    A ← APSP(M)
 4    min_cost ← A[v₀, vₛ]
 5    for round ← 1 to |V|
 6    do
 7        flag ← 0
 8        for each vᵢ ∈ NEIGHBOR(S)
 9        do vertex_cost ← NEW-VERTEX-COST(vᵢ)
10            M' ← UPDATED-ADJ-MATRIX(KG, π(S ∪ {vᵢ}))
11            ∀vⱼ ∈ S, M'[vⱼ, vᵢ] ← 0, M'[vᵢ, vⱼ] ← 0
12            A' ← APSP(M')
13            if (vertex_cost + A'[v₀, vₛ]) < min_cost
14                then min_cost ← vertex_cost + A'[v₀, vₛ]
15                    new_vertex ← vᵢ
16                    flag ← 1
17        if flag = 1
18            then
19                S ← S ∪ {new_vertex}
20            else return min_cost
21    return min_cost
```

an $n \times n$ adjacency matrix of a graph $G = (V, E)$, the APSP algorithm computes the all-pairs shortest path matrix, which gives the shortest path between any pair of vertices in the graph G. However, we cannot use this algorithm directly since the input that is available to us is a key challenge graph and not a weighted graph. We now briefly describe the algorithm UPDATED-ADJ-MATRIX, which converts a key challenge graph to a weighted graph. The main idea is that when an attacker acquires a new key, then weights on all edges having this key in the corresponding key challenge will reduce to the lower cost, otherwise they reduce to a higher cost. GREEDY–HEURISTIC proceeds by evaluating which neighboring key if acquired would give a shorter backbone path from the source vertex to the target vertex than the one currently seen. After at most $|V|$ rounds of decision-making, the algorithm returns a cost which cannot be reduced further. Invocation of the APSP algorithm inside the loop results in a worst case running time of $O(n^5)$. An insight into the algorithm is that we use both local (neighboring keys) and global (shortest path) factors to find the approximate solution.

5.3 Algorithm Benchmarking

We have performed empirical evaluations to compare BRUTE-FORCE with GREEDY-HEURISTIC. Our experiments were conducted on a Pentium 4/3GHz/1GB RAM running RedHat Linux 9.1. Since the BRUTE-FORCE algorithm has a prohibitively

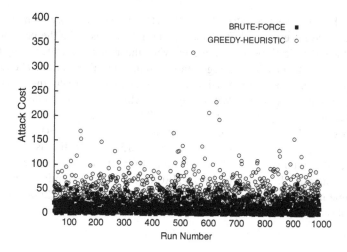

Fig. 14 GREEDY-HEURISTIC vs BRUTE-FORCE: Minimum cost of an attack

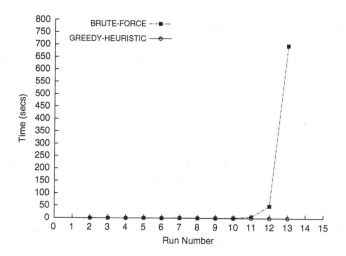

Fig. 15 GREEDY-HEURISTIC vs BRUTE-FORCE: Running time behavior

expensive running time, we have limited the size of the input to only 15 nodes. Our test data set consists of 1,000 simulation runs, and each run generates a random instance of a key challenge graph. We have compared the quality of the solutions (see Fig. 14) computed by the two algorithms as well as their running times (see Fig. 15).

When comparing the attack costs returned by the two algorithms, we have used randomly generated key challenge graphs of exactly 15 nodes for all the 1,000 runs. In Fig. 14, there are two distinct bands, a lower one which corresponds to the optimal attack costs returned by BRUTE-FORCE and a higher one which represents the attack costs returned by GREEDY–HEURISTIC. The gap is due to the inapproximability

results as shown in Sect. 5. GREEDY-HEURISTIC worked very well when the final
attack sequence is very small (3–4 nodes), and this seems to be the best case scenario for the heuristic algorithm. However, when the attack sequence is long (10–15
nodes), the heuristic produces a larger gap from the optimal solution. The explanation we give for this observation is that longer the sequence, greater the chances that
the decision-making procedure will make errors which are compounded.

When comparing the running time, the 1,000 runs had a cross-section of varying graph sizes (3–20 nodes). The running time of the BRUTE-FORCE algorithm
becomes very large even for small values of 13–15. Clearly, this is the expected
behavior as the running time of this algorithm is $O(n!)$, which is worse than exponential. On the other hand, the GREEDY-HEURISTIC has polynomial running times
for the same input. Even for graphs with a large number of nodes (200–300 nodes),
we have observed a running time of only a few minutes (15–20 min).

6   Related Work

Theoretical models allow inexpensive security analysis without real experiments or
implementation. Fault trees, privilege graphs, and attack graphs are the most relevant modeling methodologies in the context of our work. We compare and contrast
against these techniques to put our work in perspective.

6.1   Formal Models

Fault trees [13] are the first generation of formal models primarily used for system failure analysis. A fault tree is a logic (AND-OR) tree, where nodes are single
faults, edges define a combination of them, and probabilities over edges represent
the chance of their occurrence. While fault trees are suitable to model a disjunction
and conjunction of faults, they lack the expressive power to capture attacks.

The privilege graph, introduced by Dacier et al. [10] as an extension to Typed
Access Model (TAM), is a directed graph where each node represents a set of privileges on sets of objects and each arc represents privilege escalation possibly through
an exploit. This model also uses a probabilistic metric corresponding to likelihoods
of attacks. However, determining these probabilities in a meaningfulway is far more
challenging that our approach which measures the effectiveness of access control
mechanisms. Ortalo et al. [26] describe an experimental evaluation of the privilege
graph framework under certain assumptions on the memory state of an attacker,
and their work did address a few insider attack scenarios, but their implementation
required a substantial effort.

Philips and Swiler [32] proposed the attack graph model, where nodes in the
graph represent the state of a network and edges represent steps in an attack.
Building and analyzing such a graph by hand is not practical, and instead, several approaches have been proposed which use model-checking to automatically

generate attack graphs [31]. Sheyner et al. [31] showed that model checking can be used to automatically generate attack graphs. Their technique used a modified model checker to extract *all* possible traces that lead to a successful compromise. Although the process is automated, model-checking suffers from a well-known problem of state explosion which is not easily solved, and these approaches are not suitable even for networks of a reasonable size. In fact, their paper reports that even for a small network and a few atomic attacks, attack graph generation took several hours. In their followup paper [19], they performed minimization analyses to assist a security analyst in deciding which minimal set of states should be eliminated to secure the network. Ammann et al. [4] argued that modeling at granularity of atomic actions represents far more details than necessary for a security analyst; instead, they use a higher level attribute based representation. Also, by relaxing the "undo" when backtracking during graph traversal, a polynomial time vulnerability analysis algorithm is presented. In our model, we also use a coarse grained representation, and this translates to scalable model specification. On the other hand, since our model is different from traditional attack graphs, the notion of successful attacks is not a simple path.

Although in some respects, both privilege graphs and attack graphs appear similar to our work, they are in fact closer to each other than our approach. A major distinction arise in the details that are captured (see Table 1) and the nature of threat analysis. For example, in their model, the difficulty attributed to edge traversal is a static entity, while in our model, it is dynamic. Moreover, in both techniques, there is the problem of exponential state explosion, whereas our approach generates models which are polynomial-sized in the input network information. Also note that attacks in our model can succeed without privilege escalation or the presence of vulnerabilities, which is a distinct possibility for insider attacks.

State transition based approaches model penetrations and attacks as a series of state transitions from some initially secure state to some compromised state. Porras et al. [16, 29] proposed one of the earliest rule-based state transition approaches for attack representation and detection. Petri nets [18, 22] are a formal model for information flow. In this token-based model, there are two types of nodes: places and transitions. Places contain tokens, and directed arcs connect places to transitions and transitions to places as pre- and post-conditions to taking transitions. The position of the tokens indicates a particular state of execution. Multiple tokens may exist in the Petri net at any point in execution signifying that multiple states hold true. This aspect of the Petri net is similar to our model, where an attacker may have compromised multiple sub-targets.

6.2   Security Audit Tools

A multitude of commercial tools [17,24,30] are available which perform both host and network level security assessment. The audit process involves performing a laundry list of security checks and running exploits against known vulnerabilities. Since real attacks are launched, they bear a strong resemblance to real-world scenarios.

However, the coverage is limited to only known vulnerabilities. Automatically running these tools only reveals superficial security problems, and it is difficult to understand their overall impact. On the other hand, a detailed and thorough security audit is often time-consuming and expensive.

6.3 Metrics

The efficacy of a model is severely limited if it does not support quantification. Quantification allows an analyst to pose questions and obtain useful answers based on which critical infrastructural decisions can be made. The crux of quantification in most security mechanisms is not offering an absolute certainty of any given property but rather making guarantees given some assumption of the system and/or the attacker. Some research efforts have attempted to provide metrics in the context of security.

Dacier et al. [10] defined a metric called *mean effort to failure* or METF on attack state graphs. METF is based on associating transition probabilities on edges of the attack state graph representing the likelihood of a given transition. Exploring a particular path in the attack state graph gives the probability of occurrence of that path. Probabilities are useful in capturing random events like faults, but deliberate events, like attacks, can defy all probabilities. In our model, metrics are integer values rather than probabilities. We associate an integer to estimate the resistance offered by a security system to an attacker's efforts.

Manadhata and Wing propose another metric [15] for evaluating the relative security of a system based on its *attack surface*. Again the system is modeled as a state machine and the adversary's goal as a state predicate. The point they make in the paper is that security need not be measured absolutely; relative metrics are effective too. Attack surfaces evaluate a relative comparison between different versions or flavors of the same system to determine if the attack surface of the system is more exposed. Intuitively, the more exposed the attack surface of a system, the more prone it is to attack. Similarly, in our model, we make relative guarantees rather than absolute ones.

7 Conclusion And Future Work

Insider threat is a long standing security problem, but so far, without good tools and techniques, there is little that could be done to counter the threat. In this paper, we believe that we have made a significant advance by proposing a usable and generic threat assessment model and showed its applications to some typical insider threat scenarios. Indeed, we do not claim that our model is a replacement for all the existing models, but that it occupies a certain niche and complements other models.

We also believe that our modeling methodology is more generic than demonstrated in this paper and may have an appeal beyond just insider threat.

Our future work involves developing automated tools around the modeling methodology and algorithms developed in this paper to empower security analysts with techniques to measure a threat which has otherwise not been possible.

Acknowledgments This research is supported in part by by Telcordia Technologies Subcontract: FA8750-04-C-0249 from the DARPA SRS Program.

References

1. *2004 E-Crime Watch Survey: Summary Of Findings*, CERT/United States Secret Service/CSO, 2004. http://www.cert.org/archive/pdf/2004eCrimeWatchSummary.pdf.
2. *Insider Threat Study: Illicit Cyber Activity In The Banking And Finance Sector*, CERT/United States Secret Service, August 2004. http://www.secretservice.gov/ntac/its_report_040820.pdf.
3. M. ALEKHNOVICH, S. BUSS, S. MORAN, AND T. PITASSI, *Minimum propositional proof length is NP-hard to linearly approximate*, J. Symb. Log., 66 (2001), pp. 171–191.
4. P. AMMANN, D. WIJESEKERA, AND S. KAUSHIK, *Scalable, graph-based network vulnerability analysis*, in Proceedings of the 9th ACM conference on Computer and communications security, ACM Press, 2002, pp. 217–224.
5. S. ARORA, L. BABAI, J. STERN, AND Z. SWEEDYK, *The hardness of approximate optima in lattices, codes, and systems of linear equations*, J. Comput. System Sci., 54 (1997), pp. 317–331. 34th Annual Symposium on Foundations of Computer Science (Palo Alto, CA, 1993).
6. S. ARORA AND C. LUND, *Hardness of approximation*, in Approximation Algorithms for NP-Hard Problems, D. Hochbaum, ed., PWS Publishing Company, Boston, 1997, pp. 399–346.
7. R. CHINCHANI, D. HA, A. IYER, H. Q. NGO, AND S. UPADHYAYA, *On the hardness of approximating the MIN-HACK problem*, J. Comb. Optim., (2005). To appear.
8. R. CHINCHANI, A. IYER, H. Q. NGO, AND S. UPADHYAYA, *Towards a theory of insider threat assessment*, in Proceedings of the International Conference on Dependable Systems and Networks (DSN 2005, Yokohama, Japan), IEEE, 2005.
9. P. CRESCENZI, V. KANN, R. SILVESTRI, AND L. TREVISAN, *Structure in approximation classes*, SIAM J. Comput., 28 (1999), pp. 1759–1782 (electronic).
10. M. DACIER, *Towards Quantitative Evaluation of Computer Security*, PhD thesis, Institut National Polytechnique de Toulouse, December 1994.
11. I. DINUR, E. FISCHER, G. KINDLER, R. RAZ, AND S. SAFRA, *PCP characterizations of NP: towards a polynomially-small error-probability*, in Annual ACM Symposium on Theory of Computing (Atlanta, GA, 1999), ACM, New York, 1999, pp. 29–40 (electronic).
12. I. DINUR AND S. SAFRA, *On the hardness of approximating label-cover*, Inform. Process. Lett., 89 (2004), pp. 247–254.
13. J. GORSKI AND A. WARDZINSKI, *Formalizing Fault Trees*, Achievement and Assurance of Safety, (1995), pp. 311–327.
14. D. S. HOCHBAUM, ed., *Approximation Algorithms for NP Hard Problems*, PWS Publishing Company, Boston, 1997.
15. M. HOWARD, J. PINCUS, AND J. WING, *Measuring Relative Attack Surfaces*, in Proceedings of Workshop on Advanced Developments in Software and Systems Security, 2003.
16. K. ILGUN, R. A. KEMMERER, AND P. A. PORRAS, *State Transition Analysis: A Rule-Based Intrusion Detection Approach*, IEEE Transactions on Software Engineering, (1995).
17. INSECURE.ORG, *Top 75 Security Tools*, 2003. http://www.insecure.org/tools.html.
18. K. JENSEN, *Colored Petri Nets: Basic Concepts, Analysis Methods, And Practical Use*, vol. 1.2, Springer, Berlin, 1992.

19. S. JHA, O. SHEYNER, AND J. WING, *Two Formal Analyses of Attack Graphs*, in 15th IEEE Computer Security Foundations Workshop (CSFW'02), Cape Breton, Nova Scotia, Canada, 2002, pp. 49–63.

20. E. KINDLER, *Safety and liveness properties: A survey*, Bull. Eur. Assoc. Theor. Comput. Sci., 53 (1994), pp. 268–272.

21. C. LUND AND M. YANNAKAKIS, *On The Hardness Of Approximating Minimization Problems*, J. Assoc. Comput. Mach., 41 (1994), pp. 960–981.

22. E. W. MAYR, *An Algorithm For The General Petri Net Reachability Problem*, SIAM J. Comput., 13 (1984), pp. 441–460.

23. C. MEADOWS, *A Representation of Protocol Attacks for Risk Assessment*, in DIMACS Series in Discrete Mathematics and Theoretical Computer Science: Network Threats, R. N. Wright and P. G. Neumann, eds., vol. 38, December 1998.

24. NESSUS, *Security Scanner for Various Flavors of Unix and Windows*. http://www.nessus.org/intro.html.

25. P. G. NEUMANN, *The Challenges of Insider Misuse*. Prepared for the workshop on Preventing, Detecting, and Responding to Malicious Insider Misuse, Aug. 1999.

26. R. ORTALO, Y. DEWARTE, AND M. KAANICHE, *Experimenting With Quantitative Evaluation Tools For Monitoring Operation Security*, IEEE Transactions on Software Engineering, 25 (1999), pp. 633–650.

27. C. H. PAPADIMITRIOU, *Computational complexity*, Addison-Wesley Publishing Company, Reading, MA, 1994.

28. C. PHILLIPS AND L. P. SWILER, *A Graph-Based System For Network-Vulnerability Analysis*, in Proceedings of 1998 New Security Paradigms Workshop, Charlottesville, Virginia, 1998, pp. 71–79.

29. P. A. PORRAS AND R. A. KEMMERER, *Penetration State Transition Analysis A Rule-Based Intrusion Detection Approach*, in Proceedings of the Eighth Annual Computer Security Applications Conference, San Antonio, Texas, December 1992, pp. 220–229.

30. SAINT, *Vulnerability Scanning Engine*. http://www.saintcorporation.com/.

31. O. SHEYNER, J. HAINES, S. JHA, R. LIPPMANN, AND J. M. WING, *Automated Generation and Analysis of Attack Graphs*, in Proceedings of the IEEE Symposium on Security and Privacy, Oakland, CA., May 2002.

32. L. P. SWILER, C. PHILLIPS, D. ELLIS, AND S. CHAKERIAN, *Computer-Attack Graph Generation Tool*, in DARPA Information Survivability Conference and Exposition (DISCEX 11'01), vol. 2, June 2001.

33. V. V. VAZIRANI, *Approximation algorithms*, Springer, Berlin, 2001.

34. B. J. WOOD, *An insider threat model for adversary simulation*, 2000.

Toward Automated Intrusion Alert Analysis

Peng Ning and Dingbang Xu

Contents

1 Introduction

Traditional intrusion detection systems (IDSs) focus on low-level attacks or anomalies and raise alerts independently, though there may be logical connections between them. In situations where there are intensive attacks, not only will actual alerts be mixed with false alerts, but the amount of alerts will also become unmanageable.

P. Ning (✉)
Computer Science Department, North Carolina State University, Raleigh, NC 27695, USA
e-mail: pning@ncsu.edu

S.C.-H. Huang et al. (eds.), *Network Security*, DOI 10.1007/978-0-387-73821-5_8,
© Springer Science+Business Media, LLC 2010

As a result, it is difficult for human users or intrusion response systems to understand the alerts and take appropriate actions. Therefore, it is necessary to develop techniques to construct *attack scenarios* (i.e., steps that attackers use in their attacks) from alerts to facilitate intrusion analysis.

In this article, we summarize a series of research efforts aimed at addressing the above problem [26–29]. These efforts start with an approach to constructing attack scenarios based on prerequisites and consequences of attacks. Intuitively, the prerequisite of an attack is the necessary condition for the attack to be successful, while the consequence of an attack is the possible outcome of the attack. For example, the existence of a vulnerable service is the prerequisite of a remote buffer overflow attack against the service, and as the consequence of the attack, the attacker may gain access to the host. Accordingly, we correlate the alerts together when the attackers launch some early attacks to prepare for the prerequisites of some later ones. For example, if they use a UDP port scan to discover the vulnerable services, followed by an attack against one of the services, we can correlate the corresponding alerts together. It is well-known that current IDSs often miss unknown attacks or variations of known attacks. To tolerate missing detections, our method allows partial satisfaction of prerequisites of an attack. In addition, our method allows flexible alert aggregation and provides intuitive representations of correlated alerts.

We apply this alert correlation method to analyze real-world, intrusion intensive data sets. In particular, we would like to see how well the alert correlation method can help human users organize and understand intrusion alerts, especially when IDSs report a large amount of alerts. We argue that this is a practical problem that the intrusion detection community is facing. As indicated in [22], "encountering 10–20,000 alarms per sensor per day is common." To facilitate the analysis of large sets of correlated alerts, we develop several utilities (called *alert aggregation and disaggregation, focused analysis, clustering analysis, frequency analysis, link analysis*, and *association analysis*). These utilities are intended for human users to analyze and understand the correlated alerts as well as the strategies behind them.

It is often desirable, and sometimes necessary, to understand attack strategies in security applications such as computer forensics and intrusion responses. For example, it is easier to predict an attacker's next move, and decrease the damage caused by intrusions, if the attack strategy is known during intrusion response. To facilitate the extraction of attack strategies from intrusion alerts and complement static vulnerability analysis techniques (e.g., [2, 17, 33, 35]), we develop techniques to automatically learn attack strategies from intrusion alerts reported by IDSs. By examining correlated intrusion alerts, our method extracts the constraints intrinsic to the attack strategy automatically. Specifically, an attack strategy is represented as a directed acyclic graph (DAG), which we call an *attack strategy graph*, with nodes representing attacks, edges representing the (partial) temporal order of attacks, and constraints on the nodes and edges. These constraints represent the conditions that any attack instance must satisfy in order to use the strategy. To cope with variations in attacks, we use generalization techniques to hide the differences not intrinsic to the attack strategy. By controlling the degree of generalization, users may inspect attack strategies at different levels of details.

The remainder of this article is organized as follows. Section 2 presents our formal framework for correlating alerts using prerequisites and consequences of attacks. Section 3 describes several utilities for analyzing attack scenarios constructed from large collections of alerts. Section 4 presents techniques to extract attack strategies from correlated intrusion alerts. Section 5 discusses related work. Section 6 concludes this article and points out some future research directions.

2 Correlating Intrusion Alerts Based on Prerequisites and Consequences of Attacks

Our method for alert correlation is based on the observation that in a series of attacks the attacks are usually not isolated, but related as different stages of the attack sequence, with the early ones preparing for the later ones. To take advantage of this observation, we propose to correlate the alerts generated by IDSs using prerequisites and consequences of the corresponding attacks. Intuitively, the *prerequisite* of an attack is the necessary condition for the attack to be successful. For example, the existence of a vulnerable service is a prerequisite for a remote buffer overflow attack against the service. Moreover, the attacker may make progress in gaining access to the victim system (e.g., discover the vulnerable services, install a Trojan horse program) as a result of an attack. Informally, we call the possible outcome of an attack the (possible) *consequence* of the attack. In a series of attacks where the attackers launch earlier attacks to prepare for later ones, there are usually strong connections between the consequences of the earlier attacks and the prerequisites of the later ones. Indeed, if an earlier attack is to prepare for a later attack, the consequence of the earlier attack should at least partly satisfy the prerequisite of the later attack.

Accordingly, we identify the prerequisites (e.g., existence of vulnerable services) and the consequences (e.g., discovery of vulnerable services) of each type of attack. These are then used to correlate alerts, which are attacks detected by IDSs, by matching the consequences of (the attacks corresponding to) some previous alerts and the prerequisites of (the attacks corresponding to) some later ones. For example, if we find a *Sadmind Ping* followed by a buffer overflow attack against the corresponding *Sadmind* service, we can correlate them to be parts of the same series of attacks. In other words, we model the knowledge (or state) of attackers in terms of individual attacks, and correlate alerts if they indicate the progress of attacks.

Note that an attacker does not *have to* perform early attacks to prepare for a later attack, even though the later attack has certain prerequisites. For example, an attacker may launch an individual buffer overflow attack against a service blindly, without knowing if the service exists. In other words, the prerequisite of an attack should not be mistaken for the necessary existence of an earlier attack. However, if the attacker does launch attacks with earlier ones preparing for later ones, our method can correlate them, provided that the attacks are detected by IDSs.

In the following subsections, we adopt a formal approach to develop our alert correlation method.

2.1 Prerequisite and Consequence of Attacks

We propose to use predicates as basic constructs to represent the prerequisites and (possible) consequences of attacks. For example, a scanning attack may discover UDP services vulnerable to a certain buffer overflow attack. We can use the predicate *UDPVulnerableToBOF* (*VictimIP, VictimPort*) to represent the attacker's discovery (i.e., the consequence of the attack) that the host having the IP address *VictimIP* runs a service (e.g., *sadmind*) at UDP port *VictimPort* and that the service is vulnerable to the buffer overflow attack. Similarly, if an attack requires a UDP service vulnerable to the buffer overflow attack, we can use the same predicate to represent the prerequisite.

Some attacks may require several conditions be satisfied at the same time in order to be successful. To represent such complex conditions, we use a logical combination of predicates to describe the prerequisite of an attack. For example, a certain network launched buffer overflow attack may require that the target host has a vulnerable UDP service accessible to the attacker through the firewall. This prerequisite can be represented by *UDPVulnerableToBOF* (*VictimIP, VictimPort*) ∧ *UDPAccessibleViaFirewall* (*VictimIP, VictimPort*). To simplify the following discussion, we restrict the logical operators in predicates to ∧ (conjunction) and ∨ (disjunction).

We also use a set of predicates to represent the (possible) consequence of an attack. For example, an attack may result in compromise of the root privilege as well as modification of the *.rhost* file. Thus, we may use the following to represent the corresponding consequence: {*GainRootAccess* (*VictimIP*), *rhostModified* (*VictimIP*)}. Note that the set of predicates used to represent the consequence is essentially the logical combination of these predicates and can be represented by a single logical formula. However, representing the consequence as a set of predicates rather than a long formula is more convenient and will be used here.

2.2 Hyper-Alert Type and Hyper-Alert

Using predicates as the basic construct, we introduce the notion of a *hyper-alert type* to represent the prerequisite and the consequence of each type of alert.

Definition 1. A *hyper-alert type* T is a triple (*fact, prerequisite, consequence*), where (1) *fact* is a set of attribute names, each with an associated domain of values, (2) *prerequisite* is a logical combination of predicates whose free variables are all in *fact*, and (3) *consequence* is a set of predicates such that all the free variables in *consequence* are in *fact*.

Each hyper-alert type encodes the knowledge about a type of attack. The component *fact* of a hyper-alert type tells what kind of information is reported along with the alert (i.e., detected attack), *prerequisite* specifies what must be true in order for the attack to be successful, and *consequence* describes what could be true if the attack indeed succeeds. For the sake of brevity, we omit the domains associated with the attribute names when they are clear from the context.

Example 1. Consider the buffer overflow attack against the *sadmind* remote administration tool. We may have a hyper-alert type *SadmindBufferOverflow* = ({*VictimIP, VictimPort*}, *ExistHost* (*VictimIP*) ∧ *VulnerableSadmind* (*VictimIP*), {*GainRootAccess*(*VictimIP*)}) for such attacks. Intuitively, this hyper-alert type says that such an attack is against the host at IP address *VictimIP*. (We expect the actual values of *VictimIP* are reported by an IDS.) For the attack to be successful, there must exist a host at IP address *VictimIP*, and the corresponding *sadmind* service must be vulnerable to buffer overflow attacks. The attacker may gain root privilege as a result of the attack.

Given a hyper-alert type, a *hyper-alert instance* can be generated if the corresponding attack is detected and reported by an IDS. For example, we can generate a hyper-alert instance of type *SadmindBufferOverflow* from a corresponding alert. The notion of hyper-alert instance is formally defined as follows:

Definition 2. Given a hyper-alert type $T = (fact, prerequisite, consequence)$, a *hyper-alert (instance) h of type T* is a finite set of tuples on *fact*, where each tuple is associated with an interval-based timestamp [*begin_time, end_time*]. The hyper-alert h implies that *prerequisite* must evaluate to True and all the predicates in *consequence* might evaluate to True for each of the tuples. (Notation-wise, for each tuple t in h, we use $t.begin\_time$ and $t.end\_time$ to refer to the timestamp associated with t.)

The *fact* component of a hyper-alert type is essentially a relation schema (as in relational databases), and a hyper-alert is a relation instance of this schema. One may point out that an alternative way is to represent a hyper-alert as a record, which is equivalent to a single tuple on *fact*. However, such an alternative cannot accommodate certain alerts possibly reported by an IDS. For example, an IDS may report an IPSweep attack along with multiple swept IP addresses, which cannot be represented as a single record. In addition, our current formalism allows aggregation of alerts of the same type and is flexible in reasoning about alerts. Therefore, we believe the current notion of a hyper-alert is an appropriate choice.

A hyper-alert instantiates its *prerequisite* and *consequence* by replacing the free variables in *prerequisite* and *consequence* with its specific values. Since all free variables in *prerequisite* and *consequence* must appear in *fact* in a hyper-alert type, the instantiated prerequisite and consequence will have no free variables. Note that *prerequisite* and *consequence* can be instantiated multiple times if *fact* consists of multiple tuples. For example, if an IPSweep attack involves several IP addresses, the *prerequisite* and *consequence* of the corresponding hyper-alert type will be instantiated for each of these addresses.

In the following, we treat timestamps implicitly and omit them if they are not necessary for our discussion.

Example 2. Consider the hyper-alert type *SadmindBufferOverflow* discussed in Example 1. There may be a hyper-alert $h_{SadmindBOF}$ as follows: $\{(VictimIP =$ 152.1.19.5, *VictimPort* = 1235), (*VictimIP* = 152.1.19.7, *VictimPort* = 1235)$\}$. This implies that if the attack is successful, the following two logical formulas must be True as the prerequisites of the attack: *ExistHost* (152.1.19.5) $\wedge$ *VulnerableSadmind* (152.1.19.5), *ExistHost* (152.1.19.7) $\wedge$ *VulnerableSadmind* (152.1.19.7). Moreover, as possible consequences of the attack, the following might be True: *GainRootAccess* (152.1.19.5), *GainRootAccess* (152.1.19.7). This hyper-alert says that there are buffer overflow attacks against *sadmind* at IP addresses 152.1.19.5 and 152.1.19.7, and the attacker may gain root access as a result of the attacks.

A hyper-alert may correspond to one or several related alerts. If an IDS reports one alert for a certain attack and the alert has all the information needed to instantiate a hyper-alert, a hyper-alert can be generated from the alert. However, some IDSs may report a series of alerts for a single attack. For example, EMERALD [31] may report several alerts (within the same thread) related to an attack that spreads over a period of time. In this case, a hyper-alert may correspond to the aggregation of all the related alerts. Moreover, several alerts may be reported for the same type of attack in a short period of time. Our definition of hyper-alert allows them to be treated as one hyper-alert and thus provides flexibility in the reasoning about alerts. Certain constraints are necessary to make sure the hyper-alerts are reasonable. However, since our hyper-alert correlation method does not depend on them directly, we will discuss them after introducing our method.

Ideally, we may correlate a set of hyper-alerts with a later hyper-alert if the consequences of the former ones imply the prerequisite of the latter one. However, such an approach may not work in reality due to several reasons. First, the attacker may not always prepare for certain attacks by launching some other attacks. For example, the attacker may learn a vulnerable *sadmind* service by talking to people who work in the organization where the system is running. Second, the current IDSs may miss some attacks, and thus affect the alert correlation if the above approach is used. Third, due to the combinatorial nature of the aforementioned approach, it is computationally expensive to examine sets of alerts to find out whether their consequences imply the prerequisite of an alert.

Having considered these issues, we adopt an alternative approach. Instead of examining if several hyper-alerts imply the prerequisite of a later one, we check if an earlier hyper-alert *contributes* to the prerequisite of a later one. Specifically, we decompose the prerequisite of a hyper-alert into individual predicates and test whether the consequence of an earlier hyper-alert makes some of the prerequisites True (i.e., make the prerequisite easier to satisfy). If the result is yes, then we correlate the hyper-alerts together. This idea is specified formally through the following definitions.

Definition 3. Consider a hyper-alert type $T = (fact, prerequisite, consequence)$. The *prerequisite set (or consequence set, resp.) of T,* denoted $P(T)$ (or $C(T)$, resp.), is the set of all predicates that appear in *prerequisite* (or *consequence*, resp.). Given a hyper-alert instance h of type T, the *prerequisite set (or consequence set, resp.) of h,* denoted $P(h)$ (or $C(h)$, resp.), is the set of predicates in $P(T)$ (or $C(T)$, resp.) whose arguments are replaced with the corresponding attribute values of each tuple in h. Each element in $P(h)$ (or $C(h)$, resp.) is associated with the timestamp of the corresponding tuple in h. (Notation-wise, for each $p \in P(h)$ (or $C(h)$, resp.), we use $p.begin\_time$ and $p.end\_time$ to refer to the timestamp associated with p.

Example 3. Consider the *Sadmind Ping* attack through which an attacker discovers possibly vulnerable *sadmind* services. The corresponding alerts can be represented by a hyper-alert type $SadmindPing = (\{VictimIP, VictimPort\}, \{ExistHost (VictimIP)\}, \{VulnerableSadmind (VictimIP)\})$.

Suppose a hyper-alert instance $h_{SadmindPing}$ of type $SadmindPing$ has the following tuples: $\{(VictimIP = 152.1.19.5, VictimPort = 1235), (VictimIP = 152.1.19.7, VictimPort = 1235), (VictimIP = 152.1.19.9, VictimPort = 1235)\}$. Then, we have the prerequisite set $P(h_{SadmindPing}) = \{ExistHost (152.1.19.5), ExistHost (152.1.19.7), ExistHost (152.1.19.9)\}$, and the consequence set $C(h_{SadmindPing}) = \{VulnerableSadmind (152.1.19.5), VulnerableSadmind (152.1.19.7), Vulnerable\text{-}Sadmind (152.1.19.9)\}$.

Example 4. Consider the hyper-alert $h_{SadmindBOF}$ in Example 2. The prerequisite set of $h_{SadmindBOF}$ is $P(h_{SadmindBOF}) = \{ExistHost (152.1.19.5), ExistHost (152.1.19.7), VulnerableSadmind (152.1.19.5), VulnerableSadmind (152.1.19.7)\}$, and the consequence set is $C(h_{SadmindBOF}) = \{GainRootAccess (152.1.19.5), Gain\text{-}RootAccess (152.1.19.7)\}$.

Definition 4. Hyper-alert h_1 *prepares for* hyper-alert h_2, if there exist $p \in P(h_2)$ and $C \subseteq C(h_1)$ such that for all $c \in C$, $c.end\_time < p.begin\_time$ and the conjunction of all the predicates in C implies p.

The prepare-for relation is developed to capture the causal relationships between hyper-alerts. Intuitively, h_1 prepares for h_2 if some attacks represented by h_1 make the attacks represented by h_2 easier to succeed.

Example 5. Let us continue Examples 3 and 4. Assume that all tuples in $h_{SadmindPing}$ have timestamps earlier than every tuple in $h_{SadmindBOF}$. By comparing the contents of $C(h_{SadmindPing})$ and $P(h_{SadmindBOF})$, it is clear the instantiated predicate $VulnerableSadmind (152.1.19.5)$ (among others) in $P(h_{SadmindBOF})$ is also in $C(h_{SadmindPing})$. Thus, $h_{SadmindPing}$ prepares for, and should be correlated with $h_{SadmindBOF}$.

Given a sequence S of hyper-alerts, a hyper-alert h in S is a *correlated hyperalert*, if there exists another hyper-alert h' in S such that either h prepares for h' or h' prepares for h. If no such h' exists, h is called an *isolated hyper-alert*. The goal of the correlation process is to discover all pairs of hyper-alerts h_1 and h_2 in S such that h_1 prepares for h_2.

The prepare-for relation between hyper-alerts provides a natural way to represent the causal relationship between correlated hyper-alerts. In the following, we introduce the notion of a *hyper-alert correlation graph* to represent attack scenarios on the basis of the prepare-for relation. As we will see, the hyper-alert correlation graph reflects the high-level strategies or logical steps behind a sequence of attacks.

Definition 5. A *hyper-alert correlation graph* $HG = (N, E)$ is a connected DAG, where the set N of nodes is a set of hyper-alerts, and for each pair of nodes n_1, $n_2 \in N$, there is an edge from n_1 to n_2 in E if and only if n_1 prepares for n_2.

The hyper-alert correlation graph is not only an intuitive way to represent attack scenarios constructed through alert correlation but also reveals opportunities to improve intrusion detection. First, the hyper-alert correlation graph can potentially reveal the intrusion strategies behind the attacks and thus lead to better understanding of the attacker's intention. Second, assuming some attackers exhibit patterns in their attack strategies, we can use the hyper-alert correlation graph to profile previous attacks and thus identify on-going attacks by matching to the profiles. A partial match to a profile may indicate attacks possibly missed by the IDSs, and thus lead to human investigation and improvement of the IDSs. Nevertheless, additional research is necessary to demonstrate the usefulness of hyper-alert correlation graphs for this purpose.

Figure 1 shows a hyper-alert correlation graph discovered in our experiments [27]. Each node in Fig. 1 represents a hyper-alert. The text inside the node is the name of the hyper-alert type followed by the hyper-alert ID. (We will follow this convention for all the hyper-alert correlation graphs.)

The hyper-alerts can be divided into five stages horizontally. The first stage consists of three *Sadmind_Ping* alerts, which the attacker used to find out the vulnerable *Sadmind* services. The three alerts are from source IP address 202.077.162.213, and to destination IP addresses 172.016.112.010, 172.016.115.020, and 172.016.112.050,

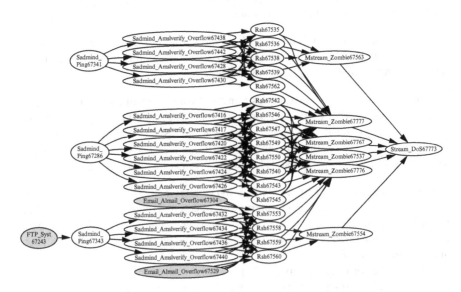

Fig. 1 A hyper-alert correlation graph discovered in our experiments

respectively. The second stage consists of fourteen *Sadmind_Amslverify_Overflow* alerts. According to the description of the attack scenario, the attacker tried three different stack pointers and two commands in *Sadmind_Amslverify_Overflow* attacks for each victim host until one attempt succeeded. All the above three hosts were successfully broken into. The third stage consists of some *Rsh* alerts, with which the attacker installed and started the *mstream* daemon and master programs. The fourth stage consists of alerts corresponding to the communications between the DDOS master and daemon programs. Finally, the last stage consists of the DDOS attack. We can see clearly that the hyper-alert correlation graph reveals the structure as well as the high-level strategy of the sequence of attacks.

To better understand the effectiveness of our method, we examine the *completeness* and the *soundness* of alert correlation. The completeness of alert correlation assesses how well we can correlate related alerts together, while the soundness evaluates how correctly the alerts are correlated. Figure 2 shows the completeness and the soundness measures computed in our experiments [27]. We also examine the effect of alert correlation in differentiating true and false alerts. Figures 3 and 4 show

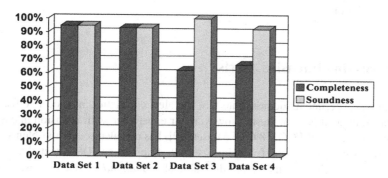

Fig. 2 Completeness and soundness

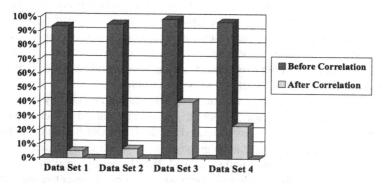

Fig. 3 False alert rate

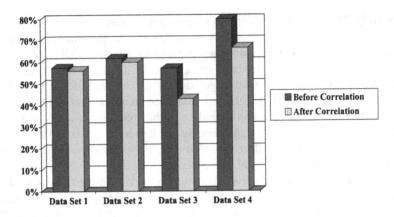

Fig. 4 Detection rate

the false alert rate and the detection rate before and after alert correlation. We can see a significant reduction in false alert rate but a slight reduction in detection rate after correlation.

3 Analyzing Intensive Alerts

Our initial experiments demonstrate that the alert correlation method is effective in analyzing small sets of alerts. However, our experience with intrusion intensive datasets (e.g., the DEFCON 8 CTF dataset [10]) has revealed several problems.

First, let us consider the following scenario. Suppose an IDS detected an *SadmindPing* attack, which discovered the vulnerable *Sadmind* service on host V, and later an *SadmindBufferOverflow* attack against the *Sadmind* service. Assuming that they were launched from different hosts, should we correlate them? On the one hand, it is possible that one or two attackers coordinated these two attacks from two different hosts, trying to avoid being correlated. On the other hand, it is also possible that these attacks belonged to two separate attempts. Such a scenario clearly introduces a dilemma, especially when there are a large number of alerts. One may suggest to use time to solve this problem. For example, we may correlate the aforementioned attacks if they happened within t seconds. However, knowing this method, an attacker may introduce delays between attacks to bypass correlation.

The second problem is the overwhelming information encoded by hyper-alert correlation graphs when intensive attacks trigger a large amount of alerts. Our initial attempt to correlate the alerts generated for the DEFCON 8 CTF dataset [10] resulted in 450 hyper-alert correlation graphs, among which the largest hyper-alert correlation graph consists of 2,940 nodes and 25,321 edges even if the transitive edges are removed. Such a graph is clearly too big for a human user to comprehend in a short period of time. Although the DEFCON 8 dataset involves intensive attacks not usually seen in normal network traffic, the actual experience of intrusion detection practitioners indicates that "encountering 10–20,000 alarms per sensor per day is common [22]." Thus, it is necessary to develop techniques or tools to deal with the overwhelming information.

In this section, we develop a set of utilities to at least partially address these problems. These utilities are provided for human analysts to examine different aspects of (correlated) alerts efficiently. Though they cannot fully solve the first problem, these utilities can help analysts get as much information as possible and make the best judgment. To address the second problem, some of the utilities are designed to narrow down the scope of alerts being analyzed or reduce the complexity of hyper-alert correlation graphs. These utilities are then integrated into one system (which we will present in the next section), which provides human analysts a platform to examine correlated intrusion alerts interactively and progressively.

Each utility takes a set of hyper-alerts as input. Depending on the output, these utilities can be divided into two classes: *hyper-alert generating utilities* and *feature extraction utilities*. A hyper-alert generating utility outputs one or multiple sets of hyper-alerts, while a feature extraction utility only outputs the properties of the input hyper-alerts. We have developed six utilities, including *alert aggregation/disaggregation, focused analysis, clustering analysis, frequency analysis, link analysis*, and *association analysis*. The first three utilities are hyper-alert generating utilities, while the last three are feature extraction utilities.

3.1 Alert Aggregation and Disaggregation

The goal of alert aggregation is to reduce the complexity of hyper-alert correlation graphs without sacrificing the structures of the attack scenarios; it allows analysts to get concise views of correlated alerts. For this reason, we also refer to alert aggregation as *graph reduction*. Alert disaggregation allows analysts to selectively disaggregate certain aggregated alerts, thus providing the ability to examine the details of select aggregated alerts.

3.1.1 Alert Aggregation

As discussed earlier, the difficulty of understanding a large hyper-alert correlation graph is mainly due to the large numbers of nodes and edges in the graph. Thus, a natural way to reduce the complexity of a large hyper-alert correlation graph is to reduce the number of nodes and edges. However, to make the reduced graph useful, any reasonable reduction should maintain the structure of the corresponding attacks.

We propose to aggregate hyper-alerts of the same type to reduce the number of nodes in a hyper-alert correlation graph. Due to the flexible definition of hyper-alerts, the result of hyper-alert aggregation will remain valid hyper-alerts. For example, in Fig. 5, hyper-alerts 67432, 67434, 67436, and 67440 are all instances of

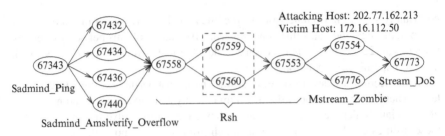

Fig. 5 A hyper-alert correlation graph discovered in the 2000 DARPA intrusion detection evaluation datasets

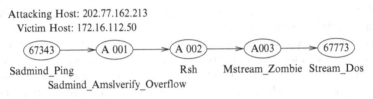

Fig. 6 A hyper-alert correlation graph reduced from Fig. 5

hyper-alert type *Sadmind_Amslverify_Overflow*. Thus, we may aggregate them into one hyper-alert. As another example, hyper-alerts 67558, 67559, 67560, and 67553 are all instances of *Rsh*, and can be aggregated into a single hyper-alert.

Edges are reduced along with the aggregation of hyper-alerts. In Fig. 5, the edges between the *Rsh* hyper-alerts are subsumed into the aggregated hyper-alert, while the edges between the *Sadmind_Ping* hyper-alert and the four *Sadmind_Amslverify_Overflow* hyper-alerts are merged into a single edge. As a result, we have a reduced hyper-alert correlation graph as shown in Fig. 6.

Reduction of a hyper-alert correlation graph may lose information contained in the original graph. Indeed, hyper-alerts that are of the same type but belong to different sequences of attacks may be aggregated and thus provide overly simplified results. Nevertheless, our goal is to lose as little information about the structure of attacks as possible.

Depending on the actual alerts, the reduction of a hyper-alert correlation graph may be less simplified so that there is too much detail in the resulting graph, or overly simplified so that some structures are hidden. We would like to give a human user more control over the graph reduction process.

We allow hyper-alert aggregation only when the resulting hyper-alerts satisfy an interval constraint of a given threshold I. Intuitively, we allow hyper-alerts to be aggregated only when they are close to each other in time. The larger a threshold I is, the more a hyper-alert correlation graph can be reduced. By adjusting the interval threshold, a user can control the degree to which a hyper-alert correlation graph is reduced.

Though simply aggregating the same type of hyper-alerts can simplify complex hyper-alert correlation graphs and thus improve their readability, one problem still

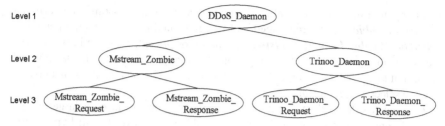

Fig. 7 An example abstraction hierarchy of hyper-alert types

remains. That is, there may be many types of alerts in a hyper-alert correlation graph. One incentive to have many types of alerts is to allow fine-grained names for different types of alerts and thus to keep more semantics along with the alerts. However, a reduced hyper-alert correlation graph may still have too many nodes and remain difficult to understand.

To allow further reduction of hyper-alert correlation graphs, we extend the above aggregation by combining *abstraction* with interval constraints. Specifically, we generalize each hyper-alert type to a more abstract one. For example, RealSecure Network Sensor 7.0 may raise two types of alerts for *mstream* zombie activities: *Mstream_Zombie_Request* and *Mstream_Zombie_Response* alerts, which represent the request sent from an mstream master program to an mstream zombie program and the response, respectively. We may abstract both of them into one type of *Mstream_Zombie* alerts. Abstraction may be performed hierarchically so that there are different levels of abstractions. For example, we may generalize *Mstream_Zombie* and *Trinoo_Daemon* into a type of *DDoS_Daemon* alert. We assign an abstraction level to each (abstract) hyper-alert type to reflect the degree of abstraction. Figure 7 shows the abstraction hierarchy for this example.

3.1.2 Alert Disaggregation

Alert aggregation controlled by interval constraints and abstraction hierarchies of hyper-alert types can reduce the size of hyper-alert graphs and present concise views of correlated alerts. However, some details of the correlated alerts and the prepare-for relations are hidden in the aggregated alerts. Alert disaggregation provides a way to examine additional details of certain aggregated hyper-alerts in the context of reduced hyper-alert correlation graphs.

Similar to alert aggregation, alert disaggregation is also performed in terms of interval constraints and abstraction hierarchies. Specifically, given an aggregated hyper-alert, we may specify an interval threshold smaller than the one used for aggregation and/or an abstraction level lower than the one used for the aggregated hyper-alert, so that this aggregated hyper-alert is divided into multiple finer-grained hyper-alerts. For example, we may choose to disaggregate an *Mstream_Zombie* hyper-alert to level 3 abstraction according to the abstraction hierarchy in Fig. 7. As a result, all the raw alerts that constitute the original *Mstream_Zombie* will be regrouped and re-aggregated based on their finer types (*Mstream_Zombie_Request* or *Mstream_Zombie_Response*), resulting in two hyper-alerts. In some sense, alert disaggregation is a re-application of a smaller interval constraint threshold and a lower-level abstraction level to the raw alerts that consti-tute the select aggregated alert.

One way to effectively use alert aggregation/disaggregation is to use large enough interval constraint threshold and the highest abstraction level for all hyper-alerts when performing alert aggregation for the first time. This will result in concise hyper-alert correlation graphs. After getting the high-level idea of the alerts in the hyper-alert correlation graphs, we may select hyper-alerts in the graph and dis-aggregate them by reducing their abstraction levels and/or the interval constraint threshold. This will regenerate the hyper-alert correlation graphs in a finer granu-larity for selected hyper-alerts. As a result, different levels of abstractions can be used for different hyper-alerts in the same hyper-alert correlation graph. Moreover, this also implies that the abstraction levels assigned to hyper-alert types have little impact on the analysis results.

3.2 Focused Analysis

Focused analysis is to help an analyst focus on the hyper-alerts in which he or she is interested. In particular, this may generate hyper-alert correlation graphs much smaller and more comprehensible than the original ones.

Focused analysis is implemented on the basis of focusing constraints. A *focusing constraint* is a logical combination of comparisons between attribute names and constants. (In our work, we restrict logical operations to AND ($\wedge$), OR ($\vee$), and NOT ($\neg$).) For example, we may have a focusing constraint $SrcIP = 129.174.142.2 \vee DestIP = 129.174.142.2$. We say a focusing constraint C_f is *enforceable w.r.t. a hyper-alert type* T, if when we represent C_f in a disjunctive normal form, at least for one disjunct C_{fi}, all the attribute names in C_{fi} appear in T. For example, the above focusing constraint is enforceable w.r.t. $T = (\{SrcIP, SrcPort\}, NULL, \emptyset)$, but not w.r.t. $T' = (\{VictimIP, VictimPort\}, NULL, \emptyset)$. Intuitively, a focusing constraint is enforceable w.r.t. T if it can be evaluated using a hyper-alert instance of type T.

We may *evaluate* a focusing constraint C_f with a hyper-alert h if C_f is en-forceable w.r.t. the type of h. A focusing constraint C_f evaluates to True for h if there exists a tuple $t \in h$ such that C_f is True with the attribute names replaced with the values of the corresponding attributes of t; otherwise, C_f eval-uates to False. For example, consider the aforementioned focusing constraint C_f, which is $SrcIP = 129.174.142.2 \vee DestIP = 129.174.142.2$, and a hyper-alert $h = \{(SrcIP = 129.174.142.2, SrcPort = 80)\}$, we can easily have that $C_f = $ True for h.

The idea of focused analysis is quite simple: we only analyze the hyper-alerts with which a focusing constraint evaluates to True. In other words, we would like to filter out irrelevant hyper-alerts and concentrate on analyzing the remaining hyper-alerts. We are particularly interested in applying focusing constraints to *atomic hyper-alerts*, i.e., hyper-alerts with only one tuple. In our framework, atomic hyper-alerts correspond to the alerts reported by an IDS directly.

Focused analysis is particularly useful when we have certain knowledge of the alerts, the systems being protected, or the attacking computers. For example, if we are interested in the attacks against a critical server with IP address *Server_IP*, we may perform a focused analysis using *DestIP* = *Server_IP*. However, focused analysis cannot take advantage of the intrinsic relationship among the hyper-alerts (e.g., hyper-alerts having the same IP address). In the following, we introduce the third utility, clustering analysis, to fill in this gap.

3.3   Clustering Analysis

Intuitively, clustering analysis is to partition a set of hyper-alerts into different groups so that the hyper-alerts in each group share certain common features. As a special case, we refer to the clustering analysis applied to a hyper-alert correlation graph as *graph decomposition*, since this operation will decompose the original correlation graphs into subgraphs on the basis of the clusters.

We use a *clustering constraint* to specify the "common features" for clustering hyper-alerts. Given two sets of attribute names A_1 and A_2, a *clustering constraint* $C_c(A_1, A_2)$ is a logical combination of comparisons between constants and attribute names in A_1 and A_2. (In our work, we restrict logical operations to AND ($\wedge$), OR ($\vee$), and NOT ($\neg$).) A clustering constraint is a constraint for two hyper-alerts; the attribute sets A_1 and A_2 identify the attributes from the two hyper-alerts. For example, we may have two sets of attribute names $A_1 = \{SrcIP, DestIP\}$ and $A_2 = \{SrcIP, DestIP\}$, and $C_c(A_1, A_2) = (A_1.SrcIP = A_2.SrcIP) \wedge (A_1.DestIP = A_2.DestIP)$. Intuitively, this is to say two hyper-alerts should remain in the same cluster if they have the same source and destination IP addresses.

A clustering constraint $C_c(A_1, A_2)$ is *enforceable w.r.t. hyper-alert types T_1 and T_2* if when we represent $C_c(A_1, A_2)$ in a disjunctive normal form, at least for one disjunct C_{ci}, all the attribute names in A_1 appear in T_1 and all the attribute names in A_2 appear in T_2. For example, the above clustering constraint is enforceable w.r.t. T_1 and T_2 if both of them have *SrcIP* and *DestIP* in the *fact* component. Intuitively, a clustering constraint is enforceable w.r.t. T_1 and T_2 if it can be evaluated using two hyper-alerts of types T_1 and T_2, respectively.

If a clustering constraint $C_c(A_1, A_2)$ is enforceable w.r.t. T_1 and T_2, we can *evaluate* it with two hyper-alerts h_1 and h_2 that are of type T_1 and T_2, respectively. A clustering constraint $C_c(A_1, A_2)$ evaluates to True for h_1 and h_2 if there exists a tuple $t_1 \in h_1$ and $t_2 \in h_2$ such that $C_c(A_1, A_2)$ is True with the attribute names in A_1 and A_2 replaced with the values of the corresponding attributes of t_1 and t_2, respectively; otherwise, $C_c(A_1, A_2)$ evaluates to False. For example, consider the clustering constraint $C_c(A_1, A_2)$: $(A_1.SrcIP = A_2.SrcIP) \wedge (A_1.DestIP = $

$A_2.DestIP$), and hyper-alerts $h_1 = \{(SrcIP = 129.174.142.2, SrcPort = 1234, DestIP = 152.1.14.5, DestPort = 80)\}$, $h_2 = \{(SrcIP = 129.174.142.2, SrcPort = 65333, DestIP = 152.1.14.5, DestPort = 23)\}$, we can easily have that $C_c(A_1, A_2) =$ True for h_1 and h_2. For brevity, we write $C_c(h_1, h_2) =$ True if $C_c(A_1, A_2) =$ True for h_1 and h_2.

Our clustering method is very simple, with a user-specified clustering constraint $C_c(A_1, A_2)$. Two hyper-alerts h_1 and h_2 are in the same cluster if $C_c(A_1, A_2)$ evaluates to True for h_1 and h_2 (or h_2 and h_1). Note that $C_c(h_1, h_2)$ implies that h_1 and h_2 are in the same cluster, but the reverse is not true. This is because $C_c(h_1, h_2) \wedge C_c(h_2, h_3)$ (i.e., h_1, h_2, and h_3 are in the same cluster) implies neither $C_c(h_1, h_3)$ nor $C_c(h_3, h_1)$.

3.4 Frequency Analysis

Frequency analysis is developed to help an analyst identify patterns in a collection of alerts by counting the number of raw alerts that share some common features. Similar to clustering analysis, frequency analysis partitions the input collection of hyper-alerts. For example, an analyst may count the number of raw alerts that share the same destination IP address to find the most frequently hit target. For convenience, we reuse the notion of clustering constraints to specify the clusters.

Frequency analysis can be applied in both *count mode* and *weighted analysis mode*. In count mode, frequency analysis simply counts the number of raw intrusion alerts that fall into the same cluster, while in weighted analysis mode, it adds all the values of a given numerical attribute (called the weight attribute) of all the alerts in the same cluster. As an example of frequency analysis in weighted analysis mode, an analyst may use the priority of an alert type as the weight attribute, and learn the weighted frequency of alerts for all destination IP addresses.

For convenience reasons, frequency analysis automatically ranks the clusters ascendantly or descendantly in terms of the results. A filter which specifies a range of frequency values may be applied optionally so that only results that fall into this range are returned to the analyst.

The frequency analysis utility is conceptually equivalent to applying clustering analysis followed by a simple counting or summing for each of the clusters. However, since frequency analysis is developed for interactive analysis, it is much more convenient for an analyst if there is a utility combining these operations together, especially when not all the clusters need to be reported to the analyst.

3.5 Link Analysis

Link analysis is intended to analyze the connection between entities represented by categorical attribute values. Examples include how two IP addresses are related to each other in a collection of alerts, and how IP addresses are connected to the alert types. Though link analysis takes a collection of hyper-alerts as input, it indeed analyzes the raw intrusion alerts corresponding to these hyper-alerts. Link analysis can identify candidate attribute values, evaluate their importance according to a user-defined metric and rank them accordingly.

Link analysis takes at least two categorical attributes, A_1 and A_2 (e.g., source IP and destination IP), as parameters. Similar to frequency analysis, link analysis may be used in *count mode* or *weighted analysis mode*. In the latter case, link analysis needs an additional weight attribute with a numerical domain. For each pair of attribute values $(A_1 = a_1, A_2 = a_2)$, link analysis with categorical attributes A_1 and A_2 counts the number of all the alerts that have $A_1 = a_1$ and $A_2 = a_2$ in count mode, or summarize the weight attribute values of these alerts in weighted analysis mode.

Given a link analysis with categorical attributes A_1 and A_2 over a collection of hyper-alerts, or equivalently, the corresponding set of raw intrusion alerts, we call each pair of attribute values a *link involving attributes A_1 and A_2*, denoted $(A_1 = a_1, A_2 = a_2)$. We then define the *weight of a link* $(A_1 = a_1, A_2 = a_2)$ as the number of alerts that have $A_1 = a_1$ and $A_2 = a_2$ in count mode, or the sum of the corresponding weight attribute values in weighted analysis mode. The *weight of an attribute value* is then the sum of the weights of the links involving the value. Specifically, the weight of $A_1 = a_1$ is the sum of the weights of all links that have a_1 as the value of A_1, while the weight of $A_2 = a_2$ is the sum of the weights of all links that have a_2 as the value of A_2.

Link analysis has two variations, *dual-domain link analysis* and *uni-domain link analysis*, depending on the treatment of the values of the two categorical attributes. In dual-domain link analysis, values of the two categorical alert attributes are considered different entities, even though they may have the same value. For example, we may perform a dual-domain link analysis involving source IP address and destination IP address. An IP address representing source IP is considered as a different entity from the same IP address representing a destination IP address. In contrast, uni-domain link analysis requires that the two attributes involved in link analysis must have the same domain, and the same value is considered to represent the same entity, no matter which attribute it corresponds to. In the earlier example, the same IP address represents the same host, no matter it is a source or a destination IP address.

The result of a link analysis can be visualized in a graphical format. Attribute values are represented as nodes in the (undirected) graph, with different sizes representing the weight of the corresponding attribute values. When uni-domain link analysis is used, all the nodes have the same shape (e.g., circle); when dual-domain link analysis is used, two different shapes (e.g., circle and square) correspond to the two different attributes, respectively. The link between two attribute values is represented by the edge connecting the corresponding nodes. The weight of each link is indicated by the color of the edge. Figure 8 shows an example of a uni-domain link analysis. Note that additional information (e.g., attribute values) about each node or link can be obtained through a user interface.

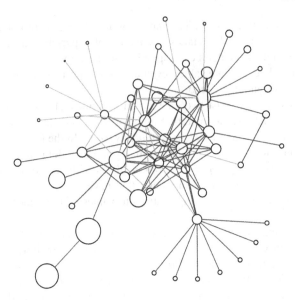

Fig. 8 Visual representation of a uni-domain link analysis (Note that edges are in different colors)

Link analysis can be considered a special case of association analysis, which is discussed next. However, due to its simplicity and the visual representation of its results, we use link analysis as a separate utility.

3.6 Association Analysis

Association analysis is used to find out frequent co-occurrences of values belonging to different attributes that represent various entities. For example, we may find through association analysis that many attacks are from source IP address 152.14.51.14 to destination IP address 129.14.1.31 at destination port 80. Such patterns cannot be easily found by frequency analysis because of the large number of attribute combinations that would need to be analyzed using frequency analysis.

Association analysis is inspired by the notion of association rule, which was first introduced in [1]. Given a set I of items, an *association rule* is a rule of the form $X \rightarrow Y$, where X and Y are subsets (called item sets) of I and $X \cap Y = \emptyset$. Association rules are usually discovered from a set T of transactions, where each transaction is a subset of I. The rule $X \rightarrow Y$ has a support s in the transaction set T if $s\%$ of the transactions in T contain $X \cup Y$, and it has a confidence c if $c\%$ of the transactions in T that contain X also contain Y.

We do not use association rules directly; instead, we use the item sets that have large enough support (called *large item sets*) to represent the patterns embedded in alert attributes. We consider each raw alert a transaction. The large item sets discovered from the intrusion alerts then represent frequent attribute patterns in the alert set.

Syntactically, association analysis takes a set S of categorical alert attributes and a threshold t as parameters. Similar to frequency analysis and link analysis, association analysis can be applied in both count mode and weighted analysis mode. In the latter mode, association analysis requires a numerical attribute (also called a weight attribute) as an additional parameter. To facilitate the weighted analysis mode, we extend the notion of support to *weighted support*. Given a set X of attribute values and a weight attribute w, the *weighted support of X w.r.t. w* in the alert (transaction) set T is

$$\text{weighted support}_w(X) = \frac{\text{sum of } w \text{ of all alerts in } T \text{ that contain } X}{\text{sum of } w \text{ of all alerts in } T}.$$

Thus, association analysis of a collection of alerts in count mode finds all sets of attribute values that have support more than t, while association analysis of a collection of alerts in weighted analysis mode returns all sets of attribute values that have weighted support more than t.

3.7 Discussion

It is desirable to develop techniques that can comprehend a hyper-alert correlation graph and generate feedback to direct intrusion detection and response processes. We consider such a technique a part of our future research plan. However, given the current status of intrusion detection and response techniques, it is also necessary to allow human users to understand the attacks and take appropriate actions. The utilities developed in this section are intended to help human users analyze attacks behind large amounts of alerts. They can make attack strategies behind intensive alerts easier to understand, but cannot improve the performance of alert correlation.

4 Learning Attack Strategies from Correlated Alerts

The correlation model can be used to construct attack scenarios (represented as hyper-alert correlation graphs) from intrusion alerts. Although such attack scenarios *reflect* attack strategies, they do not capture the essence of the strategies. Indeed, even with the same attack strategy, if an attacker changes certain details during attacks, the correlation model will generate different hyper-alert correlation graphs. For example, an attacker may repeat (unnecessarily) one step in a sequence of attacks many times, and the correlation model will generate a much more complex attack scenario. As another example, if an attacker uses equivalent, but different attacks, the correlation model will generate different hyper-alert correlation graphs as well. It is then up to the user to figure out manually the common strategy used in two sequences of attacks. This certainly increases the overhead in intrusion alert analysis.

In the following, we present a model to represent and automatically extract attack strategies from correlated alerts. The goal of this model is to capture the invariants in attack strategies that do not change across multiple instances of attacks.

4.1 Attack Strategy Graph

The strategy behind a sequence of attacks is indeed about how to arrange earlier attacks to prepare for the later ones so that the attacker can reach his or her final goal. Thus, the prepare-for relations between the intrusion alerts (i.e., detected attacks) is intrinsic to attack strategies. However, in the correlation model, the prepare-for relations are between specific intrusion alerts; they do not directly capture the conditions that have to be met by related attacks. To facilitate the representation of the invariant attack strategy, we transform the prepare-for relation into some common conditions that have to be satisfied by *all* possible instances of the same strategy. We represent such a condition as an *equality constraint*.

To clarify the notion of equality constraint, we need to explain the concept of expanded consequence set. Given a hyper-alert type T, the *expanded consequence set* of T, denoted $EC(T)$, is the set of all predicates that are implied by T's consequence set $C(T)$. Thus, $C(T) \subseteq EC(T)$. $EC(T)$ can be computed using the implication relationships between predicates [27]. Given a type T hyper-alert h, the *expanded consequence set of h*, denoted $EC(h)$), is the predicates in $EC(T)$ whose arguments are replaced with the corresponding attribute values of each tuple in h. Each element in $EC(h)$ is associated with the timestamp of the corresponding tuple in h.

In the following, we give the formal definition of equality constraint.

Definition 6. Given hyper-alert types T_1 and T_2, an *equality constraint for* (T_1, T_2) is a conjunction of equalities in the form of $u_1 = v_1 \wedge \cdots \wedge u_n = v_n$, where $u_1, \cdots, u_n$ are attribute names in T_1 and $v_1, \cdots, v_n$ are attribute names in T_2, such that there exist $p(u_1, \cdots, u_n)$ and $p(v_1, \cdots, v_n)$, which are the same predicate with possibly different arguments, in $EC(T_1)$ and $P(T_2)$, respectively. Given a type T_1 hyper-alert h_1 and a type T_2 hyper-alert h_2, h_1 and h_2 *satisfy the equality constraint* if there exist $t_1 \in h_1$ and $t_2 \in h_2$ such that $t_1.u_1 = t_2.v_1 \wedge \cdots \wedge t_1.u_n = t_2.v_n$ evaluates to True.

There may be several equality constraints for a pair of hyper-alert types. However, if a type T_1 hyper-alert h_1 prepares for a type T_2 hyper-alert h_2, then h_1 and h_2 must satisfy at least one of the equality constraints. Indeed, h_1 preparing for h_2 is equivalent to the conjunction of h_1 and h_2 satisfying at least one equivalent constraint and h_1 occurring before h_2. Assume that h_1 occurs before h_2. If h_1 and h_2 satisfy an equality constraint for (T_1, T_2), then by Definition 6, there must be a predicate $p(u_1, \cdots, u_n)$ in $EC(T_1)$ such that the same predicate with possibly different arguments, $p(v_1, \cdots, v_n)$, is in $P(T_2)$. Since h_1 and h_2 satisfy the equality constraint, $p(u_1, \cdots, u_n)$ and $p(v_1, \cdots, v_n)$ will be instantiated to the same predicate in $EC(h_1)$ and $P(h_2)$. This implies that h_1 prepares for h_2. Similarly, if h_1 prepares for h_2, there must be an instantiated predicate that appears in $EC(h_1)$ and $P(h_2)$. This implies that there must be a predicate with possibly different arguments in $EC(T_1)$ and $P(T_2)$ and that this predicate leads to an equality constraint for (T_1, T_2) satisfied by h_1 and h_2.

Example 6. Consider the hyper-alert types: *SadmindPing* = ({*VictimIP, Victim-Port*}, *ExistsHost(VictimIP)*, {*VulnerableSadmind (VictimIP)*}), and *SadmindBuffer-Overflow* = ({*VictimIP, VictimPort*}, *ExistHost (VictimIP)* ∧ *VulnerableSadmind (VictimIP)*, {*GainRootAccess (VictimIP)*}). The first hyper-alert type indicates that *SadmindPing* is a type of attack that requires the existence of a host at the *VictimIP*, and as a result, the attacker may find out that this host has a vulnerable *Sadmind* service. The second hyper-alert type indicates that this type of attacks requires a vulnerable *Sadmind* service at the *VictimIP*, and as a result, the attack may gain root access. It is easy to see that the predicate *VulnerableSadmind* is in both $P(SadmindBufferOverflow)$ and $EC (SadmindPing)$. So, we have an equality constraint *VictimIP* = *VictimIP* for (*SadmindPing, SadmindBufferOverflow*), where the first *VictimIP* comes from *SadmindPing*, and the second *VictimIP* comes from *SadmindBufferOverflow*.

We observe many times that one step in a sequence of attacks may trigger multiple intrusion alerts, and the number of alerts may vary in different situations. This is partially due to the existing vulnerabilities and the hacking tools. For example, unicode_shell [30], which is a hacking tool against Microsoft IIS web server, checks about 20 vulnerabilities at the scanning stage and usually triggers the same number of alerts. As another example, in the attack scenario reported in [27], the attacker tried three different stack pointers and two commands in *Sadmind_Amslverify_Overflow* attacks for each victim host until one attempt succeeded. Even if not necessary, an attacker may still deliberately repeat the same step multiple times to confuse IDSs and/or system administrators. However, such variations do not change the corresponding attack strategy. Indeed, these variations make the attack scenarios unnecessarily complex, and may hinder manual or automatic analysis of the attack strategy. Thus, we decide to disallow such situations in our representation of attack strategies.

In the following, an attack strategy is formally represented as an attack strategy graph.

Definition 7. Given a set S of hyper-alert types, an *attack strategy graph* over S is a quadruple (N, E, T, C), where (1) (N, E) is a connected DAG; (2) T is a mapping that maps each $n \in N$ to a hyper-alert type in S; (3) C is a mapping that maps each edge $(n_1, n_2) \in E$ to a set of equality constraints for $(T(n_1), T(n_2))$; (4) For any $n_1, n_2 \in N$, $T(n_1) = T(n_2)$ implies that there exists $n_3 \in N$ such that $T(n_3) \neq T(n_1)$, and n_3 is in a path between n_1 and n_2.

In an attack strategy graph, each node represents a step in a sequence of related attacks. Each edge (n_1, n_2) represents that a type $T(n_1)$ attack is needed to prepare

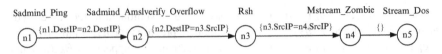

Fig. 9 An example of attack strategy graph

for a successful type $T(n_2)$ attack. Each edge may also be associated with a set of equality constraints satisfied by the intrusion alerts. These equality constraints indicate how one attack prepares for another. Finally, as represented by condition 4 in Definition 7, same type of attacks should be considered as one step, unless they depend on each other through other types of attacks.

Now, let us see an example of an attack strategy graph.

Example 7. Figure 9 is the attack strategy graph extracted from the hyper-alert correlation graph in Fig. 5. The hyper-alert types are marked above the corresponding nodes, and the equality constraints are labeled near the corresponding edges. This attack strategy graph clearly shows the component attacks and the constraints that the component attacks must satisfy.

4.2 Learning Attack Strategies

As discussed earlier, our goal is to learn attack strategies automatically from correlated intrusion alerts. This requires us to extract the constraints intrinsic to attack strategy from alerts so that the constraints apply to all instances of the same strategy.

Our strategy to achieve this goal is to process the correlated intrusion alerts in two steps. First, we aggregate intrusion alerts that belong to the same step of a sequence of attacks into one hyper-alert. For example, in Fig. 5, alerts 67432, 67434, 67436, and 67440 are indeed attempts of the same attack with different parameters, and thus they should be aggregated as one step in the attack sequence. Second, we extract the constraints between the attack steps and represent them as an attack strategy graph. For example, after we aggregate the hyper-alerts in the first step, we may extract the attack strategy graph shown in Fig. 9.

The challenge lies in the first step. Because of the variations of attacks as well as the signatures that IDSs use to recognize attacks, there is no clear way to identify intrusion alerts that belong to the same step in a sequence of attacks. In the following, we first attempt to use the attack type information to do so. The notion of *aggregatable* hyper-alerts is introduced formally to clarify when the same type of hyper-alerts can be aggregated.

Definition 8. Given a hyper-alert correlation graph $CG = (N, E)$, a subset $N' \subseteq N$ is *aggregatable*, if (1) all nodes in N' are the same type of hyper-alerts, and (2) $\forall n_1, n_2 \in N'$, if there is a path from n_1 to n_2, then all nodes in this path must be in N'.

Intuitively, in a hyper-alert correlation graph, where intrusion alerts have been correlated together, the same type of hyper-alerts can be aggregated as long as they are not used in different stages in the attack sequence. Condition 1 in Definition 8 is quite straightforward, but condition 2 deserves more explanation. Consider the same type of hyper-alerts h_1 and h_2. If h_1 prepares for a different type of hyper-alert h' (directly or indirectly), and h' further prepares for h_2 (directly or indirectly), h_1 and h_2 obviously belong to different steps in the same sequence of attacks. Thus, we should not allow them to be aggregated together. Although we have never observed such situations, we cannot rule out such possibilities.

Based on the notion of aggregatable hyper-alerts, the first step in learning attack strategy from a hyper-alert correlation graph is quite straightforward. We only need to identify and merge all aggregatable hyper-alerts. To proceed to the second step in strategy learning, we need a hyper-alert correlation graph in which each hyper-alert represents a separate step in the attack sequence. Formally, we call such a hyper-alert correlation graph an irreducible hyper-alert correlation graph.

Definition 9. A hyper-alert correlation graph $CG = (N, E)$ is *irreducible* if for all $N' \subseteq N$, where $|N'| > 1$, N' is not aggregatable.

Figure 10 shows the algorithm to extract attack strategy graphs from hyper-alert correlation graphs. The subroutine *GraphReduction* is used to generate an irreducible hyper-alert correlation graph, and the rest of the algorithm extracts the components of the output attack strategy graph. The steps in this algorithm are self-explanatory; we do not repeat them in the text.

4.3 Dealing with Variations of Attacks

Algorithm 1 in Fig. 10 has ignored equivalent but different attacks in sequences of attacks. For example, an attacker may use either *pmap_dump* or *Sadmind_Ping* to find a vulnerable Sadmind service. As another example, an attacker may use either *SadmindBufferOverflow* or *TooltalkBufferOverflow* attack to gain remote access to a host. Obviously, at the same stage of two sequences of attacks, if an attacker uses equivalent but different attacks, Algorithm 1 will return two different attack strategy graphs, though the strategies behind them are the same.

We propose to generalize hyper-alert types so that the syntactic difference between equivalent hyper-alert types is hidden. For example, we may generalize both *SadmindBufferOverflow* and *TooltalkBufferOverflow* attacks into *RPCBufferOverflow*.

A generalized hyper-alert type is created to hide the unnecessary difference between specific hyper-alert types. Thus, an occurrence of any of the specific hyper-alerts should imply an occurrence of the generalized one. This is to say that satisfaction of the prerequisite of a specific hyper-alert implies the satisfaction of the prerequisite of the generalized hyper-alert. Moreover, to cover all possible impact

---

Algorithm 1. ExtractStrategy
Input: A hyper-alert correlation graph CG.
Output: An attack strategy graph ASG.
Method:

1. Let $CG' = $ GraphReduction (CG).
2. Let $ASG = (N, E, T, C)$ be an empty attack strategy graph.
3. **for** each hyper-alert h in CG'
4.   Add a new node, denoted n_h, into N and set
       $T(n_h)$ be the type of h.
5. **for** each edge (h, h') in CG'
6.   Add $(n_h, n_{h'})$ into E.
7.   **for** each $p_c \in EC(h)$ and $p_p \in P(h')$
8.   **if** $p_c = p_p$ **then**
9.   Add into $C(n_h, n_{h'})$ the equality constraint
               $(u_1 = v_1) \wedge \cdots \wedge (u_n = v_n)$, where u_i and v_i are
               the ith variable of p_c and p_p before instantiation, resp.
10. **return** $ASG(N, E, T, C)$.

Subroutine GraphReduction
Input: A hyper-alert correlation graph $CG = (N, E)$.
Output: An irreducible hyper-alert correlation graph $CG' = (N', E')$.
Method:

1. Partition the hyper-alerts in N into groups such that the same
   type of hyper-alerts are all in the same group.
2. **for** each group G
3.   **if** there is a path $g, n_1, \cdots, n_k, g'$ in CG such that only g
       and g' in this path are in G **then**
4.   Divide G into G_1, G_2, and G_3 such that all hyper-alerts
           in G_1 occur before n_1, all hyper-alerts in G_3 occur after
           n_k, and all the other hyper-alerts are in G_2.
5. Repeat steps 2 to 4 until no group can be divided.
6. Aggregate the hyper-alerts in each group into one hyper-alert.
7. Let N' be the set of aggregated hyper-alerts.
8. **for** all $n_1, n_2 \in N'$
9.   **if** there exists $(h_1, h_2) \in E$ and h_1 and h_2 are aggregated
       into n_1 and n_2, resp.
10.   add (n_1, n_2) into E'.
11. **return** $CG' = (N', E')$.

Fig. 10 Algorithm for extracting attack strategy graphs

of all the specific hyper-alerts, the consequences of all the specific hyper-alert types
should be included in the consequence of the generalized hyper-alert type. It is easy
to see that this generalization may cause loss of information. Thus, generalization
of hyper-alert types must be carefully handled so that information essential to attack
strategy is not lost.

In the following, we formally clarify the relationship between specific and generalized hyper-alert types.

Definition 10. Given two hyper-alert types T_g and T_s, where $T_g = \langle fact_g, prereq_g, conseq_g \rangle$ and $T_s = \langle fact_s, prereq_s, conseq_s \rangle$, we say T_g is *more general than* T_s

(or, equivalently, T_s is *more specific than* T_g) if there exists an injective mapping f from $fact_g$ to $fact_s$ such that the following conditions are satisfied:

- If we replace all variables x in $prereq_g$ with $f(x)$, $prereq_s$ implies $prereq_g$, and
- If we replace all variables x in $conseq_g$ with $f(x)$, then all formulas in $conseq_s$ are implied by $conseq_g$.

The mapping f is called the *generalization mapping* from T_s to T_g.

Example 8. Consider hyper-alert types *SadmindBufferOverflow* and *Tooltalk-BufferOverflow*: *SadmindBufferOverflow* = ({*VictimIP, VictimPort*}, *ExistHost* (*VictimIP*) ∧ *VulnerableSadmind* (*VictimIP*), {*GainRootAccess* (*VictimIP*)}), and *TooltalkBufferOverflow* = ({*VictimIP, VictimPort*}, *ExistHost* (*VictimIP*) ∧ *VulnerableTooltalk* (*VictimIP*), {*GainRootAccess* (*Victim-IP*)}). Assume that *VulnerableSadmind* (*VictimIP*) imply *VulnerableRPC* (*VictimIP*). Intuitively, this represents that if there is a vulnerable Sadmind service at *VictimIP*, then there must be a vulnerable RPC service (i.e., the Sadmind service) at *VictimIP*. Similarly, we assume *VulnerableTooltalk* (*VictimIP*) also implies *VulnerableRPC* (*VictimIP*). We can generalize both *SadmindBufferOverflow* and *TooltalkBufferOverflow* into *RPCBufferOverflow* = ({*VictimIP*}, *ExistHost* (*VictimIP*) ∧ *VulnerableRPC* (*VictimIP*), {*GainRootAccess* (*VictimIP*)}), where the generalization mapping only includes $f(VictimIP) = VictimIP$.

By identifying a generalization mapping, we can specify how a specific hyper-alert can be generalized into a more general hyper-alert. Following the generalization mapping, we can find out what attribute values of a specific hyper-alert should be assigned to the attributes of the generalized hyper-alert. The attack strategy learning algorithm can be easily modified: We first generalize the hyper-alerts in the input hyper-alert correlation graph into generalized hyper-alerts following the generalization mapping, and then apply Algorithm 1 to extract the attack strategy graph.

Although a hyper-alert can be generalized in different granularities, it is not an arbitrary process. In particular, if one hyper-alert prepares for another hyper-alert before generalization, the generalized hyper-alerts should maintain the same relationship. Otherwise, the dependency between different attack stages, which is intrinsic in an attack strategy, will be lost.

The remaining challenge is how to get the "right" generalized hyper-alert types and generalization mappings. The simplest way is to manually specify them. For example, *Apache2, Back,* and *Crashiis* are all Denial of Service attacks. We may simply generalize all of them into one *WebServiceDOS*. However, there are often different ways to generalize. To continue the above example, *Apache2* and *Back* attacks are against the apache web servers, while *Crashiis* is against the Microsoft IIS web server. To keep more information about the attacks, we may want to generalize *Apache* and *Back* into *ApacheDOS*, while generalize *Crashiis* and possibly other DOS attacks against the IIS web server into *IISDOS*. Nevertheless, this does not affect the attack strategy graphs extracted from correlated intrusion alerts as long as the constraints on the related alerts are satisfied.

4.3.1 Automatic Generalization of Hyper-Alert Types

It is time-consuming and error-prone to manually generalize hyper-alert types. One way to partially automate this process is to use clustering techniques to identify the hyper-alert types that should be generalized into a common one. In our experiments, we use the bottom-up hierarchical clustering [16] to group hyper-alert types hierarchically on the basis of the similarity between them, which is derived from the similarity between the prerequisites and consequences of hyper-alert types. The method used to compute the similarity is described below.

To facilitate the computation of similarity between prerequisites of hyper-alert types, we convert each prerequisite into an *expanded prerequisite set*, which includes all the predicates that appear or are implied by the prerequisite. Similarly, we can get the expanded consequence set. Consider two sets of predicates, denoted S_1 and S_2, respectively. We adopt the Jaccard similarity coefficient [15] to compute the similarity between S_1 and S_2, denoted $Sim(S_1, S_2)$. That is, $Sim(S_1, S_2) = \frac{a}{a+b+c}$, where a is the number of predicates in both S_1 and S_2, b is the number of predicates only in S_1, and c is the number of predicates only in S_2.

Given two hyper-alert types T_1 and T_2, the similarity between T_1 and T_2, denoted $Sim(T_1, T_2)$, is then computed as $Sim(T_1, T_2) = Sim(XP_1, XP_2) \times w_p + Sim(XC_1, XC_2) \times w_c$, where XP_1 and XP_2 are the expanded prerequisite sets of T_1 and T_2, XC_1 and XC_2 are the expanded consequence sets of T_1 and T_2, and w_p and $w_c = 1 - w_p$ are the weights for prerequisite and consequence, respectively. (In our experiments, we use $w_p = w_c = 0.5$ to give equal weight to both prerequisite and consequence of hyper-alert types.) We may then set a threshold t so that two hyper-alert types are grouped into the same cluster only if their similarity measure is greater than or equal to t.

We have performed a series of experiments to study the proposed techniques [29]. Figure 11 shows one of the attack strategy graphs extracted from the 2000 DARPA intrusion detection scenario specific data set in our experiments. Based on the description of the data set [23], we know that Fig. 11 has captured most of the attack strategy. The missing parts are due to the attacks missed by the IDSs. For more information, please refer to [29].

5 Related Work

Intrusion detection has been studied for more than twenty years, since Anderson's report [3]. A survey of the early work on intrusion detection is given in [25], and an excellent overview of current intrusion detection techniques and related issues can be found in a recent book [4].

Research on intrusion alert correlation has been rather active recently. The first class of approaches (e.g., Spice [36], probabilistic alert correlation [38], and the alert clustering methods in [5] and [18]) correlates alerts based on the similarities

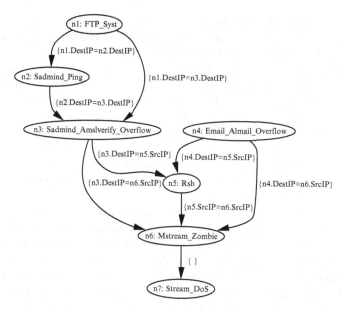

Fig. 11 An attack strategy graph extracted in our experiments

between alert attributes. Though they are effective for clustering similar alerts (e.g., alerts with the same source and destination IP addresses), they cannot fully discover the causal relationships between related alerts.

Another class of methods (e.g., correlation based on STATL [11] or LAMBDA [7], and the data mining approach [8]) performs alert correlation based on attack scenarios specified by human users or learned from training datasets. A limitation of these methods is that they are restricted to *known* attack scenarios, or those that can be generalized from known scenarios. A variation in this class uses a consequence mechanism to specify what types of attacks may follow a given attack, partially addressing this problem [9].

A third class of methods, including JIGSAW [37], the MIRADOR correlation method [6], and our approach, targets recognition of multistage attacks; it correlates alerts if the prerequisites of some later alerts are satisfied by the consequences of some earlier alerts. Such methods can potentially uncover the causal relationship between alerts, and are not restricted to known attack scenarios.

Our method can be considered as a variation of JIGSAW [37]. Both methods try to uncover attack scenarios based on specifications of individual attacks. However, our method also differs from JIGSAW. First, our method allows partial satisfaction of prerequisites (i.e., required capabilities in JIGSAW [37]), recognizing the possibility of undetected attacks and that of attackers gaining information through non-intrusive ways (e.g., talking to a friend working in the victim organization), while JIGSAW requires all required capabilities be satisfied. Second, our method allows aggregation of alerts, and thus can reduce the complexity involved in alert analysis, while JIGSAW currently does not have any similar mechanisms. Third, we develop a set of utilities for alert correlation and interactive analysis of correlated alerts, which is not provided by JIGSAW.

The work closest to ours is the MIRADOR correlation method proposed in [6], which was developed independently and in parallel to ours. These two methods share substantial similarity. The MIRADOR approach also correlates alerts using partial match of prerequisites (pre-conditions) and consequences (post-conditions) of attacks. However, the MIRADOR approach uses a different formalism than ours. In particular, the MIRADOR approach treats alert aggregation as an individual stage before alert correlation, while our method allows alert aggregation during and after correlation. As we have seen in Sect. 3, our treatment of alert aggregation leads to the three utilities for interactive alert analysis.

A formal model named M2D2 was proposed in [24] to correlate alerts using multiple information sources, including the characteristics of the monitored systems, the vulnerability information, the information about the monitoring tools, and information of the observed events. Due to the multiple information sources used in alert correlation, this method can potentially lead to better results than those simply looking at intrusion alerts. A mission-impact-based approach was proposed in [32] to correlate alerts raised by INFOSEC devices such as IDSs and firewalls. A distinguishing feature of this approach is that it correlates the alerts with the importance of system assets so that attention can be focused on critical resources. These methods are complementary to ours.

Several languages have been proposed to represent attacks, including STAT [11,14,39], Colored-Petri Automata (CPA) [19,20], LAMBDA [7], and MuSig [21]. In particular, LAMBDA uses a logic-based method to specify the pre-condition and post-condition of attack scenarios, which is similar to our method. However, all these languages specify entire attack scenarios, which are limited to known scenarios. In contrast, our method (as well as JIGSAW and the MIRADOR correlation method) describes prerequisites and consequences of individual attacks, and correlates detected attacks (i.e., alerts) based on the relationship between these prerequisites and consequences. Thus, our method can potentially correlate alerts in unknown attack scenarios.

Alert correlation has been studied in the context of network management (e.g., [13], [34], and [12]). In theory, alert correlation methods for network management are applicable to intrusion alert correlation. However, intrusion alert correlation faces more challenges than its counter part in network management: While alert correlation for network management deals with alerts about natural faults, which usually exhibit regular patterns, intrusion alert correlation has to cope with less predictable, malicious intruders.

Our approach to learning attack strategies from correlated alerts is also closely related to techniques for static vulnerability analysis (e.g., [2, 17, 33, 35]). In particular, the methods in [2, 35] also use a model of exploits (possible attacks) in terms of their pre-conditions (prerequisites) and post-conditions (consequences). Our approach complements static vulnerability analysis methods by providing the capability of examining the actual execution of attack strategies in different details (e.g., an attacker tries different variations of the same attack) and thus gives human users more information to respond to attacks.

6 Conclusion

This article summarized a series of research efforts toward automating the analysis of intrusion alerts. These efforts start with a practical method for constructing attack scenarios through alert correlation, using prerequisites and consequences of attacks. We proposed a formal framework to represent alerts along with their prerequisites and consequences, and developed a method to correlate related hyper-alerts together, including an intuitive representation of correlated alerts that reveals the attack scenario of the corresponding attacks. To facilitate the analysis of large sets of correlated alerts, we also developed several interactive utilities. Finally, to automate the analysis of intrusion alerts, we developed a method to extract attack strategies from correlated intrusion alerts.

The research described in this article is only a part of the effort toward automated intrusion alert analysis. More research is desirable to make automated intrusion analysis practical. In particular, it would be useful to integrate intrusion related information from multiple sources, such as IDSs, vulnerability scanning tools, and OS or application logs.

References

1. R. Agrawal, T. Imielinski, and A. N. Swami. Mining association rules between sets of items in large databases. In *Proceedings of the 1993 International Conference on Management of Data*, pages 207–216, 1993.
2. P. Ammann, D. Wijesekera, and S. Kaushik. Scalable, graph-based network vulnerability analysis. In *Proceedings of the 9th ACM Conference on Computer and Communications Security*, pages 217–224, November 2002.
3. J. P. Anderson. Computer security threat monitoring and surveillance. Technical report, James P. Anderson Co., Fort Washington, PA, 1980.
4. R. G. Bace. *Intrusion Detection*. Macmillan Technology Publishing, Indianapolis, 2000.
5. F. Cuppens. Managing alerts in a multi-intrusion detection environment. In *Proceedings of the 17th Annual Computer Security Applications Conference*, December 2001.
6. F. Cuppens and A. Miege. Alert correlation in a cooperative intrusion detection framework. In *Proceedings of the 2002 IEEE Symposium on Security and Privacy*, May 2002.
7. F. Cuppens and R. Ortalo. LAMBDA: A language to model a database for detection of attacks. In *Proceedings of Recent Advances in Intrusion Detection (RAID 2000)*, pages 197–216, September 2000.
8. O. Dain and R. K. Cunningham. Fusing a heterogeneous alert stream into scenarios. In *Proceedings of the 2001 ACM Workshop on Data Mining for Security Applications*, pages 1–13, November 2001.
9. H. Debar and A. Wespi. Aggregation and correlation of intrusion-detection alerts. In *Recent Advances in Intrusion Detection*, LNCS 2212, pages 85–103, 2001.

10. DEFCON. Def con capture the flag (CTF) contest. http://www.defcon.org/html/defcon-8-post.html, July 2000. Archive accessible at http://wi2600.org/mediawhore/mirrors/shmoo/.
11. S. T. Eckmann, G. Vigna, and R. A. Kemmerer. STATL: An Attack Language for State-based Intrusion Detection. *Journal of Computer Security*, 10(1/2):71–104, 2002.
12. R. Gardner and D. Harle. Pattern discovery and specification translation for alarm correlation. In *Proceedings of Network Operations and Management Symposium (NOMS'98)*, pages 713–722, February 1998.
13. B. Gruschke. Integrated event management: Event correlation using dependency graphs. In *Proceedings of the 9th IFIP/IEEE International Workshop on Distributed Systems: Operations & Management*, October 1998.
14. K. Ilgun, R. A. Kemmerer, and P. A. Porras. State transition analysis: A rule-based intrusion detection approach. *IEEE Transaction on Software Engineering*, 21(3):181–199, 1995.
15. D. A. Jackson, K. M. Somers, and H. H. Harvey. Similarity coefficients: Measures of co-occurence and association or simply measures of occurrence? *The American Naturalist*, 133(3):436–453, March 1989.
16. A. K. Jain and R. C. Dubes. *Algorithms for Clustering Data*. Prentice Hall, Englewood Cliffs, 1988.
17. S. Jha, O. Sheyner, and J. M. Wing. Two formal analyses of attack graphs. In *Proceedings of the 15th Computer Security Foundation Workshop*, June 2002.
18. K. Julisch. Mining alarm clusters to improve alarm handling efficiency. In *Proceedings of the 17th Annual Computer Security Applications Conference (ACSAC)*, pages 12–21, December 2001.
19. S. Kumar. *Classification and Detection of Computer Intrusions*. PhD thesis, Purdue University, August 1995.
20. S. Kumar and E. H. Spafford. A pattern matching model for misuse intrusion detection. In *Proceedings of the 17th National Computer Security Conference*, pages 11–21, October 1994.
21. J. Lin, X. S. Wang, and S. Jajodia. Abstraction-based misuse detection: High-level specifications and adaptable strategies. In *Proceedings of the 11th Computer Security Foundations Workshop*, pages 190–201, Rockport, MA, June 1998.
22. S. Manganaris, M. Christensen, D. Zerkle, and K. Hermiz. A data mining analysis of RTID alarms. *Computer Networks*, 34:571–577, 2000.
23. MIT Lincoln Lab. 2000 DARPA intrusion detection scenario specific datasets. http://www.ll.mit.edu/IST/ideval/data/2000/2000_data_index.html, 2000.
24. B. Morin, L. Mé, H. Debar, and M. Ducassé. M2D2: A formal data model for IDS alert correlation. In *Proceedings of the 5th International Symposium on Recent Advances in Intrusion Detection (RAID 2002)*, pages 115–137, 2002.
25. B. Mukherjee, L. T. Heberlein, and K. N. Levitt. Network intrusion detection. *IEEE Network*, 8(3):26–41, May 1994.
26. P. Ning, Y. Cui, and D. S Reeves. Analyzing intensive intrusion alerts via correlation. In *Proceedings of the 5th International Symposium on Recent Advances in Intrusion Detection (RAID 2002)*, pages 74–94, Zurich, Switzerland, October 2002.
27. P. Ning, Y. Cui, and D. S Reeves. Constructing attack scenarios through correlation of intrusion alerts. In *Proceedings of the 9th ACM Conference on Computer and Communications Security*, pages 245–254, Washington, D.C., November 2002.
28. P. Ning and D. Xu. Adapting query optimization techniques for efficient intrusion alert correlation. In *Proceedings of the 17th IFIP WG 11.3 Working Conference on Data and Application Security (DAS '03)*, August 2003.
29. P. Ning and D. Xu. Learning attack stratagies from intrusion alerts. In *Proceedings of the 10th ACM Conference on Computer and Communications Security*, pages 200–209, October 2003.
30. Packet storm. http://packetstormsecurity.nl. Accessed on April 30, 2003.
31. P. A. Porras and P. G. Neumann. EMERALD: Event monitoring enabling response to anomalous live disturbances. In *Proceedings of the 20th National Information Systems Security Conference*, National Institute of Standards and Technology, 1997.

32. P. A. Porras, M. W. Fong, and A. Valdes. A mission-impact-based approach to INFOSEC alarm correlation. In *Proceedings of the 5th International Symposium on Recent Advances in Intrusion Detection (RAID 2002)*, pages 95–114, 2002.

33. C. R. Ramakrishnan and R. Sekar. Model-based analysis of configuration vulnerabilities. *Journal of Computer Security*, 10(1/2):189–209, 2002.

34. L. Ricciulli and N. Shacham. Modeling correlated alarms in network management systems. In *In Western Simulation Multiconference*, 1997.

35. O. Sheyner, J. Haines, S. Jha, R. Lippmann, and J. M. Wing. Automated generation and analysis of attack graphs. In *Proceedings of IEEE Symposium on Security and Privacy*, May 2002.

36. S. Staniford, J. A. Hoagland, and J. M. McAlerney. Practical automated detection of stealthy portscans. *Journal of Computer Security*, 10(1/2):105–136, 2002.

37. S. Templeton and K. Levitt. A requires/provides model for computer attacks. In *Proceedings of New Security Paradigms Workshop*, pages 31 – 38. ACM Press, September 2000.

38. A. Valdes and K. Skinner. Probabilistic alert correlation. In *Proceedings of the 4th International Symposium on Recent Advances in Intrusion Detection (RAID 2001)*, pages 54–68, 2001.

39. G. Vigna and R. A. Kemmerer. NetSTAT: A network-based intrusion detection system. *Journal of Computer Security*, 7(1):37–71, 1999.

Conventional Cryptographic Primitives

Vincent Rijmen

Contents

V. Rijmen (✉)
Department of Electrical Engineering/ESAT, Katholieke Universiteit Leuven, Leuven, Belgium
e-mail: vincent.rijmen@esat.kuleuven.be

S.C.-H. Huang et al. (eds.), *Network Security*, DOI 10.1007/978-0-387-73821-5_9,
© Springer Science+Business Media, LLC 2010

1 Introduction

Modern network security systems contain cryptographic primitives as an essential building block. In this chapter, we discuss conventional cryptographic primitives, which are also known as *symmetric primitives*. The term "symmetric" stems from the fact that in order to use conventional primitives, all parties need to share the same set of secret keys. Hence, all parties have the same capabilities. This is not the case with *asymmetric primitives*, where some keys are known to one party only.

Symmetric cryptographic primitives are the work horses of cryptography because they are by far the oldest and best studied type of primitives and because they are typically orders of magnitude faster than asymmetric primitives. We describe here how symmetric primitives are used to provide two basic cryptographic services: confidentiality and integrity of messages.

The need for confidentiality of messages has been recognized from the time that writing was developed. Until the discovery of asymmetric cryptography in the 1970s, confidentiality was the only cryptographic service known. With the advent of open digital networks, which make it very easy to apply undetectable modifications to messages, the need for integrity services was recognized. Integrity services do not prohibit an intruder from modifying data, but they prohibit *undetected* alterations to data.

Confidentiality is always achieved by applying encryption primitives. However, as explained in Sects. 5 and 6, encryption primitives can also be used to provide integrity protection and many other cryptographic services.

The remainder of this chapter is structured as follows. In Sect. 2, we discuss attacks on cryptographic primitives. Subsequently, we introduce the two symmetric encryption primitives: stream ciphers in Sect. 3, and block ciphers in Sect. 4. We continue with Sect. 5 on hash functions and Sect. 6 on message authentication codes. We conclude in Sect. 7 with an outlook on open problems.

2 Attacks

We give a short overview of the types of attacks that a modern cryptographic primitive should resist. Except for error message attacks, discussed in Sect. 2.2.3, we restrict this overview to attacks that target the cryptographic primitive itself.

2.1 Cryptanalytic Attacks

Cryptanalytic attacks can be categorized according to the facilities that are assumed to be under the control of the attackers, or according to the result they achieve. In all cases, the analysis is purely based on the mathematical properties of the primitives, in contrast to the side-channel attacks, which are discussed in Sect. 2.2.

2.1.1 Classification According to Means

Perhaps, the most intuitive model is the *ciphertext-only* setting, where the attacker is assumed to have access only to the ciphertexts transmitted over the communication line. In this model, it is relatively easy to design secure primitives. Alas, the model underestimates the knowledge of a typical attacker in a typical application.

In almost all applications, an attacker has at least statistical knowledge about the content of the messages. For instance, if the message consists of English text coded in ASCII, then the distribution of the message bytes is far from uniform. In order to make the treatment more easy, it is often assumed that an attacker knows the exact content of the message for a potentially large number of ciphertexts. This is called a known-message or *known-plaintext* setting. In some applications, it is even realistic to assume that the attacker can exert some control over the messages that are transmitted. This is a *chosen-plaintext* or *chosen-ciphertext* setting.

In a *related-key* setting, it is assumed that messages have been encrypted under different keys, where the keys themselves are unknown, but the relation between the keys is known to the attacker. Such a situation might occur if an application uses a weak key update mechanism.

2.1.2 Classification According to Result

The most dangerous attacks are *key recovery attacks*, where the attacker obtains the secret key. However, in the majority of applications, much damage can be done even without full recovery of the key. For instance, in some cases, an attacker may be able to apply undetectable modifications to some message passing by, even without being able to read the message. Such an undetected modification, or *forgery*, can already have bad consequences.

Similarly, if an attacker is able to decrypt a fraction of the ciphertexts, or to collect some information on the plaintext, this is considered to be a weakness in the application. Weaknesses, for which it is not immediately clear whether they cause important security holes, are called *certificational weaknesses* of the primitive.

2.2 Side-Channel Attacks

While cryptanalytic attacks look at a purely mathematical description of a cryptographic primitives, side-channel attacks are based on weaknesses caused by imperfect implementations of these primitives in real-world applications. The firstly discovered side-channel attacks exploited weaknesses present in the implementation of the primitives themselves. Typical examples are power attacks and timing attacks, which are briefly discussed subsequently. More recently, we see side-channel attacks that exploit weaknesses at the application level. We discuss one example in Sect. 2.2.3.

2.2.1   Power Attacks

In typical computing hardware, the instantaneous power consumption differs slightly depending on the instructions being executed and even on the data being processed. Power attacks exploit the correlation between power consumption and intermediate results of the algorithms that are used by a cryptographic primitive. The attacks can be very powerful, allowing to extract a secret key from a small number of accurate power consumption measurements. Information on the instantaneous power consumption curve can be obtained directly from measurements on the power source, if accessible, or indirectly from measurements of the electromagnetic radiation produced by the equipment. Recent research results suggest that it is not possible to fully protect hardware implementations against this type of attacks [20]. Due to imperfections in logic circuits, the leakage of signals can not be avoided. However, it is possible to reduce the leakage to very low levels, making the attack very difficult in practice.

2.2.2   Timing Attacks

The second important side channel is the execution time of software routines. Carelessly implemented algorithms may exhibit a large correlation between execution time and the value of some intermediate results depending on only a few unknown bits of the key. This again allows to extract the secret key from execution time statistics. This type of attack appears to be more easy to counter, at the expense of a reduced performance: key-dependent optimizations have to switched off and sometimes dummy operations need to be inserted in order to ensure a constant execution time.

2.2.3   Error Message Attacks

Very detailed error messages may leak too much information to an attacker, thereby weakening the security of the underlying primitives. For instance, Canvel et al. [3] describes an attack against some versions of TLS/SSL. The attack exploits the fact that two independent integrity checks are performed on the messages: one based on an authentication key and one depending on the encryption key. If the content of the error message and/or the processing time depends on the number of checks that are failed, an attacker can recover the message [33].

2.2.4   Conclusions

Essential in all side-channel attacks is the fact that very few cryptographic applications maintain detailed state information. Consequently, it is very often the case that attackers can subject multiple deliberately constructed messages to the cryptographic routines and accumulate information. An application can be strengthened against all types of side-channel attacks by limiting the number of cryptographic operations that can be performed in response to requests of an unidentified party, using the same secret key.

2.3 Implications

Modern cryptographic primitives are designed to resist very powerful attacks. No weakness, even a certificational weakness, should be known. Even for such strongly secure primitives, it is possible to implement or use them wrongly, resulting in a weakness towards side-channel attacks.

History counts many examples of almost-good algorithms and almost-good ways to use them. By using standardized algorithms in standardized ways, one can maximize the assurance about an application's security [6].

3 Stream Ciphers

Stream ciphers encrypt messages one symbol at a time. Stream ciphers have a time-varying internal state. All popularly used stream ciphers are *additive* stream ciphers, which can be described as extensions of the One-Time Pad encryption scheme, which we describe at the start of this section. We continue with the description of a stream cipher, a short discussion on the requirements and a usage note. We conclude with an overview of stream ciphers in use today.

3.1 The One-Time Pad

Let the message m be described as a stream of t symbols m_i, $0 \leq i < t$, where the symbols come from an alphabet $\mathcal{A}$. In fielded systems, the alphabet is typically the set $\{0, 1\}$ or the set of byte values. In textbook examples, the alphabet is typically the set of characters: $\{$'A', 'B', ..., 'Z'$\}$. Let '+' be a binary operator such that $< \mathcal{A}, +>$ is a group. For example, if the alphabet is the set of bits or the set of bytes, then '+' is usually defined to be the bitwise exclusive-or operation. If the alphabet is the set of characters, then '+' is usually defined by mapping the characters to the numbers $0 \ldots 25$, performing an addition modulo 26 and mapping the result back to a character.

The One-Time Pad or Vernam encryption scheme is defined as follows:

$$c_i = m_i + k_i, \ 0 \leq i < t. \tag{1}$$

The c_i are the ciphertext symbols, and the k_i are the symbols of the key stream. If the k_i are generated randomly and independently, then the scheme provides *unconditional* confidentiality. This means that even a hypothetical attacker with unbounded computational resources can not decrypt a ciphertext. If the k_i are not generated randomly and independently, then the scheme may become very weak, and should no longer be called a One-Time Pad. Decryption is performed by subtracting the same key symbols again. If the bit-wise exclusive-or operation is used as the group operation, then addition and subtraction mount to the same operation.

The property of unconditional confidentiality refers to the fact that with a given ciphertext stream, for each message stream of the same length, there is a key stream that will "decrypt" the given ciphertext stream to that message stream. If all key streams are equally likely to be correct, then interception of the ciphertext stream reveals no information on the message.

3.2 Description

In most applications, it is impractical to use t independently generated key symbols. Hence, the key symbols k_i are replaced by a stream of symbols z_i, which are generated by a pseudo-random number generator seeded with a (shorter) key k. We get a system that can be described as follows:

$$c_i = m_i + z_i, \ 0 \le i < t \tag{2}$$

$$z_i = f(i, k_0, k_1, \ldots, k_p) \text{ with } p \ll t. \tag{3}$$

The pseudo-random number generator f has to be *cryptographically strong*. The construction of a cryptographically strong pseudo-random number generator is a difficult task, best left to specialists. A number of examples is discussed in Sect. 3.5.

3.3 Requirements

The output of a cryptographically strong pseudo-random number generator needs to be unpredictable. In a long sequence of output symbols, all symbols should occur almost equally often. In a short sequence, there should be sufficient deviations from the average behavior to make short-range prediction difficult. Second, for any attacker who obtains a sequence of output symbols, it should be computationally infeasible to recover the secret key.

Several other requirements have been defined, which are necessary but maybe not sufficient to achieve a secure stream cipher design. Finally, it is also desirable that the pseudo-random number generator is very efficient. One of the main perceived advantages of stream ciphers is that they can be very fast. Hence, a slow stream cipher is typically of little practical relevance, since then block ciphers offer more functionality for the same performance.

3.4 Usage

Additive stream ciphers (including the One Time Pad) can be used to protect the confidentiality of messages. They can not be used to protect the integrity or authenticity of a message. This implies that the receiver of a ciphertext which has been produced with an additive stream cipher, can not be sure that the message resulting from decryption is the same as the message that was originally sent. Integrity protection needs to be provided by other means.

Second, it is of utmost importance to ensure that the key stream is never reused. If an attacker knows that two messages were encrypted using the same key stream, then a simple subtraction of the ciphertext symbols in corresponding positions will remove the key stream symbols.

$$\left. \begin{array}{l} c_i = m_i + k \\ c_j = m_j + k \end{array} \right\} \Rightarrow c_i - c_j = m_i - m_j \qquad (4)$$

The resulting symbols are the differences of the symbols at corresponding positions in the two messages. The redundancy present in typical messages allows to recover the two original messages from the stream of differences.

3.5 Example Stream Ciphers

3.5.1 Linear Feedback Shift Registers

Pseudo-random number generators based on Linear Feedback Shift Registers (LFSRs) have received a great deal of attention in the cryptographic literature. This is partly due to the fact that LFSR circuitry is supposedly simple to implement in hardware, but probably more important is the mathematical tractability of LFSR-based designs. Despite the extensive available literature, there are few fully specified designs published.

3.5.2 RC4

RC4 is a stream cipher designed by Ron Rivest for RSA laboratories in 1987. The design is trademarked and officially a trade secret, but in 1994, a "compatible" cipher ARCFOUR has been published. This cipher has been analyzed. RC4 has a very innovative design and a good performance in software. For a long time, its security remained unquestioned. Indeed, the first results of cryptanalysis attempts did not unveil any weaknesses in the algorithm [15, 19, 25]. More recently obtained results demonstrate some weaknesses in the design. First, it appears that the second byte of the generated key stream is biased: for a fraction of 1/128 of the secret keys, this byte takes the value 0 [21]. Second, even if the first bytes of the key stream are discarded, it can still be distinguished from a truly random stream [12, 13]. Third, in applications where a part of the secret key is variable and known, e.g., the WEP protocol [38], it is possible to derive the full key [13].[1]

3.5.3 SEAL

The stream cipher SEAL [32] was designed by Rogaway and Coppersmith to be very efficient in software implementations running on a 32-bit processor. Three versions have been published, and all three have a weakness: the output can be distinguished from truly random bits. A successor, called SCREAM [16], was designed by Halevi et al. It is based on the design principles of the AES algorithm [41] and also very efficient in software implementations running on a 32-bit processor.

3.5.4 Stream Ciphers with Integrity Mechanisms

Recently, researchers are looking again into the design of stream ciphers that also provide integrity protection. This requires to leave the additive model of a stream cipher. Helix is a new example of such designs [11]. As with all cryptographic primitives, it should not be used until results from security analysis by third parties become available, but the approach is clearly interesting.

4 Block Ciphers

Block ciphers encrypt blocks of symbols at a time. They have no internal state. We start this section with the description of the substitution cipher, a predecessor of block ciphers. We continue with the description of a block cipher and a short discussion on the requirements. Subsequently, we discuss the usage modes of a block cipher, which are also called modes of operation. We conclude with an overview of block ciphers in use today.

4.1 The Substitution Cipher

The substitution cipher is based on a secret permutation of the alphabet symbols.

$$S : \mathcal{A} \to \mathcal{A} : x \mapsto y = S(x) \tag{5}$$

---

[1] Note that not all security problems of WEP can be blamed on the designer of RC4. Some of the attacks work regardless of the stream cipher that is used.

Encryption is defined as the process where each message symbol m_i is replaced by the symbol $c_i = S(m_i)$. The definition of S corresponds to the secret key k. If the size of $\mathcal{A}$ is small, then S can be stored in a table, also called a *code book*. The *Caesar cipher* is a substitution cipher, based on a simple permutation rule: every character is replaced by a character k places further down in the alphabet. According to the legend, the Roman emperor Caesar used this cipher to encrypt his confidential messages. His key was always $k = 3$.

The main distinguishing factor between substitution ciphers and stream ciphers is the fact that a substitution cipher is stateless. This leads to an important weakness present in all substitution ciphers: patterns in the message lead to patterns in the ciphertext:

$$c_i = c_j \Leftrightarrow m_i = m_j. \tag{6}$$

If the alphabet is the set of characters, and the message is written in a natural language, then this weakness can easily be exploited to recover the secret permutation S. For any natural language, the frequency distributions for single characters, digraphs and trigraphs are non-uniform. Furthermore, the frequency distributions are typical for that language. Comparison of the observed ciphertext character, digraph and trigraph distributions with the known distributions of natural languages allows to determine the language and subsequently the message [27]. Error-free message recovery is typically possible as soon as a few hundred ciphertext characters have been observed.

This weakness can be lessened by going to larger alphabets. For instance, we can group the characters into *blocks* of size b and define a permutation S_b mapping blocks to blocks:

$$S_b : \mathcal{A}^b \to \mathcal{A}^b : (x_0, x_1, \ldots, x_{b-1}) \mapsto (y_0, y_1, \ldots, y_{b-1}) = S_b(x_0, x_1, \ldots, x_{b-1}). \tag{7}$$

For growing b, the frequency distribution of the blocks will approximate the uniform distribution better and better. Since the size of the code book is proportional to $|\mathcal{A}|^b$, it becomes quickly infeasible to store it explicitly. Consequently, encryption and decryption can no longer be implemented with a table lookup into the code book. This problem is solved as follows. Instead of using completely arbitrarily selected permutations, one defines a function f to compute the table elements:

$$(y_0, y_1, \ldots, y_{b-1}) = S_n(x_0, x_1, \ldots, x_{b-1}) = f(x_0, x_1, \ldots, x_{b-1}). \tag{8}$$

The definition of the function f can be made public, except for a parameter k, the key. Such a function is called a *block cipher*.

4.2 Description

A block cipher is defined by a function f taking as input a block of b message symbols and a block of p key symbols, and producing as output a block of b ciphertext symbols. In order to make decryption possible, it is necessary that for each choice of the key symbols the inverse map from ciphertext symbols to message symbols is uniquely defined.

$$B : \mathcal{A}^b \times \mathcal{A}^p \rightarrow \mathcal{A}^b :$$

$$(x_0, \dots, x_{b-1}; k_0, \dots, k_{p-1}) \mapsto y = f(x_0, \dots, x_{b-1}; k_0, \dots, k_{p-1}) \quad (9)$$

Formally, a block cipher can be described as a family of permutations in the space of b-symbol blocks. Every value for the key defines one permutation in the family.

4.3   Requirements

From a security point of view, the ideal block cipher is the family that contains all permutations in the space of b-symbol blocks. However, such a block cipher would require excessive key lengths in order to be able to specify each permutation of the family. Second, it would be difficult to implement the function f generating the permutations. Hence, a block cipher always corresponds to a subset of all the possible permutations. For a strong block cipher, the family cannot be distinguished from a set of randomly selected permutations in the space of b-symbol blocks.

Block ciphers are an important building block in systems based on symmetric cryptography. They are not only used for encryption purpose but also for protection of integrity. A practical block cipher should satisfy at least the following requirements.

Even in the case that the attacker has at his disposition a large sample of messages, possibly chosen by him, and the corresponding ciphertexts encrypted under the target key, it should be computationally infeasible to achieve any of the following:

Key recovery: To recover the value of the secret key,
Decryption: To obtain the message corresponding to a ciphertext which is not in the sample,
Encryption: To obtain the ciphertext corresponding to a message which is not in the sample.

These properties should also hold if the set of sample messages is defined after a target message or target ciphertext has been set.

On the other side, an important perceived advantage of symmetric cryptography, is its high performance. Hence, a block cipher should be fast in comparison to asymmetric primitives. Furthermore, it should require as little storage as possible.

4.4   Usage: Modes of Operation

Similar to stream ciphers, block ciphers can be used to protect the confidentiality of messages. Even for large block lengths, the statelessness of block ciphers poses a problem. If two different messages containing common blocks are encrypted under the same key, then the corresponding ciphertexts also contain common blocks, and this is an undesirable property. Such a situation occurs for instance when two versions of the same document are encrypted. In order to avoid these weaknesses, several *modes of operation* have been defined. We discuss here briefly the three most important modes of operation and refer the reader to [40] for more details.

Block ciphers can also be used to protect the integrity of messages, discussed in Sects. 5 and 6, and to construct identification protocols.

In this section, m_i, c_i will denote b-symbol blocks of message, respectively ciphertext. Encryption of one block m_i under a key k is denoted by $E(m_i; k)$.

4.4.1   Electronic Code Book (ECB)

The ECB mode of operation is the "naive" way to use a block cipher. The message is split into blocks of length b, and each block is encrypted separately.

$$c_i = E(m_i; k) \tag{10}$$

This mode can be used if it is guaranteed that the message contains no patterns, for instance, if the message is itself a randomly generated key.

4.4.2   Cipher Block Chaining (CBC)

The CBC mode of operation is the default mode to encrypt arbitrary data. The message is split into blocks of length b. After the first block, each message block is "whitened" by adding the previous ciphertext block. Addition of two blocks is done by modular addition of the corresponding symbols. Usually, the symbols are bits; then the component-wise modular addition corresponds to bit-wise exclusive-or. The first block is whitened by addition with an *initial value IV*.

$$c_0 = E(m_0 + IV; k) \tag{11}$$
$$c_i = E(m_i + c_{i-1}; k), \ 0 < i < t \tag{12}$$

A new initial value needs to be used for every message. In a certain formal model, it can be proven that if the underlying block cipher is secure for encrypting one-block messages it is also secure when used in CBC mode to encrypt multi-block messages, provided that the initial values are generated (pseudo-)randomly and kept secret [2].

A property of the CBC mode is that each ciphertext block depends on all the previous message blocks. This property is used in the CBC–MAC authentication algorithm to provide authenticity of messages. Note, however, that the CBC *decryption* mode does not have this property: each message block depends on only two ciphertext blocks. Contrary to popular belief, encryption in CBC mode by itself does *not* provide authenticity of messages together with confidentiality, unless the message contains some adequate redundancy. Its always recommended to use separate means to guarantee the authenticity of a message.

4.4.3 Counter Mode (CTR)

The CTR mode is a relatively recently standardized mode of operation [9]. The block cipher encrypts the contents of a counter in order to produce a key stream. This key stream is subsequently used as with a stream cipher, cf. Sect. 3. For each message, the counter is initialized with an initial value IV. After every application of the block cipher, the counter is incremented with a value s.

$$c_i = m_i + z_i, \ 0 \leq i < t \tag{13}$$

$$z_i = E(IV + i \times s; k) \tag{14}$$

No counter value should be used more than once, even for different messages. This requirement has to be taken into account for the generation of the initial value and the counter step s. Again, a formal proof of security for this mode can be found in [2].

4.5 Example Block Ciphers

4.5.1 DES

The best known and, until today, the most used block cipher is the Data Encryption Standard (DES), which was designed in the 1970's and standardized in 1977 [39]. The DES encrypts blocks of 64 bits at a time, under a 56-bit key.

In 1993, a detailed design for a DES cracking machine was published [35]. In 1998, a dedicated machine was built and used to recover secret DES keys [10]. The machine simply tries out all possible keys until one is found that produces valid-looking messages. The fraction of keys surviving this test are then subjected to some further tests until the correct key has been determined. Such an attack is called *exhaustive key search*. The security of a block cipher against exhaustive key search is determined by the length of the key.

The conclusion is that the use of the DES can no longer be recommended, except if it is used in strengthened modes, for example, as discussed in Sect. 4.5.2.

4.5.2   3-DES

Soon after the introduction of the DES, multiple encryption modes were proposed. In a multiple encryption mode, the block cipher is applied multiple times to each message block, each time with a different key. It can be shown that the security of a double encryption mode against exhaustive key search only marginally better than the security of the original block cipher [7]. Consequently, triple encryption modes have become a popular means to strengthen the DES.

$$3\text{-DES}(x; k^1, k^2, k^3) = \text{DES}(\text{DES}(\text{DES}(x; k^1); k^2); k^3) \qquad (15)$$

Often, a variant on triple encryption is used, in which the middle encryption operation is replaced by a decryption operation. This mode is sometimes denoted by 3-DES–EDE.

$$3\text{-DES-EDE}(x; k^1, k^2, k^3) = \text{DES}(\text{DES}^{-1}(\text{DES}(x; k^1); k^2); k^3) \qquad (16)$$

Since the strength of 3-DES is approximately that of a (hypothetical) block cipher with the double key length of DES, it is sometimes recommended to set $k^3 = k^1$. This is called 2-key 3-DES. However, it can be shown that 2-key 3-DES is weaker than 3-key 3-DES, hence it makes sense to choose the 3 keys independently [24].

4.5.3   AES

The Advanced Encryption Standard (AES) was proposed in 2001 as a replacement of the DES [41]. The selection process consisted of an open submission phase ending in 1998, followed by an open and public evaluation period ending in October 2000. Cryptographers from all over the world submitted candidate algorithms and participated in the evaluation process.

The AES encrypts message blocks of 128 bits under keys of length 128, 192 or 256 bits. The longer key length ensures resistance against exhaustive key search for the foreseeable future. The longer block length ensures increased resistance against attacks based on multiple occurrences of the same block inside one message. Finally, the algorithm is adapted better to modern computing platforms, which makes it significantly faster than 3-DES, and on many platforms even faster than DES. For all these reasons, the AES is replacing the DES and 3-DES in many existing applications. It is definitely the preferred block cipher for applications without backwards compatibility requirements.

The AES is based on transformations with a simple description over the finite field GF(256). The fact that the AES can be expressed quite elegantly as a set of quadratic implicit equations both over GF(256) and over GF(2) has led to some controversy about its security. While it is known that solving a set of quadratic equations is a difficult problem in general, some people believe that the structure present in the particular equations describing AES will allow to solve them relatively easily [4, 26]. Full details about the design of the AES can be found in [5].

5 Hash Functions

Hash functions can be thought of as cryptographic check sums. They take as input a message of variable length and possibly a secret key. They produce an output of a fixed length. Hash functions using a secret key are also called "Message Authentication Codes" and are treated in Sect. 6.

We start this section with a description of the requirements for a hash function and a discussion of generally applicable attacks. We proceed with usage scenarios, and we conclude with some example constructions.

5.1 Requirements

The essential security properties for a hash function are one-wayness and collision resistance. These are usually specified as follows.

Preimage resistance: For all outputs y, it is infeasible to compute an input which hashes to y.

Second preimage resistance (weak collision resistance): For all inputs x, it is infeasible to compute a second input x' such that both inputs hash to the same output.

(Strong) collision resistance: It is infeasible to compute two inputs x, x' that hash to the same output.

It is easy to see that strong collision resistance implies weak collision resistance. Under plausible assumptions and excluding degenerate cases, strong collision resistance also implies preimage resistance. Some applications require a hash function which is strongly collision resistant, whereas other applications only need preimage resistance. However, nowadays, many applications use a hash function which is believed to be collision-resistant, even if only preimage resistance is required.

The term "infeasible to compute" is of course rather vague, and changing over time. What is infeasible for a large organization now might be feasible for an individual user in 10 years from now. Therefore, the computational complexity to find a collision or (second) preimage is often compared to some trivial attacks, which we discuss in Sect. 5.2.

5.2 Breaking a Hash Function

Consider a hash function h and denote by N the size of the output space of h. By definition, the size of the input space is larger than N, and hence it is clear that for all hash functions collisions exist and will be found after at most $N + 1$ tries. Furthermore, by consequence of the birthday paradox, a set of size $\sqrt{N}$ inputs contains at least one collision with a probability close to 50%. For slightly larger sets, the probability quickly approaches 100%.

These observations are true regardless of the structure of the hash function. A hash function is considered to be not collision resistant if an algorithm is known that with high probability produces collisions using less computations than $\sqrt{N}$ invocations of the hash function. Using similar reasonings, a hash function is considered to be not (second) preimage resistant if (second) preimages can be found using less effort than N invocations of the hash function.

Note that these conventions introduce a kind of efficiency criterion: from a hash function with larger output size, and hence larger size of the output space, we expect stronger resistance against attacks.

Currently, the strength of a hash function is usually equated to its collision-resistance. Almost all cryptanalytic attacks are collision attacks. It would be interesting to find out more about attacks against the property of preimage resistance.

5.3 Usage

5.3.1 Digital Signature Schemes

Collision-resistant hash functions are an essential component of all digital signature schemes. When a message m is subjected to a digital signature scheme, it is first "compressed" by means of a hash function. Only the output of the hash function is really signed. The primary reason for this approach is that signing primitives are based on asymmetric cryptography, and consequently very slow. In most applications, the only way to achieve acceptable performance is by employing a hash function to reduce the size of the input of the asymmetric components. Consequently, if one can find two messages hashing to the same value, then a signature on one of the documents will allow to forge a signature on the other document by a simple act of copying.

5.3.2 Storage of Sensitive Information

Hash functions are also used to reduce the amount of sensitive information that needs to be stored on servers. For instance, consider a password-based authentication protocol. In the most simple incarnation, the authentication server stores a list of (username,password)-tuples. Authentication is successful if the provided password matches the stored password. However, the list of passwords on the server is vulnerable to theft. In a better implementation of the protocol, the server does not store the passwords, but only the hashed values of the passwords. Authentication is then successful if the hash of the provided password matches the stored value. An attacker who has obtained the list of hashed values can not use them directly to authenticate himself/herself. Note that for this application, the hash function does not have to be collision-resistant: it suffices to use a preimage-resistant hash function.

5.4   *Example Hash Functions*

All modern hash functions in use are *iterative* constructions. That means that the variable-length inputs are first divided into blocks m_i of fixed length, which are processed sequentially by a *compression function f*. Finally, an output transformation g is applied.

$$y_0 = f(IV, m_0) \tag{17}$$

$$y_i = f(y_{i-1}, m_i), \ 0 < i < t \tag{18}$$

$$h(m) = g(y_t) \tag{19}$$

If the message length is not a multiple of the input length of the compression function, the message is extended to the desired length by means of a unique *padding rule*. Using the Merkle-Damgård construction method, any collision-resistant compression function can be used to construct a collision-resistant iterative hash function [23].

5.4.1   The MD4-Family

Two types of compression functions are in use today: custom designs and designs based on block ciphers. Almost all custom designs are based on the hash function MD4, designed in 1990 by Ron Rivest [30]. Besides MD4, the family includes MD5, extended MD4, RIPEMD and variants, HAVAL, SHA, SHA-1 and variants. While collisions for MD4 were constructed already in 1996 [8], the follow-up designs remained popular. Recently, collisions were constructed for MD5, HAVAL-128, RIPEMD [34], SHA [18] and reduced versions of SHA-1[29]. It remains an open question whether these attacks can be extended to full SHA-1 and variants. In any case, it seems there is a need for a different hash function design model.

5.4.2   Block Cipher Based Designs

Hash functions based on block ciphers use a compression function derived from the block cipher. For instance, the Davies–Meyer construction [22] works as follows:

$$f(y_{i-1}, m_i) = E(y_{i-1}; m_i) + y_{i-1}, \tag{20}$$

where $+$ denotes the bitwise exclusive-or. Other construction methods can be found in [28]. Whirlpool is a hash function based on a block cipher that has been designed only for use in the hash function [37].

Hash functions based on block ciphers are interesting because many block ciphers use basic operations that are completely different from the operations used in the MD4 family. Hence, we have reasons to believe that the recent attacks on MD4-like hash functions will not apply to them. An important disadvantage is the performance penalty. Every iteration of the compression function uses the block cipher with a new key. Hence, the block cipher key setup needs to be repeated for every block. Very few block ciphers are designed with frequent rekeying in mind. Consequently, the performance of the key setup is usually lower than raw encryption performance.

6 Message Authentication Codes

It is sometimes falsely believed that a message can be protected against deliberate modifications by computing and attaching the hash value. However, if the hash function does not take a secret key as input, it is trivial for an attacker to compute the output of the hash function over the modified message and replacing the attached hash value. Hence, when we want to protect the integrity of a message using only symmetric primitives, then we need keyed hash functions, also called Message Authentication Codes (MACs).

We start this section with a description of MAC functions and their requirements. Subsequently, we discuss the most popular constructions.

6.1 Description

A MAC function takes as input a message of variable length and a secret key. Depending on the construction, the key can have a fixed length or a variable length. A MAC function produces as output a *tag* of fixed length.

In order to protect the integrity of a message, the sender computes the MAC over that message, using the secret key he shares with the receiver. The resulting tag is attached to the message. Upon receipt, the receiver recomputes the MAC over the received message and compares the result with the tag that was sent. If both tags agree, then the receiver can be confident that the message was not modified during transport.

6.2 Requirements

The requirements for a MAC function are a cross-breed between the requirements for an un-keyed hash function and the requirements for a block cipher. Even in case the attacker has at his disposition a large sample of messages, possibly chosen by him, and the corresponding tags, it should be computationally infeasible to achieve any of the following:

Key recovery: To recover the value of the secret key,
Forgery: To produce a new message with a valid tag

Two types of forgeries can be distinguished: *substitutions*, which are based on a pair of messages that result in the same tag, and *impersonations*, which consist of a message and a valid tag that were not part of the sample set.

6.3 Examples

The most used MAC functions are based on a block cipher in CBC mode of operation, or on a dedicated design for an un-keyed hash function, e.g., HMAC. An alternative construction method is based on universal hash functions.

6.3.1 CBC–MAC

As explained in Sect. 4.4.2, if a message is encrypted with a block cipher in CBC-mode, the last ciphertext block depends on all message blocks. The CBC–MAC of a message is constructed by first "encrypting" the message with a block cipher in CBC-mode, and second apply some output transformation v on the last block of the ciphertext. The output of v is the tag [40].

Many different variations on this scheme have been proposed in order to solve security problems due to the short key length and the short block length of the popular block cipher DES. Most of the variations have subsequently been broken or shown to not live up to expectations. However, if DES is replaced by AES, then there are no known security problems with the basic CBC–MAC scheme.

Note that the CBC–MAC computations can not be shared with a CBC encryption process. If both confidentiality and integrity of the message have to be protected, then it is possible to use a block cipher in CBC mode to achieve both goals, but the secret keys used should be different. Hence, two separate passes over the message are required. Recently, new modes of operation for block ciphers have been proposed, that allow to achieve confidentiality and integrity simultaneously [14,17,31]. These modes are still being studied.

6.3.2 HMAC

Let h denote an un-keyed hash function and let '$\|$' denote concatenation of symbol streams. Then, the HMAC construction can, somewhat simplifying, be described as follows.

$$\mathrm{HMAC}(m,k) = h(k\|h(k\|m)) \qquad (21)$$

The message m is "enveloped" by the key. Since the outer invocation of the hash function operates on a short input, the performance of the HMAC construction is almost as good as the performance of h. A full description of the HMAC construction can be found in [42].

Because un-keyed hash functions are over-designed for their use in HMAC, this construction has the additional feature that even for someone who knows the key, it is computationally infeasible to construct substitution forgeries.

In the past, unkeyed hash functions were significantly faster than block ciphers. Hence, for reasonably long messages, the HMAC construction used to be significantly faster than CBC–MAC constructions. However, due to the good performance of AES and the recent cryptanalysis breakthroughs on the fastest hash functions, the difference in performance is getting smaller.

6.3.3 Universal Hash Functions

Universal hash functions were proposed in [36]. A universal hash function is actually a set of hash functions, satisfying certain properties. In an application that uses a MAC based on a universal hash function, a part of the secret key is used to select one function of the set. The selected function is applied to the message, and the output is encrypted using another part of the key.

The security of the MAC is not based on the computational infeasibility to invert a known map. Instead, one relies on the fact that the attacker does not know which function of the set has been used and hence does not know which function to invert. The set of functions is defined in such a way that guessing attacks have a low probability of success. Because there is no requirement of one-wayness on the individual functions, it is more easy to construct functions with a high performance. In principle, universal hash functions require a lot of key material, but this requirement can be alleviated by using the output of a stream cipher, cf. Sect. 3.

7 Outlook

With the conclusion of the AES selection process, it appears that application developers have now a strong symmetric primitive to ensure message confidentiality. Where it has been demonstrated that implementations of the AES can be quite efficient on a wide range of platforms, there remain application areas with special requirements which might be better served by another symmetric encryption primitive, for instance a stream cipher. The challenge for designers of stream ciphers is to come up with a design that is really faster or less costly to implement than an optimized AES implementation.

The area of integrity providing primitives appears currently to be more dynamic. Several designs that where believed to achieve the highest security level have recently turned out to contain some holes. On the one hand, this challenges the designers of symmetric primitives to come up with new designs, perhaps using completely different approaches to the problem. On the other hand, application developers are challenged to pay more attention to the exact security requirements of their application and evaluate whether the existing designs, with their known shortcomings, can still provide sufficient security.

Finally, even the best cryptographic primitive can be used wrongly and result in an application with security problems. The design of security protocols and systems remains a task for experts who have a good understanding of the characteristics that all cryptographic primitive of a given type share. Only in this way can 'silly mistakes' be avoided.

References

1. M. Bellare, A. Desai, E. Jokipii, and P. Rogaway. "A concrete security treatment of symmetric encryption: Analysis of the DES modes of operation," Proceedings of the 38th IEEE FOCS, 1997.
2. M. Bellare, A. Desai, E. Jokipii, and P. Rogaway. "A concrete security treatment of symmetric encryption," Proceedings of the 38th symposium on Foundations of Computer Science, IEEE, 1997.
3. B. Canvel, A. Hiltgen, S. Vaudenay, and M. Vuagnoux. "Password interception in a SSL/TLS channel," Advances in Cryptology – CRYPTO'03, LNCS 2729, Springer, 2003, pp. 583–599.
4. N. Courtois, and J. Pieprzyk. "Cryptanalysis of block ciphers with overdefined systems of equations," Proceedings of Asiacrypt 2002, LNCS 2501, Springer, 2002, pp. 267–287.
5. J. Daemen, and V. Rijmen. The design of Rijndael; AES – Advanced Encryption Standard, ISBN 3-540-42580-2, Springer, 2002.
6. A.W. Dent, and C.J. Mitchell. User's guide to cryptography and standards, Artech House, 2005.
7. W. Diffie, and M.E. Hellman. "Exhaustive cryptanalysis of the NBS Data Encryption Standard," Computer, 10, 1977, pp. 644–654.
8. H. Dobbertin. "Cryptanalysis of MD4," Journal of Cryptology, 11(4):253–271, Springer, 1998.
9. M. Dworkin. "Recommendation for block cipher modes of operation," NIST Special Publication 800-38A, 2001.
10. The Electronic Frontier Foundation (EFF). Cracking DES, ISBN: 1-56592-520-3, 1998.
11. N. Ferguson, D. Whiting, B. Schneier, J. Kelsey, S. Lucks, and T. Kohno. "Helix: fast encryption and authentication in a single cryptographi primitive," Fast Software Encryption 2003, LNCS 2887, pp. 330–346, Springer, 2003,
12. S.R. Fluhrer, and D.A. McGrew. "Statistical analysis of the alleged RC4 key stream generator," Fast Software Encryption 2000, LNCS 1978, pp. 19–30, Springer, 2000.
13. S.R. Fluhrer, I. Mantin, and A. Shamir. "Weaknesses in the key scheduling algorithm of RC4," Selected Areas in Cryptography SAC2001, LNCS 2259, pp. 1–24, Springer, 2001.
14. V. Gligor, and P. Donescu. "Fast encryption and authentication: XCBC encryption and XECB authentication modes," Fast Software Encryption 2001, LNCS 2355, pp. 92–108, Springer, 2002.
15. D. Golic. "Linear statistical weakness of alleged RC4 key stream generator," Advances in Cryptology – Proceedings of Eurocrypt 1997, LNCS 1233, pp. 226–238, Springer, 1994.
16. S. Halevi, D. Coppersmith, and C.S. Jutla. "Scream: a software-efficient stream cipher," Fast Software Encryption 2002, LNCS 2365, pp. 195–209, Springer, 2002.
17. C. Jutla. "Encryption modes with almost free message integrity," Advances in Cryptology Eurocrypt 2001, LNCS 2045, pp. 529–544, Springer, 2001.
18. A. Joux, P. Carribault, W. Jalby, and C. Lemuet. "Full iterative differential collisions in SHA-0," preprint.
19. L.R. Knudsen, W. Meier, B. Preneel, V. Rijmen, and S. Verdoolaege. "Analysis methods for (alleged) RC4," Advances in Cryptology – Proceedings of Asiacrypt 1998, LNCS 1514, pp. 327–341, Springer, 1998.
20. S. Mangard, T. Popp, and B.M. Gammel, "Side-Channel Leakage of Masked CMOS Gates," Proceedings of CT-RSA 2005, LNCS 3376, Springer, 2005.

21. I. Mantin, and A. Shamir, "A practical attack on broadcast RC4," Fast Software Encryption 2001, LNCS 2355, pp. 152–164, Springer, 2002.
22. S.M. Matyas, C.H. Meyer, and J. Oseas. "Generating strong one-way functions with cryptographic algorithm," IBM Technical Disclosure Bulletin, 27:5658–5659, 1985.
23. R.C. Merkle. "One-way hash functions and DES," Advances in Cryptology – Proceedings of Crypto 1989, LNCS 435, pp. 428–446, Springer, 1990.
24. R.C. Merkle, and M.E. Hellman. "On the security of multiple encryption," Communications of the ACM, 24:465–467, 1981.
25. S. Mister, and S.E. Tavares. "Cryptanalysis of RC4-like ciphers," Selected Areas in Cryptography SAC 1998, LNCS 1556, pp. 131–143, Springer.
26. S. Murphy, and M.J.B. Robshaw. "Essential algebraic structure within the AES," Proceedings of CRYPTO 2002, LNCS 2442, pp. 1–16, Springer, 2002.
27. S. Peleg, and A. Rosenfeld. "Breaking substitution ciphers using a relaxation algorithm," Communications of the ACM, 22(11):598–603, 1979.
28. B. Preneel. "Cryptographic hash functions," European Transactions on Telecommunications, 5:431–448, 1994.
29. V. Rijmen, and E. Oswald. "Update on SHA-1," Proceedings of CT-RSA 2005, LNCS 3376, pp. 58–71, Springer, 2005.
30. R.L. Rivest. "The MD4 message digest algorithm," Advances in Cryptology – Proceedings of Crypto 1990, LNCS 537, pp. 303-311, Springer, 1991.
31. P. Rogaway, M. Bellare, J. Black, and T. Krovetz. "OCB: a block-cipher mode of operation for efficient authenticated encryption," ACM Transactions on Information and System Security (TISSEC), 6(3):365–403, 2001.
32. P. Rogaway, and D. Coppersmith. "A software-optimised encryption algorithm," Fast Software Encryption 1993, LNCS 809, pp. 56–63, Springer, 1994.
33. S. Vaudenay. "Security flaws induced by CBC padding - applications to SSL, IPSEC, WTLS," Advances in Cryptology – Proceedings of Eurocrypt 2002, LNCS 2332, pp. 534–545, Springer, 2002.
34. X. Wang, D. Feng, X. Lai, and H. Deng. "Collisions for hash functions MD4, MD5, HAVAL-128 and RIPEMD," Cryptology ePrint Archive, Report 2004/199, http://eprint.iacr.org.
35. M.J. Wiener. "Efficient DES key search," Technical Report TR-244, School of Computer Science, Carleton University, Ottawa, 1994. Presented at the rump session of Crypto'93.
36. M. Wegmann, and J. Carter. "New hash functions and their use in authentication and set equality," Journal of Computer and System Sciences, 22:265–279, 1981.
37. ISO/IEC 10118-3:2003. Information technology – Security techniques – Hash-functions – Part 3: Dedicated hash-functions, 2003.
38. LAN/MAN Standard Comittee. IEEE Standard for Information Technology - Telecommunications and Information Exchange between Systems - Local and Metropolitan Area Network - Specific Requirements - Part 11: Wireless LAN medium access control (MAC) and physical layer specifications, (1999 edition), IEEE standard 802.11, 1999.
39. US National Bureau of Standards. Federal Information Processing Standards Publication 46, Data Encryption Standard, 1977.
40. National Institute of Standards and Technology (NIST). Federal Information Processing Standard 81, DES modes of operation, 1980.
41. US National Institute of Standards and Technology. Federal Information Processing Standard 197, Advanced Encryption Standard (AES), 2001.
42. National Institute of Standards and Technology (NIST). Federal Information Processing Standard 198, The keyed-hash message authentication code (HMAC), 2002.

Efficient Trapdoor-Based Client Puzzle Against DoS Attacks

Yi Gao, Willy Susilo, Yi Mu, and Jennifer Seberry

Contents

1 Introduction

It is well known that authentication, integrity, and confidentiality are the most important principles of network security. However, recent reports about a number of prominent Internet service providers that broke down because of malicious attacks [2, 3, 31, 32] urge people to realize that all security principles must be based on service availability. "Availability" in this context refers to a service that can be accessed within a reasonable amount of waiting time after a legitimate client sends a request.

Y. Gao (✉)

School of Information Technology and Computer Science, University of Wollongong, Australia

e-mail: yg70@uow.edu.au

S.C.-H. Huang et al. (eds.), *Network Security*, DOI 10.1007/978-0-387-73821-5_10,
© Springer Science+Business Media, LLC 2010

The service availability of a network server can be destructed in a variety of ways, such as internal bugs within a system, hardware limits, or malicious attacks from outside. Network-based DoS attacks, in particular, denote malicious actions, which aim at shutting down a target server and destructing its service availability via the Internet. These attacks usually attempt to block or degrade service in a designated period temporarily, rather than intrude on the server directly or damage the data permanently.

One of the most popular DoS attacks, TCP SYN flooding attacks, was reported in 1996 [2, 3, 10, 32], which succeeded in crippling Panix, a major New York Internet service provider, in early September 1996, and created similar problems for the website of the New York Times a few days later. As a rule, an SYN flooding attacker exploits spoofed IP addresses to mount a large number of initial and unresolved connection requests to a victim server, depleting its resources and rendering it incapable of responding to legitimate clients.

Distributed Denial of Service (DDoS) is a new form of DoS attack, first reported in early 2000 [8, 28, 31]. In contrast to traditional DoS attacks, DDoS attackers, in particular, are armed with self-propagation worms which can be installed on a discretionary number of vulnerable computers on the Internet. An attacker is able to harness these compromised machines in order to mount a coordinated DoS attack. These infected machines are typically divided into two groups: "Masters" and "Zombies", which play different roles in a DDoS attack. "Masters" are more like intermediaries, while "Zombies" serve as attack platforms. Communication between an attacker and the "Zombies" is not direct, but depends on the "Masters". One "Master" may control and deliver the attacker's command to a number of "Zombies". By mounting such a coordinated DoS attack, the effectiveness of a DDoS can be multiplied by 10, 100, or even 10,000 times [13].

A typical DDoS attack process can be described as follows. An attacker first scans a large range of networks to find vulnerable hosts that have weak defences against a malicious intrusion. The number of these hosts is determined by the strength of the attack that an attacker intends to launch. Second, the attacker installs "Master" or "Agent" programs on these vulnerable hosts. A machine with an "Agent" program is called a "Zombie", which carries out the actual attack. A machine installed with a "Master" program is able to communicate with a number of "Zombies" and serves as a control-handler of the attacker. An attacker can command several "Masters" directly, and "Zombies" are activated by these "Masters" at the designated time for an attack. Figure 1 shows this three-layer control. The reason for using such an architecture is to keep the attacker safe and difficult to trace. Now, all the preparation has been accomplished. The attacker only needs to cross his fingers and wait for an appropriate time to launch his DDoS attack. When a defending server suspects that it is under a DoS attack, it can only find numerous legitimate connection requests received from a large number of legitimate IP addresses, consuming all the resources of the server. However, the real owners of these "Zombies" are unwitting accomplices [16], and do not know what has actually happened on their machines.

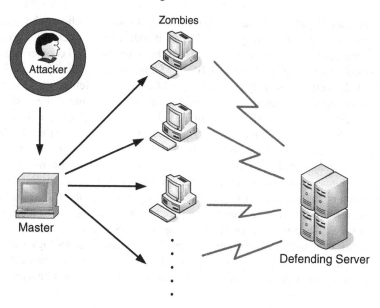

Fig. 1 Three-layer control for a DDoS attack

To prevent DoS attacks, many defence mechanisms have been proposed (e.g., [4,6,14,22,23,25]), among which client puzzle is one of the most notable and influential. Since DoS attacks mostly exploit defects in existing network protocols, the advantage of client puzzles over other proposed methods is that by improving protocols directly, it is feasible to confine DoS attacks in a harmless range for defending servers.

In a typical DoS attack, an adversary deploys unauthorized service requests to consume the limited resources of a target server. The aim of client puzzles is to impose a moderate authentication "cost"[1] on each client wishing to obtain service from a defending server. This can be achieved by asking clients to solve different cryptographic puzzles (here we call them *client puzzles*). The cost of computing client puzzles is negligible for legitimate clients, but unendurably expensive for DoS attackers who attempt to acquire considerable resources from the server. Because recent studies show that existing DDoS tools are designed carefully as to disturb "Zombie" computers and to avoid alerting their real owners. In other words, "Zombies" are unable to furtively compute puzzles for the adversary. In this way, the defending server can force the adversary to give up, because applying for more resources demands that the adversary must invest more resources himself/herself.

---

[1] In this context, "cost" means computational cost, such as CPU processing time or/and memory space.

On the other hand, client puzzles have one inadequacy. A client who requests for a service from a defending server has to install a small client-side program for the computation of puzzles. While most of the other proposed countermeasures against DoS attacks, such as Traceback IP [23], SYN cookies [6], and Ingress/Egress filtering [22] methods, merely demand a modification to a defending server or a fundamental network protocol, the potential disadvantages of these approaches are inevitable. For instance, SYN cookies are based on the assumption that an attacker launching a SYN flooding attack via spoofed IP cannot intercept all the SYN/ACK packets sent to the spoofed addresses, which is unfortunately not always true [15]. Similarly, the major idea of Traceback IP [21] is that a packet can be traced back to its source address by inserting traceback data into the packet when it passes through distinct routers to the destination, which obviously increases the traffic loads and raises much information redundancy. Compared with these, client puzzles are able to ensure service quality and protect servers against DoS attacks effectively, as long as clients install a puzzle-solving software. In today's network technology, such software can easily be implemented by a plug-in of a web browser or distributed by the servers. Hence, the requirements for this special software should not be a problem.

2   Related Work

Dwork and Naor introduced the original idea of cryptographic puzzles into junk mail defense [11], in which every successful delivery of a message requires the sender to solve a small cryptographic puzzle. By doing so, they successfully impose a large amount of computational costs on sending mass mails, while for legitimate clients, the costs to compute single puzzles are negligible.

In 1999, Juels and Brainard proposed a client puzzle protocol to defend against TCP SYN flooding attacks. The idea of the client puzzle protocol is very simple [15]. When there is no evidence of attack, a server accepts connection requests normally. If the defending server comes under a DoS attack, it distributes a unique client puzzle to each client who is applying for a connection. In order to obtain the server's resources for his/her connection, a client must compute the puzzle correctly and return the solution in time. This protocol is deployed in conjunction with the traditional time-out, which is used to control the time period for puzzle computation. Consequently, it is hard for an adversary to compute large numbers of puzzles in a short period, which can be used to differentiate legitimate requests from malicious half-open ones. In their paper, Juels and Brainard also presented a simple puzzle construction to implement their protocol although this seemed unsatisfactory and caused a lot of arguments in network forums [9, 24, 30].

In 2000, Aura et al. presented a more convincing scheme for client puzzles, which is based on Hash functions [4]. In their scheme, the server sends the parameters of a puzzle to the client, and the client performs a brute-force search and a number of computation to find the correct answer. The server distributes its resource to the client only after the solution is verified. However, the underlying problem of this puzzle scheme is that a defending server must calculate a hash function, in order to verify each solution received from clients. As a result, a possible DoS attack may occur in which an adversary sends numerous bogus answers that the server has to process. In 2004, Waters et al. [5] suggested a new technique that permits the outsourcing of puzzles. Eventhough puzzles can be used by different servers, the solution of a puzzle still requires one modular exponentiation for every defending server.

2.1 Contribution

To overcome the underlying drawbacks of the existing puzzle systems, we propose a novel client puzzle scheme that is based on a trapdoor mechanism. Our scheme is expected to possess two prominent characteristics. One is that most of the computations for puzzle generation can be fulfilled in a preconstruction phase, independent of a puzzle construction. Pre-construction can be processed during idle time, and items calculated in this phase can be reused by combining them with time parameters. The other important feature is a quick verification. No computation occurs in the verification phase, which makes DoS attacks aiming at flooding bogus solutions to exhaust system resources impossible. We show that our puzzle is computationally efficient and applicable to the existing Internet protocols. A complete security proof is also included in this chapter.

2.2 Organization of the Chapter

The rest of the chapter is organized as follows. In Sect. 3, we provide the preliminary knowledge about trapdoor functions and the Discrete Logarithm Problem(DLP). In Sect. 4, we present a formal definition of trapdoor-based client puzzles. After that, we describe our trapdoor-based puzzle scheme in detail, along with the security proof and an analysis of system efficiency. We provide the system configuration in Sect. 6 and discuss several possible improvements in Sect. 7. Finally, we conclude this chapter in Sect. 8.

3 Preliminary

3.1 Trapdoor One-Way Function

Our proposed scheme utilizes a trapdoor one-way function. Informally, a one-way function is designed to provide an algorithm which is easy to compute, yet computationally infeasible to reverse [26]. For example, given x, it is easy to compute the value of $f(x)$, but infeasible to obtain x if given $f(x)$ in polynomial time. A trapdoor one-way function is a special one-way function equipped with some secrets called "trapdoor". A trapdoor one-way function is uniformly easy to compute in one direction, but hard to reverse. Whereas in particular, it is also easy to compute x by reversing the function $f(x)$ as long as the trapdoor is known.

3.2 Security Assumption

It is well-known that the security of many famous public-key cryptosystems, such as RSA, Diffie–Hellman and DSS [17], is based on one assumption that there is a mathematically hard problem, which is difficult for cryptanalysts to solve in a polynomial time. The discrete logarithm is one of the prevalent hard problems [29].

The Discrete Logarithm Problem (DLP) is a problem that has been researched in [18, 20]: given a large prime p, a generator α of $\mathbb{Z}_p^*$, and a random element $\beta \in \mathbb{Z}_p^*$, it is hard to find the integer x ($0 \le x \le p-2$) such that $\alpha^x \equiv \beta$ (mod p). Many popular public-key cryptosystems are based on this assumption, such as the ElGamal system and the DSS [1, 12].

We provide a formal presentation of the DLP, in which p is a large prime (e.g., a 1,024-bit number).

Assumption 1. *We say that the hardness of the DLP holds, if for all probabilistic polynomial time adversaries $\mathcal{A}$, the following probability*

$$Pr[\alpha \in \mathbb{Z}_p^*, \ \beta \in_R \mathbb{Z}_p^* : \mathcal{A}(p, \alpha, \beta) = x \ s.t. \ \alpha^x \equiv \beta \pmod{p}] < \varepsilon$$

4 Definition

The aim of our trapdoor-based client puzzle system is to protect the availability of the service transferred between a web server S and legitimate clients C against DoS attacks. The system exploits a specific trapdoor one-way function, where a puzzle creator (the server S) can efficiently compute the correct solution with the knowledge of the trapdoor, while other puzzle solvers (legitimate clients C and an adversary $\mathcal{A}$) must perform a brute-force search and a number of computation to obtain the answers. The scheme consists of three efficient algorithms for generating random puzzles, solving the puzzles, and verifying the solutions of these puzzles, respectively.

Definition 1. A trapdoor-based client puzzle scheme consists of a three-tuple of polynomial algorithms (*Gen, Solve, Verify*), where

- *Gen*: Puzzle generation algorithm used by a defending server S. It takes security parameter t and a difficulty level l as input, and outputs a random puzzle $\mathcal{P}$ along with a correct solution S_s to the puzzle $\mathcal{P}$. That is

$$(\mathcal{P}, S_s) \leftarrow \mathbf{Gen}(1^t, l).$$

Indeed, a puzzle $\mathcal{P}$ comprises two elements denoted as $\mathcal{P} = (\sigma, [\alpha, \beta])$ where σ is a puzzle parameter, and $[\alpha, \beta]$ is a search range of length l. That is $l = |\beta - \alpha|$.
- *Solve*: Puzzle-solving algorithm. This is an efficient algorithm for a client C to solve the puzzles. On input $\mathcal{P} = (\sigma, [\alpha, \beta])$, it computes an answer S_c.

$$S_c \leftarrow \mathbf{Solve}(\mathcal{P})$$

- *Verify*: A deterministic algorithm performed by S. On input S_s and S_c, it outputs either one or zero.

$$\mathbf{Verify}(S_s, S_c) \in \{1, 0\}$$

Success: Define the success of a client solving a puzzle by:

$$\mathbf{Verify}(S_s, S_c) = 1, \ \ if \ S_s = S_c \ holds.$$

The diagram in Fig. 2 is a simple prototype for our trapdoor-based client puzzle scheme, in which the defending server takes charge of two positions: "Creator" and "Verifier", and a client is responsible for "Solver".

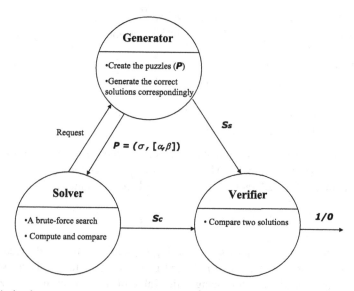

Fig. 2 A simple prototype

5 The DLP-Based Client Puzzle Scheme

5.1 Algorithm

The algorithm that we will deploy in our puzzle scheme is derived from Schnorr's Signature [7, 27], which was proposed in 1989 and could provide encryption and signature functions. Its security relies on the difficulty of computing discrete logarithms. First of all, we describe the algorithm as follows.

Let p be a large prime, and q be another prime, which is the prime factor of $p-1$. The size of p and q should be selected with care to ensure that DLP in $\mathbb{Z}_p^*$ is hard. g is a generator of the group G (order q). Denote $x \in \mathbb{Z}_q^*$ as a positive and secret integer. Let l be the difficulty lever of puzzles.

Our scheme is based on the following equations, in which random $a,\ b \in \mathbb{Z}_q^*$.

$$h = g^x \quad (\text{mod } p) \tag{1}$$

$$C = g^a \cdot h^b \quad (\text{mod } p) \tag{2}$$

$$W = a + b \cdot x \quad (\text{mod } q) \tag{3}$$

Examining the above equations, we find a transformation by assembling them together as shown below.

- Put (1) into (2).

$$
\begin{aligned}
C = g^a \cdot h^b &= g^a \cdot (g^x)^b \\
&= g^a \cdot g^{bx} \\
&= g^{a+bx} \quad (\text{mod } p)
\end{aligned}
\tag{4}
$$

- Put (3) into (4).

$$C = g^{a+bx} = g^W \quad (\text{mod } p) \tag{5}$$

Note that g and p are constant in (5). Hence, if we can maintain the constancy of W, C should be a constant as well.

From (3), we can easily verify that a and b can be chosen arbitrarily, if the secret value x is known, to obtain W. Moreover, by a given random $a' \in \mathbb{Z}_q^*$, we can compute a unique $b' \in \mathbb{Z}_p^*$ by (6) such that W is kept constant.

$$b' = (W - a') \cdot x^{-1} \quad (\text{mod } q) \tag{6}$$

Our puzzle scheme operates so that, using (3) and (5), the puzzle creator can easily compute the initial values of W and C from a pair (a, b). Then, keeping W and C constant, the creator changes the value of a' for each new puzzle and calculates a corresponding solution b' through (6). He also generates a search range associated with b', where the range length equals l (recall that l is the difficulty level). The puzzle creator should broadcast p, h, and (2), but keep g, x, q, and W secret. In consequence, the only feasible method for a puzzle solver is to perform an exhaustive search in the candidate range to find a b' that makes (2) hold.

Since he knows the trapdoor – (6), the puzzle creator performs only one addition[2] and one modular multiplication to obtain a solution for each fresh a'. On the other hand, a solver must compute a sequence of modular exponentiations for testing each instance in the given range until he finds the correct answer. Meanwhile, the creator can adjust the size of the search range – l to control the computational costs consumed by the solvers.

5.2 System Description

Now, we look at how a system using our trapdoor-based puzzle scheme works for the defending server and legitimate clients. We split the scheme into four phases, use preprocessing to calculate, and store a number of constants for puzzle construction and verification, which are expected to relieve the computational overhead of the server.

1. **Preconstruction phase**

    (a) Determine a time interval T_d and the size of A denoted by n.
    There is a trade-off between T_d and n, which requires some careful thought. In fact, the server needs to find a minimum n and a maximum T_d that satisfy the following requirement: in each time period, n is by minimum greater than the maximum connection ability of the server. It means that no instance in set A can be chosen for puzzle construction more than once in same time period. For instance, if the hourly maximum connectivity of the server is 50,000 on average, n should be from 50,001 with $T_d = 1$.
    (b) Establish A.
    A is a random and nonrepeated integer set.

    $$A = \{a_i \mid a_i \in \mathbb{Z}_q^*, \mid 1 \leq i \leq n\} \cap \{\forall a_m, a_n \in A \mid a_m \neq a_n\}$$

    (c) Compute G_A.
    G_A is computed by the server.

    $$G_A = \{g^{a_i} \pmod{p} \mid 1 \leq i \leq n, a_i \in A\}$$

    (d) Generate and encrypt t.
    t is a time parameter which is in the form of

    $$\{yymmddhh^1 hh^2\} \cap \{hh^2 - hh^1 = T_d\}.$$

---

[2] A subtraction operation can be viewed as an addition in a computer system.

We can adjust the form of t according to the designated T_d. For instance, if $T_d = 30\,\text{min}$, the form of t can be described as

$$\{yymmddhhmm^1 mm^2\} \cap \{mm^2 - mm^1 = 30\}.$$

Then, the server computes g^t (mod p) at the beginning of each new time period.

(e) Compute initial C, W, w_t and x^{-1} (mod q).

   Given a random pair $(a, b) \subset Z_q^*$, the server obtains

$$W = a + b \cdot x \quad (\text{mod } q)$$

and

$$C = g^W \quad (\text{mod } p).$$

Compute

$$w_t = W - t \quad (\text{mod } q).$$

Using the extended Euclidean algorithm, the server easily computes x^{-1} (mod q).

In the pre-construction phase, the server obtains constants $\{W, C, x^{-1} A, G_A\}$ and two periodic constants $\{g^t, w_t\}$.

2. **Construction phase**

   When receiving a request from a client C, the server S generates a puzzle $\mathcal{P} = (g^{a'}, [\alpha, \beta])$ along with its correct solution b_s. $\mathcal{P}$ is essential for a client solving a puzzle. b_s is stored on the server for verification of the answer returned from the client. This stage is described as follows.

   (a) Compute $g^{a'}$.

$$g^{a'} = g^t \cdot g^{a_i} \quad (\text{mod } p) \tag{7}$$

   where $g^{a_i} \in G_A$, t is the current time period, and g^t is a periodic constant calculated at the beginning of t. The server picks up random $g^{a_i} \in G_A$ to generate a fresh puzzle then marks this g^{a_i} to be unavailable until a new period comes. This means that when each period starts, all the elements in G_A are available. An element is marked unavailable throughout the same period, once it is chosen by the server to create a puzzle.

   (b) Generate b_s.

$$\begin{aligned}
b_s &= (W - a') \cdot x^{-1} && (\text{mod } q) \\
&= [W - (t + a_i)] \cdot x^{-1} && (\text{mod } q) \\
&= (w_t - a_i) \cdot x^{-1} && (\text{mod } q) \tag{8}
\end{aligned}$$

Note that the values of i in (7) and (8) are uniform.

(c) Obtain a search range $[\alpha, \beta] \subset \mathbb{Z}_q^*$.

$$\alpha = b_s - c \quad (\text{mod } q)$$

$$\beta = \alpha + l \quad (\text{mod } q)$$

for random $c \in [0, l)$, where l is the current difficulty level of the puzzles.

3. **Puzzle-solving phase**

Unlike the other three, this phase is performed on the client's side. We assume that a client C has installed a specific piece of software which is distributed by the server. It solves puzzles received from the server with an equation

$$C = g^a \cdot h^b \quad (\text{mod } p),$$

a triple of constants (C, h, p), and an interface for accepting puzzles from the server.

When a client receives a puzzle $\mathcal{P}$, he employs an exhaustive search (brute-force) to find the answer b_c which satisfies the equation. Due to the length of the search range $l = \beta - \alpha$, a client C needs to perform on average $l/2$ modular exponentiations to find the answer b_c.

4. **Verification phase**

Upon receiving the answer b_c from a client, the server compares it with the stored solution b_s that has been calculated in the construction phase. If they are equal, **Verify**$(\cdot)$ outputs 1, which means that authentication of the client is verified, and the server proceeds with the rest of the request. Otherwise, **Verify**$(\cdot)$ outputs 0, and the server drops the request.

$$\textbf{Verify}(b_s, b_c) = \begin{cases} 1 & \text{if } b_s = b_c \\ 0 & \text{otherwise} \end{cases}$$

5.3 Security Consideration

Theorem 1. *If (2) holds, then the solution b' computed by (6) can be verified.*

Proof: Given the initial values of (a, b), we can obtain the following result.

$$C = g^a \cdot h^b = g^a \cdot g^{bx} = g^{a+bx} = g^W \quad (\text{mod } p)$$

To create a new puzzle, we choose a' and compute the solution $b' = (W - a) \cdot x^{-1}$ (mod q). Now, we verify it in (2).

$$\begin{aligned} C = g^W = g^{a'} \cdot g^{b'} &= g^{a'} \cdot h^{(W-a') \cdot x^{-1}} \quad (\text{mod } p) \\ &= g^{a'} \cdot g^{(W-a') \cdot x^{-1} \cdot x} \quad (\text{mod } p) \\ &= g^{a'} \cdot g^{W-a'} \quad (\text{mod } p) \\ &= g^W \quad (\text{mod } p) \end{aligned}$$

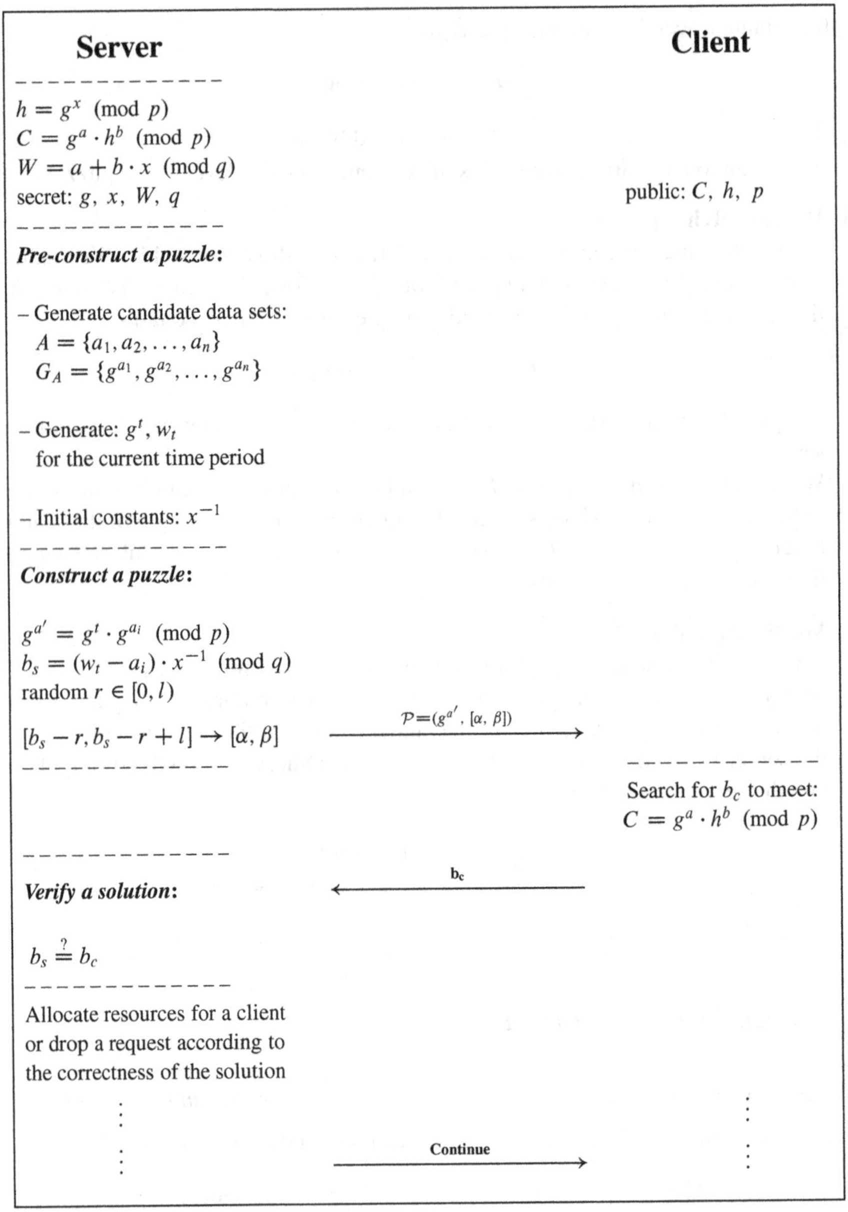

Server	**Client**

– – – – – – – – – – –

$h = g^x \pmod{p}$
$C = g^a \cdot h^b \pmod{p}$
$W = a + b \cdot x \pmod{q}$
secret: g, x, W, q public: C, h, p

– – – – – – – – – – –

Pre-construct a puzzle:

– Generate candidate data sets:
  $A = \{a_1, a_2, \ldots, a_n\}$
  $G_A = \{g^{a_1}, g^{a_2}, \ldots, g^{a_n}\}$

– Generate: g^t, w_t
  for the current time period

– Initial constants: x^{-1}

– – – – – – – – – – –

Construct a puzzle:

$g^{a'} = g^t \cdot g^{a_i} \pmod{p}$
$b_s = (w_t - a_i) \cdot x^{-1} \pmod{q}$
random $r \in [0, l]$

$[b_s - r, b_s - r + l] \to [\alpha, \beta]$ $\xrightarrow{\quad \mathcal{P} = (g^{a'}, [\alpha, \beta]) \quad}$

– – – – – – – – – – –
                                                                                          – – – – – – – – – – –

                                                                                          Search for b_c to meet:
                                                                                          $C = g^a \cdot h^b \pmod{p}$

– – – – – – – – – – –

Verify a solution: $\xleftarrow{\quad b_c \quad}$

$b_s \overset{?}{=} b_c$

– – – – – – – – – – –

Allocate resources for a client
or drop a request according to
the correctness of the solution

$\vdots$ $\vdots$
                            $\xrightarrow{\quad \text{Continue} \quad}$
$\vdots$ $\vdots$

Fig. 3 A DLP-based puzzle scheme

Theorem 2. *Our scheme is secure assuming the hardness of the Discrete Logarithm Problem.*

Proof: To illustrate our proof, first let us recall the assumption made in the Discrete Logarithm Problem. Given two elements of a group, g^v and h, it is computationally infeasible to find a non-negative integer x such that

$$h = g^x \pmod{p}$$

holds, where the size of p is appropriately chosen (e.g. 1,024 bits).

We assume there is an algorithm A that, given $C, g, h \in Z_p{}^*$, outputs a, b such that

$$C = g^a \cdot h^b \pmod{p}$$

holds with a non-negligible probability.

We will show an algorithm B that uses A to solve an instance of a Discrete Logarithm Problem, which is assumed to be hard.

To be more precise, the task of algorithm B is to output

$$x = \log_g h \pmod{p}$$

given $g, h \in Z_p^*$ for a prime p. This simulation is as follows.

First, B provides g, h, p as the public parameters to A. Then, B performs the following:

- Select a random value $\theta \in Z_q^*$, where $q \mid p - 1$.
- Compute: $C^* = g^\theta \bmod p$.

Finally, B provides C^* to A, and with a non-negligible probability, A outputs: (a, b) where:

$$C^* = g^a \cdot h^b \pmod{p}$$

holds. Now, the simulation is restarted. Again, first A is provided with the public parameters g, h, p, and finally given C^*. A will produce another forgery $(\hat{a}, \hat{b})$ where

$$C^* = g^{\hat{a}} \cdot h^{\hat{b}} \pmod{p}$$

holds. If $\hat{a} = a$ and $\hat{b} = b$ hold, then the last simulation needs to be repeated until $\hat{a} \neq a$ and $\hat{b} \neq b$. We note that A will output $\hat{a} = a$ and $\hat{b} = b$ with probability $1/q^2$.

After obtaining two values (a, b) and $(\hat{a}, \hat{b})$, B gathers the following equations:

$$C^* = g^a \cdot h^b \pmod{p}$$
$$C^* = g^{\hat{a}} \cdot h^{\hat{b}} \pmod{p}$$

Hence, B derives:

$$g^a \cdot h^b = g^{\hat{a}} \cdot h^{\hat{b}} \pmod{p}$$

which implies:

$$a + bx = \hat{a} + \hat{b}x \pmod{q}$$

or

$$x \cdot (b - \hat{b}) = \hat{a} - a \pmod{q}$$

and

$$x = (\hat{a} - a)(b - \hat{b})^{-1} \pmod{q}$$

Note that x is the solution to the DLP problem. The probability of success of B is lower bounded by $1/q^2$, which is non-negligible. Hence, we have provided the proof.

5.4 Remark

Remark 1. No client can precompute a puzzle or its solution in advance.

- In the preconstruction proces s, the defending server generates a random and nonrepeatable data set A ($A = \{a_i | 1 \leq i \leq n, a_i \in Z_q^*\}$). According to set A, the server obtains a multiplier factor set G_A ($G_A = \{g^{a_i} \pmod{p} \mid 1 \leq i \leq n, a_i \in A\}$), in which the values of g^{a_i} are consequently irregular.
- When the defending server constructs a puzzle, it performs the following computation:

$$g^{a'} = g^t \cdot g^{a_i}$$

where g^{a_i} is randomly selected from G_A. We notice that the probability of a client successfully predicting a puzzle equals $1/qn$. When q and n are big enough, precomputing a puzzle is computationally infeasible in the time period t.

Remark 2. The computational resources consumed by a client to solve a puzzle are greater than those used by the server to generate a puzzle and verify its solution.

A defending server performs two modular multiplications and three additions to create a puzzle and obtain the solution.

To produce $g^{a'}$, the server performs one modular multiplication:

$$g^{a'} = g^t \cdot g^{a_i} \pmod{p}$$

To obtain the solution, the server performs one modular multiplication and one addition:

$$b_s = (w_t - a_i) \cdot x^{-1} \pmod{q}$$

where w_t is computed at the beginning of the current time period.

To generate the search range $[\alpha, \beta]$, the server performs two additions:

$$\alpha = b_s - r$$

$$\beta = \alpha + l < N$$

To verify a solution, the server only needs to make a comparison.

$$b_s \overset{?}{=} b_c$$

Since we ensure that the sizes of p and q are large enough to resist any attacks on the DLP, the answer can only be obtained by exhaustively searching the seed range and performing modular exponentiations until the correct instance that satisfies the public equation is found. In consequence, to solve a puzzle, a client has to conduct on average $l/2$ modular exponentiations and comparisons, which are much more than the defending server does.

Remark 3. The DLP-based client puzzle scheme is better than the Hash function [4] and Diffie–Hellman [5] based puzzle schemes.

- The unique solution guarantees that the defending server can perform a simple comparison to verify puzzle solutions. This is more efficient and effective in protecting the verification phase against DoS attacks than the Hash function-based puzzle scheme, in which the defending server is required to perform a hash function for solution verifications.
- To adjust the difficulty of a puzzle, we exploit a non-negative integer l to control the length of a search range. The value of l varies according to the strength of a DoS attack. When the strength of an attack degree is low, l is correspondingly small and the cost of solving a puzzle is insignificant for a client. If an attack worsens and l enlarges, a client has to supply more resources to find a solution. On average, it requires $l/2$ modular exponentiations to solve a puzzle. Hence, our scheme is more easily measurable than the Hash function-based puzzle scheme.
- To avoid puzzle iteration, the Hash function-based scheme requires that a record of the used instances is kept for a long time, and it performs two comparisons in puzzle construction and verification respectively. However, relying on the time parameter t, our scheme can always obtain unique puzzles without wasting memory space and computational time. The items calculated in the preconstruction phase can also be reused in every new time interval.
- Apart from relying on the outsourcing for puzzle construction, the Diffie–Hellman based puzzle scheme requires a modular exponentiation to obtain a correct solution. Note that a modular exponentiation can be divided into many modular multiplications [19] and a large number of modular additions. Our DLP-based scheme, on the other hand, only needs two modular multiplications and three additions to obtain a puzzle and its corresponding solution, which is more efficient.
- Our scheme is resistant to eavesdropping attacks. As we claimed earlier, no puzzle construction information is revealed during communication between the defending server and its clients. In addition, each connection request has a unique solution, so that eavesdropping is rarely advantageous to an attacker.
- By varying the values of public instances (such as C, h, p) and constant instances (such as A, G_A), distinct web servers can obtain different puzzle schemes. This is more flexible for the current network servers that possess various capabilities.

6 System Configuration

In this section, we provide a general configuration for system parameters, which will enable the defending server to detect DoS attacks and start up the defence system in time. Our scheme begins with a regular examination to determine whether it is currently under a DoS attack. A standard parameter for an attack can be the status of buffer space consumed or the number of TCP connections. Here, we prefer the status of buffer space consumed as a standard; so let B_f denote the whole buffer space of a defending server and C_{sm} be the number of buffers consumed. We assume that there are five values of C_{sm} which reflect the strength of an attack (this can be adjusted flexibly according to the different web servers), and we call them 1–5. When less than half of B_f is consumed, the value of C_{sm} is zero, which means there is no attack alarm for a defending server. When the number of consumed buffers comes to half of B_f, the value of C_{sm} is increased to 1, indicating that the server is suspected of being under an attack. From now on, the defending server needs to construct and send out a puzzle for every client who is applying for a connection until the alarm is removed again. When the number of consumed buffers increases to 3/5 B_f, 7/10 B_f, 4/5 B_f, and 9/10 B_f, respectively, the values of C_{sm} are 2, 3, 4, and 5 correspondingly.

We have another parameter l – the difficulty level of a puzzle, which decides the length of the search range related to C_{sm}. When C_{sm} is zero, the value of l is also zero. When C_{sm} is increased to 1, l becomes 10 (the value of l can also be adjusted according to different web servers). As C_{sm} increases, the value of l appears to grow exponentially. We describe some variations below:

$$C_{sm} = 0, \quad l = 0;$$
$$C_{sm} = 1, \quad l = 10;$$
$$C_{sm} = 2, \quad l = 100;$$
$$C_{sm} = 3, \quad l = 1,000;$$
$$C_{sm} = 4, \quad l = 10,000;$$
$$C_{sm} = 5, \quad l = 100,000;$$

We can see that the difficulty of a puzzle can be increased from 0 to a figure that is computationally infeasible as an attack becomes more severe.

We describe the details of our defending system as follows.

1. $C_{sm} = 0$, **which means there is no attack alarm for our defending server.**
   When a client sends an initial connection request and an enquiry as to whether the server is under a DoS attack, the server answers "No". Then, the client and the server should continue and finish their connection according to a standard connection establishment protocol such as TCP. The period of validation for this connection is within a certain time T_v.

2. $C_{sm} \geq 1$, **which means our defending server is suspected of being under a DoS attack.**

When a client sends an initial connection request and an enquiry as to whether the server is under a DoS attack, the defending server constructs a puzzle according to the current value of l and sends back "Yes", together with a set of puzzle parameters, to the client. The server keeps a correct solution b'_{si} for every connection request i for a specified period T_w. A client uses the puzzle's parameters to solve the problem and sends the solution back. The defending server compares the two solutions and then decides whether to proceed or drop this request. A connection request should be dropped immediately if a solution received from a client is incorrect, or the time for sending back a solution is beyond T_w.

7 Discussion

In this section, we will discuss some possible attack scenarios and problems that occur when a defending server implements our trapdoor-based puzzle scheme.

- **Discussion 1**

If a malicious client floods a defending server with initial connection requests by using spoofed IP addresses or his "Zombies" (see Fig. 4), how can a server protect itself? Wasting system resources to construct and send out a puzzle for every connection request is not an efficient approach for protecting a web server. The aim of such an attack is to make a defending server perform a large number of meaningless computations for the construction of puzzles, which may lead to the possibility of exhausting the server's resources. Recall that a basic principle of client puzzles in defending against DoS attacks is to force a client to consume a

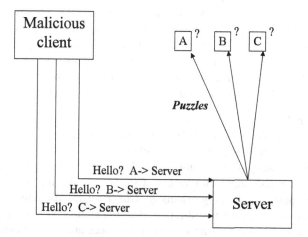

Fig. 4 A threat to our trapdoor-based puzzle scheme

large number of resources before obtaining resources from the defending server. If we do not comply with this rule, the threat of DoS attacks still exists. We propose two improved solutions to defeat this threat.

Solution 1. We propose to calculate and obtain the puzzle solution pairs $(g^{a'}, b'_s)$ in advance, and store them in a secret table on a defending server, before every new time period t starts. When there is a connection request, the server does not need to construct a puzzle by calculating the modular multiplication for $g^{a'}$ and b'_s. The server just fetches a pair of puzzle solutions $(g^{a'}, b'_s)$ from the table, keeps b'_s, and sends the value of $g^{a'}$ to the client. Hence, the only thing that the server needs to do, when there is a connection request, is to select a random integer r to generate the seed range $[b'_s - r, b'_s - r + l]$ for b'_c. The size of the table can be determined by the capability of the connectivity of the defending server.

Solution 2. Before describing our second scheme, we make the following assumption for this solution. A malicious client who deploys IP spoofing cannot intercept all the packets sent from a defending server to the spoofed addresses. When a defending server receives a connection request, it sends back a sequence number to determine whether the address is bogus. The aim of this option is to alleviate an attack via the sequence number in this first step, and then ban it in the later puzzle verification.

When a client sends an initial connection request and an enquiry as to whether the server is under a DoS attack, the server returns "Yes" and a sequence number to the received IP address. If the client is willing to accept the puzzle, he should return a value that is equal to the sequence number plus one in a strict time period T_s. After receiving the correct sequence number in a valid time period, the server generates and sends a cryptographic puzzle to the client. Otherwise, the server will drop the service request immediately. The sequence number is a filter for spoofed IP addresses, which works under the above assumption. A legitimate client has to simply solve a puzzle and send the solution in a given time T_w to obtain the final service. If the solution is correct, the server will proceed with the rest of the connection request and distribute the system's resources to the client. On the other hand, if the answer is wrong or the time for computation is beyond the given time T_w, the server will drop this request. If a connection is established, the period of validation for this connection is within a specified time T_v.

- **Discussion 2**

  Compared with a hash-based puzzle, in which a defending server does not need to store any client information while a client is solving the puzzle, our scheme requires a defending server to store a solution b'_s. These are two totally different purposes. The hash approach sacrifices CPU time in the verification process to avoid any memory becoming exhausted. Our trapdoor-based puzzle conducts a reverse activity. We note that the final decision should be made by the server administrators, who are aware of which resources are more valuable for their own systems.

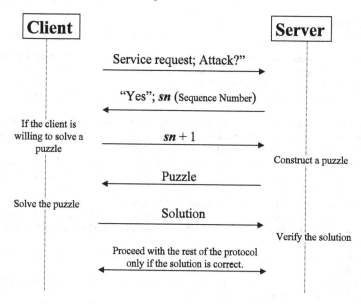

Fig. 5 Using a sequence number against IP Spoofing

- **Discussion 3**

The main goals of our client puzzle scheme are to defend network servers against DoS attacks and ensure that legitimate clients gain qualified service as long as they can solve the puzzles. However, some DoS attacks may aim to take down clients' machines, where an attacker may broadcast false puzzles to consume a client's resources.

In this case, the current solution (for example, the puzzle scheme proposed by Aura et al. [4]) is to make puzzles signed by the defending server. When receiving a puzzle, a client first verifies the signature by using the public key of the defending server and then computes it. Since the number of puzzles for a legitimate client is very small, the cost of public-key verification on the client's side is usually acceptable.

8 Conclusion

In this chapter, we have depicted a novel trapdoor-based client puzzle scheme. The puzzles generated by our scheme can conquer the potential problems of the traditional ones, such as the complexity of puzzle construction and verification. We have showed and explained that our scheme is efficient with a low computational cost and can be deployed in the current existing network protocols. Finally, we have presented that our scheme is provably secure assuming the hardness of the Discrete Logarithm Problem(DLP).

References

1. Digital signature standard (DSS). In Federal Information Processing Standards Publication 186. National Institute of Standards and Technology (NIST), 1994.
2. The New York Times, 12 September, 1996.
3. R. Aguilar, and J. Kornblum. New York Times site hacked. CNET NEWS.COM, 8 November, 1996.
4. T. Aura, P. Nikander, and J. Leiwo. Dos-resistant authentication with client puzzles. Security Protocols, 8th International Workshop, Cambridge, UK, April 3–5, 2000; revised papers, Vol. 2133 of Lecture Notes in Computer Science, pp. 170–177, Springer, 2001.
5. B. Waters, A. Juels, J. A. Halderman, and E. W. Felten. New client puzzle outsourcing techniques for dos resistance. In ACM Conference on Computer and Communications Security, pp. 246–256, 2004.
6. D. Bernstein. Syn floods - a solution. Available at http://www.op.net/jaw/syn-fix.html, 1996.
7. E. Brickell, and K. McCurley. An interactive identification scheme based on discrete logarithms and factoring. In Advances in Cryptology, Proceedings EUROCRYPT 90, LNCS 473, Vol. 5, pp. 23–29. Springer, 1991.
8. CNN. Cyber-attacks batter Web heavyweights. Available at http://www.cnn.com/2000/tech/computing/02/09/cyber.attacks.01/index.html, February 2002.
9. daN. Re: client puzzle protocol neohapsis archives. Available at http://archives.neohapsis.com/archives/nfr-wizards/2000-q1/0645.html, 2000.
10. C. Davidson. The "SYN flood" gates open for WebCom. iWorld Weekly, 16 December, 1996.
11. C. Dwork, and M. Naor. Pricing via processing or combatting junk mail. In Advances in Cryptology, Proceedings CRYPTO 92, LNCS 740, pp. 139–147, Santa Barbara, CA USA, Springer, August 1992.
12. T. ElGamal. A public key cryptosystem and a signature scheme based on discrete logarithms. IEEE Transactions on Information Theory, 31:469–472, 1985.
13. J. Elliot. Distributed denial of service attacks and the zombie ant effect. IT Professional, pp. 55–57, March 2000.
14. P. Ferguson, and D. Senie. Network ingress filtering: Defeating denial of service attacks which employ ip source address spoofing. IETF, RFC 2267, January 1998.
15. A. Juels, and J. Brainard. Client puzzles: A cryptographic countermeasure against connection depletion attacks. In S. Kent, (Ed.), Distributed Systems Security (SNDSS), pp. 151–165, 1999.
16. F. Kargl, J.Maier, and M. Weber. Protecting web servers from distributed denial of service attacks. In Proceedings of the 10th International WWW Conference, Hong Kong, May 1–5, 2001.
17. C. Kaufman, R. Perlman, and M. Speciner. Network Security: Private Communication in a Public World (2nd Edition). Prentice Hall PTR, 2002.
18. A.K. Lenstra, and H.W. Lenstra, Jr. Algorithms in number theory. In J. van Leeuwen, (Ed.), Handbook of Theoretical Computer Science, Vol. A, pp. 673–715, MIT/Elsevier, 1990.
19. C. Mclvor, M. Mcloone, and J. Mccanny. Modified montgomery modular multiplication and rsa exponentiation techniques. In IEE Proceedings - Computers & Digital Techniques, Vol. 151, pp. 402–408, November 2004.
20. A. Oldyzko. Discrete logarithms in finite fields and their cryptographic significance. In Advances in Cryptology, Proceedings EUROCRYPT 84, LNCS 209, pp. 224–314, Springer, 1984.
21. K. Park, and H. Lee. On the effectiveness of probabilistic packet marking for ip traceback under denial of service attack. IEEE INFOCOM 2001, pp. 338–347, 2001.
22. K. Park, and H. Lee. On the effectiveness of route-based packet filtering for distributed dos attack prevention in power-law internets. In Proceedings of ACM SIGCOMM'2001, August 2001.
23. K. Park, and H. Lee. Advanced packet marking mechanism with pushback for ip traceback. In ACNS04 PROGRAM - Academic Track, June 8–11, 2004.
24. M. B. Rash. client puzzle protocol. Available at http://honor.trusecure.com/pipermail/firewall-wizards/2000-february/007944.html, 2000.

25. L. Ricciulli, P. Lincoln, and P. Kakkar. TCP SYN flooding defense. In In Communication Networks and Distributed Systems Modeling and Simulation Conference (CNDS'99), 1999.
26. B. Schneier. Applied cryptography : protocols, algorithms, and source code in C. Wiley, 1996.
27. C. Schnorr. Efficient signature generation for smart cards. In Advances in Cryptology, Proceedings CRYPTO 89, LNCS 435, pp. 239–252, Springer, 1990.
28. L. Sherriff. Virus launches ddos for mobile phones. Available at http:// www.theregister.co.uk/ content/1/12394.html.
29. C. Wang, C. Lin, and C. Chang. Signature schemes based on two hard problems simultaneously. In the 17th International Conference on Advanced Information Networking and Applications, pp. 557–560, 2003.
30. G. Weijers. re:client puzzle protocol. Available at http://archives.neohapsis.com/archives/ nfr-wizards/2000-q1/0558. html, 2000.
31. M. Williams. Ebay, amazon, buy.com hit by attacks. IDG News Service, 9 February 2000.
32. B. Ziegler. Hacker tangles panix Web site. Wall Street Journal, 12 September 1996.

Attacks and Countermeasures in Sensor Networks: A Survey

Kai Xing, Shyaam Sundhar Rajamadam Srinivasan,
Major Jose "Manny" Rivera, Jiang Li, and Xiuzhen Cheng

Contents

1 Introduction

A wireless sensor network (WSN) comprises a large number of sensors that collaboratively monitor various environments. The sensors all together provide global views of the environments that offer more information than those local views provided by independently operating sensors. There are numerous potential applications of WSNs in various areas such as residence, industry, military, and many others. For instance, people can use WSNs to build intelligent house, to gather machine information for real-time control in factories, and to track enemy movements in battle fields.

K. Xing (✉)
School of Computer Science and Technology, Suzhou Institute for Advanced Study,
University of Science and Technology of China, Hefei, Anhui, 230027 China
e-mail: kxing@ustc.edu.cn

S.C.-H. Huang et al. (eds.), *Network Security*, DOI 10.1007/978-0-387-73821-5_11,
© Springer Science+Business Media, LLC 2010

To collect data from WSNs, base stations and aggregation points [1] are commonly used. They usually have more resources (e.g., computation power and energy) than normal sensor nodes which have more or less such constraints. Aggregation points gather data from nearby sensors, integrate the data and forward them to base stations, where the data are further processed or forwarded to a processing center. In this way, energy can be conserved in WSNs [2, 3], and network life time is thus prolonged.

WSNs have some special characteristics that distinguish them from other networks such as the Internet. The characteristics, listed as follows, demand careful considerations for protocol and algorithm designs that can lead to the use of WSNs in the real world:

- Sensors have limited resources, such as energy, memory, and computation capacity. Light-weight protocols and algorithms are preferred to achieve longer sensor life.
- Sensors have limited reliability, partially because of the resource constraints.
- WSNs usually have dynamic topologies. Apart from sensors' leaving the network for reliability issues, new sensors may be added or activated and join the WSNs.
- WSNs can well have a large number of sensors.
- WSNs are usually centralized in terms of data processing and sometimes control as well. Data flow from sensors toward a few aggregation points, which further forward the data to base stations of a fewer number. Base stations could also broadcast query/control information to sensors.

Among the designs of WSNs, security is one of the most important aspects that deserves great attention, considering the tremendous application opportunities. This chapter leads readers to this area by presenting a survey of various potential attacks and solutions in WSNs. To ease the presentation, we classify the attacks based on the layering model of Open System Interconnection (OSI) (actually only four layers are used). We will present the mechanisms and effects of the attacks in four layers (physical, MAC, network, and application), along with some potential countermeasures. A summary discussion is at the end.

2 Physical Layer

The physical layer is concerned with transmitting raw bits of information over wired/wireless medium. It is responsible for signal detection, modulation, encoding, frequency selection and so on, and is hence the basis of network operations.

2.1 Attacks in the Physical Layer

Many attacks target this layer as all upper layer functionalities rely on it. Adversaries can do "nontechnical" things such as destroying sensors, or conduct "technical" actions such as wiretapping. In general, the following three types of attacks are categorized as physical layer attacks:

- Device Tampering
- Eavesdropping
- Jamming

2.1.1 Device Tampering

As imaginable, the simplest way to attack is to damage or modify sensors physically and thus stop or alter their services. The negative impact will be greater if base stations or aggregation points instead of normal sensors are attacked, since the former carry more responsibility of communications and/or data processing. However, the effectiveness of these attacks against physical sensors is very limited due to the high redundancy inherent in most WSNs. Unless large amount of sensors are compromised, the operations of WSNs will not be affected much.

Another way to attack is to capture sensors and extract sensitive data from them. As more complicated attacks (e.g., spoofing and denial of services) are made possible by this step (based on the sensitive data), such attacks are probably more threatening.

2.1.2 Eavesdropping

Without senders and receivers' awareness, eavesdropping [4–6] attackers monitor the traffic in transmission on communication channels and collect data that can later be analyzed to extract sensitive information. WSNs are especially vulnerable to such attacks since wireless transmission is the dominant method of communication used by sensors. During transmission, wireless signals are broadcast in the air and thus accessible to the public. With modest equipment, attackers within the sender's transmission range can easily plug themselves into the wireless channel and obtain raw data. By and large, the capability of eavesdropping depends on the power of antennas. The more powerful the antennas, the weaker signals attackers can receive, and thus the more data can be collected. Since eavesdropping is a passive behavior, such attacks are rarely detectable.

2.1.3 Jamming

Unlike device tampering attacks that are physical, jamming attacks disrupt the availability of transmission media. The approach is to introduce intense interference to occupy the channels and bereave normal sensors of the chances to communicate. With a device jamming its surrounding sensors, adversaries can disrupt an entire sensor network by deploying enough number of such devices. The problem of such attacks is that jamming devices have the risk of being identified, since sensors close to a jamming device may detect higher background noise than usual.

2.2 Countermeasures in the Physical Layer

Some attacks in the physical layer are quite hard to cope with. For example, after sensors are deployed in the field, it is difficult or infeasible to prevent every single sensor from device tampering. Therefore, although there are some mechanisms that attempt to reduce the occurrences of attacks, more of them focus on protecting information from divulgence.

2.2.1 Access Restriction

Obviously, restricting adversaries from physically accessing or getting close to sensors is effective on all the attacks aforementioned. It is good to have such restrictions if we can, but unfortunately, they are either difficult or infeasible in most cases. Therefore, we usually have to fall back on another type of restrictions: communication media access restriction.

A few techniques exist nowadays that prevent attackers from accessing the wireless medium in use, including sleeping/hibernating and spread spectrum communication [7]. The former is fairly simple as it switches off sensors and keeps them silent until the attackers go away. However, its effectiveness is at the expense of sacrificing the operations of WSNs. The latter is more intelligent with frequencies varying deliberately. This technique uses either analog schemes where the frequency variation is continuous, or digital schemes (e.g., frequency hopping) where the frequency variation is abrupt. By this way, attackers cannot easily locate the communication channel and are thus restrained from attacking. With current technology, powerful devices are required to perform such functionalities. Therefore, spread spectrum communications are not yet feasible for WSNs that are usually constrained in resources. Nonetheless, given the rapid advancement of technologies, this technique is very promising in the future.

Directional antenna [8–12] is another technique for access restriction. By confining the directions of the signal propagation, it reduces the chances of adversaries accessing the communication channel. Again, similar to spread spectrum communication, its production cost is high at present and unsuitable for large-scale sensor networks, but may be more useful in the long run.

2.2.2 Encryption

In general, cryptography is the all-purpose solution to achieve security goals in WSNs. To protect data confidentiality, cryptography is indispensable.

Cryptography can be applied to the data stored on sensors. Once data are encrypted, even if the sensors are captured, it is difficult for the adversaries to obtain useful information. Of course, the strength of the encryption depends on various factors. A more costly encryption can yield higher strength, but it also drains the limited precious energy faster and needs more memory.

More often, cryptography is applied to the data in transmission. There are basically two categories of cryptographic mechanisms: asymmetric and symmetric. In asymmetric mechanisms (e.g., RSA [13–15]), the keys used for encryption and decryption are different, allowing for easier key distribution. It usually requires a third trusted party called Certificate Authority (CA) to distribute and check certificates so that the identity of the users using a certain key can be verified. However, due to the lack of a priori trust relationship and infrastructure support, it is infeasible to have CAs in WSNs. Furthermore, asymmetric cryptography usually consumes more resources such as computation and memory.

In comparison, symmetric mechanisms are more economical in terms of resource consumption. As long as two nodes share a key, they can use this key to encrypt and decrypt data and securely communicate with each other. However, the problem of lacking a priori trust relationship and infrastructure support persists. How to establish a shared key for two communicating parties is a challenging issue.

For key establishment, some researchers have proposed random key distribution schemes [16–18], in which each sensor randomly picks a set of keys from a large pool. As a result, each sensor has a shared key with any of its neighbors with some probability after deployment. Alternatively, we can have a full pairwise scheme in which each sensor shares a unique key with any other sensor in the network. Thus, any pair of sensors is guaranteed to share a key. However, since each sensor needs to store $n - 1$ (assuming the total number of sensors is n) keys, this scheme suffers from a high memory cost of $O(n)$.

In the peer intermediaries scheme for key establishment protocol (PIKE) [19], authors use intermediary sensors as trusted parties to establish symmetric keys. Each node shares a unique key with each of $O(\sqrt{n})$ nodes[1]. When nodes i and j need to communicate but have no common key, they first find out a node k that shares a unique pairwise key with each of them. A path key will be computed for i and j through k. This protocol improves the memory cost to $O(\sqrt{n})$ compared to the full pairwise scheme, but sacrifices some security due to the possible unreliability of intermediary sensors.

Another key predistribution scheme is proposed by Du et al. [20], in which multiple key spaces based on Blom's method [21] are computed off-line, and each sensor is preloaded randomly with information from one or more key spaces. As long as two sensors have information from the same key space, they can compute a shared key. In Blom's method, a key space is defined by a matrix pair (G, D), where G is public while D is private. Each node stores a column of G and a row of A, which is computed from G and D. To get a shared key, two nodes first exchange their

---

[1] We use the terms "node" and "sensor" interchangeably in this chapter.

columns of G, then compute the shared key using their private rows of the matrix A. It allows any pair of nodes to find a secret pairwise key by using $\lambda + 1$ units of memory space. Blom's method has the $\lambda - secure$ property, which means as long as no more than λ number of sensors are compromised, the corresponding key space remains perfectly secure.

Two in-situ based key management schemes, iKMS and sKMS, have been proposed in the literature [22, 23]. In iKMS, service sensors, with each carrying a key space, and worker sensors, with no a priori knowledge, are deployed at the same time. Worker sensors obtain security information through an asymmetric secure channel from service nodes after deployment and then compute shared key with their neighbors. In sKMS, homogeneous sensors are preloaded with several system parameters, and they differentiate their roles as either service nodes or worker nodes after deployment. Each service node constructs a key space based on Blom's method and distributes the key information to a number of worker sensors through a secure channel established by Rabin's algorithm. sKMS is "perfect" in against node capture attack, achieves high connectivity (close to 1) in the induced key-sharing graph, and consumes a small amount memory in worker sensors.

3 MAC Layer

Sensors rely on Medium Access Control (MAC) layer to coordinate their transmissions to share the wireless media fairly and efficiently [24]. In wireless MAC protocols, typically nodes exchange control packets (e.g., CTS and RTS in IEEE 802.11) to gain the right for data transmission over the channel for a certain period of time. Node identifications are embedded in the packets to indicate senders and receivers.

3.1 Attacks in the MAC Layer

Due to the openness of wireless channels, the coordinations between sensors based on MAC protocols are subject to malicious manipulation. Adversaries can disobey the coordination rules and produce malicious traffic to interrupt network operations in the MAC layer. They can also forge MAC layer identifications and masquerade as other entities for various purposes.

3.1.1 Traffic Manipulation

The wireless communication in WSNs (and other wireless networks) can be easily manipulated in the MAC layer. Attackers can transmit packets right at the moment when legitimate users do so to cause excessive packet collisions. The timing can be readily decided by monitoring the channel and doing some calculations based on the MAC protocol in effect. The artificially increased contention will decrease signal quality and network availability and will thus dramatically reduce the network throughput [25, 26]. Besides, in widely used MAC schemes where packet transmissions are carefully coordinated, attackers can compete for channel usage aggressively disobeying the coordination rules [27–29]. This misbehavior can break the operations of the protocols and result in unfair bandwidth usage. In either way, the network performance is degraded. Eventually, the collisions and unfairness lead traffic distortion.

3.1.2 Identity Spoofing

MAC identity spoofing is another common attack in the MAC layer [30]. Due to the broadcast nature of wireless communications, the MAC identity (such as a MAC address or a certificate) of a sensor is open to all the neighbors, including attackers. Without proper protection on it, an attacker can fake an identity and pretend to be a different one. A typical MAC identity spoofing attack is the Sybil attack [31,32], in which an attacker illegally presents multiple MAC identities.

To gain access to the network or hide, an attacker can spoof as a normal legitimate sensor. It can even spoof as a base station or aggregation point to obtain unauthorized privileges or resources of the WSN. If successful, the entire network could be taken over.

Spoofing attacks are usually the basis of further cross-layer attacks that can cause serious consequences. For example, Sybil attacks [31, 32] may expose legitimate information to the adversary or provide wrong information for routing to launch false routing attacks (Sect. 4.1.1).

3.2 Countermeasures in the MAC Layer

To counter attacks in the MAC layer, current research focuses on detection. It allows for many kinds of further actions to stop the attacks, such as excluding the attacking nodes from interactions. There also exist some prevention approaches, which are mainly against spoofing attacks.

Many solutions presented below are actually proposed for ad hoc networks. We believe that they can be easily extended to WSNs.

3.2.1 Misbehavior Detection

Because attacks deviate from normal behaviors, it is possible to identify attackers by observing what has happened. Various data can be collected for this purpose, and various actions can be taken after detection.

In a countering scheme [33] for the IEEE 802.11 protocol, a receiver assigns and adjusts the backoff values to be used by the corresponding sender. Whenever detecting the sender's misbehavior in manipulating backoff value, the receiver may add some penalty to the next backoff value assigned to the sender. The idea was applied to ad hoc networks [29] and similarly can also be applied to WSNs.

Another solution uses "watchdogs" [34] on every node to monitor whether or not the neighbors of a node forward the packets sent out by this particular node. A neighbor not forwarding packets will be identified by the watchdog as a misbehaving node. A similar scheme for MANET [35, 36] requires an intrusion detection system (IDS) on each node. The IDS monitors all the local activities (of users, system, and communication) in the neighborhood. If abnormal behaviors are detected, the IDS will trigger some local actions, for example, alerting the local user. In addition, the IDS may request neighboring nodes to cooperate for a global intrusion detection. Each node will propagate its information to its immediate neighbors. If the majority of such information received by a node indicates intrusions, the misbehaving nodes can be identified and precluded from the network.

Some other solutions use ratings to distinguish between good and bad nodes. In CORE [37], the rating is called "reputation" and is evaluated based on each entity's collaborativeness in communication. Misbehaving nodes will eventually gain a "bad" reputation and thus be excluded from communication by others. The mobile intrusion detection system (MobIDS) [38] is a variation of the reputation mechanism. The MobIDS on each node overhears the forwarded packets by its next hop and checks whether its neighbor sensors faithfully forward the packet or not. In addition, an iterative probing mechanism is used: when sending a packet, a sensor encrypts an intermediary node id in the packet head; when receiving the packet, the corresponding intermediary node, if normal, is supposed to decrypt the packet head and sends back a reply to the sender. During the overhearing and probing, observations between $[-1, 1]$ are generated. A positive value represents a positive behavior while a negative value indicates otherwise. With these observations, a node has a local rating of its neighboring nodes. The rating is securely distributed to neighboring nodes with a signature. After a node collects enough local ratings for a certain node, it will average these ratings and generate a global rating for that node. Based on the global rating, that node may or may not be excluded from the communication.

Game theory has also been used for misbehavior detection. These approaches assume that misbehaving nodes take greedy actions to gain better performance, such as higher share of bandwidth, and leverage the optimal point called "Nash equilibrium". Konorski [39] proposes a misbehavior-resilient backoff algorithm for ad hoc networks in which all nodes can hear each other. By adjusting the backoff value, the network may reach a fair equilibrium for bandwidth allocation. Cagalj et al. [40] considers those selfish nodes that reduce the contention window size in CSMA/CS ad hoc networks to gain higher throughput/bandwidth. At the operating point of "Nash equilibrium", all the nodes with similar traffic constraints and the same contention window size should get similar throughput. Based on this assumption, each node measures the throughput of all nodes at the point of equilibrium. If a node is observed to have a different throughput from others, it could well be a misbehaving one.

Note that the ideas presented above, such as using watchdog, rating nodes, or comparing nodes' behavior at "Nash equilibrium," can also be used to develop misbehavior detecting techniques in other layers, as long as attackers' misbehavior deviates from normal. Nonetheless, considerations have to be given based on the layer-specific features, for example, how and what to watch, what metrics are used to rate nodes, and what behavior is abnormal at "Nash equilibrium", and so on.

3.2.2 Identity Protection

Identity can be treated as yet another kind of information whose legitimacy needs to be guaranteed. Therefore, cryptography-based authentication can be used to prevent identity spoofing. Since most authentication schemes are designed for the network layer and the application layer, we will postpone the discussion of authentication schemes to Sect. 4.2.1. Readers should keep in mind that the authentication techniques discussed there can also be applied to identity protection in the MAC layer.

In addition to authentication, other security measures also exist for this problem. Most of them are for false identify detection, as presented in the following:

- Radio resource testing was proposed to counter Sybil attacks [31]. It assumes that attackers consume more channel resources but can only use one single channel each time. By assigning different channels to neighboring nodes, the verifier can identify Sybil attackers through unused assigned channels.
- Position verification can be used to detect immobile attackers. If different identities appear at the same position, the node at that place can be identified as an attacker.
- Code attestation is based on the assumption that the code running on attackers or compromised nodes is different from that running on normal nodes. Therefore, attackers can be identified by validating the code running on them, for example, by verifying the memory content. One technique to verify the code running in a remote embedded device is proposed in SWATT [41]. Its design ensures that the result returned by the embedded device can be correct only if the memory contents are correct. The verifier first sends a challenge to the embedded device, for which the latter computes a response through the verification procedure. After that, the verifier locally computes the answer to the challenge. By checking the two answers, the embedded device can be verified.
- Sequence checking is the method to check the sequence number in the header of 802.11 frames. First, a pattern of legitimate sequence number activity for each MAC address is established. If the behavior of a node deviates from its sequence pattern, this node can be identified as an attacker.
- Identity-key association [32] can also help reduce false identities. The key idea is to associate the node identity with keys used by the node in communication. An attacker can impersonate a node in front of another only if the communication key shared by them is cracked.

4 Network Layer

In the network layer, the key issues include locating destinations and calculating the optimal path to a destination. By tampering with routing service, such as modifying, routing information and replicating data packets, attackers can fail the communication in WSNs.

4.1 Attacks in the Network Layer

As in most other networks, sensors collaborate for routing in WSNs. However, the collaboration between sensors are susceptible to malicious manipulation in WSNs. Adversaries can gain access to routing paths and redirect the traffic, or distribute false information to mislead routing direction, or launch DoS attack against routing (such as flooding packets in order to block/interrupt the traffic in the network), acting as black holes to swallow (i.e., to receive but not forward) all the received messages, selectively forwarding packets through certain sensors, etc.

4.1.1 False Routing

As the name suggests, false routing attacks [42] are launched by enforcing false routing information. There are three different approaches of enforcement [42]:

- Overflowing routing tables.
- Poisoning routing tables.
- Poisoning routing caches.

Overflowing Routing Tables. If the routing table of a normal network node overflows, the node will have to discard and thus ignore later incoming routing information. Therefore, attackers can inject a large volume of void routing information into the network. The injected information will eventually occupy the majority of the routing table space on normal nodes and cause overflow.
As an example, in the network of Fig. 1a, node 13 ('S') is the source, node 12 ('D') is the destination, and node 11 ('A') is the attacker. If A was a normal node, the routing table of it would be as shown in Fig. 1b. S would then be able to communicate with D. However, as an attacker, A keeps sending into the network wrong routing information about nonexistent nodes. The routing table of S will hence become the one in Fig. 1d, and the network will be visioned by S as in Fig. 1c. The visioned network does not contain any paths between S and D, and restrains S from communicating with D.

Routing table poisoning. In this type of attacks, compromised nodes inside the network modify route update packets before sending or forwarding them out, that is, make "poison". Such modifications result in wrong routing tables of all nodes

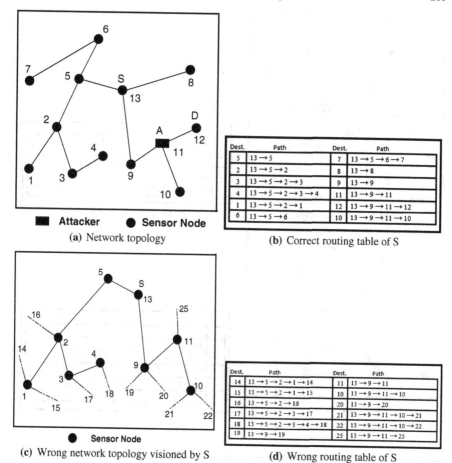

Attacker ● **Sensor Node**

(a) Network topology

(b) Correct routing table of S

(c) Wrong network topology visioned by S

(d) Wrong routing table of S

Fig. 1 A Network before and after the attack of overflowing routing tables

inside the network. For example, in a network (Fig. 2a) with a compromised node (node 11) 'A', a source (node 13) 'S', and a destination (node 12) 'D', without poisoning, the routing table of S is as in Fig. 2b. With poisoning, it may become one in Fig. 2d, giving a wrong vision of the network (Fig. 2c) to S.

Poisoning routing tables will direct traffic onto wrong paths and may result in congestion or even collapse of networks. It may also lead to further attacks by putting attackers into the desired route.

Route Cache Poisoning. The third kind of false routing attacks can be achieved by poisoning the cache. Some on-demand routing protocols [43] require each node to maintain a cache with the most recent route information. This cache can be poisoned by the adversary by using a technique similar to the attack used for poisoning the routing table.

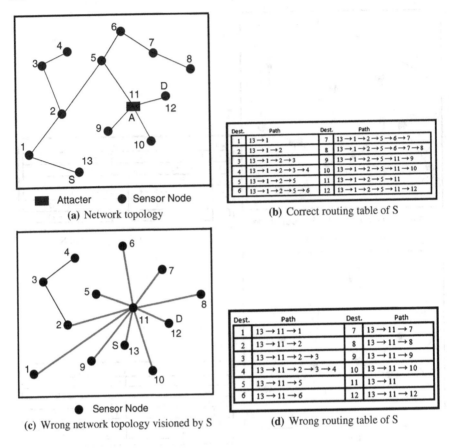

(a) Network topology

(b) Correct routing table of S

(c) Wrong network topology visioned by S

(d) Wrong routing table of S

Fig. 2 A network before and after the attack of poisoning routing tables

In summary, there are three types of false routing attacks. A false routing attack can be used to place the adversary in its desired route to divert route traffic from one part of the network to another, to restrain traffic on certain paths, and to bring down a part of or the entire network.

4.1.2 Packet Replication

In this type of attacks, attackers resend (replicate) packets previously received from other nodes. The packets can be broadcasted to the entire network (called *flooding attack*) or to a particular set of nodes. They can also resent irrespective of whether the sender is sending any new packets or not. With large amount of packets replayed, both the bandwidth of the network and the power of the nodes are consumed in vain, which leads to the early termination of network operations.

4.1.3 Black Hole

The black hole attack is one of the simplest routing attacks in WSNs. In a black hole attack, the attacker swallows (i.e., receives but does not forward) all the messages he receives, just as a black hole absorbing everything passing by. By refusing to forward any message he receives, the attacker will affect all the traffic flowing through it. Hence, the throughput of a subset of nodes, especially the neighboring nodes around the attacker and with traffic through it, is dramatically decreased.

Different locations of the attacker induce different influences on the network. If the attacker is located close to the base station, all the traffic going to the base station might need to go through the attacker. Obviously, black hole attacks in this case can break the communication between the base station and the rest of the WSN and effectively prevent the WSN from serving its purposes. In contrast, if a black hole attacking node is at the edge of the WSN, probably very few sensors need it to communicate with others. Therefore, the harm can be very limited.

4.1.4 Sinkhole

Sinkhole is a more complex attack [44] compared with black hole attack. Given certain knowledge of the routing protocol in use, the attacker tries to attract the traffic from a particular region through it. For example, the attacker can announce a false optimal path by advertising attractive power, bandwidth, or high quality routes to a particular region. Other nodes will then consider the path through this attacker node better than the currently used one and move their traffic onto it.

Since affected nodes depend on the attacker for their communication, the sinkhole attack can make other attacks efficient by positioning the attacker in busy information traffic. Many other attacks, such as eavesdropping, selective forwarding and black holes, etc., can be empowered by sinkhole attacks.

4.1.5 Selective Forwarding

Selective forwarding attacks include two cases. In one case (Message Selective Forwarding), the attacker selectively sends the information of a particular sensor; in the other case (Sensor Selective Forwarding), the attacker sends/discards the information from selected sensors. The former attack is considered as the application layer attack and will be discussed in Sect. 5.1.2, while the latter attack is considered as in the network layer and is the focus of this subsection.

Obviously, this attack can take place only when the attacker is on the route of packet transfer in a multi-hop network [45]. If the attacker happens to be on the route, it can just discard the packets from some selected nodes at its will. Otherwise, before the attack can be launched, it needs to position itself in the routing path using other attacks such as the Sybil attack, sinkhole attack, and routing table poisoning attack.

4.1.6 Wormhole

A wormhole attack [46] requires two or more adversaries. These adversaries have better communication resources (e.g., power, bandwidth) than normal nodes, and can establish better communication channels (called "tunnels") between them. Unlike many other attacks in the network layer, the channels are real. Other sensors probably end up adopting the tunnels into their communication paths, rendering their output under the scrutiny of the adversaries.

4.2 Countermeasures in Network Layer

Since the functionalities of the network layer require the close collaboration of many nodes, all these nodes have to be enclosed for security consideration. It is therefore relatively difficult to mitigate attacks. Nonetheless, some countermeasures are available as follows:

- Routing Access Restriction.
- False Routing Information Detection.
- Wormhole Detection.

4.2.1 Routing Access Restriction

Routing may be one of the most attractive attack targets in WSNs, as we saw in the previous subsection. If we can exclude attackers from participating in the routing process, that is, restrict them from accessing routing, a large number of attacks in the network layer will be prevented or alleviated.

Multipath routing is one of the methods to reduce the effectiveness of attacks launched by attackers on routing paths [47–49]. In these schemes, packets are routed through multiple paths. Even if the attacker on one of the paths breaks down the path, the routing is not necessarily broken as other paths still exist. This alleviates the impact of routing attacks, although does not prevent these attacks.

A general way is to use authentication methods [50–54]. With authentication, it can be easily determined whether a sensor can participate in routing or not.

Authentication can be either end-to-end or hop-to-hop [52]. In end-to-end authentication, the source and destination share some secret and can thus verify each other. SEAD [55] and Ariadne [56] are two secure routing protocols based on end-to-end authentication. When a node receives a routing update, it will always verify the sender of the update before accepting the update. In hop-to-hop authentication, each message in transmission is authenticated hop-by-hop. Therefore, the trust between the source and the destination is built upon the trust on all the intermediate nodes in the path. It is not as secure as end-to-end authentication, but is not so expensive as it does not require every pair of nodes shares some common secret. Binkley and Trost [51] designed a link-level authentication mechanism for ad hoc routing in which IP and MAC addresses are used for hop-by-hop verification. Zhu et al. [53] propose an interleaved hop-to-hop authentication scheme that provides $t - security$: the injected false data packets can be detected when no more than t nodes are compromised. In this scheme, each sensor u_i associates itself to the sensor u_j that is $t + 1$ hops closer to the base station. u_i is called the lower association node of u_j, and u_j is called the upper association node of u_i. Data are authenticated hop-by-hop between associated nodes until they reach the base station.

Hop-to-hop authentication can be combined with multipath routing and result in multipath authentication [52]. The paths can be physical, meaning that messages are routed through multiple physically different communication paths. The paths can also be virtual, if they are actually on the same physical path, but are differentiated by other means such as encryption keys. Multipath authentication offers a tradeoff between resource constraints and security and provides an in-between security level.

4.2.2 False Routing Information Detection

Sometimes attackers do have chances to send false routing information into the network, for example, during route discovery stages. If the false information does not lead to network failure such as broken routes, we really cannot do much about it. Otherwise, we can apply the idea of misbehavior detection discussed in Section 3.2.1.

For example, watchdog [34] or IDS [35, 36, 38] may find that some node fails to route messages along the routing path due to the wrong information it keeps. This anomaly of route failure may trigger out an alarm. Nodes can start to trace the source of false routing information. Reputation [37, 38] can also be maintained, depending on whether nodes are providing valid routing information. Nonetheless, how to trace the source of routing information can be a very difficult problem.

4.2.3 Wormhole Detection

Wormhole attacks are difficult to deal with because the information they inject into the networks is real. The most recent research work on the countermeasures focuses on the following techniques:

- Using synchronized clocks [57]. With the assumption that all nodes are tightly synchronized, each packet includes the time at which it is sent out. When receiving the packet, the receiver compares this value to the time at which it receives the packet. With the knowledge of transmission distance and consumed time, the receiver is able to detect if the packet has traveled too far. If the transmission distance is far beyond the maximum allowed travel distance, probably it is under wormhole attacks.
- Using directional antennas [8]. Directional antenna is used to discover neighboring nodes identified by zone. The zones around each sensor are numbered 1 to

N oriented clockwise starting with zone 1 facing east. After receiving signals from unknown nodes, a node can get approximate direction information based on received signals and identify the unknown node by zone. After that, it cooperates with its neighboring nodes to verify the legitimacy of the unknown node, for example, by checking whether the unknown node is known by the neighboring nodes.

- Using Multidimensional Scaling–Visualization of Wormhole (MDS-VOW) [58]. MDS-VOW first constructs the layout of the network. If there exist wormhole attackers, the shape of the constructed network layout will show some bent/distorted features.

5 Application Layer

The application layer implements the services seen by users. Two examples of important applications in WSNs are data aggregation and time synchronization, where data aggregation sends the data collected by sensors to base stations, and time synchronization synchronizes sensor clocks for cooperative operations.

5.1 Attacks in the Application Layer

Attacks in this layer have the knowledge of data semantics and thus can manipulate the data to change the semantics. As the result, false data are presented to applications and lead to abnormal actions. In this section, the following attacks will be discussed:

- Clock Skewing
- Selective Message Forwarding
- Data Aggregation Distortion

5.1.1 Clock Skewing

The targets of this attack are those sensors in need of synchronized operations (e.g., [59–61]). By disseminating false timing information, the attacks aim to desynchronize the sensors (i.e., skew their clocks).

For example, in IEEE 802.11 (which can be applied to WSNs), nodes are required to be synchronized with the access point. Beacon packets are broadcasted by the access point periodically. The packets contain timing information to be used by nodes for clock adjustment. Attackers can send false beacon packets with wrong timing information [59, 62]. Once nodes adjust their clocks based on the wrong information, they will be out of synchronization with the access point. Although true beacon packets later can bring them back to synchronization, the nodes will oscillate between the two states and be unstable.

5.1.2   Selective Message Forwarding

For this attack, the adversary has to be on the path between the source and the destination and is thus responsible for forwarding packet for the source. The attack can be launched by forwarding some or partial messages selectively but not others. Note that the attack is different from the other selective forwarding attack in the network layer (Sect. 4.1.5). To launch the selective forwarding attack in the application layer, attackers need to understand the semantics of the payload of the application layer packets (i.e., treat each packet as a meaningful *message* instead of a monolithic unit), and select the packets to be forwarded based on the semantics. In comparison, the selective forwarding attack in the network layer only requires attackers to know the network layer information, such as the source and destination addresses. Attackers decide whether to forward packets according to those kinds of information only and therefore operate at coarse granularity (Fig. 3).

5.1.3   Data Aggregation Distortion

Once data are collected, sensors usually send them back to base stations for processing. Attackers may maliciously modify the data to be aggregated them and make the final aggregation results computed by the base stations distorted. Consequently, the base stations will have an incorrect view of the environment monitored by the sensors, and may take inappropriate actions.

Data aggregation can be totally disrupted if black hole or sinkhole attacks (Sect. 4.1.3) are launched. In this scenario, no data can reach the base stations. However, for those attacks, only the network layer knowledge is required. Therefore, they are categorized as network layer attacks.

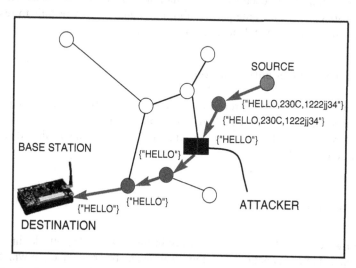

Fig. 3 A selective message forwarding example

5.2 Countermeasures in the Application Layer

As presented above, attacks in the application layer rely on application data semantics. Therefore, the countermeasures focus on protecting the integrity and confidentiality of data, no matter whether it is for control or not.

5.2.1 Data Integrity Protection

In general, authentication can be used to protect any data integrity. As discussed in Sect. 4.2.1, nodes can use end-to-end, hop-to-hop, or multipath authentication depending on the cost they can afford and the security level they desire.

When authentication is not adopted, for example, for feasibility reasons, or when data integrity is somehow compromised, the misbehavior detection techniques as discussed in Sect. 3.2.1 can be applied. The differences lie in the data to be observed in order to collect proofs of anomalies. Taking the clock skewing attack as an example: to detect such attacks, timing information in synchronization packets should be watched.

When readings (the data collected by sensors about the monitored environment) are considered, some specific detection mechanisms have been proposed and are referred to as *false reading detection*. With an assumption that the faulty/compromised sensors produce readings remarkably deviated from the normal condition, an outlier detection algorithm [63] can locate such sensors by comparing their readings with those of their neighbors. In the online deviation detection scheme [64], an estimation of the data distribution is computed through the input data stream of the WSN. If the current reading of a sensor remarkably deviates from the data distribution (namely the normal readings in the WSN), this sensor will be detected as an outlier. There is also a centralized approach [65]. Base stations launch marked packets to probe certain sensors and try to route packets through them. If a sensor fails to respond, the base stations may conclude that this node is dead.

5.2.2 Data Confidentiality Protection

Encryption is an effective approach to prevent attackers from understanding captured data. Similar to authentication, the principles of encryption do not change for use in different layers. Readers are referred to Sect. 2.2.2 for the detailed discussion of encryption in WSNs.

6 Discussion

Although we discuss the attacks separately in this chapter, the attacks in fact are often launched in combination. The combination can be cross-layer, in which multiple attacks in different layers are launched in a collaborative way. For example, the Sybil attack (in the MAC and network layer) provides identity spoofing for adversaries to do the wormhole attack (in the network layer). The combination can also be intra-layer, in which multiple attacks in the same layer occur simultaneously. For example, in the network layer, a wormhole attack can be launched to lure traffic to a compromised node that does sinkhole attack. Such combinations complicate the situation of WSN security and demand further research on countermeasures.

Besides, the same kind of attacks may be present in multiple layers, although they use different techniques. For instance, denial of services (DoS) attacks exist in physical layer, MAC layer, and network layer [27]; Sybil attacks exist in both MAC layer and network layer [32]. For each kind of such attacks, since their fundamentals are the same, our discussion on their characteristics is usually more detailed in one layer than in others.

We also notice that not only the same kind of attacks but also the same kind of countermeasures can appear in multiple layer. For example, misbehavior detection techniques can be applied to almost all the layers we discussed. Again, we usually discuss these techniques in more details in one layer than in others.

7 Conclusion

In this chapter, a survey is given on existing and potential attacks in WSNs. The attacks are classified according to the OSI stack model. For each layer of physics, MAC, network and application, we have discussed several typical attacks that exploit the characteristics of that layer. We have also covered the countermeasures and potential solutions against those attacks, and mentioned some open research issues. Hopefully by reading the chapter, the readers can have a better view of attacks and countermeasures in WSNs and find their way to start secure designs for these networks.

References

1. J. ibriq and I. Mahgoub, "Cluster-based routing in wireless sensor networks: issues and challenge," in *SPECS'04*, 2004, pp. 759–766.
2. Y. Xu, J. Heideemann, and D. Estrin, "Energy conservation by adaptive clustering for ad-hoc networks," in *Poster session of MobiHoc'02*, 2002.
3. Y. Xu, J. Heidemann, and D. Estrin, "Adaptive energy-conserving routing for multihop ad hoc networks," may 2000, submitted for publication.
4. M. Franklin, Z. Galil, and M. Yung, "Eavesdropping games: a graph-theoretic approach to privacy in distributed systems," *J. ACM*, vol. 47, no. 2, pp. 225–243, 2000.
5. M. Abadi and J. Jürjens, "Formal eavesdropping and its computational interpretation," in *TACS '01: Proceedings of the 4th International Symposium on Theoretical Aspects of Computer Software*. London, UK: Springer, 2001, pp. 82–94.
6. K. D. Murray, *Security Scrapbook Espionage and Privacy News of the Week*. [Online]. Available: http://www.spybusters.com/SS0210.html
7. [Online]. Available: http://www.faqs.org/rfcs/rfc1455.html

8. L. Hu and D. Evans, "Using directional antennas to prevent wormhole attacks," in *Network and Distributed System Security Symposium(NDSS)*, 2004.

9. R. R. Choudhury, X. Yang, N. H. Vaidya, and R. Ramanathan, "Using directional antennas for medium access control in ad hoc networks," in *MobiCom '02: Proceedings of the 8th annual international conference on Mobile computing and networking*. New York: ACM, 2002, pp. 59–70.

10. S. Yi, Y. Pei, and S. Kalyanaraman, "On the capacity improvement of ad hoc wireless networks using directional antennas," in *MobiHoc '03: Proceedings of the 4th ACM international symposium on Mobile ad hoc networking & computing*. New York: ACM, 2003, pp. 108–116.

11. M. Takai, J. Martin, R. Bagrodia, and A. Ren, "Directional virtual carrier sensing for directional antennas in mobile ad hoc networks," in *MobiHoc '02: Proceedings of the 3rd ACM international symposium on Mobile ad hoc networking & computing*. New York: ACM, 2002, pp. 183–193.

12. R. Ramanathan, "On the performance of ad hoc networks with beamforming antennas," in *MobiHoc '01: Proceedings of the 2nd ACM international symposium on Mobile ad hoc networking & computing*. New York: ACM, 2001, pp. 95–105.

13. L. Zhou and Z. J. Haas, "Securing ad hoc networks," *IEEE Network*, vol. 13, no. 6, pp. 24–30, 1999.

14. J.-P. Hubaux, L. Buttyán, and S. Capkun, "The quest for security in mobile ad hoc networks," in *MobiHoc '01: Proceedings of the 2nd ACM international symposium on Mobile ad hoc networking & computing*. New York: ACM, 2001, pp. 146–155.

15. "Providing robust and ubiquitous security support for mobile ad hoc networks," in *ICNP '01: Proceedings of the Ninth International Conference on Network Protocols (ICNP'01)*. IEEE Computer Society, 2001, p. 251.

16. H. Chan, A. Perrig, and D. Song, "Random key predistribution schemes for sensor networks," in *SP '03: Proceedings of the 2003 IEEE Symposium on Security and Privacy*. Washington, DC: IEEE Computer Society, 2003, p. 197.

17. L. Eschenauer and V. D. Gligor, "A key-management scheme for distributed sensor networks," in *CCS '02: Proceedings of the 9th ACM conference on Computer and communications security*. New York: ACM, 2002, pp. 41–47.

18. D. Liu and P. Ning, "Establishing pairwise keys in distributed sensor networks," in *CCS '03: Proceedings of the 10th ACM conference on Computer and communications security*. New York: ACM, 2003, pp. 52–61.

19. H. Chan and A. Perrig, "Pike: Peer intermediaries for key establishment in sensor networks," in *IEEE Infocom*, 2005.

20. W. Du, J. Deng, Y. S. Han, and P. K. Varshney, "A pairwise key pre-distribution scheme for wireless sensor networks," in *CCS '03: Proceedings of the 10th ACM conference on Computer and communications security*. New York: ACM, 2003, pp. 42–51.

21. R. Blom, "Non-public key distribution," in *Advances in Cryptology: Proceedings of Crypto '82*, 1982, pp. 231–236.

22. L. Ma, X. Cheng, F. Liu, M. Rivera, F. An, and J. Li, "ikms: An in-situ key management scheme for wireless sensor networks," 2005.

23. F. Liu, X. Cheng, and L. Ma, "S-kms: A self-configured key management scheme for sensor networks," 2005.

24. [Online]. Available: http://www.eweek.com/encyclopedia_term/0,2542,t=MAC+layeri=46426,00.asp

25. V. Gupta, S. Krishnamurthy, and M. Faloutsos, "Denial of service attacks at the mac layer in wireless ad hoc networks." [Online]. Available: http://www.cs.ucr.edu/~krish/milcom_vik.pdf

26. I. A. Jean-Pierre, "Denial of service resilience in ad hoc networks." [Online]. Available: http://lcawww.epfl.ch/Publications/aad/aadHK04.pdf

27. A. D. Wood and J. A. Stankovic, "Denial of service in sensor networks," *Computer*, vol. 35, no. 10, pp. 54–62, 2002.

28. P. Michiardi and R. Molva, "Prevention of denial of service attacks and selfishness in mobile ad hoc networks," in *Institut Eurecom Research Report RR-02-063*, 2002.

29. A. A. Cardenas, S. Radosavac, and J. S. Baras, "Detection and prevention of mac layer misbehavior in ad hoc networks," in *Proceedings of the 2nd ACM workshop on security of ad hoc and sensor networks*, 2004.

30. E. D. Cardenas, "Mac spoofing–an introduction," 2003. [Online]. Available: http://www.giac.org/practical/GSEC/Edgar_Cardenas_GSEC.pdf

31. J. R. Douceur, "The sybil attack," in *IPTPS '01: Revised Papers from the First International Workshop on Peer-to-Peer Systems*. London: Springer, 2002, pp. 251–260.

32. J. Newsome, E. Shi, D. Song, and A. Perrig, "The sybil attack in sensor networks: analysis & defenses," in *IPSN'04: Proceedings of the third international symposium on Information processing in sensor networks*. New York: ACM, 2004, pp. 259–268.

33. P. Kyasanur and N. H. Vaidya, "Detection and handling of mac layer misbehavior in wireless networks." in *DSN*, 2003, pp. 173–182.

34. S. Marti, T. J. Giuli, K. Lai, and M. Baker, "Mitigating routing misbehavior in mobile ad hoc networks," in *MobiCom '00: Proceedings of the 6th annual international conference on Mobile computing and networking*. New York: ACM, 2000, pp. 255–265.

35. Y. Zhang, W. Lee, and Y.-A. Huang, "Intrusion detection techniques for mobile wireless networks," *Wirel. Netw.*, vol. 9, no. 5, pp. 545–556, 2003.

36. Y. Zhang and W. Lee, "Intrusion detection in wireless ad-hoc networks," in *MobiCom '00: Proceedings of the 6th annual international conference on Mobile computing and networking*. New York: ACM, 2000, pp. 275–283.

37. P. Michiardi and R. Molva, "Core: a collaborative reputation mechanism to enforce node cooperation in mobile ad hoc networks," in *Proceedings of the IFIP TC6/TC11 6th joint working conference on communications and multimedia security*. Deventer, The Netherlands, The Netherlands: Kluwer, B.V., 2002, pp. 107–121.

38. F. K. Andreas, "Sensors for detection of misbehaving nodes in manets." [Online]. Available: http://medien.informatik.uni-ulm.de/forschung/publikationen/dimva2004.pdf

39. J. Konorski, "Multiple access in ad-hoc wireless lans with noncooperative stations." in *NETWORKING*, 2002, pp. 1141–1146.

40. M. Cagalj, S. Ganeriwal, I. Aad, and J.-P. Hubaux, "On cheating in csma/ca ad hoc networks," in *EPFL Technical Report*, 2004.

41. A. Seshadri, A. Perrig, L. van Doorn, and P. K. Khosla, "Swatt: Software-based attestation for embedded devices." in *IEEE Symposium on Security and Privacy*, 2004, pp. 272–282.

42. C. R. Murthy and B. S.Manoj, "Transport layer and security protocols for ad hoc wireless networks," in *Ad Hoc Wireless Networks – Architectures and Protocols*, 2004.

43. C. E. Perkins and E. M. Royer, "Ad-hoc on-demand distance vector routing," in *WMCSA '99: Proceedings of the Second IEEE Workshop on Mobile Computer Systems and Applications*. IEEE Computer Society, 1999, p. 90.

44. C. Karlof and D. Wagner, "Secure routing in wireless sensor networks: Attacks and countermeasures," *Elsevier's AdHoc Networks Journal, Special Issue on Sensor Network Applications and Protocols*, vol. 1, no. 2–3, pp. 293–315, September 2003.

45. D. Ganesan, B. Krishnamachari, A. Woo, D. Culler, D. Estrin, and S. Wicker, "An empirical study of epidemic algorithms in large scale multihop wireless networks," 2002.

46. Y. Hu, A. Perrig, and D. Johnson, "Wormhole detection in wireless ad hoc networks," 2002. [Online]. Available: citeseer.ist.psu.edu/hu02wormhole.html

47. D. Ganesan, R. Govindan, S. Shenker, and D. Estrin, "Highly-resilient, energy-efficient multipath routing in wireless sensor networks," *SIGMOBILE Mob. Comput. Commun. Rev.*, vol. 5, no. 4, pp. 11–25, 2001.

48. W. Lou, W. Liu, and Y. Fang, "Spread: Enhancing data confidentiality in mobile ad hoc networks," in *IEEE INFOCOM*, 2004.

49. P. Papadimitratos and Z. J. Haas, "Secure data transmission in mobile ad hoc networks," in *WiSe '03: Proceedings of the 2003 ACM workshop on Wireless security*. New York: ACM, 2003, pp. 41–50.

50. K. Hoeper and G. Gong, "Models of authentication in ad hoc networks and their related network properties," in *Tech Reports*, 2004. [Online]. Available: http://www.cacr.math.uwaterloo.ca/techreports/2004/cacr2004-03.pdf

51. J. Binkley and W. Trost, "Authenticated ad hoc routing at the link layer for mobile systems," *Wirel. Netw.*, vol. 7, no. 2, pp. 139–145, 2001.
52. H. Vogt, "Exploring message authentication in sensor networks," in *1st European Workshop on Security in Ad Hoc and Sensor Networks (ESAS 2004)*, 2004.
53. S. Zhu, S. Setia, S. Jajodia, and P. Ning, "An interleaved hop-byhop authentication scheme for filtering false data injection in sensor networks," 2004.
54. A. Perrig, R. Szewczyk, V. Wen, D. E. Culler, and J. D. Tygar, "SPINS: security protocols for sensor netowrks," in *Mobile Computing and Networking*, 2001, pp. 189–199. [Online]. Available: citeseer.ist.psu.edu/perrig01spins.html
55. Y.-C. Hu, D. B. Johnson, and A. Perrig, "Sead: Secure efficient distance vector routing in mobile wireless ad hoc networks," in *4th IEEE Workshop on Mobile Computing Systems and Applications* (WMCSA '02), jun 2002, pp. 3–13. [Online]. Available: citeseer.ist.psu.edu/hu02sead.html
56. Y.-C. Hu, A. Perrig, and D. B. Johnson, "Ariadne: A secure on-demand routing protocol for ad hoc networks," in *Proceedings of the Eighth Annual International Conference on Mobile Computing and Networking* (MobiCom 2002), Sept. 2002, (in press). [Online]. Available: citeseer.ist.psu.edu/article/hu02ariadne.html
57. Y. Hu, A. Perrig, and D. Johnson, "Packet leashes: A defense against wormhole attacks in wireless ad hoc networks," 2001. [Online]. Available: citeseer.ist.psu.edu/hu01packet.html
58. W. Wang and B. Bhargava, "Visualization of wormholes in sensor networks," in *WiSe '04: Proceedings of the 2004 ACM workshop on Wireless security*. ACM, 2004, pp. 51–60.
59. E. Shi and A. Perrig, "Designing secure sensor networks," *IEEE Wireless Communications*, vol. 11, no. 6, pp. 38–43, 2004.
60. A. Perrig, R. Szewczyk, J. D. Tygar, V. Wen, and D. E. Culler, "Spins: security protocols for sensor networks," *Wirel. Netw.*, vol. 8, no. 5, pp. 521–534, 2002.
61. J. Elson and D. Estrin, "Time synchronization for wireless sensor networks," in *IPDPS '01: Proceedings of the 15th International Parallel & Distributed Processing Symposium*. Washington, DC: IEEE Computer Society, 2001, p. 186.
62. G. Khanna, A. Masood, and C. N. Rotaru, "Synchronization attacks against 802.11," in *Networks and Distributed Systems Symposium (NDSS) Workshop*, 2005.
63. M. Ding, D. Chen, K. Xing, and X. Cheng, "Localized fault-tolerant event boundary detection in sensor networks," in *Proceedings of IEEE INFOCOM*, Miami, FL, March 2005.
64. T. Palpanas, D. Papadopoulos, V. Kalogeraki, and D. Gunopulos, "Distributed deviation detection in sensor networks," *SIGMOD Rec.*, vol. 32, no. 4, pp. 77–82, 2003.
65. J. Staddon, D. Balfanz, and G. Durfee, "Efficient tracing of failed nodes in sensor networks," in *WSNA '02: Proceedings of the 1st ACM international workshop on Wireless sensor networks and applications*. New York: ACM, 2002, pp. 122–130.

Index

A

Access restriction, 260
Access structures
  compartmented structures, 22
  multilevel structures, 21–22
  optimal metering scheme (OPT), 20
  threshold structures, 21
Active attacks, 127
Ad hoc on-demand distance vector
  (AODV), 124
Ad-hoc wireless networks
  advantages, 120
  characteristics, 120
  design challenges in, 126–127
  group rekeying for, 73–74
  routing protocols
    broadcasting in, 125–126
    factors affecting, 121
    hybrid, 124–125
    major requirements, 121
    proactive, 122
    reactive, 123–124
  secure routing mechanisms, comparison,
    141–142
  security attacks on routing protocols
    attacks using modification, 128–129
    classification, 127–128
    denial of service (DoS) attack, 130–131
    fabrication attacks, 129–130
    impersonation attacks, 128
    replay attacks, 130
  security mechanisms and solutions, routing
    protocols
    ARAN, 135
    ARIADNE, 132–133
    broadcast authentication, 140–141
    CONFIDANT, 136–137
    data encryption and digital
      signatures, 131
    MAC, 131
    rushing attack prevention (RAP),
      137–138
    secure efficient ad hoc distance
      vector, 132
    secure routing protocol, 134–135
    security aware routing, 133–134
    security protocols for sensor networks
      (SPINS), 136
    sybil attack, 139
    wormhole attack, 138
  security services in, 126–127
Advanced encryption standard (AES), 225
Alert aggregation, 191–193
Alert disaggregation, 193–194
Anonymous credential system with anonymity
  revocation, 41
Anonymous e-cash, 41–42
Application layer
  attacks
    clock skewing, 272
    data aggregation distortion, 273
    selective message forwarding, 273
  countermeasures in, 274
Approximation algorithm, 161
Approximation ratios, 161
ARIADNE, 132–133
A secure routing protocol for ad hoc networks
  (ARAN), 135
Association analysis, 198–199
Asymmetric and symmetric cryptography, 261
Attacker tracing, 87–88
Attacks, 154
  in application layer, 272–273
  cryptanalytic, 214–215
  detection and management, 94–95
  implications, 217

S.C.-H. Huang et al. (eds.), *Network Security*, DOI 10.1007/978-0-387-73821-5,
© Springer Science+Business Media, LLC 2010